The Rhetorical Poetics
of the Middle Ages

Prof. Robert O. Payne *"And gladly wolde he lerne, and gladly teche."*

The Rhetorical Poetics of the Middle Ages

Reconstructive Polyphony

Essays in Honor of Robert O. Payne

Edited by
John M. Hill and
Deborah M. Sinnreich-Levi

Madison • Teaneck
Fairleigh Dickinson University Press
London: Associated University Presses

Associated University Presses
440 Forsgate Drive
Cranbury, NJ 08512

Associated University Presses
16 Barter Street
London WC1A 2AH, England

Associated University Presses
P.O. Box 338, Port Credit
Mississauga, Ontario
Canada L5G 4L8

The paper used in this publication meets the requirements of the American National Standard for Permanence of Paper for Printed Library Materials Z39.48-1984.

Library of Congress Cataloging-in-Publication Data

The rhetorical poetics of the Middle Ages : reconstructive polyphony : essays in honor of Robert O. Payne / edited by John M. Hill and Deborah M. Sinnreich-Levi.
    p. cm.
Includes bibliographical references and index.
ISBN 0-8386-3810-4
    1. Poetry, Medieval—History and criticism.   2. Chaucer, Geoffrey, d. 1400—Criticism and interpretation. 3. Rhetoric, Medieval. 4. Poetics. I. Hill, John M. II. Sinnreich-Levi, Deborah M. III. Payne, Robert O.
PN688.R49 2000
809.1'02—dc21   99-27895
                                            CIP

Contents

6 CONTENTS

Robert O. Payne: In Memoriam

BORN IN HERMISTON, OREGON, ON 4 DECEMBER 1924, ROBERT O. Payne, the scholar and teacher, deeply loved few things more in life than medieval poetry of the fourteenth century, particularly Chaucer's and the poetry of the alliterative revival. Out of that love came the intellectual whirl of teaching and seminar discussion as well as development of his students. One must say also that Robert O. Payne loved serious fishing, at which he was unusually skilled.

A tallish, white-haired scholar when I first met him in an undergraduate Chaucer class at the University of Washington, he had, by 1965, taught vigorously at Baltimore City College and the University of Cincinnati. His teaching was filled with big, complex issues; he made Chaucer seem important not only as a great English poet but also as a risky, wide-ranging intellectual, all too aware of how vulnerable ideas and good works are to cultural and linguistic change, to decay, misunderstanding, and loss out of time. By 1963, he had already published *The Key of Remembrance: A Study of Chaucer's Poetics,* and he seemed not only to know intimately the arguments of every Chaucer scholar who had ever published, but to possess all their books.

Payne was so passionately engaged with the search for truth about Chaucer's works that he accorded the scholars he reviewed a generous, perceptive summary of their arguments—this before demolishing those he found wanting, doing so with a logical clarity possessed by few Chaucerians of his or any other generation. Payne usually saved his most elegant efforts for his career-long critique of the kind of pseudo-historical, neo-patristic scholarship identified with the work of such Chaucerians as D. W. Robertson and B. F. Huppe. Aside from informed reviews of his colleagues' books, he would go on to publish an influential chapter on rhetorical poetry in the *Companion to Chaucer Studies* (1968), along with several essays on Chaucer's "Legend of Good Women" in the 1970s, coming in the next decade to a seminal essay on self-images of the poet in fourteenth- and fifteenth-century English and Scottish poetry. He showed how the crucial, Aristotelian idea of *ethos* plays out in the experimental hands of late medieval poets (*Studies in Medieval*

7

Culture 16 [1984]). Two years later, he published a widely reviewed book on Chaucer's works in general, *Geoffrey Chaucer,* for
the Twayne English Authors series (1986).

Throughout his career, Payne continued to expand the philosophical implications of that 1963 book, a study centered in part on
the rhetorical issues permeating Chaucer's masterpiece, *Troilus and
Criseyde*—a poem Payne first approached in his Johns Hopkins dissertation in 1953. Today, thirty-four years later, *The Key of Remembrance* is still widely read by Chaucerians and students of medieval
rhetoric largely because it is the richest introduction we have to
Chaucer as poet-rhetorician.

In the classroom, Payne was a generous spirit, both pointed and
encouraging in his comments. He read Chaucer's poetry beautifully, often with a knowing familiarity, as though only further study
would clue us in to how exciting, radical, and even "modern"
Chaucer really was. For Payne, deep engagement with Eliot, Frost,
Stevens, Moore, Bishop, Berryman, and others only enhanced his
sense of Chaucer as a great poet. Bob had many dissertation students, and to each he gave the benefits of extended equality and his
searching mind. He would return drafts of chapters with comments
that could cause one to change direction completely, happily. Perhaps this discouraged some, although I never met such a student of
his. Without fail, the many students I know feel grateful, both for
his scrutiny and for his unfailing support. Bob did not know how
to make an apprentice; for his students he was, rather, a midwife to
the birth of scholars.

Bob died on 9 February 1994. On 10 February 1995, a colloquium at the Graduate School and University Center, C.U.N.Y.,
honored him *in memoriam.* His wife Betty and her sister, Bea,
along with numerous colleagues, old friends, and dissertation students, joined for intellectual discussion and remembrance. The
event took shape in a sound studio-classroom at the Graduate Center mainly because no common room could accommodate the number of people who came. The large, industrial-tech space, with its
arrays of lights and electronic gear, seemed both strange and deeply
right for a medievalist gathering in Bob's honor. There was nothing
of the luddite or of the aesthetic snob in Bob; he honored good art,
music, sculpture, architecture, wherever he found it. The study of a
great medieval poet is part of the study of great art, wherever and
whenever it occurs.

Thirteen of Bob's former graduate students came to say something about him and their working time with him. Organized by
Scott Westrum, the part of the colloquium that testimonials formed

occurred in the early afternoon. It was my privilege to preside, but as we said what we had to say, a remarkable prose concert shaped itself. One after another, with silence in between, some of Bob's students spoke of him as they knew him and as his mentoring had affected them. They said of him that he taught them how to listen to Chaucer, how to perceive feeling, how to stretch across the centuries and confront Chaucer as a living presence. They said that, invariably, he set them serious tasks that puzzled him in big ways; that to them, he never condescended; that, indeed, he could be playful; and that he taught them to look both historically and within medieval poetry for the processes of its own creation. For his students, Bob was host, companion, jouster, mentor, friend. As both a nascent Platonist and a New Critic, he taught more by observation, style, and voice than by precept, although he was always ready to ground any observation in a jargon-free, yet complex, textual and cultural matrix. His students came because he mattered to them, because he took them seriously, and because one's teacher becomes oneself through one's own enactments with students—his progeny also, as one respondent fittingly noted. The program became, in the partial words of another respondent, a "scene of rendezvous" where intelligence, feeling, "dignity, and friendship" came together. It could only have been better had Bob suddenly appeared, nodding to us all in his slightly bemused, fisherman-scholar fashion.

John M. Hill

Introduction

JOHN M. HILL

In *The Key of Remembrance* (1963), Robert O. Payne proposes a rhetorical poetics for medieval vernacular poetry in general and for Chaucer's poetry in particular. In doing so, he definitively moves away from the negative evaluations of rhetoric in relationship to the poetical power then prevalent, having been so since the days of Manly and Rickert. By showing the deep integration in medieval poetry of rhetorical practices and poetical processes, Payne opens up a vast landscape for critical exploration. Other scholars followed his lead or else have undertaken parallel work in continental literature—no one with greater scope, however, than Douglas Kelly, *Medieval Imagination* (1978), and Paul Zumthor, *Toward a Medieval Poetics* (1972, 1992). Kelly emphasizes the medieval French poet's rhetorical control regarding intentions and effects, especially given the clarifying techniques of amplification through variation and repetition. Zumthor acknowledges the pervasive presence of rhetorical construction in medieval poetry but finds that presence invasive rather than significantly constitutive. For him, medieval rhetorical art is not the source of medieval vernacular poetry or poetics.

In striking contrast to these scholars, Payne focuses on the ways in which rhetorical practices become problematic for Chaucer, such that Chaucer creates new poetry in large part by wrestling with the dicta of the Second Rhetoric. It is in Chaucer's dilemmas, discoveries, and attempted solutions that Payne finds the grounds for a serious poetics, one that, in some sense, applies to many medieval poets, whether writing before, during, or after Chaucer's time. That poetics consists of questions and produces dilemmas and corresponding practices regarding the ways in which poetic intentions find adequate expression, given the plethora of rhetorical devices and the vagaries of meaning and effect seemingly built into any process of complex figuration.

The poetry Payne analyzes contains experiments, in effect, as Chaucer tries to transcend the dilemmas that provoke his best work.

11

In this connection especially, Payne sees Chaucer resorting to the
dream frame throughout his poetical career in various efforts to
align the confusing truths of authority with the less than clear les-
sons of experience and the imaginative lure of dreams.

As Chaucer's poetry becomes a poetry of the indeterminate and
the hard-to-reconcile, it opens up to all sorts of post-medieval insights, especially those we have gained in our modern and even
postmodern efforts at analyzing and understanding the inner work-
ings of metaphorical language; the psychology of emotion and perception; and the social, personal, and epistemic relativity, even
constructibility, of truth statements. That this is so justifies the gathering in the present volume of rhetorically inspired essays in a time
when medieval studies have exploded in many directions. We need
to step back now and refocus on the rhetorical poetic Payne
broaches on Chaucer's behalf, and on just how our contemporary
approaches to medieval poetry and poetics either build on Payne's
openings or complement them in powerful ways. Before introducing the various essays gathered here, however, we should first review Payne's sense of the rhetorical poetic and its attendant
problems in relation both to Zumthor's idea of a medieval poetics
and Kelly's sense of how medieval poets worked rhetorically.

When Zumthor turns directly to rhetoric, he acknowledges its
common, medieval aspirations: "to perceive, grasp, and express not
the details of experience but a kind of stable and theoretically universal quintessence" (*Medieval Poetics* 29). That aspiration ensures
a "durable but uneven influence" for rhetoric on vernacular
poetry—the underlying sources for which, however, lie elsewhere
(*Medieval Poetics* 30). Tradition—understood as a kind of self-en-
coding—and particular, evolutionary acts of language are those
sources. In part, this may be to admit the obvious: that poets invent
neither their own language nor the large body of literary conventions within which they work. But exactly how is it that traditions
encode themselves, or that language can be said to act indepen-
dently of human uses and formulations?

Zumthor must finally discount rhetoric's influence, seeing rhetoric as invasive, because Rhetorica would insert both an idea of controlling, individual agency and one of permanence, of stable
quintessence latent in all things, into what is deeply fluid, somewhat freeform, and entirely communitarian for Zumthor—the pervasive "mobility" of medieval texts, by which Zumthor means that
medieval texts are far from fixed. Indeed, they are variants of each
other within given traditions of narrative or story or song; no variant is that "text" that all similar variants in some way have the

potential to be. In confronting that so-called mobility, Zumthor invents "the Work," a "potential" never fully realized in any version, say, of *The Song of Roland* or of an Arthurian romance.

This physical potential is neither a transcendent idea nor one inherent elementally in the individual work. It is neither Platonic, in the sense that individual variants collectively approximate, whether deviating away from or pointing toward, the form that all are variants of; nor is this potential structural in the sense of implying a rough system of interrelated, sometimes substitutable parts—such as is the case, for example, in the kind of morphology Vladimir Propp works out for folktale types. Moreover, Zumthor does not mean the physical potential of doing work or of moving from a fixed point to some other point or state. Rather, he thinks of "potential" as latency within a vast, evolving, physical system. That system has no mind—much as the linguistic systems we abstract can have no mind, no presiding intelligence or even shaping energy. For Zumthor, individual innovations, whether in folksong or literary text, are merely harbingers of evolution within a system likened to autonomous language. In their appearances, those harbingers, those innovations produced somehow by (presumably convention-respecting) performers and poets, are like mutations in utterances otherwise spoken to the requirements of particular communities—communities which, through those innovations, somehow communicate with themselves. Once materialized, those harbingers become potentially catalytic texts within a text-producing system that, like language itself, is "a matrix of limitless possibilities" (*Medieval Poetics,* 53). Unlike evolution in the natural world, where reproductive fitness in competitive environments determines the success or failure of a mutation, in Zumthor's wonderland the innovations simply bubble up and interact with the literary norms of given communities. Variant bird songs, so to speak, interact integratively with the standards from which they deviate. And so an infinite number of variants and interactions is possible—an idea we lose sight of when we insist on seeing texts as deliberately shaped by human agents operating inventively within the variable and, to some extent, supercedable norms of literary competence peculiar to given traditions of story or song.

Indeed, the idea of innovative and surprising agency is precisely what Zumthor would banish from his poetics, especially in relationship to Rhetorica, which he rightly sees as essentially magisterial and controlling in her transcendental ambitions. His idea of mobility may indeed, then, be how rhetorical and poetical intervention looks from outside the rhetorical world, after one has dismissed

authorial intention and control, along with all the attendant problems of conflicted purposes, relatively intractable matter, surprising
developments, and vagarious effects—effects especially on a wide
variety of differentially responding hearers and readers. But, even
in his poetical cloud chamber of innovations interacting with momentarily established, communitarian standards, how can Zumthor,
in fact, escape the rhetorical when he invokes the historical circumstances of songs or poems responding to and being shaped by the
communicating community? "Mouvance" simply reinstates rhetoric elsewhere: as a mysterious, communitarian production, issuing
organically in both the repetitious and the innovative.

If we move from the synthesizing abstractions of autonomously
evolving systems to the rhetorical scene of purposeful speaker and
speech, with communities of speakers and hearers, authors and
readers, we find ourselves once again contemplating that "deep-felt
aspiration" Zumthor ascribes to medieval rhetorical doctrine. Here,
Douglas Kelly takes us nearer medieval poetical practice than
Zumthor can from his organic, evolutionary perspective, although
we may find ourselves agreeing with him that the springs of creativity in vernacular poetics are not quite reached.

Kelly gives the textbooks of the Second Rhetoric their full due.
He sees rational extension in them and probes what they may well
mean even if they do not always say so. Deeply magisterial and
controlling, rhetorical imagination, as Kelly sees it, moves from
particular images and ideas to the mental archetypes those images
imitate or else re-present. However, those re-presentations by description and other devices are thought of as amplifications in a top-
down procedure that suggests ineffable reality beyond the senses,
yet a reality somehow available to the mind through the mind's
rationalistic processes (*Medieval Imagination,* 28). Thus, incorpo-
real and abstract realities are made visible, as it were, in one or
more re-presentations—usually more, in that copious approximations, through synonymy, can give us a refined feel for the abstract
and invisible ideas and processes in question.

How does the rhetorical poet form an idea of those abstractions
and processes, in the first place? He must have already decided on
an idea of them before deploying metaphors, images, and secondary ideas, as it were, in his efforts at refinement and ever sharper
refocusing through his amplifications. This top-down logic is magisterial and seems to deform everything. It certainly is not how
communities might communicate with themselves in innovative,
evolving ways. It can hardly take us to the wellsprings of vernacular
poetry, of creativity, because it cannot account for surprise, discov-

ery, or change (something to which Zumthor's scheme, at least, is a response). Instead, in Kelly's presentations, we have art subordinated; that is, art serves idea. Authorial intention is clear and always controlling, in relation to which innovation can only seem a mistake, an unwanted sport, unless it cleverly continues the logic of ever-refining amplification. One might protest, then: Doesn't context matter? Don't contextual effects matter emotionally and confusingly? And isn't synonymy an illusion? Different semantic domains express complex, sometimes contradictory values. Related domains diverge as much as they overlap. Thus, contrary to Kelly's claim, we cannot easily grasp authorial meaning through the author's descriptions and repetitions unless description is somehow impoverished, stripped of ambiguity—indeed, of complex figuration, deep syntax, and both emotional and psychological resonance.

The loss of the latter, in effect, is one of the consequences of a top-down view of rhetorical poetry. How, indeed, does one arouse emotional conviction in one's audience (one of rhetorical poetry's key aims, as distinguished from mere emotional heat)? In his *Rhetoric,* Aristotle takes us into a psychology of passions (pathos), without which psychology, the rhetorician or the rhetorical poet is little better than a verbal engineer or the constructor of maxims for the vulgar. Medieval rhetorical handbooks do not repeat Aristotle's discussion of the passions, but often medieval vernacular poets either intuit the role of the passions or else face the passions as necessary but problematical aspects of their own work and in their own understanding of what they have read, heard, and are trying to reinvigorate for their contemporaries—that is, those interventions into the works (however understood) of their predecessors we call their poems.

In relation to Chaucer, Kelly's presentation of rhetorical imagination is especially unsatisfying, in that Chaucer seems bent on confronting puzzles—the puzzles of contradictory and often refractory truths in the poems and books of his predecessors, puzzles aggravated by his own emotional and experiential bents, as much as they are illuminated, even as he struggles with the often confounding issues of complicated rhetorical means and effects. Chaucer seems to replace controlling intention of the top-down sort with questioning. Questioning often evolves into inquiry informed by desire and assisted problematically by rhetorical techniques—inquiry that leads the poet and his readers into contradictory and therefore fascinating material, however problematically either the poet's ideas or his literary efforts align with Truth.

That rhetorically inspired, emotionally informed, and troublingly assisted inquiry is what Robert O. Payne sees most at work in Chaucer's poetry. It thus becomes a central feature of Chaucer's rhetorical poetics. However, in the course of elaborating just *how* Chaucer makes poetry out of the problems of controlling and completing good, rhetorical interventions into the works of his predecessors, Payne raises some key issues that only begin to yield their full potential to the resources of modern and postmodern analyses. These issues concern polysemy, polyphony, contextuality, and emotional efficacy.

Given that classical *inventio,* the discovery of ideas, disappears in medieval theory; and given that poetry then finds itself relegated to communicating authoritative truths—as a handmaiden to doctrine—what follows? First, the burden of composition, as Kelly rightly notes, shifts to amplification and abbreviation in a rhetoric, if you will, of colorful italics, of emphases. As Payne notes, in his turn, this produces a labor of style that seeks both the affective and the effective in "the rearrangement and emphasis achieved by amplification and abbreviation" (*Key,* 48). Although a kind of instructional poetry is possible in these terms, they do not describe the total effectiveness and impact of the poetry that results: "verbal embroidery" can radically alter both the colors and the patterns of the poet's source text or texts, thus becoming re-creative in surprising ways and with surprising effects. As a dynamic of change enters into the process of emphasis and affective heightening, much can, and often does, happen for which the rhetoric textbooks are unprepared. We begin to deal with shifting meaning and ambiguity, with all the openness of referential signs and sign systems, with polysemy and engaged semiotics.

If, in medieval theory, moral tension is what draws emotional response, then how does the morally problematic affect us, and how does the poet then control emotional response when moral perceptions are up for grabs? The working out of a competition between moral views in fit decoration not only confounds our sense of easy truth but also our sense of beauty, which fit decoration can hardly serve in a perplexed moral environment. To elucidate this development successfully, where it occurs, we need at least the supplementation of modern theories.

We need, too, modern aesthetics, situational ethics, and the psychologies of feeling and cognition. We may further need the cultural particularizations that feminism, Marxism, and Freudianism can provide—particularizations that can interact with organic and post-organic aesthetic theories concerning the nature of the literary object itself. In these supplementations, the cry that medieval rhetorical poetry is the art of clothing the already discovered truth in fitting, affectively convincing language becomes the nostalgic echo of a never fulfilled project—an echo that conceals its own, diverse truth: that, as Payne phrases the matter, "there are many kinds of utility and effect, and a confounding variety of means of achieving them" (*Key,* 61). Moreover, the poet's epistemological "key," which is the remembrance of old truths in old books, is not simply a storehouse of useful statements, proverbs, maxims, and moral and prudential ideas; rather, it is, in Payne's treatment, the calling up affectively of already selected, interpreted, evaluated, and emphasized truths—the desire-laden interpretation and hopeful disposition of interpretations! Here, we move from polysemy to a polyphony of voices socially and textually imbedded in circumstantially varied ways.

Here, that vision of the past about which Chaucer may well have remained devout—the past as a history intellectually unified and significantly ordered—begins to recede swimmingly. It becomes a chimerical horizon as soon as the serious rhetor in Chaucer, the poet, tries to make sense of it, given his concerns, his experience, his present. Chaucer's rhetorical and poetical practice separates him even further from standard, rhetorical precepts. Also, insofar as Chaucer questions what is foundational and what is not, what is primary truth and what is secondary commentary, what is ornamental and what is ornamented, what is text and what is gloss—just so far does his enterprise open up to—indeed, seem to call for—both the insights of modernist relativity within whatever dream of the ultimately determined and the reflections occasioned by a postmodern perception of contextual as well as chaotic flux. Here, subjectivity appears in both positive and negative ways, given the instrumentality of feeling—of a "pitous heart" when one (Chaucer) writes the old story into English. Chaucer's feeling for the old story's pathos and for language—the story's original tongue as well as his own vernacular—is crucial to revivifying it, to assaying the old story and effectively re-presenting it. Indeed, in this regard, feeling may be crucial even to *remembering* the old story.

For Payne, a kind of melancholy haunts Chaucer's powers of remembrance—the melancholy of desperate repair, of saving, fixing, and thus holding onto the lore (the truths) preserved for us in the past. This is not quite the dream Zumthor posits for rhetoric's aspirations—that universal quintessence rhetoric would express. For Payne, Chaucer's melancholy has much to do with desire and its less-than-present, less-than-satisfactory objects. The effort to mediate desire becomes the psychological justification for that famous

persona—the Chaucerian narrator, who then is Chaucer's defense
against, as well as organizing response to, awareness of contradiction and inconsistency in his material. Just where does that defense
root itself? Or: what exactly are the failures in a given set of rhetorical efforts that generate a need for the comic persona so characterized?

In turning to *Troilus and Criseyde,* Payne offers Chaucer's most
ambitious and illuminating effort as poet-rhetorician, beginning
with the issue of how a "fitting style can distribute" a decorative
emphasis that can reactivate an old story (*Key,* 177). In this case,
however, trouble appears almost from the beginning, in the person
of the intrusive narrator, who becomes a strategy of presentation, as
magician and commentator. Theoretically, elements of style should
emphasize moments in whatever overall plan is narratively set in
motion. The presence of a less than magisterial narrator, however,
bedevils everything, bringing in doubt, the indefinite, and the un-
said as responses, whether the narrator's own or those of any supposed audience. This bedevilment, of course, is of a piece with the
illusion of reality Chaucer produces in *Troilus and Criseyde,* much
of which "comes not from the actual processes of characterization,
but from the affective immediacy of the moral and emotional problems within which the existence of the characters are defined" (*Key,*
182). Because of this affective immediacy and because of Chaucer's skill with dialogue—his powers of differentiated voicing—we
tend to forget, according to Payne, the typicality and representative-
ness of Chaucer's central characters in *Troilus.*

Chaucer's procedures here produce a great moment: dialogue becomes a way, through subtle voicing, to complicate otherwise flat
characters. We need typicality so that rhetorical emphasis has a line
on which to work. But when typicality disappears in moments of
surprise, movement, and mystery, there is no help from the handbooks or from rhetorical theory in general. Moreover, just how does
Chaucer establish a manipulable, "affective immediacy," given the
moral dilemmas posed in and through his characters? Does he work
intuitively, creatively, or, in some ongoing contextual way, dramatically? Again, from the perspective of medieval rhetorical theory,
there is no help in the handbooks, not even hints. Thus, just here, a
major development in medieval poetry appears. In Chaucer's effort
to control the story after having created the affective immediacy
Payne notes Chaucer resorts finally to moral perspectivism—
brilliantly, in that much of the affective impact of the story concerns moral issues or else is intensified that way. The moral plane,
however, does not get us satisfactorily out of the poem, which, as

Payne rightly sees, becomes a profoundly moral universe without a moral.

Moral issues become ratiocinative when rendered successfully in perspectival terms: that is, in proper perspective we can see Pandarus's morality correcting Troilus's, and vice versa. Troilus's morality is incomplete, but ours is not demonstrably better—and so on. Such balancing does not adequately express emotional situations, however: the pull, if you will, of the affective. At best, trying to fine-tune mutually correcting perspectives can keep us close to the portentousness of emotional drama, to the depths involved, the human constants, and the operations of desire. But to plumb those depths we need post-medieval technologies, beginning, perhaps, with notions of how everything in social worlds is open to construction, change, and reconstruction.

In Chaucer's case, Payne carefully draws out an impressive pattern of moral and lyrical emphases in *Troilus*—good rhetorical practice that implicates a governing or else informing perspective. But that pattern of inset lyrics does not so much make meaning as stab at it, at what seems latent in the material. These approximations are as half-blind and groping as they are insightful. Here, the labor of style does not produce definitive meaning; at most, it proposes various meanings problematically. As that happens, we cross metaphysical boundaries, so to speak, and watch as Chaucer explores an organic dimension of an otherwise Platonic underlay in medieval rhetorical theory. As we cross those boundaries, we happen upon any number of problems—a large one being the question of ultimate grounding for any truth about anything. This sounds like a postmodern terminus because it is.

Any controlled elaboration eventually will run afoul of the suppleness of natural language and of our doubts about indubitable fact whenever the facts we seek are complex and extended, open to structural interpretation and corroboration by communities of interpreters. Medieval rhetorical theory cannot deal well with that relativity any more than it has something notable to say about the treacherous effects of contextualization or about the effects of lively intercourse between minimally realized characters (who should but do not always keep to a set-piece game plan for Chaucer). Style should control implication and move us along from one level of consideration to another. But can it, in fact, do so when the story becomes dramatically vivid and affectively immediate? The answer is "no," because contexts change awareness and understanding, making judgment with any deep conviction difficult if not impossible. We need attention to linguistic contexts and to ongoing narrative strands which only modern theory has a way of addressing analytically. Here, I. A. Richards' remark on old and new *Rhetorics* is pointedly germane: "but where the old Rhetoric treated ambiguity as a fault in language, and hoped to confine or eliminate it, the new Rhetoric sees it as an inevitable consequence of the powers of language and as the indispensable means of our most important utterances—especially in Poetry and Religion" (Richards, 115). For Richards, meaning is "an abridgment of contexts settled in the word: the word means what has been abridged, not something to which it directly and narrowly refers." A sign stands for "an absent cause and conditions" (Richards, 113).

We are a long way from medieval theory here but not from the practice Payne highlights in his eventual estimate of Chaucer's effects in *Troilus*. Sometimes imagery in the work offers us both a way of morally judging a situation (an immediate, narrow reference) and a way of confronting countervailing sympathies—as when Troilus is said to sit down on the side of his bed, this sorrowful man "Ful lik a ded ymage, pale and wan" (IV:235). Whenever this happens, we may find ourselves reading against the grain and reaching for help, again, to postmodern conceptions of centers and margins as we consider what is emphasized and what, in the form of awarenesses of something else, has been partly repressed (one of the abridged absences). If we read against the grain, is that perverse of us, or is it, in fact, something Chaucer's work invites (as might the practice of other poets)? In Book III, for example, religious imagery seems to establish a line of measurement at Troilus's expense, measuring the corruption of his higher reason. But that imagery also has countervalues perhaps abridging "absent cause and condition" while hazarding a present, judgmental reference. Were Chaucer's practice determinedly moral, we could speak, regarding Book III and Troilus's conceptions of Love, of an emerging line of measurement that would be Chaucer's—or, at least, would be the one he would settle on if he could. But he finally does not. Why? Because he cannot bring all the abridged effects and values he generates regarding earthly joy and sobering, celestial perspective down to a resolution in this poem, such that, through ample clarifications, we convincingly feel the supposedly terrible inadequacy of Troilus's unaided reason. Rather than defer his end until the appropriate moment, or break off the entire, vast effort, Chaucer continues to let his rhetorical practice (the labor of style) actually produce obstacles to, or else subversions of, that end!

Payne notes this development at an emotionally realized level in the poem. When Chaucer's narrator remains objective, his aphoristic judgments parallel those being accumulated in the whole evaluative apparatus of the poem. But when he succumbs, so to speak, to the effectiveness of his own style and sees them [the characters] momentarily living and complete within their inevitable (and therefore unconscious) historical and human limits, the current of his sympathies immediately begins to flow counter to his main moral drift in the poem.   (*Key,* 207)

Unless we morally marginalize human sympathies and their objects here, we, too, must follow suit in that counterflow to the poem's "main moral drift." As we follow, we feel ourselves at sea without theoretical moorings—once again in a postmodern predicament of sorts for which our recourse must be to the insights of postmodern analyses. At this point, we part company with Chaucer's efforts to align the mutable with the immutable in some measurable and defining way.

We have reached one of several impasses in *Troilus* that are "impasses in the pursuit of intelligence of love, just as they are in the fabrication of the art which will activate that intelligence" (*Key,* 219). Knowledge and art come up short, then—just as technique, however purposeful, always will when attempting to do what feeling and understanding cannot: truly align the mutable with the immutable; repair the past once and for all for the present; love and never lose.

Whereas Chaucer's very effort validates the poem's moral generalizations, the poem nevertheless becomes a reminder of everyone's "limitedness and partiality" in the application of the moral principles that seem ultimate. Though not his aim, this is where Chaucer's probing has led him. Rhetorically, the moral perspectives Chaucer poses are like nuclear control rods: they keep the human reactions affecting us from going critical and destroying the poem. Thus for Payne, Chaucer's wrestling with moral issues on his and our behalf becomes a form of self-discovery and moral discovery—not a stage on the way to uplift and resolution. *Troilus and Criseyde* has no moral, yet it is a deeply moral poem. As such, it is certainly an unlooked-for rhetorical and poetical achievement. To engage it requires all the modern awareness we can summon individually and collectively, as surely as it requires a grounding in medieval rhetorical technique and purpose.

In the essays that follow, this grounding in medieval rhetorical purposes will be assumed more often than not, except when a renovative view is offered as in Mary Carruthers' and Johanna Prins' essays. The contributors to this volume have taken up several over-

lapping rhetorical-poetical issues from modernist and postmodernist perspectives, focusing more often than not on the constructing
and reconstructive directions taken by poets working with competing genres, planes of reference, styles, and voices.

Both Johanna Prins and Mary Carruthers focus on the traditional
uses of rhetoric, the one on oblique, individualized uses of a courtly
register in Dutch drama, and the other on the ways in which memory and rhetorical composition are inherently involved with each
other. Prins sees a mixture of courtly and bourgeois rhetoric in the
Abel plays. The interplay rhetorically is that of the brutal and practical in relation to an ideal of empathy and forgiveness. For Carruthers, medieval memory and rhetorical composition have cognitive,
technological, and social interrelationships. By showing the social
and memorative conventions involved in the opening of *The Book
of the Duchess,* especially as they relate to the narrator's initial
perturbation before opening the book in which he finds the story of
Ceys and Alcione, Carruthers emphasizes the social and productive
aspects of the work of grief and recollection. Indeed, remembering
is composition, and composition is a remembering in some symmetrical, if not commutative, sense.

What is it that one remembers, and to what ends? At the strictly
entertaining level, Deschamps, in Deborah Sinnreich-Levi's discussion, articulates a vernacular poetics of natural music, delight, and
medicinal pleasure. This activity is congruent with Charles Owen's
focus on Chaucer's skillful appropriation and redirection in his vernacular of received prosodic forms, especially the French octosyllabic couplet. Owen shows how Chaucer takes a foreign form and
adapts it to English, simultaneously rendering it colloquial enough
for subtle voicing.

That confrontation with the foreign, of course, lies at the heart of
rhetorical intervention and interpretation regarding the works and
techniques of the past. Taken a step further, it raises the issue of
influence between poets, poems, genres, and traditions, which, in
turn, in another step, takes us to confrontations of a dialogical and
polyphonic kind.

In matters of direct, acknowledged influence, medieval poets
often are either explicit or altogether mum—aggressive appropriation being the name of the game (which only looks like rampant
plagiarism to us). That appropriation, of course, is always selective,
interpretative, even surprisingly instrumental. Joel Feimer, for example, sees Chaucer working selectively with prior treatments of
the women whose legends he recapitulates in *The Legend of Good
Women.* Under the God of Love's edict, Chaucer tells of good

women who have been martyrs for love; but he does so ironically, editing portraits of notorious women such as Cleopatra and in the process, distinguishing himself from Boccaccio's similar endeavors. Rhetorical reshaping becomes an act of ironic portraiture, critiquing "fyn loving" rather than upholding the God of Love's command. Feimer sees Chaucer engaged in an interesting rhetorical and poetical task: how to turn a troubling and influential tradition of Love on its head without reinforcing its moralizing overtly.

Dante, in Anne Schotter's treatment, works with an idea of influence that is maternal and generative rather than agonistic. In the medieval interception and reanimation process, Dante sees himself as working in a cooperative way, nurtured by his predecessors, rather than in a competitive way such that he must absorb and overcome those who came before. A feminist perspective helps us see this more clearly than we might otherwise, Schotter suggests, because we can both think about a non-agonistic model and focus on the cult of the Virgin as a historically significant development for the maintenance of nurturing models of influence. William McClellan elaborates a problematic version of direct, acknowledged influence when he looks through Bakhtinian lenses at Chaucer's relationship to Petrarch, as focused especially through Chaucer's Clerk. McClellan shows us that rhetorical interventions, especially those that would reorient a received tale from one plane (say, an allegorical one) to another (say, an ethical one) cannot be wholly innocent. They are interpretations with some appropriating and deviating force, yet not necessarily ones that come to a confident, complete reappropriation.

The question of influence can easily modulate into the oppositional or else tensely interactive when we move from poets drawing upon poets to poems and traditions incorporating either differentiable genres or metafigures for poetry itself. Sealy Gilles discusses the rhetorical issue of how a stabilizing genre, the gnome, can become unstable when it becomes personal lament through insistent repetition in contexts of complaint—as in *The Wanderer*. Diane Marks shows how, in his Laura sonnets, Petrarch implicitly opposes metaphors for rhetorical poetry; rather than embrace the traditional idea of poetical language as veil, Petrarch picks up the idea of the knot. In doing so, he attacks the traditional charge that poets lie; more importantly, he integrates ideas of flesh and spirit, agent and thought, words and truth. Simultaneously he intimates the (knotted) complexity of reading and writing poetry, of rightly understanding and then rightly suiting words to thoughts such that one can materialize ideas in a rhetoric that is adequate to them. Gale Sigal argues that the alba stands in oppositional relationship to courtly lyric and pastoral, as well as to the norms of social hierarchies considered historically. In that opposition, the alba creates its own impassioned world, wherein intense voices express a mutuality of love as well as loss between reciprocally bound male and female, whose sex roles are, in fact, fluid.

The world of the alba suggests the efficacy of rhetorical self-construction in opposition to all other genres, and indeed to historical reality. Here, the rhetorical issue is precisely the construction through voices of a rhetorically managed reality that is everything for the lovers, much as its social counterpart, the social construction of belief, becomes a key rhetorical maneuver in Robert Hanning's discussion of a tale from the *Decameron*. For Hanning, forensic competition and social construction go hand in hand rhetorically. Boccaccio exploits forensic rhetoric and the social contexts, hierarchies, and constructs that efficacious forensic practices depend on. Legal and quasi-legal fictions are rhetorically constructed in some transactional arrangement with social fictions—the social constructs by which we live.

Burt Kimmelman takes this double construction—of a "reality" and of a rhetoric—as involving mutually entangled "rhetorics," those of experience and poetry. The Chaucerian persona becomes Chaucer's myth of himself and his poetic enterprise, the persona becoming a way of wrestling rhetorically with questions of experience and abstracted knowledge, while becoming an image of the less than magisterial poetry produced. A rhetorical dialectic emerges that underscores the continual interplay between the world's impingements on the mind and the mind's ideas of that world.

A similar interplay appears in Martin Stevens's essay, but now focused less on world and poem than on the poems and their literary foils and premises themselves. That is, Chaucer's poetry is seen as in constant dialectic with its own rhetorical premises, a rhetoric of self-reflexivity, which, through parodic attention to bodies of texts lying behind the "parody" text, raises the issue of narrative competence. The relationship between source or parodied text is inherently dialogical or heteroglossic. Reflexivity is a relativized yet system-bound notion: the "system" is inscribed within itself, as in a "chaotic" iteration.

Taking this to the limit of catching the uncatchable, Ellen Martin narrows the focus even more to address the blurred boundaries between *sentence* and ornament as directly as possible. Her essay tries to catch the poet in the very act of confronting his own acts of

multiple figuration, of indecisive interpretation regarding the por-
tentous works and meanings of others. Those acts, however, do not
preclude a continuing search for truth, no matter how subjective or
self-examining they become. Indeed, Chaucer's figurations offer up
images or stand-ins for truth—stand-ins that suggest *The House of
Fame*'s latent content; as a rhetorician's dream, that latent content
is the poetic material of troping. In this poem, Chaucer continually
deflects an equally continuing quest for a topic, one effect of which
is to frustrate the appearance of any mastery that would suppress
invention and the multiplicity of possible meanings displayed in
the poem's sequences of inventions, tropes, allusions, disruptions,
catalogues, and so on. Thus, for Martin, *The House of Fame* is
about the freedom to invent without giving up either the plenum of
possible meanings or the pursuit of truth (if only as an idea).

We think these essays admirably extend the spirit of Robert O.
Payne's work on medieval rhetoric and poetics, perhaps especially
in the cases of those applying modernist and postmodernist perspectives. To keep the past alive in one's sense of values is the heart
of the rhetorical enterprise for Chaucer, for Payne, and for us in
response to Chaucer and to Payne's pioneering work. In that quest
we can hardly reduce our aesthetic sensibilities to whatever we can
glean historically from medieval treatises on verbal art and its purposes, although renovative understandings of those treatises can be
surprising. We need to use every theoretical understanding we have
of art and poetry if we are to understand what medieval poets have,
in fact, done in practice, whatever they thought they were doing in
theory.
    It is in the spirit of those remarks that the essays gathered here
should be read. Robert O. Payne would have had us read Spenser,
Yeats, and Stevens in our effort to understand Chaucer. Our contributors in many cases would also have us read feminist criticism,
Barthes, Bahktin, Foucault, Derrida, Freud, Lacan, Winnicott and
others, as well as medieval rhetoricians and theologians. Once we
have read all of this, Chaucer and his medieval predecessors and
successors can no longer look as they might have to some of their
local audiences. For Payne and for the contributors to this volume,
a rhetorical poetics reflects concerns between speaker and hearer—
for language, emotion, idea, understanding, and temporality—
shared by most medieval poets in lively and complex ways. This is
so much the case that we can hardly forgo any understanding we
have of poetry and art in our engagement with works of the past.
    That we can hear many voices and register the play of heteroglos-

sia especially in Chaucer's work does not, of course, mean that other medieval poets are equally accessible to us in the same ways. Each essay makes its own case for the particular awareness through which it responds to provocative invitations in the poetry studied—whether French, Italian, English, or Dutch. The outcomes, we think, are not so surprising. In many ways the poets and poems themselves—poems written in a profoundly rhetorical age—have anticipated the studies gathered together here, studies written in a new age newly fascinated with the post-Burkean "rhetorics" of everything from sexual behavior to politics and science.

Works Cited

Kelly, Douglas. *Medieval Imagination: Rhetoric and the Poetry of Courtly Love.* Madison: University of Wisconsin Press, 1978.

Manly, John Matthews. "Chaucer and the Rhetoricians." Proceedings of the British Academy, 12. London, 1926.

——— and Edith Rickerts, eds. *The Text of the Canterbury Tales.* 8 vols. Chicago: University of Chicago Press, 1940.

Payne, Robert O. *The Key of Remembrance: A Study of Chaucer's Poetics.* New Haven: Yale University Press, 1962.

Richards, I.A. "A Context Theory of Meaning and Types of Context." *Richards on Rhetoric: I.A. Richards, Selected Essays (1929–1974).* Ed. Ann E. Berthoff. Oxford: Oxford University Press, 1991. 111–117.

Zumthor, Paul. *Toward a Medieval Poetics.* Tr. Philip Bennett. Minneapolis: University of Minnesota Press, 1992; *Essai de poètique médiévale.* Paris: Seuil, 1972.

The Rhetorical Poetics
of the Middle Ages

Eustache Deschamps' *L'Art de dictier*:
Just What Kind of Poetics Is It?
Or: How Robert O. Payne Launched My
Career in Deschamps Studies

DEBORAH M. SINNREICH-LEVI

Bob PAYNE WAS THE FIRST MODERN SCHOLAR TO RECOGNIZE THE IMPOR-
tance of Eustache Deschamps' *L'Art de dictier*. He came across it
in the course of his own graduate work, puzzled over it, and never
stopped thinking about it—and never stopped making others think
about it. In the 1980s, I was initiated into Bob's perennial ritual and
became one of countless graduate students assigned *L'Art de dictier*
as the topic for an oral report in his seminar on medieval rhetoric.
He did not mention how few libraries had the text; he didn't mention how little criticism there was; he didn't mention the frustration
of previous students handed this assignment (but *they* did). I have
come to appreciate that Bob perceived *L'Art de dictier*'s importance, but never completed parsing out how it fit into the history of
rhetorical and poetic treatises. He knew someone would eventually:
I owe him a great debt for handing me a challenge, a dissertation, a
book, and a career in Deschamps studies.

L'Art de dictier is the earliest *ars poetica* in French. Written in
1392 by the prolific courtier-poet Eustache Deschamps, its stated
purpose is to teach the reader to compose poetry and songs; however, it is apparently incomplete, dissimilar to earlier vernacular
treatises, and sometimes confusing in its recommendations, thus
causing some critics to dismiss it. But Deschamps, poised on the
crux between earlier poetics composed in Latin which linked the
lyric to music and the newer theories which focused on the text
alone, had several concerns to balance. Clearly intended as an instructional manual, *L'Art de dictier* is the product of a tremen-
dously successful poet and reflects the poetic practice of his day. It
assumes a knowledgeable audience of noble literati who could follow its telegraphic style. It also reflects fourteenth-century philo-

29

sophical and medical attitudes concerning the therapeutic qualities of pleasure, music and literature, as well as the importance of popular genres within the courtly tradition. It is not, however, the weak link in the chain of rhetorical treatises that Payne thought.

Eustache Deschamps lived from about 1346 to 1406 or 1407. Not much is known about his youth except that he was raised in the house of Guillaume de Machaut.[1] He studied the seven liberal arts, as well as astrology and law, at the University at Orléans in the 1360s, and, although he seems not to have earned a degree, his education colored his poetics. The curriculum at Orléans was noted for its stress on the practical application of the liberal arts, in addition to theoretical study (Rashdall II:144). L'Art de dictier reflects both this early liberal arts education and the experience of a lifetime of practical courtly service. He spent his life serving the houses of Orléans, Anjou, and Burgundy, rising from his first position as a squire to gentleman usher, sergeant-at-arms, chatelain, and bailiff. He wrote occasional poetry commemorating all the significant doings of his times. Among his approximately 1,500 poems collected in the unique manuscript of his complete works,[2] there are also many on a broad spectrum of secular and religious topics. Deschamps wrote hundreds of virelais, rondeaux, chansons royales, lais, and balades, preferring this last to any of the other forms. His work in all these genres was admired and emulated by such contemporaries as Chaucer and Christine de Pizan.

Many believe Deschamps' influence on Chaucer can be seen in the lengthy borrowings from Le Miroir de mariage seen in The Merchant's Tale and The Wife of Bath's Prologue, as well as in the influence of the Lai de franchise on the Prologue to The Legend of Good Women. Deschamps' balades were also known to Chaucer and influenced his shorter poems.[3] Deschamps expressed his own admiration for Chaucer in a balade whose refrain styles him "Grant translateur, noble Geoffroy Chaucier" (Balade 285). Christine de Pizan acknowledges her debt to Deschamps in a letter in 1403, calling him "cher maître et ami," and he acknowledges her in Balade 1242, styling her "Muse eloquent entre les .ix."[4] Deschamps thus was accepted by some of the greatest poets of his time as a colleague and a model; even if his treatise was not known to them, his poetic practices were.

How can one begin to understand L'Art de dictier, the first vernacular poetics in French? A useful comparison is L'Art de dictier and other vernacular artes poeticae. Those closest in spirit to L'Art de dictier, even if no clear lines of influence can be demonstrated, are the Old Provençal artes poeticae, also written by courtier-poets;

but there is no evidence as to whether Deschamps was familiar with them. Deschamps was not ignorant of the Latin poetic tradition, and it is clear he did not perceive himself writing in a vacuum. However, although there is no way of establishing what contact, if any, he had with Old Provençal, these treatises seem more like his kind of work because of their content and intent. They share limited grammar discussion, a lack of rhetorical devices would-be versifiers should adopt or avoid, short prescriptions for forms, and exemplary strophes as models for inspiration. It has been shown elsewhere that he was familiar with the works of Rabanus Maurus, Boethius, Priscian, and others (SATF XI, passim), but no one has ever proposed sources for *L'Art de dictier*. Deschamps commends his treatise to the correction of those "qui mieulx et plus saigement . . . scevent et scavroient mieulx faire" (those who know . . . better and more wisely) than he (*L'Art* 102–3). Ernest Langlois suggests no sources for *L'Art de dictier*, although "[il] ne doute pas qu'il ait existé dès le milieu du XIVe siècle 'des *Arts de seconde rhétorique*, que nous ne connaissons pas,' mais que dénoncent suffisament des allusions précises" (in SATF XI: 157). Such speculation on the actual sources of specific aspects of the texts themselves is not as satisfying as comparing *L'Art de dictier* with earlier vernacular works, because there are no clear lines of influence. The juxtapositioning of various other treatises against *L'Art de dictier*, however, can show us how Deschamps' concerns differed from or continued earlier traditions. There is not enough space here, though, to illuminate the various differences between *L'Art de dictier* and other *artes poeticae*, Latin or vernacular.[5] Deschamps does not discuss at all, or discusses in totally unexpected or obscure ways: figures of thought and diction, music, phonology, versification, genre theory, rhyme, audience, style, tone, and the levels of diction appropriate thereto—all requisite components of earlier rhetorical handbooks. What, then, *does* Deschamps discuss in *L'Art de dictier*?

One of the main features of *artes poeticae* in Latin and other traditions had long been grammar; yet, Deschamps manages to dismiss grammar in one of the extremely short introductory paragraphs that begin *L'Art de dictier*. For him, grammar had become merely a craft. Grammar is the first and principal art, but it has this name from its basic functions—it is a basic skill without which no other arts can be learned. It is the art "par lequel l'en vient et aprant tous les autres ars par les figures des letres de A, B, C, que les enfans aprannent premierement, et par lesquelz aprandre et scavoir l'en peut venir a toute lettre science, et monter de la plus petite lettre jusques a la plus haulte" ([by which] one comes to learn all the other arts by means of the letters of the alphabet which children learn first. By learning and understanding these, one can arrive at all knowledge and rise from the least letter all the way up to the most exalted science) (*L'Art* 54–55). This utilitarian attitude toward grammar is similar to the stance Deschamps takes on the other liberal arts—even music, which eventually gets his greatest attention, as we will see.

For what audience did Deschamps intend this practical treatise? He wrote in French about composing in the vernacular: he did not have to make the case for using the vernacular that Dante did in *De vulgari eloquentia* about a hundred years earlier: by Deschamps' time, vernacular composition on serious subjects had become accepted in France. His contemporary, Nicole Oresme, for example, had published several treatises in French before the composition of *L'Art de dictier* (Patterson I:73). Deschamps never indicates any awareness that he is writing in the vernacular rather than the contemporarily still more scholarly Latin. The only significant reference he makes to French, as opposed to any other language, is at the end of a passage discussing the qualities of vowels and consonants, in which he says that the letters of the alphabet are the medium "par lesquelles tout langaige latin et francois est escript et profere" (through which French and all other languages are written and pronounced) (*L'Art* 68–69). Indeed, Deschamps indiscriminately mixes Latin and French words in his phonological examples.[6] He does advocate an understanding of linguistics, discussing vowels and consonants, apparently in an effort to achieve euphony in composition. Lyric poetry, which Deschamps discussed as natural music, is enhanced by euphonious diction. And, since he composed almost exclusively in French, his privileging the vernacular is the clearest indication of his judgment of its primacy. This favorable attitude may date from Deschamps' youth, for he heard lectures in French when he studied at Orléans (Rashdall II:144). Deschamps clearly posited an audience literate in a vernacular who would compose in that same vernacular in the same way the troubadour theoreticians posited an Old Provençal audience who would not be resistant to composing in Old Provençal.[7] The poets who were to have followed Deschamps' instruction must have been courtly, since he gives short shrift to specific genres of poetry such as the sirventes and the pastourelle which are not suited to the court but, rather, belong only at the Puys d'amours (*L'Art* 82–83, 94–95). Deschamps makes only oblique references to refrains and musical settings, using technical vocabulary without defining it, so he must have expected his audience to be familiar with the technical language of music and poetry. Therefore, it would seem that he wrote for a circle of French-speaking, noble literati who, though perhaps not exactly poets, aspired to understand poetry and possibly to write it themselves.

Deschamps sought to teach by use of brief explanations, relying on exemplary strophes to make his points clear where he could or would not. In addition to the exemplary strophes he supplies, poetic examples of his own work and that of others were abundantly available to his audience for use. Indeed, he says that certain genres are easy enough to come by, that "whoever might fear he couldn't retain" all the theory could just pick up a lyric "for they are numerous enough," so that he had no need to include lengthy, complete examples in his "little book" (*L'Art* 96–97). Indeed, he speaks in several places of the need to be brief, to keep his little book from getting too long. He viewed it as a brief but clear how-to manual that would have been burdened by too weighty discourse and explanation. Such abbreviated instructions support the deduction that Deschamps was writing for a circle of initiates familiar with contemporary poetic practices. And Deschamps' elevating music beyond its traditional function in mathematics, preferring mimetics to formulas, moves the discussion into a realm previously uninhabited. He found the composition of poetry trivial and intuitively clear to those appropriately gifted for it. Certainly, no one not already familiar with the genres he describes would be likely to be able to compose them relying solely on his idiosyncratic treatise.

L'Art de dictier is composed of two main parts, a treatise on the seven liberal arts and a prescriptive poetics. Music receives considerably more attention than the rest of the liberal arts. That Deschamps felt compelled to touch on all the arts—in order to wrap his treatise on poetics in a larger, more recognizable and orthodox format—is the probable result of the combination of his academic education and quotidian experience. The descriptions of the arts are remarkable in the stress placed on their practical applications, reflecting his Orléans education and his career, for Deschamps must have found little use for the liberal arts in theory and considerable use for their practical application. Thus, grammar is the tool by means of which we learn everything else; rhetoric wins our disputes and enhances our reputation; geometry constructs our buildings and vessels; arithmetic tallies our property and calculates our coinage, and astronomy guides our agriculture and health care. It is music, finally, as the "medecine des vii ars" which, by means of lyrics and melody, refreshes "le couraige et l'esperit des creatures ententives aux autres ars" (hearts and spirits of men intent on the other arts), as well as those exhausted by nature (*L'Art* 60–61).

The section on music is more than twice as long as those on the other six arts combined. Music can be divided into two kinds, natural and artificial. For Deschamps, artificial music is produced either by instruments or by the human voice. Natural music is lyric poetry; whereas he says the two kinds of music go well together, natural music is vastly superior, since it can be taught to no one unless he is already gifted for it, and since it can be performed under circumstances where artificial music cannot be. The section on music concludes with a discussion of linguistics and euphonics. It was necessary to class poetry in a discussion of the arts of the trivium and the quadrivium, but discussing lyric poetry as a kind of music was unusual. A more likely aegis for it would have been rhetoric; certainly Payne understood the history of poetics as a part of the history of rhetoric. Deschamps' further distinction between the application of natural and artificial music is noteworthy for its divergence from earlier theoretical applications of those terms. Ever since classical antiquity, music had been studied as a branch of mathematics. A complex set of mathematical theorems shaped early medieval music theory, so it was grouped in the quadrivium along with geometry and astronomy as an art based on arithmetic. Deschamps redefined music as lyric poetry, not necessarily accompanied by any instrumental music. This definition makes him the first French poet to declare the lyric's independence. The various lyric forms Deschamps composed in are set free to develop without the constraints of the musical settings of the *formes fixes*.

The balance of *L'Art de dictier* is taken up with brief prescriptions for the composition of various genres of poetry and exemplary poems or strophes. The genres discussed are the balade, the sirventes, the virelai, the rondeau, and the lai. Other genres mentioned but not discussed are the chanson royal, the sote balade, the balade amoureuse, and the pastourelle. These brief prescriptions add to the poetic theories expounded in the first sections but not systematically. It is the section devoted to music that bears the greatest investigation.

Deschamps' definition of music departs from that of earlier theoreticians. Boethius, for example, begins by dividing music, a study based on arithmetic, into three kinds: the music of the spheres, human music, and instrumental music. The first is a guiding principle of unity in the universe; the second, an Aristotelian method of binding the rational and irrational parts of the soul; the last, the physical means of production. (None of these orthodox domains interested Deschamps.) It is in a further subdivision of this last class that Boethius eventually mentions the lyric. He says that the musical art is yet again divided into three classes, none of which is really music: "One class has to do with instruments, another invents songs, a third judges the work of instruments and songs. . . . The second class . . . is that of the poets, which is borne to song not so much by speculation and reason as by a certain natural instinct. Thus this class also is to be separated from music" (*De institutione musica,* in Strunk 84–86). It is only the pure theoretician's music that is Boethian authentic music—the "skill of judging . . . rhythms and melodies . . . founded in reason and speculation." This academic music did not interest Deschamps. Many other theoreticians after Boethius discussed music and poetry, and others have variously traced the development of musical and poetic theories,[8] but in the role of "natural instinct," Deschamps rejects the Boethian exclusion of song from music.

Deschamps divides music into natural and artificial music; natural music is lyric poetry, produced by the spoken voice, artificial music is instrumental or choral music. The latter is a skill that can be taught to *anyone*; the former can be taught to no one who lacks innate talent. Music, indeed, rhetoric and poetics, had been treated throughout the Middle Ages as technical crafts that could be learned; Deschamps' *ars* approaches a sense of art; that is, it is dependent on talent. And, although writers in the Boethian tradition had held that the only pure music is neither that of the instrumental performer nor of the poet but that of the musical theoretician, such grounding in musical theory escapes notice in *L'Art de dictier* almost completely.

Deschamps says of artificial music: "L'artificiele est . . . appelee artificiele de son art, car par ses vj notes, qui sont appellees us, re, my, fa, sol, la, l'en puet aprandre a chanter . . . le plus rude homme du monde, ou au moins tant faire que, suppose ore qu'il n'eust pas la voix habile pour chanter . . . , scaroit il et pourroit congnoistre les accors ou discors avecques tout l'art d'icelle science. . . ." (The artificial is . . . called artificial because of its art, for through its six notes, which are called *ut, re, mi, fa, sol, la,* one can teach . . . the most uncultivated man in the world to sing. . . . Or, supposing that he did not have a suitable voice for singing . . . , at least one could teach him enough so that he would know and be able to recognize the harmonies and discords using all the art of this science) (*L'Art* 60–64).

Such artificial music actually is inferior; it is merely a craft. The least cultivated can be taught to perform or at least appreciate its work. It is not as respectable as Boethius' "authentic music." But Deschamps' natural music is a loftier creation:

> L'autre musique est appelle naturele pour ce qu'elle ne puet estre aprinse a nul, se son propre couraige naturelment ne s'i applique, et est une musique de bouche en proferant paroules metrifiees, . . . Et ja soit ce que ceste musique naturele se face de volunte amoureuse a la louenge des dames, et en autres manieres, selon le materes et le sentement de ceuls qui en cest musique s'appliquent, et que les faiseurs d'icelle ne saichent pas communement la musique artificiele ne donner chant par art de notes a ce qu'ilz font, toutevoies est appellee musique ceste science naturele pour ce que les diz et chancons par eulx faiz ou les livres metrifiez se lisent de bouche, et proferent par voix non chantable, tant que les douces paroules ainsi faictes et recordees par voix plaisant aux escoutans qui les oyent, si que au puy d'amours anciennement et encores acoustomez en pluseurs villes et citez des pais et royaumes du monde.

> (The other music is called natural because it cannot be taught to anyone unless his spirit is naturally inclined to it. It is an oral music producing words in meter. . . . And even though this natural music originates from amorous desire in the praise of women, and in other ways, according to the subjects chosen and the inclination of those who apply themselves to this music; and even though those who make natural music generally don't know artificial music or how to give their lyrics an artful melody, nevertheless, this natural science is always called music because the *diz, chançons,* and *livres metrifiez* that they compose are read out loud and produced by a voice that can't sing in such a way that the sweet words thus composed, recited aloud, are pleasing to those who hear them, as it used to be at the Puys d'amours of old and as it is still the custom in several towns and cities of the countries and kingdoms of world.)
>
> (*L'Art* 62–64)

Deschamps finds natural music superior because it involves talent. It is linked to the tradition of the love lyric and is sweet even if recited by those who can't sing or if devoid of musical accompaniment.[9] The inspiration for lyric poetry may spring from passion and be a tool in the seduction of women, or it may have other sources—a point so clear it needs no explanation. Deschamps espouses an expressive poetics that rises from whatever urges the poet must express or whatever subjects he must explain. The lyric's art resides in its words, not in its melody. Most important, it gives great pleasure to its audience—pleasure caused by the euphony of its language and the sweetness of its content. Language has no direct link to (and no direct bearing on) content, but both content and language can contribute a positive quality—a euphonious sweet-ness—to the lyric. Unlike other theoreticians such as Dante, who dwell on the importance not only of the sound of language and poetry but also on the ideas and sentiments they convey, Des-champs makes no comment about the appropriateness of language to content beyond the stipulation that the lyrics of natural music have a certain eloquence (*L'Art* 64–65). Poetry also has a social dimension and history. Some poems can be graded competitively at the Puys—a poetic competition with a widespread, if popular, reputation—but courtly poetry is somehow different. Certain forms are more appropriate for courtly audiences than for common cir-cles, yet all forms can be explained by a shared theory of inspira-tion and exert their effects on their audiences by the same means.

Deschamps was not alone among fourteenth-century French poets who sought to bring popular genres, "sottise," to the court (Poirion 364). Indeed, both Froissart and Villon took prizes at local poetry competitions for exactly such poems (Bec I:162). Machaut and Charles d'Orléans also composed such poems. But Deschamps himself composed few poems in the genres usually brought before the Puys d'amours, although he does include brief comments in *L'Art de dictier* on their form and content. He mentions the pas-tourelle and the sote balade just long enough to say he will not speak of them. He does, however, reiterate his expression theory in this context: "Item, quant est aux pastourelles et sotes chancons, elles se font de semblables taille et par la maniere que font les balades amoureuses, excepte tant que les materes se different selon la volunte et le sentement du faiseur. Et pour ce n'en faiz je point icy exemple pour briefte et pour abregier ce livret" (As for pas-tourelles and sotes chansons, they are similar in length and style to balades amoureuses, except their contents are different according to the desire and sentiment of the poet. Therefore, I won't include any examples here for the sake of brevity and abridging this little book) (*L'Art* 94–95). Deschamps himself wrote few pastourelles but did not disparage them; he was the only major fourteenth-cen-tury writer to have made any effort at all to bring this more rural genre to the court, substituting a light, satirical style for their nor-mal vulgarity (Poirion 364) (although he did write at least four sote balades, all quite scabrous).[10] He composed no balades amoureuses and mentions them only in the above comparison. He did compose at least 136 chansons royales and mentioned that genre in *L'Art de dictier* in a list of genres suitable to the Puys d'amours. Because it was usually built on five rhymes, this genre was considered techni-cally difficult to compose. Many of Deschamps' chansons royales were, in fact, based on only three or four rhymes demonstrating his technical excellence and his ability to integrate this popular genre into his courtly corpus. Similarly, Deschamps does not discuss the rondeau in *L'Art de dictier*, except to say that it was suitable for the Puys d'amours; but he composed about 170 rondeaux, seven of which appear in *L'Art de dictier*.[11]

Deschamps apparently wrote no sirventes, although he tells us,

> Serventois sont faiz de cinq couples comme les chancons royaulx; et sont communement de la vierge Marie, sur la divinite; et n'y souloit [on] point faire [de] refrain, mais a present on les y fait, servens comme en une balade; et pour ce que c'est ouvrage qui se porte au puis d'amours, et que nobles hommes n'ont pas acoustume de ce faire, n'en faiz cy aucun autre exemple."

> (Sirventes are made of five strophe like the chansons royales and are commonly about the Virgin Mary or the Divinity. It was not the custom to write any refrains for them, but now one does write them, serving as in a balade. Because this is a work which belongs at the Puys d'amours and which it has not been the custom for noble men to compose, I will not include any other examples here.) (*L'Art* 82–83)

All these mentions of popular genres indicate how deeply Deschamps was interested in the poetic practices of his day—even those he disparages as too popular for his own purposes. His sense of their widespread popularity, however, forced him to include these rural genres and adapt or adopt them for courtly use, thus guaranteeing their futures. Noble men might not have composed in these forms before; Deschamps may not have been trying to encourage their spread; but they have a place in fourteenth-century lyric—Deschamps' natural music—that he could not ignore.

The balade, an accepted courtly form, was Deschamps' own favorite; he composed more than 1,000 balades, all with three isometric strophes and most with envoys. Deschamps himself seems to have been responsible for the addition of envoys to this fixed form, for, as he points out, "it was not formerly the custom to compose envoys at all except in chansons royales" (*L'Art* 79). Nevertheless, most of Deschamps' balades do not follow all the rules he prescribes in *L'Art de dictier*; thus, by testimony of his own poetic practice, they are not absolutely binding. Theory, then, was not as important to Deschamps as practice. He did, however, compose hundreds of poems before beginning *L'Art de dictier*. Moreover, his rules are not always clear or consistent. He uses technical vocabulary without defining it and often confusingly. But one of his

prescriptions includes what is possibly the first formal recommen-
dation to alternate masculine and feminine rhymes.[12] Deschamps
thought balades whose lines were all of equal length (and he
counted the last syllable of a line with a feminine rhyme) were
neither "pleasing nor of such good form" (*L'Art* 72–73). This injunction reinforces his earlier stress on euphony. Other instances of
interesting tidbits are scattered throughout *L'Art de dictier,* but this
is not the place to discuss them in detail.

Both natural and artificial music are sweet by themselves; however, their union produces an even finer product, a product of which
some think Deschamps may have had a momentary jealousy since
it seems he could not produce it himself.[13]

> Et aussi des deux musiques sont si consonans l'une aveques l'autre, que
> chascune puet bien estre appellee musique, pour la douceur tant du
> chant comme des paroles qui toutes sont prononcees et pointoyees par
> doucour de voix et ouverture de bouche; et est de ces deux ainsis comme
> un mariage en coniunction de science, par les chans qui sont plus
> anobliz et mieulx seans par la parole et faconde des diz qu'elle ne seroit
> seule de soy. Et semblablement les chancons naturels sont delectables
> et embellies par la melodie . . . de la musique artificiele.

> (And these two kinds of music are so consonant with each other, that
> each one can well be called music, as much for the sweetness of the
> melody as for that of the words that are all pronounced and made dis-
> tinct by the sweetness of the voice and the opening of the mouth. It is
> as if these two were married in a union of knowledge through the melo-
> dies which are more ennobled and fitting because of the text and the
> eloquence of the lyrics than either would be alone. Similarly, *chançons
> natureles* are made delightful and embellished by the melody . . . of
> artificial music.)

> (*L'Art* 64–65)

The primacy of natural music transcends the limitations of artificial
music. The two kinds of music enhance each other, but there are
times when natural music's superior qualities clearly are preferable;
for example, artificial music cannot be produced in such places as
the private chambers of the nobility or in the sickroom where there
is special need of its restorative powers. One does not always have
enough people—or room for them—to perform artificial music. Artificial music is sometimes just too loud to be appropriate or efficacious. Although each kind of music is pleasant alone,

> les diz des chancons se puent souventefoiz recorder en pluseurs lieux
> ou ilz sont moult voulentiers ois, ou le chant de la musique artificiele

n'aroit pas tousiours lieu, comme entre seigneurs et dames estans a leur prive et secretement, ou la musique naturele se puet dire et recorder par un homme seul, de bouche, ou lire aucun livre de ces choses plaisans devant un malade, et autres cas semblables ou le chant musicant n'aroit point lieu pour la haulteur d'icellui, . . . [les] voix . . . necessaires a ycellui chant proferer par deux ou trois personnes pour la perfection du dit chant.

(. . . the lyrics of the songs can often be recited in places where they are most willingly heard—even where artificial music would not always be performed, as among lords and ladies in private and secret. Natural music can also be uttered and recited by one man alone aloud; or any book of these pleasing things can be read before a sick person. It is the same in other cases where the performance of the melody would not be possible because of its loudness and [the] . . . voices . . . necessary for two or three people to perform this song properly.) (*L'Art* 64–67)

Deschamps' recognition of music's healing qualities caused by the pleasure it engenders adds another peculiarly medieval dimension to his theory. In the Middle Ages, pleasure was viewed as medically therapeutic. This therapeutic value was both a hygienic and recreational nature. The salutary effects of the former were comparable to those of proper diet and regular bowel movements. Such analysis of the effects of pleasure or cheerfulness date at least as far back as the *Isogoge* of Johanitius, which was cited extensively by Hugh of St. Victor (Olson, *Literature as Recreation,* 40) and can be seen to have been widely accepted doctrine from the introduction to the *Decameron*: Boccaccio's narrators flee the plague-ridden city and engage in delightful occupations, including storytelling, in hopes of deriving similar salutary effects to what their moderate diet will afford them. "[T]here is a great deal of evidence that educated people in the fourteenth century believed that enjoyment of music and fiction would decrease the likelihood of their being struck by the plague" (197–98). As for pleasure's recreational effects, they were noted by such early writers as Aristotle who, in his *Ethics,* advocated resting the soul from mental strain (as the body is from physical labor) by means of amusement (96). Aquinas and other medieval thinkers developed this line of thinking.[14] "Deschamps' view of lyric as natural music involves the logical fusion of hygienic and recreational ideas. The power of music . . . to repair mind and body is the medical fact that justifies the ethical inclusion of refreshment as a legitimate activity within the framework of liberal pursuits" (148–49). Olson has also shown that Deschamps' mentor Machaut subscribed to these theories which influenced his writing.

Although Deschamps shared Machaut's views on the therapeutic nature of literature and music, his own work differs radically from that poet-musician's in that Deschamps divorced the lyric from the musical setting that had always accompanied it.[15] There is a setting for only one of his poems, and he did not write it.[16] Speculation about jealousy and competence aside, we do not know what Deschamps' musical skills may have been; they are irrelevant to the consideration of his poetics. Deschamps saw lyric poetry as a greater art than instrumental music, as capable of standing apart from it—indeed, requiring separation from it, depending on the social situation.

It is finally time to address Payne's analysis of *L'Art de dictier*. Payne, who identified as a fundamental concern of the rhetorical handbooks "an elegant and orderly style and the use of language to persuade" ("Chaucer" 42), was disturbed by the lack of overt focus in *L'Art de dictier* on *elocutio* and *dispositio* and its replacement by this material and self-aggrandizing definition. Payne said, "the surface materials of poetry are lies and illusions, its effects emotional rather than rational. . . . only the ends of poetry—the service of truth—could justify its imaginative and irrational means, and only the maintenance of systematic and categorical order among its means could keep them from getting out of hand" (43). No wonder he found Deschamps' poetic theory thin and lacking in a moral commitment (*Key* 55).

When Payne first addressed *L'Art de dictier* in *The Key of Remembrance,* he situated Deschamps between Dante and Chaucer. Directly or indirectly, he said, even vernacular poets had to have been influenced by the ideas of the Latin *artes poeticae*. Vernacular poets absorbed standards of composition from earlier vernacular poetry, Latin poetry, or the various *artes poeticae*. "[S]erious and artistically self-conscious vernacular poets, sharing in general the rhetoricians' assumptions about the nature and value of poetry," inevitably realized that the particulars of style as analyzed by the Latin-oriented *artes poeticae* were not completely useful in managing the vernacular (53). Payne was convinced that the vernacular poet "had somehow to construct his own equivalent of the worthy poetry defined in Latin by the schoolmasters" (53). Deschamps followed in Dante's footsteps, both being "sufficiently concerned with the problem that they provide us with theoretical expositions as well as a body of poetry to help bridge the gap between Latin theory and vernacular practice" (54). As I argue elsewhere, however,

Deschamps actually did not share all of Dante's concerns. Deschamps no longer has to defend the vernacular: there is no sense that he is even aware that his is the first French poetics. Dante's *De vulgari eloquentia* "is not a manual of style so much as a survey of prosody" (55). In this, it resembles *L'Art de dictier*. Although *De vulgari eloquentia* does present a much more developed and coherent poetics, Payne complains that Deschamps "has next to nothing to say about the moral commitment for which gave rational consistency to the theory and affective power of the practice of poetry" (55). However, looking for the same moral threads in Dante's and Deschamps' work ties *L'Art de dictier* to a procrustean bed. Payne found in Deschamps' medicinal and recreational applications of music "a faded and indirect moral apology" for poetry but I would now argue for Deschamps' perception of the therapeutic, rather than the moral nature of poetry. Nowhere in *L'Art de dictier* is there discussion of the moral suasion ascribed to poetry in earlier poetics. Thus, when Payne had difficulty situating Deschamps neatly between Deschamps and Chaucer in the long line of rhetorical poets, it is no wonder that he found *L'Art de dictier* lacking.

It is to Bob Payne's credit as a scholar, teacher, and mentor that he handed me *L'Art de dictier* as a problematic, faulty treatise in need of apology and graciously accepted it back in a new light: the first French poetics which *does* have ties to both the vernacular and Latin traditions, which *does* reflect the poetic practice of a certain time and a certain well-recognized poet, but which is also strong in its own traditions: liberal arts, music, popular genres, and therapeutic medicine.

Notes

1. There has long been speculation that Deschamps was Machaut's nephew, based on a single, uncorroborated report in *Les Règles de la seconde rhétorique*: "Apres vint Eustache Morel, nepveux de maistre Guillaume de Machaut, lequel fut bailli de Senliz et fut tressouffisant de diz et balades et autres choses" (Then came Eustache Deschamps, master Guillaume de Machaut's nephew, who was the bailiff of Senlis and a prolific writer of songs and balades and other works [cited in SATF XI:12]. (SATF stands for Société des Anciens Textes Français. The SATF edition is still the only complete collection of Deschamps' poetry. All references to Deschamps' work will be to this edition except for references to *L'Art de dictier* which will be to the Colleagues Press edition.) I. S. Laurie argues convincingly against any blood relationship (Laurie, in Sinnreich-Levi, *Eustache Deschamps: His Works and His World*, 2–3).
2. Bibliothèque Nationale Fonds Français, 840.
3. See Bryan and Dempster 207 and 333; Chaucer 839, 860. For Deschamps'

contribution to Chaucer's literary environment, see Olson, "Deschamps' *Art de dictier.*" Wimsatt has played down Deschamps' influence on Chaucer. I. S. Laurie argues strongly against such influence.

4. See SATF XI:91–92, 92 n. 1; VI:251.

5. In my edition of the text, I conduct a detailed comparison of *L'Art de dictier* with *De vulgari eloquentia* and various Old Provençal poetics.

6. Deschamps uses "Julien," "Vivien," "Jacob" and "vates" in a discussion of the euphonics of consonantal [i]; he uses "Gaza" and "dixit" as examples of double consonants (*L'Art* 68–69).

7. See Marshall for editions and a fine discussion of Old Provençal poetics. See *L'Art de dictier* for an expanded discussion of Deschamps' poetics and that of the troubadours.

8. For a discussion of Boethian theory and *L'Art de dictier,* see Dragonetti. For other discussions of Deschamps' theories and those of musical theoreticians, see Bower, Laurie, Varty, and Wimsatt.

9. It is also linked to the lyrics of those troubadours and later poets who complain of the awful performances of lesser jongleurs and other entertainers who massacre their works. Eventually, such complaints evolve into the like of Chaucer's rebuke to his scrivener as the medium of transmission evolves from the lyric performed by a jongleur with musical accompaniment to a poem transcribed by a hand other than the poet's.

10. Sotes Balades 1216, 1363, 1455, 1488.

11. Some of the rondeaux in the SATF edition of Deschamps' complete works (which is based on the sole complete manuscript, MS. Bibliothèque Nationale Fonds Français 840) may not be Deschamps' (SATF XI:124 n.2).

12. Others have credited Ronsard with the invention of the alternation of masculine and feminine rhyme (Lote II:121).

13. Varty concludes his study noting that if Deschamps had been a musician, he would have had to admit that inspiration is not limited exclusively to the poet, but to the musician as well; that technique is an insufficient skill for the good musician even as it is for the good poet.

14. For a detailed tracing of the development of these ideas, see Olson, *Literature as Recreation,* esp. chaps. 2 and 3.

15. Wimsatt points out that many of Machaut's lyrics were also written without musical accompaniment ("Chaucer and Deschamps").

16. The musical setting for Balade 123, found in Musée Condé Ms. 1047, fol. 52ro, was composed by F. Andrieu. It is the only extant setting for a Deschamps poem (SATF XI:24).

Works Cited

Bec, Pierre. *La Lyrique française au moyen âge (xii–xiie siècles): contributions à une typologie des genres poétiques médiévaux: études et textes.* 2 vols. Paris: Picard, 1977.

Bower, Calvin. "Natural and Artificial Music: The Origins and Development of an Aesthetic Concept." *Musica Disciplina* 25 (1965):17–33.

Bryan, W. F., and Germaine Dempster, eds. *Sources and Analogues of Chaucer's* Canterbury Tales. New York: Humanities Press, 1958.

Chaucer, Geoffrey. *The Works of Geoffrey Chaucer.* 2nd ed. Ed. F. N. Robinson. Boston: Houghton Mifflin, 1957.

Deschamps, Eustache. *L'Art de dictier.* Ed. and trans. Deborah M. Sinnreich-Levi. East Lansing, MI: Colleagues Press, 1994.

———. *Oeuvres complètes de Eustache Deschamps.* 11 vols. Ed. Gaston Raynaud and August Henri Edouard, le Marquis de la Queux de Saint-Hilaire. Paris: Firmin-Didot, 1878–1903; rpt. New York: Johnson Reprint Co., 1966.

Dragonetti, Roger. *"L'Art de dictier* d'Eustache Deschamps." *Fin du moyen âge et renaissance: mélanges de philosophie française offerts à Robert Guiette.* Ed. Henri Pirenne. Antwerp: Nederlandesche Boekhandel, 1961. 49–64.

Laurie, I. S. "Deschamps and the Lyric as Natural Music." *Modern Language Review* 49 (1964): 561–70.

Lote, Georges. *Histoire du vers français.* 3 vols. Paris: Hatier, 1965.

Marshall, J. H., ed. *The* Razos de trobar *of Raimon Vidal and Associated Texts.* London: Oxford University Press, 1982.

Olson, Glending. "Deschamps' *L'Art de dictier* and Chaucer's Literary Environment." *Speculum* 48 (1973):714–23.

———. *Literature as Recreation in the Later Middle Ages.* Ithaca: Cornell University Press, 1982.

Payne, Robert O. "Chaucer and the Art of Rhetoric" *Companion to Chaucer Studies.* rev. ed. Ed. Beryl Rowland. New York: Oxford University Press, 1979.

———. *The Key of Remembrance.* New Haven: Yale University Press, 1963.

Patterson, W.F. *Three Centuries of French Poetic Theory: A Critical History of Poetry in France (1328–1630).* 3 vols. New York: Russell & Russell, 1966.

Poirion, Daniel. *Le Poète et le prince: l'évolution du lyrisme courtois de Guillaume de Machaut à Charles d'Orléans.* Paris: Presses Universitaires de France, 1965.

Rashdall, Hastings. *The Universities of Europe in the Middle Ages.* 3 vols. Ed. F. M. Powicke and A. B. Embden. Oxford: Oxford University Press, 1936.

Sinnreich-Levi, Deborah M., ed. *Eustache Deschamps, Fourteenth-Century Courtier Poet: His Work and His World.* New York: A.M.S. Press, 1998.

Strunk, Oliver, ed. *Source Readings in Music History: Antiquity and the Middle Ages.* New York: Norton, 1965.

Varty, Kenneth. "Deschamps' *L'Art de dictier.*" *French Studies* 19 (1965):164–68.

Wimsatt, James. "Chaucer and Deschamps' 'Natural Music'": *The Union of Words and Music in Medieval Poetry.* Ed. Rebecca A. Baltzer, Thomas Cable, and James I. Wimsatt. Austin: University of Texas Press, 1991:132–50.

———. *Chaucer and His French Contemporaries: Natural Music in the Fourteenth Century.* Toronto: University of Toronto Press, 1991.

Chaucer: Beginnings

CHARLES W. OWEN

OF THE POETS WHOSE DEVELOPMENT ADDS A DIMENSION TO THEIR AP-
peal and influence, Chaucer is unique. No less than half his major
works were left unfinished, and his masterpiece, *The Canterbury
Tales,* is a collection of fragments. If he had had the kind of persistence that impelled him always to finish what he had begun, we
should have had from him not only a complete *Anelida and Arcite*
and a less enigmatic *House of Fame,* but also the innumerable
Saints' Legends of Cupid projected in Alcestis' command:

> Thow shalt, while that thou lyvest, yer by yere,
> The moste partye of thy tyme spende
> In makyng of a glorious legende
> Of goode wymmen, maydenes and wyves,
> That weren trewe in lovyng al hire lyves   "F" 485[1]

For the tidiness of completed works, we should have lost the imperfect but vivid Canterbury pilgrimage; the Pardoner and Wife of
Bath would have yielded to Alcestis their part in Chaucer's energies; and the complete pattern of his development as an artist,
infinitely less important to us, would still have resembled Shakespeare's in its general lines, with the *Book of Troilus* paralleling the
tragedies and the *Legend* representing the decline of artistic intensity into tragicomedy. As it is, we have a poet whose devotion to
his art was spasmodic and whose skill and insight continued to
develop through the interruptions of his other career, despite the
unfavorable influences of poetic convention, of court obligation, of
religious feeling.

One of the most deceptive of all stylistic qualities was Chaucer's
ease of manner. He was not prolific in his poetic output. The period
of most intense activity in the mid-1380s—which crowded together
in a very few years the *Palamon and Arcite,* the *Troilus,* the *Legend,*
and the early work on *The Canterbury Tales*—gave way to a time
of uncertainty, to shifting of tales, to changes of plan, to work on
The Wretched Engendryng, the *Astrolabe,* and the *Equatorie,* per-

haps to a cessation of literary work of any but the most casual kind, certainly to a brief resumption of work on *The Legend of Good Women.* New combinations of poetic elements, as in the *Squire's Tale,* sometimes failed to fuse. Not one of the fragments of *The Canterbury Tales* turned out to have both a beginning and an end. The interruptions, the changes in plan reflect not only the confidence in continuing creativity, but the personal and original standards that Chaucer's experience of men and books had developed over the years. He was not afraid to leave behind his failures. He was certainly not interested in repeating successes. *The Canterbury Tales,* a fragment composed of fragments, has a potential often realized for the interaction of its elements; it projects the complexity of its imitated world the more vividly for the confidence of its author in implicit relationships. This confidence was not typical of the poetry of the Middle Ages. It is, however, present in Chaucer's earliest work. Apparently the climate of medieval thought and belief made it at least available. Its presence in *The Book of the Duchess,* as well as in *The Canterbury Tales,* suggests the continuity that underlies the remarkable development in Chaucer's art. It is a question whether the change or the consistency underlying change is the more striking element in this development.

Clearly, the change, great as it was, received its impetus from within rather than from without. It resulted from a growth in Chaucer's awareness and his responses rather than from the pressures of audience or patron. No considerations of advancement or advantage impelled Chaucer to lay aside the dream allegory for direct narrative or to develop the enlarged metrical possibilities of the pentameter in place of the octosyllabic or to abandon the courtly orientation of *Palamon and Arcite* and *Troilus* for the wider range of *The Canterbury Tales.* On the contrary, the evidence would seem to show that, among possible patrons, *The Book of the Duchess* would have been more pleasing than *The Parlement of Foules* and this, in turn, more pleasing than *The Miller's Tale* or *The Pardoner's*—that, in short, if anybody's taste was being flattered in the way Chaucer's art developed, it was most likely his own and that of his social equals—not that of the king and the great nobles on whom his fortune depended.

As in *The Canterbury Tales,* the basic fiction in *The Book of the Duchess* is that it is not in fact a fiction, that the narrator purportedly is telling us about something that actually happened to him. We watch this narrator, an insomniac, respond to a book he has read, a book, incidentally, which itself is a fiction. True, Chaucer's sources for this book are easily identified in the *Metamorphoses,* the *Ovide Moralisé,* and possibly Machaut's *Dit de la fonteine amoureuse.* But the book in Chaucer's poem distinguishes itself from the other accounts of Ceys and Alcyone by having a man replace Iris as Juno's messenger to the "goddes of slepyng." This comically insistent male changes the whole tenor of the episode in Morpheus' cave, gives it an emphasis that justifies the effect it is to have on the narrator. The fictive book contains much the narrator tells us he is skipping over—the entire account, for instance, of Alcyone's sorrow after she sees her husband's drowned body, before her own death "withinne the thridde morwe." It is worth emphasizing that the narrator is not only a solitary reader but one who reads carefully and goes back over the book to check the accuracy of his reading. His scholarly assiduity adds to the comedy of the connection between the book and the dream. In presenting a narrator who is clearly a fiction, whose autobiography is less important for the meaning of the poem than the Black Knight's which forms a part of it; in ascribing to this narrator opinions about the relation of the poem's parts transparently inadequate, Chaucer sets the reader free. The implicit meanings are the ones that count.

We watch the narrator read, and we see with amusement his naive response to the story of Ceys and Alcyone. We recognize the part his insomnia plays in his misreading. The miracle of sleep leads to a refreshing dream. The narrator changes roles in mid-dream, becoming a listener and interlocutor as the Black Knight takes on the burdens of troubled love. The dreamer's difficulty in understanding what the Knight is trying to tell him compels his grief-stricken companion first to relive the experience of love and then to face the finality of loss. The drama of the colloquy thus brings into conflict despair and incomprehension. The resolution of the conflict is action on two levels. The knight returns home from the forest. The narrator, awakened from his dream, writes his poem. The last words, "now hit is doon," simultaneously bring to an end both the narrator's writing and our reading. Reader and narrator thus experience the poem together, the interpretation of its "queyntness" an open question for both.

The reading and misreading, the listening and the failure to hear correctly in this Chaucer's earliest poem prefigure the House of Rumor, the parlement of raucous birds, and the tale–telling pilgrims on Canterbury Road. Drama involves people listening as well as talking. Each mind makes its own fiction of what transpires. This fiction, in turn, shapes response. A meaning emerges that no one vision controls and that resists final definition. Experiment with this basic pattern will mark Chaucer's art throughout his career. It will influence his meter and his use of language as well as the structure of his poems. It will affect his attitude to allegory and the way he regards time. It will lead to a fascination with the problems inherent in human freedom and with the fictions we live and create.

At the beginning of his career, in *The Book of the Duchess,* we find Chaucer at his most courtly, reflecting the dominant influence of the *Roman de la Rose* and the current literary taste as represented by Machaut and Froissart. Not only the occasional nature of the poem, but its function in Chaucer's career as courtier proclaim themselves, albeit delicately, with a clarity not to be found in any of Chaucer's later narratives. Despite its limitations, despite the confinement of purpose and the diffuseness of much of the verse, the poem breathes a life into its conventions and has elements of originality. The conception of the climax of the poem in terms of drama, the delicate balance between grief and joy in the experience of both the dreamer and the Black Knight, the discretion of tone through which so much of sympathy and consolation for the noble patron is conveyed, give it a distinct and secure place in English elegiac literature. The series of interesting parallels between the parts of the poem, echoes of phrase and motif, a complexity of emotional relationships, have made it one of the most fully and intellectually appreciated of Chaucer's poems in our own day.[2] The dream convention itself receives an infusion of fresh life from the surface authenticity of sudden detail and irrational sequence, and especially from the suggestion of deeper forces at work in the psychology of the dreamer. The poem has a frame story which includes, as an important element, the writing of the poem; it has a voice that speaks in constant counterpoint with intention and therefore implies more than it states; it gives to occasional details the unassimilated obstinacy of real objects.

Critics have tended to underestimate the extent to which *The Book of the Duchess* foreshadows his mature triumphs. Chaucer borrows freely from Ovid, from the *Roman de la Rose,* and from his contemporaries, Machaut and Froissart. He shows at the same time a surprising degree of independence and an understanding of what the nature of his own language permitted. He accepted, for instance, as axiomatic the "scarsete of rhyme" in English. In both *The Book of the Duchess* and *The House of Fame,* he confined himself to the octosyllabic meter, following Guillaume de Lorris and Jean de Meun rather than his own contemporaries. In doing so, he both avoided and created difficulties for himself. He avoided the complicated metrical exercises that were so prominent a feature of Machaut's and Froissart's *dits*—the complaints with their hundred distinct rhymes, the *lais* with the intricately patterned line lengths and rhyme schemes for each of the twelve sections. At the same time, he denied himself the interesting variations that the ballade of *The Legend of Good Women* or the roundel of *The Parlement of Foules* provided. The complaint and the love song of the Black Knight are so unobtrusive as to be indistinguishable in terms of form; they contribute nothing to what Chaucer clearly recognized as the problem with octosyllabics in English, the danger of falling into a monotonous dog-trot. What is genuinely eight-count in French is reduced by stress to four in English. We go from the longest possible span without cesura to the shortest possible line for extended use in poetry when we transfer the meter from French to English.[3]

The difference is worth illustrating. Here is one of several descriptions of bird-song from the *Roman de la Rose* that Chaucer first translated and then adapted to his own purpose in *The Book of the Duchess*:

> Grant servise douz e plaisant
> Aloient li oisel faisant;
> Lais d'amors e sonez cortois
> Chantoient en lor serventois,
> Li un en haut, li autre en bas;   705
> De lor chant, n'estoit mie gas.
> La doucor e la melodie
> Me mist au cuer grant reverdie;
> Et quant j'oi escoute un poi
> Les oisiaus, tenir ne me poi   710
> Qu'adonc Deduit veoir n'alasse . . .   711[4]

> (A great litany sweet and pleasant
> The birds kept on performing,
> Lays of love and courtly sonnets
> They sang in their close harmony,
> The ones above, the others below,   705
> Of their song no possible mockery.
> The sweetness and the melody
> Made in my heart great rejoicing,
> And when I had listened a while
> To the birds, I couldn't help   710
> Going right away to see Mirth . . .)

In this brief sample, the easy grace of the meter is apparent. The French poet has no need for variations other than those the feminine rhymes afford. Word length and phrasing work within the eight-count rhythm, providing at once variety and the fulfillment of order. One line opens and closes with a three-syllable word; the next one has eight monosyllables. Later, five monosyllables lead up to a four-syllable feminine ending. The passage has a single run-on line. Although we get single examples of leonine rhyme (701, 702) and rime riche (709, 710), the rhyme neither dominates nor fails to influence meaning. On the one hand, there is not the straining for leonine rhyme fashionable a century later. On the other, the rhyme "serventois" draws its meaning from linguistic association rather than precise literary reference, and the line ending in "gas" marks time with the meaning to complete the couplet.

The Chaucerian translation of the passage is surprisingly accurate.[5]

Ful fair servise and eke ful swete
These briddis maden as they sete.
Layes of love, ful wel sownyng   715
They songen in her jargonyng;
Summe high and summe eke lowe songe
Upon the braunches grene spronge.
The swetnesse of her melodye
Made al myn herte in reverye.   720
And whan that I hadde herd, I trowe,
These briddis syngyng on a rowe,
Than myght I not witholde me
That I ne wente inne for to see
Sir Myrthe. . . .   725

The couplets in the English are only slightly more dominant than in the original, but they seem much more so. In part due to the fillers, the "fuls" and "ekes" of the opening lines, in part due to the wrenching of accent in "sownyng" and the reaching for a rhyme in "I trowe," the effect results primarily from the very regularity that was so pleasing in the French. Thanks to the stresses in English, the rhythm is now four-count, and the single substitution in the third line and the run-on at the end of the passage are not sufficient to break the monotony. The poet understands the meter sufficiently to avoid the pitfall of too many lines that break in the middle. But the end-stopped couplets with stresses and syllable-count almost entirely regular illustrate beautifully the inherent dangers of the form for this kind of poetry in English.

If Chaucer was responsible for the "A" fragment of The Romance of the Rose, he learned from both his own failures and the weaknesses of the French poet he was translating. The facility of rhyme in French and the inherent grace of the meter tempted Guillaume de Lorris into repeated descriptions of birds singing as the dreamer entered the garden. Chaucer gathered suggestions from all of these descriptions and gave them more than decorative function as his insomniac narrator dreams he is waking in *The Book of the Duchess*:

Me thoughte thus: that hyt was May,
And in the dawenynge I lay
(Me mette thus) in my bed al naked
And loked forth, for I was waked
With smale foules a gret hep   295
That had affrayed me out of my slep
Thorgh noyse and swetnesse of her song.
And, as me mette, they sate among
Upon my chambre roof wythoute,
Upon the tyles, overal aboute,   300
And songen, everych in his wyse,
The moste solempne servise
By noote that ever man, I trowe,
Had herd; for som of hem song lowe,
Som high, and al of oon acord.   305
To telle shortly, att oo word,
Was never herd so swete a steven,
But hyt had be a thyng of heven,
So mery a soun, so swete entewnes,
That certes, for the toun of Tewnes   310
I nolde but I had herd hem synge;
For al my chambre gan to rynge
Thurgh syngynge of her armonye. . . .   313

The great difference from the earlier passage is not just the skillful use of the run-on and of substitutions, not even the frequent breaking of the couplet as the unit of meaning. Rather, it is the discovery of the long cadence, of the sense variously drawn out, beyond the limits of expectation in counterpoint with the rhythmic compulsions of form and language. What had earlier obtruded as weaknesses, the use of "I trowe" for rhyme, the repeated reminders of the dream, the whole line devoted to fillers ("To telle shortly, at oo word"), even the fashionable word-play with "Tewnes," are successfully contained by the cadence. Especially noteworthy is the syncopated rhythm of "The mooste solempne servise / By noote. . . ."

That Chaucer found his own way with octosyllabics so quickly speaks highly for his independence and his sensitivity to language.

French poetry was clearly developing its own critical vocabulary during Chaucer's lifetime. The *Leis d'amor* had appeared in southern France while Chaucer was still a boy, and his admirer, Deschamps, was to produce an *Art de dictier* in the final decade of Chaucer's life. To the extent that there were genres in English courtly poetry, they were simply adopted from the French—the terms *ballade, virelay,* and *envoy* proclaiming their derivation. Technical terms in France were not confined to naming the genres, but extended to classification of rhymes as well. Machaut uses the terms in his poetry, an indication that he expected his audience to know them, too:

> Retorique versifier
> Fait l'amant et metrefier
> Et si fait faire jolis vers
> Nouviaus et de metres divers.   150
> L'un est de rime serpentine,
> L'autre equivoque ou leonine,
> L'autre croisie ou retrograde,
> Lay, chanson, rondel ou balade;
> Aucune fois rime sonant   155
> Et quant il li plaist, consonant,
> Et li aourne son langage
> Par maniere plaisant et sage.   (Prologue V:158)

> (To put his rhetoric into verse
> And into meter, the lover labors,
> And so he fashions beautiful lines,
> Fresh and in varied verse-forms.   150
> One is in serpentine rhyme,
> Another equivocal or leonine,
> Another crossed or retrograde,
> Lay, song, rondel, or balade,
> Occasionally, assonance,   155
> And when he pleases, consonance,
> And he adorns his language
> In a pleasant and sagacious manner.)

Chaucer's intimacy with the poetry of his French contemporaries proclaims itself in the opening lines and throughout *The Book of the Duchess*; he must have been fully aware of the preoccupation with rhyme across the Channel, but he resisted the temptation to follow Machaut up this critical blind alley. If his fifteenth-century followers were no better poets than the *grands rhetoriqueurs,* the fault lay in their own misjudgments and in the linguistic change that distorted his verse for their ears.

Not all of Chaucer's effects in *The Book of the Duchess* were so happy as his description of bird-song. He tries at times for the verbal ingenuity that was so tedious a feature of his models, offering rhetorical virtuosity as an artistic equivalent for emotional intensity. After more than thirty lines on the greatness of his sorrow, the Black Knight continues:

> For y am sorwe, and sorwe is y.
> Allas! and I wol tel the why:
> My song is turned to pleynynge,
> And al my laughtre to wepynge, 600
> My glade thoghtes to hevynesse;
> In travayle ys myn ydelnesse
> And eke my reste; my wele is woo,
> My good is harm, and evermoo
> In wrathe is turned my pleynge 605
> And my delyt into sorwynge . . .

And so, for eleven more lines, to Fortune and the chess game, which modulates after 70 lines back into the sorrow theme for a final 24. This set piece, for such it is, must have taken no slight expenditure of time and effort. To find such varied ways for the limited content—to counterpoint rhythm of thought and language, now reversing the opposing terms, now doubling the one or the other and running over the lines, now quickening the tempo by doubling the oppositions per line (see lines 610–11)—required all the young poet's ingenuity. The passage has to be read on the surface, as it were. Then it rewards us with the dazzle of such a 20-syllable octosyllabic couplet as:

> For there nys planete in firmament
> Ne in ayr ne in erthe noon element 694

It takes a special attitude, however, a suspension of normal critical standards, to appreciate such a virtuoso performance. *The Book of the Duchess* has won critical attention in our own day for quite other qualities.

For the most part, Chaucer resists the temptations of prolix artificiality. The Black Knight's formal complaint lasts only eleven lines; we shall see later with what restraint the dreamer responds to the Knight's direct statement of his sorrow's cause. Occasionally, Chaucer experiments with a single run-on syllable before a pause—

disastrously in the following lines, where the repetition of the
rhyme approaches the effect called in French "rime retrograde":

> This lady, that was left at hom,
> Hath wonder that the king ne com
> Hom, for it was a longe terme.   79

But much more successfully in these:

> And therwith she yaf me a ryng;
> I trowe hyt was the firste thyng;
> But if myn herte was ywaxe   1275
> Glad, that is no nede to axe!
> As helpe me God, I was as blyve
> Reysed as fro deth to lyve —
> Of al happes the alderbeste,
> The gladdest, and the moste at reste.   1280

The sense of happiness attained against hope and beyond expectation receives, in the run-on and assonance of "glad," a metrical
equivalent. A similar effect two lines later in "reysed," a feminine
run-on without assonance, gives an increment of meaning to the
rather trite "blyve," which the rest of the line explains. The final
couplet sets up a pattern of assonance in the two successive stresses,
"al happes," but then modulates, in meaning as well as sound,
through the middle term "gladdes," to the rhyme and the lover's
feelings "moste at reste." Here, grammar yields to meaning, to the
happiness that makes of the external and the internal one harmoni-
ous world. Close analysis of a passage like this one hardly does
justice to the lack of strain, the unobtrusiveness of Chaucer's verse.
It labors where the verse moves as naturally as conversation. But it
confirms the poet's developing skill with language. It shows him
capable not just of surmounting the difficulties of octosyllabics, but
of adapting subtleties of rhythm and sound to meaning. As we shall
see, the mastery, though not consistent in *The Book of the Duchess,*
is capable of a variety of effect.

Chaucer makes original use of forms, themes, and passages that
come to him from the *Roman de la Rose* and his contemporaries;
his versification continues to find unobtrusive ways of meeting the
challenges inherent in English octosyllabics. Machaut and, after
him, Froissart had injected a new and personal note into the love
vision. Some of their poems omit the dream entirely; others relegate
it to a mere episode in what purports to be straight autobiography.
Machaut, in the *Dit de la fonteine amoureuse,* turns an overheard

lover's complaint into 800 lines of verse, presents them to the despairing nobleman, and accompanies him to the fountain where a dream takes place for both poet and lover, leaving behind tokens of its reality. In the *Jugement du roi de Beheinne,* no dream occurs. The lover overhears a dispute between a man and a woman over who has suffered the more, the woman whose lover is dead or the man whose mistress has deserted him for another. He suggests that the disputants submit their case to the King for judgment. The King decides for the man. The poet's association with the King and his ability to pay him the kind of tribute a man of taste will most appreciate are perhaps the most important, though only implicit, meanings of the poem. Froissart's *Paradys d'amour* is almost entirely a dream, but it has the Poet's plight in love as its central concern. His despair is admonished by Plaisance and Esperance, who take him to the Court af Love in the *paradys* for a renewal of his submission. He receives the reward of being accepted as servant by his lady. His later *Espinette amoureuse* has the dream as a minor element in a detailed account of his experiences with his lady.

Chaucer adapts to his own purposes this autobiographical tendency. The fiction of autobiography becomes a framework for the dream. The emphasis is not on the narrator, as in both Machaut and Froissart, but on the book he reads in his waking moments and on the Black Knight in his dream. The one clear thing we know about the narrator, his insomnia, motivates and distorts his reading, finds cryptic reflections in the dream, and by the end of the poem which includes its writing, has disappeared as a symptom of a mysterious eight-year-old "sicknesse." It is an anomaly of the autobiographical fiction that at the beginning the narrator shows no recognition of the sleep implicit in the dream or of the healthy and creative activity he is engaged in while writing the poem. By having his narrator fail to see any but the most superficial connections, the poet leaves the definition of his meaning to his audience. The narrator in *The Book of the Duchess* is the clearly recognizable original of the naive persona who "stands in" for the author in most of Chaucer's works. Like his fellow in the later *The Parlement of Foules,* he sees between the book he has been reading and his experience asleep a mechanical connection that, because of the unawareness of deeper psychological relationships, carries comic overtones. From his book, he has learned of the existence of a god of sleep:

> Me thoghte wonder yf hit were so;
> For I had never herd speke or tho
> Of noo goddes that koude make 235

Men to slepe, ne for to wake,
For I ne knew never god but oon.   237

As in *The Parlement of Foules,* the deeper significance of what he
dreams comes through because of his simple honesty, distorted by
no intervention of intellect and accompanied only by a fresh amazement at the uniqueness of experience. There are significant differences, however. The narrator in *The Book of the Duchess* is
changed, as he is not in the *Parlement,* by his experience. Furthermore there are some indications that his naivete is, in part, assumed.
The elaboration of his vow to the God of Sleep has a comic exuber-
ance and ends with a sophisticated reservation:

                          this shal he have
         Yf I wiste where were hys cave.   262

His profession of ignorance as to any possible interpretation has a
mock-heroic quality as he insists on the impenetrability of his
dream to Joseph and Macrobius, and by implication compares himself to Pharaoh and Scipio. In this respect, he foreshadows somewhat the character of the narrator in *The Canterbury Tales,* who
clearly has chosen the simplicity he shows the Host and the other
pilgrims as a better instrument for both observation and judgment.
The narrators in Chaucer's poems, though related by a common
simplicity of manner and a reluctance to make critical comments,
are nicely adjusted to their functions.
    Chaucer's originality in *The Book of the Duchess,* as later in the
Troilus and *The Canterbury Tales,* points in two directions in his
narrative: greater use of realistic detail and an emphasis on pattern
and design. To some extent, these two seemingly disparate tendencies reinforce each other. The parallels between book and dream,
between the predicaments of narrator and Black Knight, enable him
to make his reference to John of Gaunt's loss more discreet and to
develop the dream verisimilitude with a psychological depth that
adds a dimension of significance to the poem. The most prominent
parallel is that between Alcyone's loss of her husband Ceys and the
loss suffered by the Black Knight. Because of the naive character
of the narrator, this parallel is never made explicit. Its unobtrusiveness is a first instance of Chaucer's willingness to let the values of
his poems emerge from behind the humorous counterpoint of his
narrator's comment, in this instance the delighted discovery that a
God of Sleep exists. Thus, the chord of lament sounds in purely
fictive terms at the beginning of the poem with no overt reference

to Blanche's death and Gaunt's grief. The ghost of Ceys, in bidding farewell, offers a consolation to his wife that epitomizes the pathos of loss and represents one of the tonal limits of the poem—a consolation Chaucer does not presume to offer later to John of Gaunt through John's surrogate, the Black Knight.

> And farewel, swete, my worldes blysse!
> I praye God youre sorwe lysse.   210
> To lytel while oure blysse lasteth.   211

The sounds of the final line, especially the l's, in combination with the final iambs of the two preceding lines create a metrical equivalent for a litany of loss. The position of "blysse," too soon for the rhyme and yet more than a rhyme (rime riche with "blysse" and near identical with "lysse"), gives the very sound a meaning.

The delicacy with which Chaucer expresses his allegorical meaning is furthered by the less obvious parallel between the narrator's predicament and the events of his dream. The suggestions of a real dream sequence after the narrator falls asleep, and the psychological connections between the waking plight and the dream make it possible to read the poem on a level quite apart from its allegorical reference. Not until the final lines of the poem does Chaucer give clues for the uninitiate as to who the Black Knight is. Meanwhile, the dreamer's experience is meaningful in itself. It suggests in the very beginning of his vision the beneficent effect of sleep as he dreams of awaking to a brighter world where no hint of his malaise intrudes. The suggestions of spring, of dawn, of an unencumbered nakedness in bed, and the long description of heavenly bird–song (already commented on), the accord with nature and himself that the dreamer now feels, express effectively the renewal of life and energy that sleep is bringing—the dream of well-being to match the revitalizing slumber. The succeeding description of walls and windows which permit the inveterate reader to absorb books, both text and gloss, without the labor of reading defines in a new way the welling up of power and health in the narrator's being.

With a swiftness that reflects the peculiar logic of dreams, the narrator no sooner hears the sounds of preparation for a hunt than he finds himself on horseback riding out of his room to join in the sport. His eagerness to engage in activity contrasts with his lethargic despair while awake and reflects anew the restorative powers of sleep. In the account of the hunt, Chaucer shows the same reticence with respect to the small detail he had earlier shown in the thematic parallelism of book and dream. Events succeed each other, making each its sharply visualized impact. Consistent though they are with the conventions of medieval hunting, they also have a dreamlike rapidity of transition, a selectivity of emphasis that suggests an intrusion into the dream of the narrator's malaise. His imagination follows the hunt through its sounds fastening on the "ruse" by which the hart escapes, on the failure of the hounds, and on the huntsman as he (in a headless line)

> Blew a forloyn at the laste.   386

As if to dissociate himself from an elusive "hert" and to deny the implications of "forloyn," the narrator tells us in the very next line:

> I was go walked fro my tree   387

Leaving his post, leaving his horse, strangely freed from the formal obligations of the hunt, he is overtaken by the fawning whelp in a line that imitates the dog's bewilderment with a surplus of syllables:

> That hadde yfolowed, and koude no good   390

Trying to catch it, the dreamer is led into a delightful grove, peopled with deer of all kinds, with squirrels and other "beestes," which, unshadowed by even a memory of the hunt, he can linger in, enjoy and observe in all its detail (for some 44 lines of delighted description in which the dreamer first concentrates on the path and its myriad flowers, only slowly raising his eyes to the squirrels and the treetops they inhabit).

> But forth they romed ryght wonder faste
> Doun the woode; so at the laste
> I was ware of a man in blak,   445
> That sat and had yturned his bak
> To an ook, an huge tree.   447

In the figure of the Black Knight, the distancing and objectifying of grief perfects itself. The dreamer can sympathize with the sorrow of another, having created and accepted in his dream an image of the finality of his own quest:

> Anoon ryght I gan fynde a tale
> To hym, to loke wher I myght ought

Have more knowynge of hys thought.
"Sir," quod I, "this game is doon.
I holde that this hert be goon;   540
These huntes konne hym nowher see."   541

Chaucer does not insist on the suggestive detail, on the double
meanings and psychological substitutions, in which the conventions
of the hunt and of courtly love coalesce. He has the restraint now,
as he does later in his treatment of the old man in *The Pardoner's
Tale,* to avoid saying too much about his little dog, to allow him to
appear and disappear without comment. The tree which the dreamer
leaves at the sound of a "forloyn" may well be the psychological
equivalent of the tree against which the Black Knight is leaning, as
the rules of the hunt may be of the code of courtly love. But Chaucer does not obtrude these explanations upon us any more than he
does the allegorical relevance of the dream. When we come to the
repetitions of the phrase "at the laste" (which occurs seven times
in the poem), we do well to doubt that we are here encountering a
delicate feeling for the power of significant repetition rather than
the inexperienced resort to a stock connective.[6] Whatever we may
think of any specific instance, the general pattern of the dream is
clear in its significance. It epitomizes the universal function of
sleep; it confirms the word *wonder* that echoes through the poem;
and when the dreamer awakens, it inspires him to the creative effort
of imitating in verse the experience he has had:

This was my sweven; now hit ys doon.   1334

The completed poem is both an account and a confirmation of the
dreamer's recovery, and it parallels the therapy the Black Knight
receives within the dream, the therapy of communicating to another
the "wonder" of his experience of love.

The exploitation of parallel and contrast for implicit meaning,
effective in *The Book of the Duchess* and so often to be met with
later in Chaucer's poetry, aids him in establishing the objectivity,
the narrative distance characteristic of his most distinctive work. It
sets him off from the didacticism so prevalent in medieval literature
and points in the direction of withdrawal from overt judgment, a
faith in the responses of his audience and in the meanings that fact
and detail carry implicitly. The relevance of the dramatic to these
general tendencies in Chaucer's art is apparent. His ability to imitate the rhythms of speech in verse developed steadily as his genius
for comedy drew him from the romantic and courtly in medieval

tradition toward the projection of voice. Even in so early a work as *The Book of the Duchess,* we find him resorting to a dramatic solution for problems of narrative emphasis. By inventing a whole new character for Juno's messenger and realizing the visit to Morpheus in dramatic terms, he breaks the sophisticated suavity of his model in Ovid's *Metamorphoses* and prepares for the impression the story is to make on the narrator—for his amusing discovery that a God of Sleep exists. Rhythmic control enables him to convey stage direction and speech with comic effect and to imitate the haste of the messenger with a skillful line of summary.

> This messenger com fleynge faste
> And cried, "O ho! awake anoon!"
> Hit was for noght; ther herde hym non.   180
> "Awake!" quod he, "whoo ys lyth there?"
> And blew his horn ryght in here eere,
> And cried, "Awaketh!" wonder hye.
> This god of slep with hys oon ye
> Cast up, axed, "Who clepeth ther?"   185
> "Hyt am I," quod this messenger.
> "Juno bad thow shuldest goon"—
> And tolde hym what he shulde doon . . .   188

The opposition between breathless urgency and sleepy reluctance is conveyed in these lines through speech, action, sound, and rhythm. We get the linking of the disparates in the two couplets (179f and 183f), with the addition in the second couplet of the run-on into the next line and a succession of five long syllables ("oon ye/Cast up axed"), the amusing failure by the messenger to identify himself ("Hit am I"), the single line of summary at the end that at once avoids repetition and imitates haste, these instances of comedy intensified by prosody prefigure the enhancement of meaning through prosodic effect in Chaucer's later works.

More complicated in function and uneven in skill is the scene between the dreamer and the Black Knight. The Knight, with the role of greatest emotional intensity, is the least successful element in the poem. We have already seen an example of the artificiality that marks the expression of his grief. The affectation of the courtly style also mars, though not so seriously, his account of his lady and of his love for her. By opposing to the Knight's long explanations the persistent obtuseness of the dreamer Chaucer creates a series of dramatic interruptions, where we hover on the brink of disclosure. We know what the conclusion will be. The conflict creates the suspense not of how it will end but of when. With each intervention of the dreamer, we expect the resolution to take place. But the description of the lady adds another element. Interested now in the Knight's relation to her, we fear the resolution will take place before we know the full story. The colloquy thus serves a variety of purposes. The persistent questioning about information the dreamer has already received (in the Knight's song) suggests the frustrations of nightmare, the knowing and not being able to bring the essentials of knowledge to clear focus, the repeated attainment of what turns out to be the same objective—it functions as an element of dream verisimilitude. Furthermore, the dreamer's comments stimulate the knight into affirming the value of his experience:

> "Bet? Ne no wyght so well," quod he   1045

And again, when the dreamer has compared the Knight's "chaunce" to "shryfte withoute repentaunce":

> "Repentaunce! nay, fy!" quod he,   1115
> "Shulde I now repente me
> To love? Nay, certes. . . ."   1117

The fear of premature resolution increases with our interest in the story. Such a resolution appears inevitable with the direct question "What loss is that?" (1139); fortunately, the dreamer continues his questioning:

> "Nyl she not love yow? ys hyt soo?   1140
> Or have ye oght doon amys,
> That she hath left yow? Ys hyt this?
> For Goddes love telle me al."   1143

We experience the Knight's dedication, his writing of the short love song, the agony of hesitation over telling his lady directly, her denial of his suit, his asking her again "another yere," and the fulfillment of their life together:

> "And thus we lyved ful many a yere
> So wel, I kan nat telle how."   1297

We come to the end of the story seven words later, in the adverb *now*, rhyming with the Knight's inexpressible happiness but meaning the opposite in his monosyllabic echo:

> "Sir," quod I, "where is she now?"
> "Now?" quod he, and stynte anoon.
> Therwith he wax as ded as stoon,   1300
> And seyde, "Allas, that I was bore!
> That was the los that here-before
> I tolde the that I hadde lorn.
> Bethenke how I seyde here-beforn
> 'Thou wost ful lytel what thow menest;   1305
> I have lost more than thou wenest.'
> God wot, allas! Ryght that was she!"
> "Allas, sir, how? What may that be?"
> "She ys ded!" "Nay!" "Yis, be my trouthe!"
> "Is that youre los? Be God, hyt ys routhe!"   1310
> And with that word ryght anoon
> They gan to strake forth; al was doon,
> For that tyme, the hert-huntyng. . . .   1313

Aesthetic satisfaction on the reader's part thus accompanies the memories of fulfilled love in the mitigation of the Knight's grief. The dreamer's laconic comment and his lapse into a silence that expresses his sympathy better than words unite with the sudden end of complaint, of dialogue, of hunt, of dream, of poem, and of the writing of the poem to reinforce this aesthetic satisfaction.

Not the least of the beauties of this passage (which begins with two headless lines) is the implication in the single word of the Knight—

> "Now?" quod he, and stynte anoon   1299

the implication of how far from the present grief he had been carried, the shock of return from the blissful fulfillment he had been reliving. Chaucer manages in this passage to epitomize the experience of loss with its poignancies of memory and grief. His skill with dialogue and his tendency to see narratives in terms of dialogue thus manifest themselves in his earliest original work.

The Book of the Duchess is unique as an elegy in putting as much emphasis as it does on the positive without expressing faith in an afterlife. For a loss whose finality it never seeks to minimize,[7] it offers the therapy of memory. By defining what it is he has lost, the Black Knight is forced to recognize the value to him of the relationship he had with his love. This value remains, and at the moment of greatest awareness and intensity coexists with the despair at her death:

"Now?" quod he, and stynte anoon. . . .   1299

The Black Knight will never be the same after this moment of expanded being. By its very delicacy of statement, however, the poem
maintains a reserve toward Blanche. The dreamer as surrogate at
two removes from Chaucer expresses sympathy for the Knight and
indirectly for John of Gaunt. Any personal feeling Chaucer felt at
the death of Blanche, he chose not to express in this most courtly
of his poems. Curiously it is this personal note that finds expression
in some lines written a few years later by his contemporary Froissart. The French poet's tribute to Queen Philippa and the Duchess
Blanche throws into relief what Chaucer's poem is and is not.
Froissart is responding to the request by Philosophy that he name
those whose generosity he has experienced:

> "Volentiers! Premiers vous exemple   230
> La bonne, qui pourist en terre,
> Qui fu roine d'Engleterre;
> Phelippe ot nom la noble dame,
> Propisces li soit Diex a l'ame!
> J'en suis bien tenus de pryer   235
> Et ses largheces escryer,
> Car elle me fist et crea,
> Ne onques voir ne s'effrea
> Ne ne fu son coer saoules
> De donner le sien a tous les.   240
> Aussi sa fille de Lancastre —
> Haro! mettes moi une emplastre
> Sus le coer, car, quand m'en souvient,
> Certes souspirer me couvient,
> Tant sui plains de malencolie. —   245
> Elle morut jone et jolie
> Environ de vingt et deux ans;
> Gaie, lie frische, esbatans,
> Douce, simple, d'umble samblance;
> La bonne dame ot a nom Blanche.   250
> J'ai trop perdu en ces deux dames,
> J'en tors mes poins, j'en bac mes palmes."
>   (*Le Joli Buisson de Jonece* 230–52)

> (Willingly! First I give you as example   230
> The good woman rotting in the ground
> Who was queen of England.
> The noble lady had the name Phelippe —
> May God be propicious to her soul.

I am surely bound to pray for her   235
And celebrate her generous bounty,
For she made and fashioned me
Nor was she truly ever put off by fear
Nor was her heart ever sated
From giving of her substance to all.   240
Also her daughter of Lancaster —
Haro! put soothing ointment
On my heart, for when I remember her,
Sighing certainly becomes me,
I'm so full of melancholy. —   245
She died young and beautiful
At the age of about twenty-two,
Gay, happy, fresh, striking,
Sweet, simple, unassuming.
The good lady had Blanche for name.   250
I've lost too much in these two ladies.
For them I twist my hands, I beat my palms.)

This natural statement of grief for the two great ladies dead of the
plague in the same year confirms the praise the Black Knight heaps
on his lady in *The Book of the Duchess*. Its considerable art remains
throughout in the service of Froissart's emotion. Attention to some
of its detail will help illustrate one final time the distinction between
French and English octosyllabics, and especially the French emphasis on rhyme. The variations in the Froissart are, for the most part,
those provided by word length and phrasing. At the moment of
greatest emotion, the poet permits himself the exclamation "Haro"
and breaks the couplet with the only genuine run-on line in the
passage. It is worth noting how natural the word order is, how un-
forced the rhythmic effects. Froissart risks the repetition seven
times running of a 4-4 division of the lines beginning "Elle morut /
jeune et jolie," counting on the grammatical distinctions to avoid
monotony and perhaps wanting a ritualistic regularity to give emphasis to the poignance of her early death. The passage is not as
artless as it first appears. The rhymes from "pryer" to the final
couplet are leonine with the interesting exception of "et deus ans—
esbatant." They include the unusual combinations "saoules—a tous
les," "Lancastre—emplastre," and "samblance—nom Blanche."
The final line, with its seven monosyllables, is also worth noting.
The relation of "J'en tors" to "J'ai trop" in the previous line gives
an equivalence in sound for the involuntary kinesthetics of the
poet's grief, also emphasized by the not-quite-perfect rhymes of the
last two couplets. The artifice adorning what is also a direct and

natural expression of feeling gives the passage a courtly delicacy it would be almost impossible to reproduce in English octosyllabics.

The contrast with *The Book of the Duchess* points up the reserve of the English poet, the distance between Chaucer the man and his narrator.

Notes

1. Quotations from Chaucer are from *The Riverside Chaucer,* with the following exceptions in *The Book of the Duchess*: 179, For "O, how!", "O ho!"; 201, for "songe", "songen"; 211, for exclamation point, period; 262, parentheses omitted; 307, for dash at end of line, comma; 308, for dash at end of line, comma.

2. See, for instance, Clemen chap. 1; Bronson; Lawlor; Baker; Manning; Winny chap. II; Spearing 49–73; Boitani 140–49; Mehl chap. 3; Lawton 52–57; Stevenson esp. her analysis of the rhymes in the Knight's Song to his Lady, 9; and finally the refreshing account of the poem in Pearsall 82–93. A more radical approach, with which I find myself only partly in sympathy, is reflected in Dennis Walker's two pieces. Walker insists that consolidation takes place only for the reader, not for the dreamer or the Black Knight within the poem. See also Aers. Mention should be made of James Wimsatt's work in the French sources and of Willaim Calin, "Machaut and Chaucer II: Literary Considerations," a paper given at the 21st International Congress, Kalamazoo, 1986, and his book, *A Poet at the Fountain.*

3. For an illuminating discussion of the special importance of the cesura in French poetry and its use in different meters in medieval French poetry, see Lote vol. I, esp. 83–116 and 213–33. French octosyllabics occasionally have the cesura; verses longer than the octosyllabic always have it. The count beyond eight apparently was thought too large to be perceived automatically. Hence, the decasyllabics in French break normally into four-syllable, six-syllable hemistichs; the alexandrines invariably (until the late eighteenth century) into six, six. The cesura is distinguished from the rhyme in being derived from the heightening of pitch at the end of a phrase, as opposed to the dropping of pitch at the end of a sentence (see Lote I:264–90). Comments on Chaucer's octosyllabics have failed to note the special role of the cesura in French metrics, as opposed to its casual use in English poetry (Howard 142–47).

4. Quoted from the Langlois edition, vol. II. Two variants probably present in Chaucer's text are, in the first line, "Biau servise e doux et plaisant"; and, in the final line, "Que dant Deduit. . . ." For other descriptions of bird-song in the first part of the *Roman* drawn on by Chaucer in *The Book of the Duchess,* 291ff., see 67–83, 95–102, 478–96, and 644–80.

5. For extended comment on the translation's "literal reproduction of its source," see Eckhardt, esp. 46ff.

6. The phrase occurs nine times in the 2,158 lines of *The House of Fame,* twice in the 699 decasyllabics of *The Parlement of Foules.*

7. Even the metamorphosis of Ceys and Alcyone is omitted. See Ovid, *Metamorphoses,* IX:731ff.

Works Cited

Aers, David. "Chaucer's *Book of the Duchess*: An Art to Consume Art." *Durham University Journal* 38 (1976–77):201–5.

Baker, Donald. "Imagery and Structure in Chaucer's *Book of the Duchess*." *Studia Neophilologica* 30 (1958):17–26.

Chaucer, Geoffrey. *The Riverside Chaucer*. Ed. Larry D. Benson. Boston: Houghton Mifflin, 1987.

Boitani, Piero. *English Medieval Narrative in the Thirteenth and Fourteenth Centuries*. Tr. Joan Krakover Hall. Cambridge: Cambridge University Press, 1982.

Bronson, Bertrand. "*The Book of the Duchess* Reopened." *PMLA* 67 (1952):863–81.

Calin, William. *A Poet at the Fountain: Essays on the Narrative Verse of Guillaume de Machaut*. Lexington: University Press of Kentucky, 1974.

Clemen, Wolfgang. *Chaucer's Early Poetry*. Tr. C. A. M. Sym. London: Methuen, 1963.

Eckhardt, Caroline. "The Art of Translation in *The Romaunt of the Rose*." *Studies in the Age of Chaucer* 6 (1984):41–63.

Froissart, Jean. *Oeuvres de Froissart: Poésies*. Vol. 2. Ed. Auguste Scheler. Brussels: Victor Devaux, 1870–72.

Howard, Donald. *Chaucer: His Life / His Works / His World*. New York: E. P. Dutton, 1987.

Lawlor, John. "The Pattern of Consolation in *The Book of the Duchess*." *Speculum* 31 (1956):626–48.

Lawton, David. *Chaucer's Narrators*. Cambridge: Boydell & Brewer, 1985.

Lorris, Guillaume de, and Jean de Meun. *Roman de la Rose*. Ed. Ernest Langlois. Société des Anciens Textes Français. Paris: Firmin-Didot, 1914–24.

Lote, Georges. *Histoire du vers français. Ouvrage publié avec le concours du Centre de la recherche scientifique*. Paris: Boivin, 1949–1988.

Machaut, Guillaume de. *Oeuvres*. Vol. 1. Ed. Ernest Hoepffner. Société des Anciens Textes Français. Paris: Firmin-Didot, 1908–21.

Manning, Stephen. "Chaucer's Good Fair White, Woman and Symbol." *Comparative Literature* 10 (1958):97–105.

Mehl, Dieter. *Geoffrey Chaucer: An Introduction to His Narrative Poetry*. Cambridge: Cambridge University Press, 1986.

Pearsall, Derek. *The Life of Geoffrey Chaucer: A Critical Biography*. Oxford: Blackwell, 1992.

Spearing, A. C. *Medieval Dream Poetry*. Cambridge: Cambridge University Press, 1976.

Stevenson, Kay Gilliland. "Readers, Poets, and Poems Within the Poem." *Papers on Language and Literature* 25 (1989):19–35.

Walker Dennis. "Narrative Inclusiveness and Consolatory Rhetoric in the *Book of the Duchess*. *Chaucer Review* 18 (1983):1–17.

———. "The Psychological Realism of Fictional Characters: Another Perspective." *Neuphilologische Mitteilungen* 86 (1985):337–42.

Wimsatt, James I. *Chaucer and his French Contemporaries: Natural Music in the Fourteenth Century*. Toronto: University of Toronto Press, 1991.

Winny, James. *Chaucer's Dream Poems*. New York: Harper & Row, 1973.

"The Mystery of the Bed Chamber": Mnemotechnique and Vision in Chaucer's *The Book of the Duchess*

Mary Carruthers

IN THIS ESSAY, I WOULD LIKE TO RECONSIDER SEVERAL FEATURES OF Chaucer's *The Book of the Duchess* in a somewhat different context than has been accorded them before. These matters are the "dream vision" nature of the narrative, including the highly decorated nature of the "bed chamber" in which the dreamer awakens in his vision; the stress given to the dis-ease and anxiety of the narrator prior to his dream of the Man in Black; and the way in which grief and remembrance work together to make this elegy into a commemoration—a social remembering via literature—of the noble lady, Blanche.[1] These may seem to us now only distantly related, but they are linked conventions that bring together the themes of grieving and remembering with the procedures of inventing compositions.

Although memory has long been assumed to be in some elementary fashion the task of *The Book of the Duchess,* most modern treatments have sought the psychological motives of the characters in the poem, focusing on the grief of the Man in Black as a trauma to be cured and placing the dreamer in the position of "confessor" or therapist, wittingly or not. The "sicknesse/That I have suffred this eight yeer" (36–37)[2] has been attributed to the poet's grief for Blanche, or to conventions of love poetry or political expediency, or to a more generalized melancholia, and his concomitant sleeplessness to the standard symptoms of a diseased humor. The considerable attention accorded to the dream visions in this poem has gone to defining exactly what the truth-value of Chaucer's vision might be, arguing from the terminology first defined in Macrobius' commentary.[3]

Starting from the premise that all memorials are social in their function, *The Book of the Duchess* can be profitably studied, I think, in the context of particular rhetorical practices and conventions which both poet and audience shared, especially those providing a procedural model for composition, including, especially, composition of literature. As an elegy for a public figure, *The Book of the Duchess* is a memory poem requiring memory-work on the part of all its participants—dreamer, characters, and audiences within and without the poem.[4] I emphasize the notion of memory-*work,* for, in this culture, "memoria" was a great deal more consciously schematic, institutionalized, and public than the private and subjective emphasis which psychoanalytic theory has given to it. As Maurice Halbwachs, one of the first social philosophers in this century to examine the socially constructive necessity of "public memory," has argued, it is our *dreams* that are fully private, for in dreams individually focused modern psychologies, such as Freudian, can find the area where consciousness is isolated and most turned in upon itself. But, "[n]o memory is possible outside frameworks used by people living in society to determine and retrieve their recollections" (Halbwachs 41–42).[5] Memory, by its very nature, is constructive as well as conservative; it is social and so rhetorical—a view of the subject that is wholly medieval in its emphases.

If we were asked now to describe how we compose something, we would probably say that we compose by using our "imagination." Thus, when we read in a medieval description of religious meditation or in a medieval poem that composition begins in "recollection," we tend to assume one of two things: either that medieval people had no concept at all of "creativity" in our sense and that they were devoted to a more or less slavish reiteration of other people's creations; or we assume that what they call "recollection" is something completely other than anything we would recognize as "memory"—and that they made a category error by using the wrong term. So, in her 1911 study, *Mysticism,* Evelyn Underhill felt compelled to apologize for "[t]he unfortunate word *Recollection,* which the hasty reader is apt to connect with remembrance" (Underhill 314).[6]

This statement and others like it assume that the process of composing has always been the same, as though composition were a universal, natural procedure like breathing that always has involved the same steps and the same unchanging mental "faculties"—that is, "observation" and "imagination." In this early twentieth-century scheme of things, "memory" is always and only a faculty of repeating previously experienced and stored "information." This view of human cognition seems to assume, as well, that descriptions of mental activities are always efforts to define by classification: what "is" memory, what "is" imagination, what "are" the emotions. It allows little room for the possibility that what these terms describe are not psychic "objects" (the memory, the recollection, the imagination) but aspects of a single procedure taking place unceasingly in a human mind. Of course, when pressed, every philosopher and psychologist will tell you that he or she is perfectly aware that the "faculties" cannot be separated out from the seamless process of thinking—but the vocabulary and form of scholastic analysis militates against this and in favor of faculty distinctions.[7]

But the "psychological faculties" are a creation of human analytical procedure, not of God (or of Nature). If we could learn instead to think habitually of human cognition in terms of process or "way" (the *via* of the ancient liberal arts) and then focus on the cognitive way called "composition," we might understand that this process could be presented and analyzed as "recollective" because it was assumed to begin with acts of remembering, mnemonic activities that "draw in" other memories. The result was something like what we now call "using our imagination," even to the point of visionary experience. But the medievals called it "recollection," and they were neither wrong nor foolish nor naive to do so.

Imagination is important in both ancient and medieval analysis of composition because images were considered to be essential to thinking. When I was much younger, I used to wonder whether I thought with words or with ideas. Some of my students now say they think with "concepts"—they "get a concept" of something. Premodern cultures were sure that humans think "in images," that our minds compose thoughts within a medium of images, that our minds "think with" recollected pictures. Evelyn Underhill wrote of visionary experiences that they are "picture[s] which the mind constructs, it is true, from raw materials already at this disposal: as the artist constructs his picture with canvas and paint" (Underhill 271). *Recollection* is an unfortunate word only to a culture whose idea of "memory" is restricted to rote reiteration, and demoted from cognition altogether. For the process of constructing from "raw materials already at [the mind's] disposal" is a procedure of engaging memory.

In a common monastic idiom, one "remembers" death, heaven, and hell—that is, one makes a mental vision or "seeing" of invisible things from the matters of one's memory. A twelfth-century monk wrote that "[t]he frequent recollection of the city of Jerusalem and of its King is to us a sweet consolation, a pleasing occasion for meditation."[8] A professor at Bologna, Boncompagno da Signa, writing a textbook of rhetoric in 1235, includes in his discussion of rhetorical *memoria* sections "de memoria paradisi" and "de memoria inferni," and comments that "we must assiduously remember the invisible joys of Paradise and the eternal torments of Hell" (Boncampagno da Signa 278). The sources for such remembering are both literary and visual: commentaries, murals, miniatures, sculptures, windows. Sometimes they might also include things one actually had seen in the past; Boncompagno, for example, says that when he "remembers" Hell, he remembers (among other things) an eruption of Mt. Etna he had once seen. This is a cognitive "way" for knowing the future in the present by means of "gathering" (*collectio*) previously remembered materials—Invention as Recollection—and it is this procedure I want to explore in this essay.[9]

Before considering *The Book of the Duchess,* I would like to examine two familiar moments of pure "imagination," as we now would call it, pure literary "vision." The first is the initial vision of Boethius' *Consolation of Philosophy.* The work begins with a poem of complaint (meter I.1), followed by some narrative prose, thus:

> While I, in silence, hoped to cogitate this composition within myself [Haec dum mecum tacitus ipse reputarem] and to inscribe using a stylus my tearful protest a woman was seen by me to be standing up over my head [adstitisse mihi supra verticem visa est mulier] . . . (I. pr. i, 1–3)[10]

I would like to call attention to some features of this famous narrative that may seem trivial because they are so commonplace. First, notice that Boethius is engaged in "silent" composition, that is "meditation" or what I have called "memorative composition." The poem he is working on (that is, meter 1) is at a stage before it gets written down with a stylus, the stage of "invention" and "disposition," whose product is often called *res* to distinguish it from *dictamen,* the stage at which the *res* is "clothed" with words, and from the *liber scriptus,* when it is (perhaps, if it is worthy) written down in a fair copy.[11] In fact, from what he tells us, he is in the final drafting stages, almost ready to write his composition out with a stylus but still wanting to mull it over ("reputarem")—that is, still composing.

Second, notice that it is during this activity of mental composing that the woman of grave countenance "became see-able to me" [mihi . . . visa est mulier] standing upright over the composing poet—who is in his bed. We are not told whether or not his eyes, at this point, are closed; later manuscript paintings of this scene show him either with eyes closed or eyes open.[12] But his mind is not only conscious; it is fully engaged in the recollective composition of his poem, performed as the rhetoric handbooks all counsel by means

of mental imaging techniques such as the lady-figure (Philosophy)
which "disposes" the matter (*res*) of his work.

The poet carefully regards his vision of the lady, painting it in
the eye of his (and our) mind. Then Philosophy spies the Muses
"nostro adsistentes toro" [standing about our bed] (I. pr. 1, 26–7).
They leave in confusion. And then Boethius, weeping and astonished ("obstipui": I. pr. 1, 46), fixes his countenance on the ground
and, in silence still (the adjective "tacitus" is repeated), begins to
watch for whatever will come next:

> But I, whose gaze immersed in tears became blurred, nor could I discern
> who that woman might be, . . . was stunned, and, with my gaze fixed
> upon the ground, in silence, began to watch out for what she might do
> next [At ego cuius acies lacrimis mersa caligaret nec dinoscere possem,
> quaenam haec esset mulier . . . obstipui uisuque in terram defixo quid-
> nam deinceps esset actura, exspectare tactitus coepi]. (I. pr. 1, 44–48)

Notice first the emphasis in this narrative on acts of seeing. I have
already mentioned how Lady Philosophy is said to become "see-
able" by the meditating poet. Notice that the Muses are called "has
scenicas meretriculas" (I. pr. 1, 29), literally "these prostitutes to-
be-looked-at-as-though-on-a-stage." Isidore of Seville, quoting
Varro, says that the word *scenicus* comes from the activity of "gaz-
ing" (as, of course, do both "theater" and "theory") (Isidore of
Seville xviii:42–43; cf. x:253). And finally, Boethius says he
watches Lady Philosophy—"exspectare" from the verb *spectare*,
"to look" (I. pr. 1, 47).

And he is in his chamber in his bed. A common modern explanation for this detail is that it is there because the *Consolation of
Philosophy* is a dream vision. While I know that is its current literary classification, I find this argument from genre—as though such
classifications were anything more themselves than useful modern
mnemonic shorthand—anachronistic, tautological, and misleading
as an explanation for the phenomenon being analyzed.

Every composition in medieval cultures was thought to begin as
an act of mental seeing. The reason Boethius is lying down in his
bedchamber, as his narrative makes clear, is not in order to sleep
but to compose poems. He is silent, and he is lying in bed because
those two physical attitudes are among the postures commonly
thought to induce the mental concentration necessary for "memory-work." One fifteenth-century manuscript painter showed Boethius in bed with his eyes closed and his head angled toward
Philosophy, who stands beside the bed—clearly the painter understood that she is being "seen" mentally, inwardly.

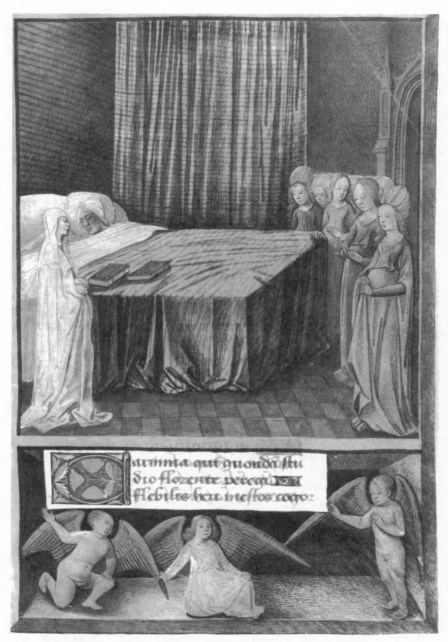

Lady Philosophy appears to Boethius in his bed, while the Muses gather at its foot. Notice that Boethius' eyes are shut; notice also how flat the bed-clothes are about his body, suggesting that is has less physical weight in the bed that the two books, whose shadows are prominently featured. From a French manuscript of 1476; London, British Library, MS Harley 4335–4339, f. 27r. Photo: The British Library, reproduced with permission.

Finally, in the passage quoted above, notice that in order to watch Philosophy, Boethius looks at the ground ("visuque in terram defixo"). That is a very peculiar detail. The manuscript images I have seen of this encounter show Boethius lying on his back (with his eyes open or closed) or standing at a desk while the lady dictates to him. But the text says that after Philosophy banishes the Muses, Boethius begins to weep copiously and throws himself prostrate, face downward.

Lying prostrate and weeping "in silence" (that is, in meditation) became a standard posture in the Middle Ages for literary invention. In the late twelfth century, the monk Eadmer ascribes just such behavior to Saint Anselm during the initial composition of his *Proslogion,* and more than a century later, Bernard Gui says that Saint Thomas Aquinas did the same thing as he composed his *Summa theologica.*[13] In monastic thought, this inventional state is linked, by Bernard of Clairvaux among others, to *Song of Songs* 5:2, "Ego dormio, et cor meum vigilat" ("I sleep but my heart is awake").[14] One must keep in mind that "heart" was a commonplace synonym for "memory." Learning "by heart" is an English translation of the Latin *recordari,* linked by Varro to the root *cor, cordis,* "heart"; Italian has preserved the Latin verb in *recordarsi,* French in *recorder* (Varro vi:46; [I:214–15]).

In his 23rd sermon on *The Song of Songs,* Bernard of Clairvaux describes the process of what he calls "the mystery of the bed chamber [secretum cubiculi]," divine contemplation. The first stages are characterized by "restlessness," an active mind "disposing" matters, "arranging" things. The language is that of the rhetorical analysis of literary composition, Inventio and Dispositio being the initial stages of creation.[15] This mental activity, which Anselm's biographer Eadmer described as being like an illness ("inquietude" is dis-ease), is what is referred to in the verse, "Ego dormio et cor meum vigilat."

Roman rhetorical practice also associated composition with lying down. During Cicero's dialogue *De Oratore,* the chief speakers, Marcus Antonius and Lucius Crassus, adjourn twice (between books of the dialogue) in order to collect their thoughts on the subjects put to them by the younger members of the party. Marcus Antonius prefers to compose by walking with Cotta in the portico ("in porticu," a structure that provides the "intercolumnia" often recommended as backgrounds for memory-work). But Lucius Crassus retires to his invention-chamber:

> what [Cotta said] he chiefly noticed was that Crassus devoted all this midday interval to the closest and most careful meditation; and that as

he [Cotta] was well acquainted with the look [Crassus] wore when he had to make a speech and with the fixed gaze of his eyes when he was meditating, and had often witnessed this in important lawsuits, on the present occasion he was careful to wait till the others were reposing, when he came to the room [exedra] where Crassus was reclining on a couch [lectulus] placed there for him, and as he perceived that he was deep in meditation, at once retired; and that almost two hours were spent in this manner without a word being spoken. (Cicero, *De oratore* III.v.17)

The Roman *exedra* was a sort of large bay or recess within a larger space——it could also be a small chamber off a larger area (such as the peristyle). At least from the Republican period on, like other rooms in Roman houses, it was painted with images arranged in scenes or panels, often painted "intercolumnia," between columns, one of the architectural forms most closely associated with the

Cubiculum M, in the Villa of Fannius Synestor at Boscoreale, Roman, 40–30 BCE. The installation is modern, and neither the floor mosaic nor couch and stool (since removed) came from the same villa. New York, The Metropolitan Museum of Art, reproduced with permission.

"places" of memory-work.[16] Thus, we may think of Crassus as selecting for his invention process a fully decorated chamber. Notice that the couch has been specially placed there for him. And since the dialogue takes place at his own villa, we can also presume that this *exedra* is Crassus' own particular room, his "study," used for his business, for conversation with particular friends, for reading and contemplation. I imagine Crassus' chamber as a room rather like that from the late Republican villa of P. Fannius Synestor at Boscoreale. That room is just large enough for a single couch. Its walls are all painted in panels "intercolumnia" with what appear to be scenes from a theater. It opens off a much larger space, for it is now in the columned Great Hall of the Metropolitan Museum of Art. The effect is indeed (as Vitruvius noted of these painted *exedrae*) like stage sets, a "theater" of architectural forms that apparently was assumed to be conducive to inventional meditation—not, I think, because it provided subject matter but because the ordered familiarity, the rote quality, of such pictures in one's most tranquil space could help provide an order or "way" for thinking, functioning for invention somewhat as a mandala-picture does in traditions of Tibetan contemplation.[17]

Quintilian also assumed that a person needing to compose would go to bed. He describes someone desperate to "invent" a composition by "[lying] back with eyes turned to the ceiling, trying to fire [his] imagination by muttering . . . in the hope that something will present itself" (X.iii.15). Equally, he counsels (as did Martianus Capella, in a tradition that remained strong) that nighttime, when silence reigns and distractions are minimized, is the best time for the meditative stages of composing (the *res* and *dictamen*), which require intensive concentration (X.iii.25–30; cf. Martianus Capella 269).[18] Writing with a stylus is better done, he says, in daylight. This advice reverberates within the poetry of *The Song of Songs*, 3:1, "In lectulo meo, per noctes, quaesivi quem diliget anima mea" ("In my bed, through the night, I have sought him whom my soul loves.")

My second example of literary "seeing" starts off a long narrative. Aeneas, washed ashore at Carthage after a great storm, comes unseen into the city and into the temple of Juno which Dido has erected, "rich in gifts and the presence of the goddess" (I.447). Here, to his amazement, he sees a series of pictures on its walls, each showing a scene of the battle for Troy:

> he scans each object, while he marvels at the city's fortune, the handicraft of the several artists and the work of their toil, he sees in due order

the battles of Ilium, the warfare now famous throughout the world, the sons of Atreus, and Priam, and Achilles, fierce in his wrath against both. He stopped and weeping cried: "What land, Achates, what tract on earth is now not full of our sorrow?" . . . So he speaks, and feasts his soul on the insubstantial picture [animum pictura pascit inani]." (*Aeneid* I:454–60, 464)

Memorial material is called up, reassembled, brought together ("com-posed") by the agency of a picture, upon which the mind "grazes" in a recollective, meditative rumination. Memorial cultures are storytelling cultures, and the picture-artifact is also a story-artifact.[19] The artifact presents—makes present in memory—the occasion for a composition, the "starting point" of recollection, as these mural paintings do for Aeneas, as the shield presents stories of the Greeks to Achilles, as the "swordhilt of giants" chased with scenes of the Flood does to Hrothgar. These artifacts are only textual, although ones much like them have been found: for example, the "Frank's Casket" or the "Iliac Tablet" in the Capitoline museum in Rome.[20] It is no coincidence that Simonides of Ceos, the "inventor" of the ancient mnemonic art of "picturing" images in backgrounds, is also identified (by Plutarch) with the maxim "ut pictura poesis."

A number of works, both Roman and medieval, begin with an initial "picture," and the technique has acquired a name although the one used by scholars is modern, *Bildeinsatz*.[21] Cicero's *De Natura Deorum* begins with a cosmic "picture"; so, far more elaborately, does Martianus Capella's treatise on the liberal arts, with its picture-narrative of "the wedding of Mercury and Philology." Philosophy's robe is an example; so too is the intricate beginning picture of Dame Nature in Alain de Lille's Boethian poem, *The Complaint of Nature*. The technique is common still in the fourteenth century; I described in *The Book of Memory* friar Robert Holcot's *picturae*, which he says he "placed" mentally in the initial verses in Hosea in order to remember the themes of the commentary, clearly as his invention-tool for sermons and lectures (*Book of Memory* 230–31).[22]

Bildeinsatz starts off a work by aiding the memory of both the fictional onlooker and the reader/hearer with a summary of the principal "matters" of the work to follow seen as a set of painted or sculpted, embroidered or mosaic images—the careful technique of the artificer is often stressed, for technical memory is being addressed. These "pictures" are almost always described as being within a room, often on the walls of a chamber, though sometimes they are on the floor or even the ceiling. It is not hard to see the relationship of this figure to the textbook advice to an orator to fashion *imagines agentes,* grouped narratively as "scenes" within "background places," whose relative positions cue the order and subjects of his composition. *Bildeinsatzen* have the rhetorical quality called *enargeia*; often this figure is conflated with *ekphrasis,* the description of a building or other artifact (such as the Temple of Juno in *Aeneid* I). But narrowly defined (which is a good place to start, though I wish to broaden the definition shortly), such a picture differs from *ekphrasis* in two ways. It is at the beginning of a work, a trope of preamble, whereas *ekphrasis* can occur at any point in a work. Because of its location, it acts as the elementary foundation, the *dispositio* of what follows. Placement is critical. These literary "pictures" start off a complex work—in computer-speak, they "initialize" it. The images' placement within the initializing arrangement rings changes on the three basic modes of associative recollection: they may be "alike," they may be "opposite," they may be "neighborly" or "contiguous."[23] In memory technique, these traits refer to an image's relative position in a composition, rather than to its conceptual status. Their placement sets the associative pathways onto which one hooks up additional material in various directions from the foundational images.

These compositional tropes resonate in the initial activities of the narrator of *The Book of the Duchess.* The elegy—a poem of remembrance—begins with the poet unable to sleep, ill, in a state of dazed melancholy and near to death because of it, "For sorwful ymagynacioun / Ys alway hooly in my mynde" (14–15). The "sicknesse" is caused by melancholy (23) and manifests itself both by the sorrowful imagining mentioned in line 14 and "fantasies" that are always in his head and draw him away from his routines and ordinary nature. Moreover, these idle thoughts have oppressed him for eight years. "Fantasies" of the "ymaginacioun" that oppress and dis-ease the mind are a trope of the initial stages of composition, as we have just seen. Chaucer's characterization of these as "fantasies" puts his images in the class of those in which recollection is conducted, the *phantasia* of meditative image-making. His melancholy, fear of death, and the emotional accidia or "torpor" which he says he suffers from at the beginning of the poem: these are the conventional signs of someone who is trying to get his recollective machinery started, the "inquietude" that precedes fruitful meditation. Bernard of Clairvaux writes that the preparatory stage of the mystery of the bedchamber is "not a place of repose. . . . The contemplative who perchance reaches that place is not allowed to rest and be quiet"; this languorous restlessness is what is characterized in the key text, "ego dormio et cor meum vigilat."[24]

Given the conventional nature of this emotional state as a prelude to invention, Chaucer's reference to his eight years' "sickness" seems best understood, as others have suggested, to refer to the interval between Blanche's death and the poem's composition, placing the poem's date in the mid-1370s.[25] One should not expect autobiographical or other individualistic psychological explanations for this well-worn, Roman and monastic, trope of composition. Nor should we understand this state as the insecurity of an unskilled poet, or even of a skilled poet wanting to poke fun at his bumbling persona. Chaucer and his audience understood this anxiety—even of eight years' duration—as a craftsman's prelude to serious work.

The dreamer goes to his bed and calls for a book in which he reads a tale (Ceyx and Alcione) about the death of a spouse. Although the story itself is grief-filled, the reader-poet remains in his torpor until he is finally stirred to action by a novel scheme for sleep, and makes his first composition, the prayer to Morpheus. He then falls asleep ("ego dormio") and has a visionary dream: "ryght upon my book / Y fil aslepe, and therwith even / Me mette so ynly swete a sweven" (274–76). In this vision he is awakened by a birds' chorus. The poet opens his "eyes"—his mind's eyes—and sees the sun streaming through the brilliant glass of his bedchamber, in which the stories of Troy are painted. He also sees, as mural paintings, all the tales and commentaries of *The Romance of the Rose*. Between them, these two works contain much of the *dicta et facta memorabilia* of late medieval society. Notice also that these works are painted in pictures, not just of the Troy stories, but also of *The Romance of the Rose,* for part of its "glose" is the program of pictures with which it was conventionally furnished.[26] In mnemotechnical terms, this bed chamber is ornamented with images which cue *memoria rerum,* those "matters" which serve to initiate all literary craft.

The conventions of memory-work resonate through the dream itself. The dreamer rides forth from his chamber into a "forest" (*silva,* a common image for a disordered mind, one without the paths that inventory its contents, where as a result "the straight way is lost"). Here he finds a "hart hunt" in progress, which he watches from a tree. When the hunt is suspended after the dogs lose the hart's scent, the narrator wanders from his tree, and led by a puppy, finds his way into the forest's darkest secret heart.[27] Here he finds a Man in Black, sitting against a great tree (a common pose of both grief and meditation). This Man in Black, ill, in a state of dazed melancholy and near to death because of it, is composing a "lay," which he proceeds to recite without any music—unlike the birds, he has only "a maner song, / Withoute noote, withoute song" (471–72). He then tells a story about a chess game he has played with Fortune (and lost by losing his queen). The poet misses the metaphor—it does not resonate for him. So the mourning knight tries again to explain his grief, and in a sustained act of remembering that proceeds primarily by gathering in much associated matter from common stories, he is able finally both to re-member his dead spouse and also his first song. Unlike the first lay, this recollection is a true song, though it is not clear whether the Man in Black actually sings it to the dreamer.[28]

The poem is often described as a kind of psychodrama, in which the dreamer, either willfully or not, plays the role of therapist to the Man in Black, eventually enabling him to "face up to" his grief, stop "hiding behind" fictions, and thus "get on with his life" (I assume). But to put it so crudely is also to point up the modern, individualist bias in such a reading. The psychically healing nature of the dialogue may better be understood using a model closer to confession than to psychotherapy, although the confession model is also very limited in use for this poem.

The elegaic poem is like a confession only because both activities are dependent on memory-work. Each involves a sustained, deliberate act of remembering, though their goals are different. Both also begin in grief, mourning (for one's self, for another) as the matrix of remembering. Nor is grief restricted to composing elegies and confessions; for, as we have seen, the deliberate production of melancholy, a "sorwful ymagynacioun" even to the point of tears, was a commonplace means (though not the only possible one) of initiating one's cognitive, mnemonic image-making.[29]

The compositional nature of penance, like all prayer, was recognized—one "makes" a confession as one "makes" any composition, from the matters of one's memory.[30] The goal of such "h(e)art-hunting" is "restoration," not of the individual in any modern psychological sense, but of the person as a citizen of God, of *civitas Dei*. Confession, unlike psychiatry, focuses primarily on community. Through the penitential "art of memory"—the orderly examination of "conscience" (a word which, in many contexts, interchangeable with "memory" in Middle English)—one restores balance and achieves, however temporarily (in this life), a harmony.

So the "hart-hunt" is an inventory pun for this poem. It is enriched by the other dominant game image in the poem—chess. By the fourteenth century, chess games also had a common association with penitential mnemonics. Best known is the confessional manual, *The Game of Chess,* by the Dominican friar Jacopo da Cessolis, but chessboards and matches are common as a mnemonic images in the margins of prayer books. Why chess? Because it is preeminently a game of memory. It is a game of patterns, one that depends on "finding" images in places, the essential technique of memory. And these remembered patterns enable the invention of each new game. One could think of a chess game as a narrative made up by two people engaged in an exchange of remembered plays—each move leads to new story possibilities as the game develops. The interplay of past, present, and future that constitutes the invention of each game is also (as Augustine wrote long before chess was known in the West) the particular provenance of memory, for memory also "invents" time.

The method of mnemonic invention is that of deliberate compositional "gathering," a vast collation of matter held together by associations of various sorts—conceptual, yes, but also (and often more effectively) by puns of both sound and sight. These chains of sensory associations construct a chorus or "entunement"—"diverse voices make sweet music," as Justinian says in Dante's *Paradiso* (Canto 6.124). And now we should remember those birds, whose sweet "entewnes" (in-tuning) the poet wants to listen to "for all the toun of Tewnes" (the town, *civitas,* of Tunes—for once I agree with D. W. Robertson in hearing in this pun a distant echo of paradise) (Huppé and Robertson 46–47).

In mnemonic reading, words in the text are treated primarily as cues for and nodes within associational chains arrived at through recollection. The reader learns to treat text as "brief," or *brevitas* or "breves" (like musical notes): summary distillations that require exfoliation and dilation in the reading, remembering mind. Thus, reading is itself at the same time an activity of storing and one of composing, simultaneously using and making memory images.

The Book of the Duchess proceeds in part by puns, both paronomastic (as in *tewnes* and *herte*) and visual, like the punning which mirrors the postures, health, and activities of the poet in those of the Man in Black. Add to that the fundamental assumption in medieval medicine that disease results from imbalance in the humors (including melancholy), and one understands the importance of harmony in this poem. Harmony leads to birds, birds to Ceyx and Alcione, Alcione, as halcyon, to harmony again.[31] Metamorphosis connects to resurrection—the *Ovide moralisé* sets up that frame. The "heart-hunting" of this poem, far from being a journey to find "the inner man," is a journey outward to "find" an entire library of textual melodies. It takes the form of a chorus, not of birds only but also of stories—the Man in Black remembers his dead lady by making her "picture" from the images provided by the common stories he so plentifully "gathers in" to his composition. His mourning is completed in the way his private, dis-eased, tuneless "imbalance" is, as it were, "civilized" and "composed" by being woven into the stories that make up shared, communal memories. As the poem makes clear, this activity does not enable the Man in Black to "forget" his grief or "get over" the death of Blanche. Precisely, it enables him to remember her continually, but publicly. The poem was, after all, composed as an act of public mourning, and its basic dialogic structure brings the knight's mourning into the public sphere.

The public nature of these acts of memory is critical, for they are, as I have argued elsewhere, rhetorically, not psychologically, conceived.[32] The mourning knight seeks to remember his dead lady not in order to "recover" her as she once actually was ("She ys ded" after all), nor does Chaucer seek to "transcend" her death by making both her person and the knight's grief into something timeless and forever unchanging. Rather, the memory-work of both the dreamer and the Man in Black results, as it were, in the "publication" of Blanche. The mnemonically generated pattern-making in which the knight engages, "gathering" around the figure of his lady all the associations of public *res memorabilia,* makes Blanche also part of the common story. The point is not individual transcendence but communal historicizing; for, in Halbwachs' words, "our recollections depend on those of all our fellows and on the great frameworks of the memory of society" (43). Such memory frameworks were understood most often in Chaucer's culture as shared stories or "matter," like those in Ovid, *The Romance of the Rose* and the Troy-books.

"Recollecting" is not at all the same thing as "transcendence," nor does it lead to "permanence." Halbwachs' memory frameworks, for which the medieval mnemotechnical term is *formae,* are structures one may use to mold and shape, to attach and order and dispose, to help construct one's own compositions. Such structures are useful precisely because they are not unalterable and changeless, but constantly refashioned and historicized in the "exchange," the economy, of rhetoric.[33]

In that program, grief plays a particular role as an agent of new creation. As I have tried to demonstrate, the context and sources for this trope are not to be found in psychological writings, but in rhetorical lore common to Chaucer and his court audience. I realize that this shifts the locus of critical attention away from the personal trauma of the knight to a public sphere in which the activities of both the poet and the audience assume considerable significance. But I do not think this poem is primarily an effort to console a bereaved individual by seeking to assure him that from death comes life or that Blanche lives eternally. Blanche is dead, and that is "routhe" (1310) to us all. The poem, in short, concerns itself with our grief more immediately than with Blanche's death and salvation (a matter, after all, better addressed through the prayers of the Church). *The Book of the Duchess* is an act of public mourning, of public remembering, and the emotion of grief itself is its focus. While the "hert-huntyng" may be done "[f]or that tyme" (1313), we are meant to understand that it will continue, at least on each public anniversary of the duchess's death.

Notes

1. Phillipa Hardman, "Memorial Monument," offers the first full-length study of this poem, not as a "dream vision" but as a memorial work, and tries to define what implications for both the provenance and meaning of the poem such a consideration might carry. She has fruitfully linked aspects of the poem to contemporary funerary sculpture and provided an essential understanding of this poem as an artifact of a "memorial culture." An instructive meditation on "memory" in Chaucer, and especially in *The Book of the Duchess,* is Louise Fradenburg, "'Voice Memorial'": Fradenburg's analysis, conducted in psychoanalytical concepts, focuses on questions of subjectivity in grieving and loss.

2. All citations are to *The Riverside Chaucer.*

3. The most recent general account of medieval dream theory in its philosophical dimension is Steven Kruger, *Dreaming in the Middle Ages,* which does not discuss Chaucer particularly, but does contain much useful information about the dissemination and reputation of Macrobius' categories. See also, the important discussion of the truth value of dream images in Robert R. Edwards, *Ratio and Invention.*

4. Previous efforts to relate Chaucer's dream-vision poems specifically to mnemonic techniques such as the making of "backgrounds" and the placement therein of "agent images" include Beryl Rowland's, Richard Kelly's, and my own "Italy, *Ars memorativa,* and Fame's House." Some of the theoretical issues involved in the "mnemonic criticism" of literary texts are explored by William Engel, my reply to his essay, "Inventional Mnemonics and the Ornaments of Style," and further discussions of the matter by Lina Bolzoni, "A Reply to Mary Carruthers," and Sylvia Huot, "Inventional Mnemonics, Reading and Prayer." General studies of what might be called "inventive" or "cognitive" uses of memory can be found in Lina Bolzoni and Pietro Corsi, eds., *La Cultura della Memoria*; Susanne Küchler and Walter Melion, *Images of Memory*; and my own *The Book of Memory.*

5. Halbwachs' entire collection—but especially the second part on "The Legendary Topography of the Gospels in the Holy Land" (a condensed version of

Halbwachs' 1941 monograph on this subject)—should be of great interest to all medievalists interested in what one might call the "rhetoric of place." See also, the interesting case studies discussed in James Fentress and Chris Wickham, *Social Memory*.

6. For all its Victorian psychologizing, Underhill's study remains full of keen observation, a mine of source material.

7. Coleman cautions wisely against the tendency in writing about mental activities and procedures to divide "faculties" from one another (*Ancient and Medieval Memories,* esp. 231–32).

8. An anonymous meditation, from the *Exhortatio ad amorem claustri et desiderium lectionis divinae* (ed. *Analecta monastica* II) (Leclercq 62 and note).

9. The modeling of memory as a dual process of "dividing" and "gathering" is analyzed at length, with many examples, in *The Book of Memory,* esp. chap. 6.

10. The Latin text is cited from E. K. Rand's edition for the Loeb Classical Library. The translation is my own, based on the admirable one by Richard Green, which is too polished to quite convey the literal sense of the Latin words.

11. These stages of composition are described in detail with illustrative examples, in *The Book of Memory,* chap. 6.

12. See, for example, the illustrative plates in Pierre Courcelle, *La Consolation de Philosophie*.

13. Eadmer reports that Anselm experienced sleeplessness, loss of appetite, and a feeling that he had been "infested" by his intense mental wrestling with the argument of his composition (Southern 30); Bernard Gui reported that Thomas Aquinas "never set himself to study or argue a point, or lecture or write or dictate without first having recourse inwardly—but with tears—to prayer . . ."; while "writing on Paul's epistles, [Thomas] came upon a passage which quite baffled him until . . . he fell to the ground and prayed with tears; then what he desired was given to him and it all became clear" (Foster 37–38).

14. Underhill has an excellent discussion of monastic (and mystical) "(in)quietude," traditionally linked to this verse (316–27).

15. Quoted from Bernard of Clairvaux, Sermon 23, sect. iv. (II:33–36). The initial stage of "restlessness," Bernard says, is only the entrance to the bedroom proper, for, in a turn on the standard trope, he reserves the bed itself for the state of divine union that the mystics call "rest." Still, "restlessness," a kind of preliminary "sleep," is necessary to get to "rest." The idea that sleep can be a state of memorial, cognitive activity is also a well-known medieval trope. Pierre Riché notes that medieval hagiographers applied the text of Sg 5:2 to instances of children learning the psalms by reciting them bit by bit until they slept and then awakening with perfect knowledge of the texts (223–24). The injunction to "sleep on it!" is a modern turn on this ancient trope of cognition.

16. A fascinating study of the relationship of composition and architectural space, including the terms of the pseudo-Ciceronian architectural mnemonic, is in Leach (esp. chap. 2, "*Loci et Imagines*: The Development of Topographical Systems in Roman Landscape.") *Intercolumnia* are listed in the most complete surviving description of the ancient architectural mnemonic, in the *Rhetorica ad Herennium,* iii. 30, and continued to be featured as significant mnemonic loci in advice from the Middle Ages and Renaissance.

17. On the Boscoreale room and Vitruvius' comments, see Ling (29–31). On the function of mandala-paintings and medieval meditational *picturae,* see Zinn.

18. Other instances from antiquity are given in *The Book of Memory* (86). A late instance of this same compositional trope occurs in a headnote supplied by the

fifteenth-century English scribe, John Shirley, to John Lydgate's "Gaude Virgo Mater Christi." The poem is said to have been composed "by Daun Iohan þe munke Lydegate *by night as he lay in his bedde* at Londoun" (my emphasis; see Boffey 65). Shirley may well be emphasizing the *gravitas* of Lydgate's meditation by associating it with this long-standing trope; that doesn't mean, of course, that Lydgate, a monk, did not also actually compose at night lying in bed.

19. The classic modern study of the primary importance of "stories" to the human ability to remember is Barlett.

20. The Iliac tablets are a relatively common type of artifact; although there is disagreement on their purpose, many scholars think they served some pedagogical function. A good discussion of these, as well as the whole genre of narrative pictures in antiquity, can be found in Brilliant.

21. On the convention of *Bildeinsatz* in ancient literature, see esp. Keuls. Leach talks about the way literary *picturae* are used to structure subsequent works (esp. 85–89).

22. These *picturae* were transcribed from the manuscript source by Smalley (172–78). I have discussed the temple murals in Chaucer's *Knight's Tale* as mnemonic *picturae* in "Seeing Things."

23. These categories, taken from Aristotle's discussion in "De memoria et reminiscentia," were the subject of commentaries by both Albertus Magnus and Thomas Aquinas; see *The Book of Memory,* 62–64.

24. Bernard of Clairvaux, Sermon 23:11, *On the Song of Songs* (II:35). The conventional mournfulness of the poet-visionary in Chaucer's French models should be understood in this tradition too. See also Hill.

25. One should keep in mind that the reading "eight" in line 37 rests solely on Thynne's 1532 edition, and that numbers in manuscripts are notoriously subject to miscopying. A summary of various suggestions for the date is found in the notes of *The Riverside Chaucer*; as is apparent, I agree with those who have suggested a date some years after Blanche's death.

26. On the picture program of *The Romance of the Rose* as an essential aspect of its "reading," see Huot, The Romance of the Rose *and Its Medieval Readers.*

27. Years ago, John Steadman suggested that the puppy might be associated with the dogs conventionally (at this time) carved in aristocratic tomb sculptures, like a pillow beneath the feet of the lady: see "Chaucer's 'Whelp'." This suggestion is given new force by Phillipa Hardman's argument that *The Book of the Duchess* should be understood in conjunction with the building and dedication of Blanche's tomb in 1374 ("Memorial Monument"). The various arguments as to whether dogs are or are not associated with virtues or vices (see *The Riverside Chaucer* note on BD 489–96) are somewhat off the point: as an example of the author's meditative "gathering," Chaucer's puppy is an instructive jumble of disparate sources, both words and images.

28. Hardman has argued that Chaucer's use of the verb *told* (1181) indicates that the Man in Black is speaking, not singing, his remembered song. Given the wide semantic range of *told* at this time, I don't think one should try to pin the meaning down here with great precision, for the verb can mean "recount" or "tell over," and one might well "recount" a song by singing all or part of it. In any event, the text is clear that this is "song," something the earlier lay is without. See Hardman, "Ars Celare Artem."

29. In his treatise "De memoria et reminiscentia," Aristotle, articulating commonplaces, characterizes melancholy as the humor most conducive to reminiscence. Because it is cold and wet, the melancholy humor creates and gathers

memory images readily—one must be careful, however, to maintain a balance, for overly melancholic temperaments, being too wet, cannot retain impressions for long, and also tend to make helter-skelter crowds of disorderly images. See *The Book of Memory* (49–50); and Sorabji, a translation with extensive commentary on Aristotle's treatise.

30. Indeed, the title, "art of memory," in the Middle Ages and early Renaissance, was applied to works that are not precepts of mnemotechnique but are specifically examinations of conscience. The earliest one of this sort that I have found, as a separate treatise, is the "tractatus de memoria" of Hugo of Rouen (twelfth century). Shoaf has aptly commented on the *herte* pun and penitential psychology.

31. I disagree with Fradenburg, who argues that Chaucer's abrupt killing-off of Alcione indicates solely that she is being excluded by the poet from the metamorphosis (and thus from resurrection) she shares with Ceyx in Ovid's version (188–90). In any rhetorical occasion, the individuals in the audience are invited to perform their own memory-work with the materials presented, and well-known matters are often deliberately suppressed in expectation that the audience will fill them in. This constitutes a portion of the "dialogue" of a text. Obviously, members of the audience will make different constructions—but that is part of the point of "remembering," the source of its ethical "usefulness."

32. I analyzed the famous scene of Heloise taking the veil, in tears, before an audience, quoting lines from Lucan, as a model of rhetorically conceived moral action: "the entire ethical situation in Abelard's account is socially and rhetorically conceived: it requires a recollecting subject, a remembered text, and a remembering audience"; *The Book of Memory* 178–83. These three necessary components are present in *The Book of the Duchess* as well.

33. The connection between "historical" understanding and the rhetorical concept of "equity" is described by Eden. Interesting observations on the relationships of legal fictions and memory are to be found in Haverkamp.

Works Cited

Bartlett, F. C. *Remembering: A Study in Experimental and Social Psychology.* Cambridge: Cambridge University Press, 1932.

Bernard of Clairvaux. *On the Song of Songs.* Tr. Kilian Walsh. 4 vols. Kalamazoo, MI: Cistercian Publications, 1983.

Boethius. *The Consolation of Philosophy.* Ed. E. K. Rand. Loeb Classical Library. Cambridge, MA: Harvard University Press, 1962. Tr. Richard Green. Library of Liberal Arts. New York: Macmillan, 1962.

Boffey, Julia. *Manuscripts of English Courtly Love Lyrics in the Later Middle Ages.* Woodbridge: Boydell & Brewer, 1985.

Bolzoni, Lina. "A Reply to Mary Carruthers, 'Inventional Mnemonics and the Ornaments of Style'." *Connotations* 3 (1993–94):37–41.

———, and Pietro Corsi, eds. *La Cultura della Memoria.* Bologna: il Mulino, 1992.

Boncompagno da Signa. *Rhetorica novissima.* In *Scripta anecdota glossatoria.* Ed. A. Gaudenzo. Bibliotheca iuridica medii aevi, vol. 2 Bologna: n.p., 1892.

Brilliant, Richard. *Visual Narratives: Storytelling in Etruscan and Roman Art.* Ithaca: Cornell University Press, 1984.

Carruthers, Mary. "Seeing Things: Locational Memory in Chaucer's Knight's Tale." *Art and Context in Late Medieval English Narrative.* Ed. Robert R. Edwards. Cambridge: Boydell & Brewer, 1994. 93–106.

———. "Inventional Mnemonics and the Ornaments of Style: The Case of Etymology." *Connotations* 2 (1992–93): 103–14.

———. *The Book of Memory.* Rev. ed. Cambridge: Cambridge University Press, 1992.

———. "Italy, *Ars memorativa,* and Fame's House." *SAC* Proceedings 2 (1987):179–87.

Chaucer, Geoffrey. *The Riverside Chaucer.* Ed. Larry D. Benson et al. Boston: Houghton Mifflin, 1987.

[Cicero]. *Rhetorica ad Herennium.* Ed. and tr. H. Caplan. Loeb Classical Library. Cambridge, MA: Harvard University Press, 1954.

Cicero. *De oratore.* Ed. and tr. E. W. Sutton and H. Rackham. 2 vols. Loeb Classical Library. Cambridge, MA: Harvard University Press, 1942–48.

Coleman, Janet. *Ancient and Medieval Memories: The Reconstruction of the Past.* Cambridge: Cambridge University Press, 1992.

Courcelle, Pierre. *La Consolation de Philosophie dans la tradition littéraire.* Paris: Etudes Augustiniennes, 1967.

Eden, Kathy. "Equity and the Origins of Renaissance Historicism: The Case for Erasmus." *Yale Journal of Law & the Humanities* 5 (1993):137–45.

Edwards, Robert R. *Ratio and Invention: A Study of Medieval Lyric and Narrative.* Nashville, TN: Vanderbilt University Press, 1989.

Engel, William. "Mnemonic Criticism & Renaissance Literature: A Manifesto." *Connotations* 1 (1991–92):12–33.

Fentress, James, and Chris Wickham. *Social Memory.* Oxford: Blackwell, 1992.

Foster, Kenelm, ed. and tr. *Biographical Documents for the Life of St. Thomas Aquinas.* Oxford: Blackfriars, 1949.

Fradenburg, Louise O. "'Voice Memorial': Loss and Reparation in Chaucer's Poetry." *Exemplaria* 2 (1990):169–202.

Halbwachs, Maurice. *On Collective Memory.* Ed. and tr. Lewis A. Coser. Chicago: University of Chicago Press, 1992.

Hardman, Phillipa. "The *Book of the Duchess* as a Memorial Monument." *Chaucer Review* 28 (1993–94):205–15.

———. "'Ars Celare Artem': Interpreting the Black Knight's "Lay" in Chaucer's *Book of the Duchess.*" *Poetica* 37 (1993):49–57.

Haverkamp, Anselm. "Rhetoric, Law, and the Poetics of Memory." *Cardozo Law Review* 13 (1992):1639–53.

Hill, John M. "The *Book of the Duchess,* Melancholy, and that Eight-Year Sickness." *Chaucer Review* 9 (1974–75):35–50.

Huot, Sylvia. "Inventional Mnemonics, Reading and Prayer: A Reply to Mary Carruthers." *Connotations* 3 (1993–94):103–9.

———. *The Romance of the Rose and Its Medieval Readers.* Cambridge: Cambridge University Press, 1993.

Huppé, Bernard F., and D. W. Robertson. *Fruyt and Chaf: Studies in Chaucer's Allegories.* Princeton: Princeton University Press, 1963.

Isidore of Seville. *Etymologiarum sive Origines libri xx.* Ed. W. M. Lindsay. 2 vols. Oxford Classical Texts. Oxford: Oxford University Press, 1911.

Kelly, Richard. "The Mnemonic Structuring of Medieval Literature." *Oxford Literary Review* 3:1 (1978):13–19.

Keuls, Eva. "Rhetoric and Visual Aids in Greece and Rome." *Communications Arts in the Ancient World.* Ed. E. A. Havelock and J. P. Hershbell. New York: Hastings House, 1978. 121–34.

Kruger, Steven F. *Dreaming in the Middle Ages.* Cambridge: Cambridge University Press, 1992.

Küchler, Susanne, and Walter Melion, eds. *Images of Memory: On Remembering and Representation.* Washington: Smithsonian Institution, 1991.

Leach, Eleanor Winsor. *The Rhetoric of Space: Literary and Artistic Representations of Landscape in Republican and Augustan Rome.* Princeton: Princeton University Press, 1988.

Leclercq, Jean. *The Love of Learning and the Desire for God.* Tr. C. Misrahi. New York: Fordham University Press, 1961.

Ling, Roger. *Roman Painting.* Cambridge: Cambridge University Press, 1991.

Martianus Capella. *De nuptiis philologiae et mercurii.* Ed. A. Dick. 1925; rpt. Stuttgart: Teubner, 1969.

Quintilian. *Institutio oratoria.* Ed. and tr. H. E. Butler. 4 vols. Loeb Classical Library. Cambridge: Harvard University Press, 1922.

Riché, Pierre. *Ecoles et enseignement dans le Haut Moyen Age.* Paris: Picard, 1989.

Rowland, Beryl. "Bishop Bradwardine, the Artificial Memory, and the House of Fame." *Chaucer at Albany.* Ed. R. H. Robbins. New York: Burt Franklin, 1975. 41–62.

Shoaf, R. A. "Stalking the Sorrowful H(e)art: Penitential Lore and the Hunt Scene in Chaucer's *The Book of the Duchess.*" *JEGP* 78 (1979):313–24.

Smalley, Beryl. *English Friars and Antiquity in the Early Fourteenth Century.* New York: Barnes and Noble, 1960.

Sorabji, Richard. *Aristotle on Memory.* Providence, RI: Brown University Press, 1972.

Southern, R. W., ed. and tr. *The Life of Anselm by Eadmer.* London: Thomas Nelson, 1962.

Steadman, John M. "Chaucer's 'Whelp': A Symbol of Marital Fidelity?" *Notes and Queries* n.s. 3 (1956):374–75.

Underhill, Evelyn. *Mysticism.* 1911; rpt. New York: Dutton, 1961.

Varro. *De lingua latina.* Ed. and tr. R. G. Kent. 2 vols. Loeb Classical Library. Cambridge, MA: Harvard University Press, 1938.

Virgil. *Aeneid.* Ed. H. R. Fairclough. 2 vols. Loeb Classical Library. Rev. ed. Cambridge, MA: Harvard University Press, 1978.

Zinn, Grover A., Jr. "Mandala Symbolism and Use in the Mysticism of Hugh of St. Victor." *History of Religions* 12 (1972–73):317–41.

Chaucer's Selective "Remembraunce": Ironies of "Fyn Loving" and the Ideal Feminine

Joel Feimer

As ROBERT O. PAYNE HAS ESTABLISHED IN *THE KEY OF REMEMBRANCE,* Chaucer was among the most careful and self-reflective of medieval makers. Following the "orthodox tradition in medieval aesthetics," Chaucer practiced poetry as "a process of manipulating language so that the wisdom evolved in the past will become available, applicable, and operative in the present" (Payne 89). As Payne observes, this was an essential and abiding feature of Chaucer's narrative and semiotics. Chaucer understood the power of poetry to move its audience, but he was also aware of the problems entailed by the poet's perceptions of good and evil (89–90), the difficulties resulting from the "treacherously corruptible" nature of language, and the "linguistic erosion" that time wreaks on the "agencies of poetic effect" (85). In his discussion of the "G" text of the Prologue to *The Legend of Good Women,* Payne establishes Chaucer's abiding interest in these issues, which informed and directed his life's work. The visionary trial of Chaucer's naive persona-narrator by the God of Love and his convicting "defense" by the compassionate Alceste underscore the irresolvability of these questions, of which defiance of resolution and the resulting confusion are also perennial features. Payne asserts that, as "a possible formal escape from the circularity of the old, compulsive, book-experience-dream pattern, *The Legend of Good Women* takes Chaucer exactly nowhere" (111).

After reading and rereading Chaucer's works over the past twenty years, and reflecting on Professor Payne's remarks, I think Chaucer establishes this "nowhere" as a state of being, a tension to be experienced by the narrator and witnessed by the reader. However, because of the nature of literary remembrance as developed by Chaucer in his poems, this tension can never be resolved. It will never attain closure because the process of literature and the questions it raises remain open as living experiences for audience, maker, and persona-narrator alike. The processes of making and reading, however, entail choices on the part of the poet and the audience. In *The Legend of Good Women,* the sliding (Chaucer's term) context of literary creation, enables Chaucer the maker to present an agenda that is in accord with the antifeminist orthodoxies of his time.

In *The Legend of Good Women,* the lack of resolution in the prologues underscores the ironies experienced in reading, or rather witnessing, Chaucer's versions of the legends themselves. As a comparison of three of Chaucer's tales of women martyred for love with Boccaccio's presentation of them will reveal, Chaucer's persona-narrator does have an agenda, which the God of Love correctly suspected. By dutifully fulfilling his penance for his portrait of the faithless Criseyde, Chaucer's persona-narrator presents a series of narratives drawn from a vast fund of authorities, which he modifies to fulfill the letter of his penance, to compose a hagiography of women faithful to the tenets of the God of Love and martyred in his cause by the men they love. However, as the following analysis will show, the spirit of these stories ironically will replicate the crime of which the persona-narrator has been accused, convicted, and sentenced: the production of compositions in "Despit of love" ("F" 372, "G" 352). At least one recent critic has asserted that:

> The narrator might well be awake to the implications of his storytelling and thereby poking fun at Cupid by giving him a poem whose effect is just the opposite of what the tyrannical male god demanded. (Hansen 2)

Several other critics concur with Hansen, that the narrator is consciously, even playfully, subversive in fulfilling the letter, but not the spirit of his penance (Delany 99, 190; Dinshaw 71–72, 85–87). But I prefer those readings which recognize that the persona-narrator's completion of his assigned task is shaped by the ironies, ambivalences, and tautologies inherent in the system of "fyn loving" he is supposed to defend (Payne 108–15; Martin 204). While the persona-narrator's awareness may be arguable, the maker's is not. Indeed, the ironies are more complete if the persona-narrator remains true to his naiveté, his self-professed ineptness.

Chaucer's *Legend of Good Women* creates an ideal of feminine perfection, using stories of classical heroines from the mythographic tradition transmitted to the Middle Ages by such writers as Hyginus, Fulgentius, the Third Vatican Mythographer, and, ultimately, Chaucer's contemporary, Boccaccio (Seznec 11–36, 84–

146; Feimer 153–58, 261–81). Chaucer draws from and modifies the mythographic tradition to establish a mythos for the medieval god, Amor, and for his court of noble lovers (Kiser 15–17, 71–72). The noble women whom Chaucer the narrator encounters in his secular love vision are all constrained to serve Amor by the power sexual passion wields over them and by the conventions of "fyn loving" or *fin'amor* to which they must subscribe by virtue of their social position (Ferrante 71–73). Thus, Chaucer delves in old fields, stories about the heroines of classical antiquity, to undermine the medieval tradition of refined love. He applies the key of memory to the spiritual manacles of the god of Love.

The setting and the structure of the vision in the two prologues to *The Legend of Good Women* establish a mythopoeic process for the narrator's experience, while the stories of the heroines provide mythographic authority for what he will reveal about the nature of love. Ironically, Chaucer's revelation of the problematic qualities of refined love will be made under the guise of a penance imposed on his fictional self by the god of Love. Thus, the secular dream visions of the two prologues to the poem provide counterpoint to, as well as setting for, the legends of the heroines. The penitential project imposed by Love is to compose a comprehensive lovers' *legenda aurea* in the vein of such encyclopedic works as Boccaccio's *De Claris mulieribus*.

Far from being promiscuously inclusive, Chaucer's portraits of good women are extremely selective and narrowly focused on his theme, to the point where he modifies traditional material to conform to his stated purpose (Kiser, 97), as a comparison with a few of Boccaccio's examples of famous women will demonstrate. In contrast to Boccaccio's mythographic sketches, the narratives of Chaucer's good women reveal that they have all earned their sainthood in lovers' paradise through their martyrdom in the cause of love. The restricted parameters of Chaucer's presentation of the ideal feminine are established in the prologues to *The Legend of Good Women*. Here, the narrator encounters the classical heroine, Alceste, who holds the supreme position among Love's martyred ladies by virtue of the selfless sacrifice of her own life so that her husband might live. Alceste's example becomes the figure against which the sufferings of other ladies in the cause of refined love are measured. Fidelity in love, especially to a faithless lover, becomes the primary virtue. Such a context reduces women to signs that are at the mercy of interpretation (Delany 88–90, 206; Hansen 8, 11, 13–14; Martin 203). At the risk of contextualizing the context even further, I would like to cite the observations of the novelist, Christine Brooke-Rose, who has undercut the hypocritical nature of the system of refined love in her description of women as semiotic objects:

> The social exchange of women was for pleasure, release *and* (emphasis hers) procreation, which had to be patrilineal, hence the "protection" of women, etc. *All other developments,*[1] towards more grace in the winning, on the one hand, and harder bargaining in the buying—higher dowries—on the other, are mere displacements and refinements. (313)

The context of refined love established in the prologues embraces a variety of heroic types of classical women and justifies some startling transformations from their traditional portraits, such as are found in Boccaccio's *De Claris mulieribus*. For example, Cleopatra's devouring lust is cleansed of its enormities when it becomes refined love. Thisbe's foolish rebellion against the objections of her parents becomes concern for fidelity to the troth she has pledged Piramus. Most startling is the presence of Lucretia among Chaucer's good women, since her martyrdom is the result of rape, not *fin' amor*. It may be that Lucretia's fate and Tarquin's crime indicate the extreme of Chaucer's critique of refined love.

A comparison of the consciously mythographic *De Claris mulieribus* with the ironically hagiographic *Legend of Good Women* will reveal both how much these works have in common and how much freer is Chaucer's work. Through their use of irony, both texts underscore the problematic nature of the medieval concept of refined love and of the ideal of feminine perfection it establishes. Chaucer's work, however, boldly employs the Christian concept of martyrdom as a sign of justification in the profane dogma of refined passion. Chaucer blends hagiographic form and mythographic content to expose the pathological effects of refined love on those noble women and men who are constrained by their rank to profess it. His adaptation of the form of Christian martyrdom as a vehicle for the profane content of classical narrative creates a powerful, yet subtle, satiric tenor. Boccaccio does not use this device because his purpose is both less focused and less far-reaching critically.

Boccaccio's *De Claris mulieribus* and Chaucer's *Legend of Good Women* develop complementary attitudes toward human passion and the ideal feminine. Boccaccio's stated purpose is to praise women who "quocunque ex facinore orbi vulgato sermone notissimas novero" (Proem 24.6) (have become renowned to the world through any sort of deed) (Trans. Guarino xxxviii),[2] while Chaucer's is to provide a secular martyrology of faithful women. Fame and goodness become problematic terms when applied to individual women in these works. Fame may be derived from any sort of deed, and the price of goodness is extremely high.

An examination of Boccaccio's dedicatory letter and Chaucer's prologues, as well as the respective portraits of the heroines mentioned above, reveals a number of significant variations and divergences in technique and content, but ultimately a startling consensus in attitude toward women between these two works. Boccaccio commences his dedication, "in eximiam mulieribus sexus laudem ac amicorum solatium, potius quam in magnum rei publice commodum, libellum scripsi" (18) (I wrote a little book in praise of women for the pleasure of my friends more than as a service to the community). As we will see, Boccaccio's idea of praise for women is somewhat controversial, and his disclaimer concerning service to the community is not completely candid. Similarly, Chaucer's mandated purpose is:

> Thow shalt, while that thou lyvest, yer by yere,
> The moste partye of thy tyme spende
> In makyng of a glorious legende
> Of goode wymmen, maydenes and wyves;
> That weren trewe in lovyng al hire lyves;
> And telle of false men that hem bytraien
> That al hir lyf ne do nat but assayen
> How many women they may doon a shame;
> For in youre world that is now holde a
> game.   ("F"481–89, "G" 471–78)

Alceste's command to the narrator is more specific than Boccaccio's "mulieribus sexus laudem." The dreamer-narrator is to compose a hagiography of women, maids, and wives who were true in love, and conjointly of the men who betrayed them. It is as if praise of women's fidelity is not possible without condemning lechery in men. This rigid polarity does not admit variation; instead, it reveals a pathology of refined love for the beloved object who experiences both spiritual and physical symptoms which cause suffering and, in the case of Chaucer's good women, invariably, death.

Neither is Boccaccio's expanded explanation of *laudem,* which is found in the preface to *De Claris mulieribus,* without its problems. He queries:

Et si extollendi sunt homines dum, concesso sibi robore, magna perfecerint, quanto amplius mulieres, quibus fere omnibus a natura rerum mollities insita et corpus debile ac tardum ingenium datum est, si in virilem evaserint animum et ingenion celebri atque conspicua audeant atque perficiant etiam difficillima viris, extollende sunt? (24.4)

(If men should be praised whenever they perform great deeds (with strength which Nature has given them), how much more should women be extolled (almost all of whom are endowed with tenderness, frail bodies, and sluggish minds by Nature), if they have acquired a manly spirit and if with keen intelligence and remarkable fortitude they have dared undertake and have accomplished even the most difficult deeds?) (Trans. Guarino xxxvii)

Therefore, according to Boccaccio, given women's natural deficiencies of physical strength, moral character, and intellect, any woman who performs a noteworthy accomplishment deserves to be singled out for praise. More significantly, Boccaccio goes on to declare that he will include the notorious as well as the virtuous in his compendium of women who merit notice (24). In the interest of accuracy, Boccaccio includes the narratives of famous, evil women, advising his intended patroness, "sic obscenis sepositis, colliges laudanda" (20) (thus set aside the offensive, consider those deserving praise). The portraits of notorius women comprise roughly one-third of *De Claris mulieribus*. The substantial number of vicious women who merit notice establishes a foil against which the accomplishments of the virtuous women may be contrasted. Boccaccio believes that, given their deficient natures, women are more susceptible to vice than they are capable of virtue. Indeed, any woman who has performed a virtuous deed worthy of remembrance has somehow transcended her nature and acquired a *virilem animum,* a manly spirit, or soul.

The "G" text of Chaucer's Prologue to *The Legend of Good Women* provides a startling contrast to Boccaccio's remarks. This is a list of authorities the dreamer-narrator might have reworked instead of translating the heretical story of *Troilus and Criseyde* into English. The list includes Livy and Saint Jerome. The passage contains the following comment on faithful women:

> For to hyre love they were so trewe
> That, rathere than they wolde take a newe,
> They chose to be ded in sondry wyse,
> And deiden, as the story wol devyse. (288–91)

In the course of their sufferings in the cause of love, women are offered only two options—dishonor or death. When one understands that dishonor is not an available choice to a virtuous woman, he discovers the crux of the god of Love's remark: fidelity to one's lover, no matter how false or vile he may be, and martyrdom in the cause of love comprise the validation of the virtuous woman and assure her a place in Love's paradise.

The ironies of the prefatory comments in both these works set up problematic contexts for the stories they introduce. For Boccaccio, a virtuous woman is an anomaly and therefore worthy of regard. In Chaucer's elaborate fiction of the dreamer-narrator's penitential examination by the god of Love and Alceste, any virtuous woman is condemned to and defined by extinction.[3] Thus both authors establish an orthodoxy of antifeminism behind a facade of encomium.[4]

Boccaccio is more straightforward in portraying his heroic women. Through his use of the adjective *claris,* he is able to present his examples of wicked women as established by the mythographic tradition without modifying their narratives. Chaucer, on the other hand, must edit his portraits to conform to the qualities of the good woman established in the prologues (Hughes-Hallett 1, 113–15, 121–23). An excellent example of both authors' fidelity to their stated objectives is found in their respective portraits of Cleopatra, who debuts in English in *The Legend of Good Women* (Frank 37–40).

More fully realized, Boccaccio's account provides a significant contrast to Chaucer's. In *De Claris mulieribus,* Cleopatra (138) is portrayed as a woman who

> ad imperandum, per nephas tamen, ipsi regno pervenerit, nulla fere, nisi hac et oris formositate vere claritas nota, refulsit, cum e contrario avaritia crudelitate atque luxuria omni mundo conspicua facta sit. (138.1)

> (came to rule through crime. She gained glory for almost nothing else than her beauty, while on the other hand she became known throughout the world for her greed, cruelty, and lustfulness.) (Trans. Guarino 192)

She establishes her single rule in Egypt by poisoning her brother. When the Romans arrive, Cleopatra is undaunted. She defies Pompey and seduces Caesar "cum formosissima esset et oculorum scintillantium arte atque oris" (138.7) (with being most beautiful, and with scintillating eyes, and artful eloquence). After Caesar is murdered by the Senate, Cleopatra ensnares Antony with "pulchritudine sua et lascivientibus oculis" (138.10) (with her beauty and lascivious eyes). In her lechery and cupidity, she becomes the plaything of oriental kings, but she is a whore with a mission: to rule the Roman empire.

As Boccaccio develops the narrative, in Antony's desire to possess Cleopatra, he promises to give her the world but is unable to deliver it. Instead, outraged at Antony's setting aside his sister Octavia for the wanton Cleopatra, Octavian attacks, defeating the lustful pair in a series of pitched battles. The most famous of these is Actium, which Cleopatra is instrumental in helping Antony lose. When Antony finally commits suicide, Cleopatra attempts to seduce Octavian, who virtuously rejects her. Cleopatra then resolves to join Antony in death.

Boccaccio provides two versions of her end. In the first, she opens her veins in Antony's tomb and applies asps to her wounds. In the alternate account, Antony forces her to drink a poison she had prepared for him. Neither of Boccaccio's endings is in complete accord with Chaucer's version, nor with the more famous Shakespearian *Liebestod*. In Boccaccio's narrative, Cleopatra is an example of all the worst in woman: concupiscence, cupidity, treachery, murder, and the illicit desire for power to which women are always susceptible according to the antifeminist tradition (Rogers 3–22). In *De Claris mulieribus,* Cleopatra is portrayed as an excellent example of those female obscenities about which Boccaccio cautioned his patron.

Chaucer's Cleopatra is pale by comparison (Frank 41; Hughes-Hallett 128). She is singled out by Love in both prologues as the inaugural martyr of the dreamer's penitential legend ("F" 566, "G" 542). In Chaucer's version, Cleopatra's youthful enormities, the murder of her brother and the seduction of Caesar, are missing. Instead, the story begins with Antony, who becomes "Rebel unto the toun of Rome" (591) in response to his own good fortune, and who falsely repudiates the unsuspecting Octavia to take another wife (592–94). He thereby earns the enmity of both Rome and Caesar (Boccaccio's Octavian). At this point in the tale, the narrator laments Antony's death because he had been a noble warrior until the power of love subdued him:

> But love hadde brought this man in swich a rage,
> And hym so narwe bounden in his las
> Al for love of Cleopataras,
> That al the world he sette at no value. (598–602)

Not the seductive blandishments of Cleopatra, but the snare of love, has caused the falling out between Antony and Rome. Throughout

Chaucer's edited narrative, Cleopatra is faithful to Antony and committed to their love unto death. When Antony commits suicide at the close of the sea battle, the devoted Cleopatra oversees his burial, embalming his body in costly spices and placing it in a shrine (671–77). She then has a pit dug and filled with adders. At its brink, Cleopatra declaims her devotion to Antony:

> And in myself this covenaunt made I tho,
> That ryght as ye felten, wel or wo,
> As fer forth as it in my power lay,
> Unreprovable unto my wyfhod ay,
> The same wolde I fele, lyf or deth—
> And thilke covenant, whil me lasteth breth,
> I wol fulfille; and that shal ben wel sene,
> Was nevere unto hire love a trewer quene. (688–95)

She then jumps into the pit and it stung to death by the adders. The audience is further informed that Cleopatra chose to be buried there, and that she "hire deth receyveth with good cheere" (700). In tracing the theme of Cleopatra from classical writers to the twentieth century, Lucy Hughes-Hallett asserts that Cleopatra's fidelity as a wife became an essential quality of her character, noting that this feature of her legend is first developed by Chaucer in *The Legend of Good Women* (113–31).

The Narrator concludes with the declaration:

> And this is storyal soth, it is no fable.
> Now, or I fynde a man thus trewe and stable,
> And wol for love his deth so frely take,
> I preye God let oure hedes nevere ake!
> > > Amen! (702–5)

This is a remarkable statement when one recalls the narrator's descriptions of Antony in love's bondage. Nevertheless, the portrait of Cleopatra thus presented is in accord with the narrator's stated purpose to relate stories of women who are martyrs to the god of Love, even if it does contain some self-contradiction.

Chaucer's characters and narrative are substantially different from Boccaccio's. To sanctify Cleopatra, more than half her traditional life's story had to be excised and the remainder transformed. The culprit of Chaucer's account is not Cleopatra but love. In her person, she is worth the world, and none dares call this lust. However, how does one interpret the curious manner of her death, a fate more appropriate for one of Dante's sinners than a saint of the god of Love?[5] The mixing of Cleopatra's body with the serpents in the pit dug before Antony's grave raises specters of insincerity on the part of the narrator, which his ironic assertion of the truth of the story only intensifies. Given the syntax of the last four lines, the narrator must dread chronic migraines.

The narrative of Thisbe (*De Claris mulieribus* 13) is closer to the avowed purpose of both works, but still, it is not without its ironies. For both Boccaccio and Chaucer, the tale of Piramus and Thisbe is informed by the tragic conclusion of their love. The basic facts of the story are essentially the same in each version: the young lovers grow up to pledge their troth, the physical barrier of the wall, symbolizing the more significant obstacle of their parents, their proposed tryst, and its fatal dénouement.

According to Boccaccio, fate plays a significant part in the tragedy, "egit iniqua sors ut, crescentibus annis, cum ambo formosissimi essent, puerilis amor in maximum augeretur incendium illudque inter se" (13.2) (iniquitous fate made it so that with the growing years, because both were most comely, childish love grew to the greatest conflagration between them). Thus, for Boccaccio, fate endowed the youthful lovers with physical beauty, which is the wellspring of their sinful passion. Boccaccio comments at the close of the narrative:

Florentis etatis amor crimen est, nec horrendum solutis crimen; in coniugium ire poterat. Peccavit fors pessima et forsan miseri peccavere parentes. Sense quippe frenandi sunt iuvenum impetus, ne, dum repentino obice illis obsistere volumus, desperantes in precipitium inpellamus. (13.12–14)

(Youth's love is a sin, but not a horrible transgression for those who are single, since it can result in marriage. Wicked Fortune sinned, as perhaps did their wretched parents. Certainly, the ardor of the young should be curbed slowly, lest wishing to oppose them with sudden impediments we drive them to despair and perdition.) (Trans. Guarino 25)

In addition to evil fortune, a passion that could not be overcome by walls or parental vigilance is the culprit here; yet, the passion of Pyramis and Thisbe might have had a lawful outlet in marriage, without which the human race would cease to exist. Youthful ardor is made more powerful by wrongheaded parental objections, which force the lovers to the deceptions and desperate measures that result in their tragedy. Thus, passion and eagerness to fulfill it, impelled by frustration, bring Pyramis and Thisbe to the fatal trysting place and aid evil Fortune in accomplishing their fate.

Chaucer provides essentially the same narrative but with a few additions that alter its tone. For example, when the narrator mentions that Thisbe's home if Babylon, he comments:

> The whyche toun the queen Semyramus
> Let dychen al aboute, and walles make
> Ful hye, of hard tile wel ybake. (707-9)

While the contextualizing reference to Semiriamis is present in Ovid's version (*Metamorphoses* 4.57), neither Boccaccio in his narrative of Thisbe, nor an anonymous twelfth-century version of the tale in Old French, which Chaucer knew, include it (Cormier 12; Delany 122–24). Both Dante (*Inferno* 5.52–60) and Boccaccio, in a chapter devoted to her notorious career (*De Claris mulieribus* 2), establish Semiramis as a type of lust. Her name provides a tinge of irony for the story of female truth in love that follows. Dante comments that Semiramis "libitio fe'licito in sua legge" (*Inferno* 5.56) ("made lust licit in her laws") in order to legitimate her own libidinousness (notice the pun on happiness). Moreover, the walls with which she surrounds Babylon provide both a foreshadowing and a foil to the barrier that separates Thisbe from Piramus.

A second point, which is juxtaposed to the first in the tale, is the insistence of both Thisbe and the narrator on her fidelity in love. Raymond Cormier (3–12) and Sheila Delany (123–25) have noticed that Thisbe's concerns originate in a twelfth-century "translation" of Ovid's narrative. Thisbe forsakes her friends "for to save hire trouthe" (798); she returns to the trysting place after being frightened off by the lioness so that Piramus will not doubt her (857). Her final words are:

> But God forbede but a woman can
> Ben as trewe in lovynge as a man!
> And for my part, I shal anon it kythe. (910–12)

This statement is supported by the narrator's comment:

> For it is deynte to us men to fynde
> A man that can in love been trewe and kynde.
> Here may ye se, what lovere so he be,
> A woman dar and can as wel as he. (920–23)

One cannot help but wonder at these words. Indeed, the message is ironic if one considers the character men display in the legends; but, more important, one must consider the end to which fidelity has brought Thisbe. Furthermore, when Thisbe's martyrdom is set within the context of Babylon and its lustful queen, the irony of Thisbe's claim to truth in love becomes manifest. It is rather truth in lust. Finally, Piramus' own suicide undercuts the import of Thisbe's and the narrator's statements (Delany 191–93). The narrative demonstrates that Piramus and Thisbe are bound by a self-destructive passion attributed to true love, or in the Prologues' terms, "fyn loving," as impregnable as any wall.

More than Cleopatra's or Thisbe's, the story of Lucretia illustrates the problematic nature of Boccaccio's and Chaucer's works. In the mythographic tradition—which, in Lucretia's case, commences with Livy—this heroine is certainly famous and praiseworthy in Boccaccio's sense. In the context of Chaucer's *Legend,* she appears to be good in the most straightforward sense of the word. In *De Claris mulieribus,* this noble Roman matron suffers the horrors of rape at the hands of a lust-maddened tyrant. After she ensures that revenge will be taken, and that her reputation for virtue is secure, she absolves herself of sin before taking her life, "ego me, si peccato absolvo, supplicio non libero; nec ulla deinceps impudica, Lucretie vivet exemplo" (98.7) (I, though I absolve myself from sin, do not liberate myself from punishment, nor will any other woman live shamefully through Lucretia's example). Boccaccio makes Lucretia's a tragedy of unfortunate beauty, similar to Thisbe's, but this time Lucretia's fair form provokes a crime against her for which she must bear the ultimate responsibility. Her case differs little from that of Dorigen in Chaucer's *The Franklin's Tale.* Boccaccio comments:

Infelix equidem pulcritudo eius et tanto claris, nunquam satis laudate, pudicitia sus dignis preconiis extolenda est, quanto acrius ingesta vi ignominia expiata; cum ex eadem non solum reintegratum sit decus, quod feditate facinoris iuvenis labefactarat ineptus, sed consecuta sit roman libertas. (98.9)

(Hers was an unfortunate beauty. She cleansed her shame harshly, and for this reason she should be exalted with worthy praise for her chastity, which can never be sufficiently lauded. Because of her action, not only was her reputation restored, which a lewd young man had tried to destroy, but Rome was made free.) (Trans. Guarino 103)

What is curious is that Boccaccio praises Lucretia for her suicide. For ancient Romans raised in the tenets of Stoicism, self-slaughter was an act of courage. However, for a Christian audience familiar with the tale of Judas, suicide is an act of despair and self-damnation. Setting that issue aside for the moment, the less obvious, but more significant, aspect of Lucretia's tale is the tragic consequence of being endowed with extraordinary beauty and virtue. One is left with the uncomfortable conclusion that when a beautiful woman desires to be virtuous, her only recourse in a world where anyone may be incited to passion by her attributes is death. Furthermore, feminine virtue in this context is reduced to chastity. A woman may possess other admirable qualities, but what matters most to Boccaccio—and, it would seem, to Lucretia—is that she be reputed chaste.

Chaucer's Lucrece is caught in a similar predicament. Her beauty and virtue are the boast of her husband, the objects of Tarquin's animal lust, and the pride of the Latin authors, Livy and Ovid, whom Chaucer cites as his sources (1683). However, Chaucer adds one more authority to the list of writers who praise Lucrece (1690), Saint Augustine of Hippo, who mentions her in *The City of God* (1.19). On the surface, this would seem to be confirmation of Lucrece's virtue from a Christian viewpoint (Frank 93–110), while acknowledging the problem of praising a pagan act of suicide. However, if one reads what Augustine has to say about Lucrece, one must wonder what Chaucer meant by the allusion. Augustine comments, "Quod ergo se ipsam, quoiam adulterum pertulit, etiam non adultera occidit, non est pudicitae caritas, sed pudoris infirmitas" (1.19) (And accordingly, since she killed herself for being subjected to an outrage in which she had no guilty part, it is obvious that this act of hers was prompted not by the love of purity, but by the overwhelming burden of her shame) (Trans. Dods 25). Augustine proceeds to compare Lucrece to some unnamed Christian women who had suffered similar outrages but who had declined the option of suicide because it was a criminal act. Augustine concludes the contrast:

Habent quippe intus gloriam castitatis, testimonium conscientiae; habent autem coram oculis Dei nec requirunt amplius, ubi quid recte faciant non habent amplius, ne devient ab auctoritate legis divinae, cum male devitant offensionem suspicionis humanae. (*Civitas Dei* 1.19)

(Within their own souls, in the witness of their own conscience, they enjoy the glory of chastity. In the sight of God, too, they are esteemed pure, and this contents them; they ask no more: it suffices them to have the opportunity of doing good, and they decline to evade the distress of human suspicion, lest they thereby deviate from the divine law.) (Trans. Dods 25)

In the light of this information, the reference to Saint Augustine is startling. It renders Lucrece's act wrongheaded and sinful because it was concerned with earthly reputation rather than divine judgment (for a disclaimer, see Frank 97–99; for concurrence, see Kiser 104–5).

Sheila Delany suggests that the narrator's seemingly uncomprehending reference to Augustine's sympathy for Lucrece is a "deliberate falsification" (204–5) and demonstrates that a "Pauline-Augustinian orthodoxy" is "fundamental to the Chaucerian sensibility" (231). She also shows that the act of suicide is "evidence of Lucrece's complicity in reducing herself to a sign," and further that

> It is a story of semiotics, because she kills herself as the irrefutable sign of her real feelings, which might not otherwise be believed by the public at large (1843–44). Unwilling to risk a wrong interpretation of herself, Lucrece forces the issue. (She reckoned, of course, without the Christian exegete Augustine.) (206)

Such a reading of Lucrece's legend indicates that Chaucer's project is, in reality, a critique of refined love and its god, which ironically is developed as a defense. It also clearly demonstrates the impasse to which noble women are brought by the necessity of defining their honor in sexual terms, while they are elevated (reduced might be a more appropriate term) to the status of objects who inspire passion and who must then suffer the consequences of that inspiration.

In concluding his version of the tale, Chaucer's narrator comments that Lucrece was considered a saint in Rome "as in hir lawe" (1872), which may indicate that Lucrece is meant to be judged according to pagan standards of virtue, or that, as a pagan without the benefit of Christian revelation, Lucrece could not have made the correct moral decision in her predicament. The narrator's final comment on women in general develops the lesson of Lucrece's fate. He claims women are all stable of heart and:

> . . . Crist himselve telleth
> That in Israel, as wyd as is the lond,
> That so gret feyth in al that he ne fond
> As in a woman: and this is no lye. (1879–82)

The reference to Christ recalls the Christian context Chaucer creates for Lucrece's tragedy with his citation of the "grete Austyn" (1690). Thus, the naive narrator's final comment renders the preceding encomium profoundly ironic. Lucrece may have been the most virtuous of women according to the precepts of pagan moral law, but she is certainly damned according to Christian doctrine. As Delany observes of Chaucer's legends in general, "erotic intensity does not certify general morality, and neither does men's malfeasance certify women's virtue" (208). Furthermore, one must notice that Lucrece's story is not modified to conform to *The Legend of Good Women*'s stated purpose of praising Love's faithful servants. Rather, Chaucer's heroine is a victim of lust. There is no development of Lucrece's love for Colatyn, and her domestic devotion is sketched only as a plausible inspiration for Tarquin's bestial passion. In any case, Lucrece's tale raises some important questions concerning the effects and purposes of Chaucer's lovers' *legenda*, not the least of which are those that proceed from their essential irony in tone and content. Several recent critics see these ironies as elements of a conscious agenda on the part of an aware, feminized, if not feminist narrator (Delany 187–88, 192, 205–7, 234; Dinshaw 74, 85–87; Martin 209–10). However, whereas Chaucer the author consciously wove the intertextual and referential fabric of his work from the semiotic threads of the classical and medieval traditions, the ironies resultant from the maker's art include the persona-narrator's obtuseness. Delany uses the adverb *obtusely* to modify the narrator's comment on Antony's declining fortunes under the influence of his passion for Cleopatra. As I have observed, the narrator's lack of comprehension is an essential aspect of the maker's purpose. That the narrator brings his material together and presents his experiences without fully understanding, or even "misreading," them renders their presentation objective. The fault can more clearly be seen to lie in the system described, since the "nyce" narrator is only the uncomprehending transmitter of his experiences. As Delany comments on the system circumscribed by *The Legend of Good Women*, "In communication, we have confusion; in love cupiditas; in society and sexual relations, power" (232). Although I concur with her observation, I must narrow its focus. It is not passionate love in general that is the topic of *The Legend of Good Women*, or even heterosexual love, as Hansen asserts (2–5), but the specific form of passion known to Chaucer and his audience as "fyn loving," the *fin'amor* plaintively celebrated by the troubadours, assiduously learned by Chaucer's Man in Black, professionally practiced by Troilus' anti-type, Diomede, a passion often mislabeled "courtly love." It is the form of relationship to which noblewomen and men are constrained by their class. *The Legend of Good Women* may indeed be seen as a document composed "in despit of Love" and the tenets of *fin'amor*. For what right-minded individual would choose to endure the fortunes of Cleopatra, Thisbe or Lucrece or, for that matter, Antony or Piramus? Tarquin is the most offensive case which reduces the project of loving in a refined way to its essential, hypocritical flaw. Constraint in passion, stripped of the lofty lover's rhetoric, is rape, as Dorigen's lengthy meditation on her plight suggests (*Franklin's Tale* 1355–1456). Chaucer's concern in the legends is with the multifarious impact of this fact of refined love. "Fyn loving" renders language duplicitous and personal relationships abusive. Ultimately it poses a profound threat to the fabric of society and the structure of the political order as the figures of the "lovers" Antony and Tarquin witness.

Both Boccaccio and Chaucer come to praise the subjects of their respective works. However, their encomia provide little consolation to what, in their opinion, is the frail, fair sex. The portraits of women that comprise these texts are fraught with paradox and irony, especially in the juxtaposition of context and content. As presented in these collections, beauty is either a weapon or a trap for women; passion is both their instrument and their bane; virtue is circumscribed by the narrowest of definitions; and women are provided with little or no opportunity to transcend the limits that these works impose. Women are either the victims or the victimizers of the men to whom they are bound by refined love. There is no possibility for resolving this impasse in either *De Claris mulieribus* or *The Legend of Good Women*. For Boccaccio, Cleopatra, Thisbe, and Lucretia are three aspects of a continuum that establishes the complex nexus of the ideal feminine. Cleopatra devours her lovers, and she would have consumed her world had she not been balked by Octavian. Prompted by youthful passion, Thisbe flouted parental authority and completed her fateful tryst on the point of her dead lover's sword. In opposition to Cleopatra, Lucretia is destroyed by the destructive passion her beauty inspires.

In contrast, Chaucer's narrator may insist on the "trouthe in love"of all his heroines, but he shapes their stories in such a way that the problems, dilemmas, and tragic consequences of such truth are underscored by a characteristic irony arising from the naiveté of his persona. The idealized presentations of feminine types in *De Claris mulieribus* and *The Legend of Good Women* are infused with a radical antifeminism which exhibits an essential mistrust of woman, of her beauty, and of her strength of character (when it is allowed her); they express a profound admiration for, as well as intimidation by, the passions women inspire.

A close reading of Chaucer's *The Legend of Good Women* in the light of the medieval mythographic tradition reveals an original, if negative, approach on the English maker's part to inventing a mythos for the god of Love. Instituted as the dreamer-narrator's penance for writing poems in despite of love, it becomes the narrator's ultimate, if unwitting, offense. In Chaucer's view, women such as Cleopatra are as much victims of their passions as is Thisbe of her fate, or Lucrece of Tarquin's lust. "Fyn loving" promotes only sorrow, and those chosen to be its object are doomed to suffer tragic ends. This presentation of the themes of love may be observed throughout Chaucer's works from *The Book of the Duchess* to *The Canterbury Tales.* White, Dido in *The House of Fame,* the formel eagle, Emily, Dorigen, and even Criseyde and the Wife of Bath—all derive their significance from a mythos of refined love developed by Chaucer from the classical heroines of the mythographic tradition.

Notes

1. Emphasis mine.
2. Translations of Boccaccio's Latin not attributed to Guarino are my own.
3. For discussions of woman's definition by death in *The Legend,* see Dinshaw 76–78; Martin 210.
4. For a discussion of Chaucer's antifeminism, see Weissman 93–110.
5. See *Inferno* 5.63, for Cleopatra among the lustful, the mixing of sinners and serpents takes place among the thieves, *Inferno* 24–25.

Works Cited

Alighieri, Dante. *Divina Commedia.* 3 vols. With an English trans. by J. A. Carlyle. Rev. H. Oelsner. London: Dent, 1900.

Augustine, St. Aurelius. *The City of God.* Tr. Marcus Dods. Intro. Thomas Merton. New York: Modern Library, 1950.

———. *The City of God Against the Pagans.* Vol. 1. Tr. George E. McCracken. Loeb Classical Library. Cambridge, MA.: Harvard University Press, 1957.

Boccaccio, Giovanni. *Concerning Famous Women.* Tr. Guido A. Guarino. New Brunswick, NJ: Rutgers University Press, 1963.

———. *De Mulieribus claris.* Ed. Vittorio Zaccaria. *Tutte le Opere di Giovanni Boccaccio.* 10. Ed. Vittore Branca. Milan: Mondadori, 1969.

Brooke-Rose, Christine. "Woman as Semiotic Object." *The Female Body in Western Culture: Contemporary Perspectives.* Ed. Susan Rubin Suleiman. Cambridge, MA.: Harvard University Press, 1985. 305–16.

Chaucer, Geoffrey. *The Riverside Chaucer.* 3d ed. Ed. Larry D. Benson et. al. Boston: Houghton Mifflin, 1987.

Cormier, Raymond, ed. and tr. *Three Ovidian Tales of Love: Piramus et Tisbé, Narcisus et Dané, and Philomena et Procné.* New York: Garland, 1986.

Delany, Sheila. *The Naked Text: Chaucer's Legend of Good Women*. Berkeley: University of California Press, 1994.

Dinshaw, Carolyn. *Chaucer's Sexual Poetics*. Madison: University of Wisconsin Press, 1989.

Feimer, Joel N. "The Figure of Medea in Medieval Literature: A Thematic Metamorphosis." Diss., CUNY, 1983.

Ferrante, Joan M. *Woman as Image in Medieval Literature: From the Twelfth Century to Dante*. New York: Columbia University Press, 1975.

Frank, Robert Worth, Jr. *Chaucer and* The Legend of Good Women. Cambridge, MA: Harvard University Press, 1972.

Hansen, Elaine Tuttle. *Chaucer and the Fictions of Gender*. Berkeley: University of California Press, 1992.

Hughes-Hallett, Lucy. *Cleopatra: Histories, Dreams, and Distortions*. New York: Harper Perennial, 1990.

Kiser, Lisa J. *Telling Classical Tales: Chaucer and the Legend of Good Women*. Ithaca: Cornell University Press, 1983.

Martin, Priscilla. *Chaucer's Women: Nuns, Wives, and Amazons*. Iowa City: University of Iowa Press, 1990.

Ovid. *The Metamorphoses*. 2 vols. Tr. Frank Justice Miller. Loeb Classical Library. 1916. Rep. Cambridge, MA: Harvard University Press, 1977.

Payne, Robert O. *The Key of Remembrance: A Study of Chaucer's Poetics*. New Haven: Yale University Press, 1963.

Rogers, Katherine M. *The Troublesome Helpmate: A History of Misogyny in Literature*. Seattle: University of Washington Press, 1976.

Seznec, Jean. *The Survival of the Pagan Gods: The Mythological Tradition and Its Place in Renaissance Humanism and Art*. Tr. Barbara F. Sessions. Bollingen Series 38. 1953. Princeton: Princeton University Press, 1972.

Weissman, Hope Phyllis. "Antifeminism and Chaucer's Characterizations of Women." *Geoffrey Chaucer: A Collection of Original Articles*. Ed. George D. Economou. New York: McGraw-Hill, 1975. 93–110.

The Interior of His Mind: Exegesis in *The House of Fame*

ELLEN E. MARTIN

"How can you waste such power on a broken dream?"
Ralph Waldo Emerson to Arthur Hugh Clough, letter,
17 May 1858

BOB PAYNE CONTINUOUSLY ASSURED HIS CHAUCER CLASS THAT "*THE House of Fame* is a busted poem.*" I wondered what a "busted poem" might be—even how such could be—but liked the phrase "busted poem" so well that I did not want to see it defined too quickly. I will now attempt to describe it, but, I hope, not delimit it: a certain lack of limitation is essential to a "busted poem," and especially, I suggest, a blurred *limes* between sentence and ornament.

I. He Builds Binaries and Finds Them Wanting

Looking at it as a rhetorically structured narrative, Payne saw (or I think he thought he saw) an attempt to comprehend all the varieties of language in one plot, which failed because, in the action of a quest for "tidings," the narrator-poet could not visit any idiom without by his presence actually changing its character.[1] As he reads the *Aeneid* in Book I, the text shifts between writing and painting under his eyes.[2] When he listens to the eagle in Book II, pedagogy turns into parody, parody into fear, and fear into silliness. Understanding is left to choose between the sublimely frivolous and the comically lethal. Is he trying to tell the ultimate joke: the one where you die laughing? Undecided what to do with Dante, Chaucer drops him—and then must wonder whether Dante (in the person of the eagle) will drop him, as if in a vengeful echo of his own vision of being consumed by the sun towards which the golden eagle had borne him in *Purgatorio* 9. But Chaucer, while contriving a curious poetic anti-sun confronting Dante, does not pay the dues

106

of mounting a viable competition with him. He more radically risks making either himself or Dante look foolish. Poetic extinction is a real possibility when one's commentary on texts drives them each to the point of reversing their intentions. Contemplating exposure to things that might overwhelm his powers to represent them, Chaucer adopts a deflationary stance vis-à-vis authority, and thereby casts his apprehension in the form of an aesthetic question: How can the intrusive imagination, that changes what it renders, represent things without falsifying or suppressing its own insight? Without, indeed, at some disturbing point deflecting its powers away from the projected revelation? If Chaucer can find a way to allow for, and even represent, the occasional repression of representing, then he will make available to his readers his own ambivalence about the very idea of witnessing and reporting significance. In such a transference of poetic fear onto the reader, he would achieve a comedic sublime.

My own strategy for diagnosing Chaucer's tactical retreats, for catching his comic muse in the act, is to look at the poem's dealings with the matter of medieval exegesis, biblically derived and poetically potent, and explicitly linked to interpretive theories for both medieval and modern readers. Exegesis reads one thing "out of" another (while eisegesis reads stuff "into" things), and offers a generational pattern by which one's reading begets an indirectly figured meaning with the material furnished by an author's writing. It is likely that we speak commonly of exegesis, reading-out-from, even when we are reading-into, and elide the term eisegesis, first because we see previous interpreters getting away with it, and second, because we think we might be supposed or obliged to be reading-from when we secretly want very much to read-into, but are not sure we can justify it. Exegesis does not, however, clone the originating text, but rather uses the deferral of generational difference to alter the family resemblance between text and meaning. Exegetical interpretation extends the text by metonymy, not repetition. More radical differences arise between discourses conceived of as related than between discourses regarded as plainly distinct. While reading-into is thought to be the more arbitrary, and therefore groundless or dangerous, procedure, the reading-out-from generates more unexpected mutations of material. To read an exegetic gloss out from a text is to confound the rhetoric of the text with the impulsiveness of interpretation (or to recognize that in reading or writing one has already confounded them). The generational reading-out-from provides a metonymic relay between text and gloss, between rhetorical material and interpretive method, that leads one to see that the material asks for interpretations and that the method has a rhetoric of its own. By acknowledging the marriage between rhetoric and interpretation, we can resume confidence in some phenomenal link between Chaucer's poem and any understanding of it, but resume that confidence without giving up its "busted" or mutating character.

In exegesis, one has a widely practiced medieval hermeneutic that assumes, as modern psychoanalysis does, the existence of latent meanings, unintended by the author, which would also be undiscovered by the reader but for indirect methods of interpretation. Augustine claims in the *De Utilitate Credendi* that the most rich and rewarding reading occurs "when some truth is understood from another's writing, when he who wrote would not have understood it. In this kind [of misreading] there is no little usefulness, but indeed, if you consider more closely, the whole fruit of reading is therein complete."[3] Reading comes to fruition, primarily when and not entirely until, the reader allows interpretation to "seek out new worlds" in the text, even to the extent of boldly going where no authority has gone before; it ripens further when an author acknowledges, even to the extent of providing rhetorical space for it, the inevitable occurrence of unintended meanings in the work. The implication of medieval exegetical method itself is that even reading literally and for intended meaning is simply one form of the "misreading" by which a reader addresses the given words in a way that frees them from the "given" quality that authorial formulation temporarily lays upon them. Reading and misreading, together with writing and miswriting, realize all the possible intentions and thus liberate meaning from the measure of singular intention. All these acts of mis/read/writing are set out in the *House of Fame,* but it is the least noted act of "miswriting" that Chaucer most explicitly puts forward in his search for an idiom that will make most comprehensively sure that all the possible meanings have been provided for in his text. The more of it he can miswrite—that is, write so that it insists on being reread under the creating correction of any reader—the vaster the realm of meaningfulness he will have made available to exploration, and the less he must commit himself to any one signified.

The catalogue of doubts about dreams announces at the poem's opening its concerns with how meaning attaches to variable signifiers. It then presents the possibly authoritative *Aeneid* in descriptions that slide between a tablet reproducing the text itself and pictorial illustrations referring to that text. The double metaphor of inscription and depiction establishes the unfixed relationships between text and interpretation. Perhaps the tablet is the text and the pictures the gloss; perhaps the pictures are the presence of the story and the tablet's words a mediating gloss. Chaucer's equivocation imagines a nonself-reliant text that stands in need of a glossator. Readers must constantly re-decide whether they are looking at text, gloss, or both. Chaucer avoids managing too artfully his poetic means, arranging instead for a text whose rhetorical means will overwhelm its signifying ends. He thus provides a diversionary analogy to the prospect of truth overwhelming his text, in the bracket of a fantasy of his verbal powers overwhelming another. With the roles of force and collapse taken by varying elements, he has faced his consummation and deflected it, too. Another effect of the means' outflanking the ends is to include within the set of the poem's means the undoing of those means. Such undoing may be understood both psychoanalytically, as a defense against authorial anxiety, and logically, as a gesture undermining the identity principle. To frame this set that includes contradictory items, Chaucer allows the simplistic binary system of means and ends, signifiers and signifieds, rhetoric and interpretation, to stand, relying on its very inadequacy to index for us the category of the excrescent, the ornament that eludes interpretation's estimates.

Thus, the *House of Fame* opens as a text regarding commentary as necessary (it controls the advent of meaning) and continues as one recognizing that commentary does not decide ultimate meanings (it leaves open the possibility of surprise meaning). Textual exegesis is a necessary, but not conclusive, exercise; the signifying occurs during the process of reading, not as a result of it.[4] Tesserae of scriptural imagery occur often enough in the poem to form a recognizable thread in its program; but they are also infrequent enough to occupy an ornamental place, and it is not as ornaments that exegemes have usually been treated. The new use of exegetical matter as figure rather than as decoder is itself a trope that recasts intention as experiment, and systemic reference as a lace of excess and lack. The binary of figure and key also blurs, for once one sees that the exegetical material is figurative just as other tropes are, one also senses that their hint of truth is still a needed part of the skeptical text. Why does Chaucer take up both these stances?

He has wonderfully set up a contrast between substantive referentiality and arbitrary referentiality, corresponding to the two ways of conceiving an exegeticizable language, as either divinely created (*allegoria in factis*) or humanly instituted (*allegoria in verbis*) allegory. On one hand, he looks at an authoritative tiding that is itself concerned with the right execution by heroes of divine imperatives. (The medieval factor of Aeneas as cad is the loose thread here, hinting at something unaccounted for in the classical story, a concern not limited to courtly literature with the treachery of misrepresenting desires by simplistic symbolic substitutes, a concern that recurs with the inadequacies of each of the discourses of Vergil, Dante, the eagle, classical invocation, history, epic, Fame, Rumor, and tidings, each of which proposes a "sentence" too limited to evoke in him the fear that alone convinces him of meaning's proximity.) On the other, he pictures arbitrariness of reference in the palace of Fame and the ballroom of Rumor, where desserts are meted out without measure, and language distorts the stories it reports. Between books I and III, the eagle's informed but incredible discourse on sound mediates the scenes of substance and crapshoot. The masterful Dante is invoked, and his vision rendered as volubility. Conflating his topic and his way of talking, the eagle tells not the truth about tidings but a story about truth. And with *that,* Chaucer can scare himself as Dante's covering arrogance could not.[5] Having contrived this binary system, Chaucer seeks not a *tertium quid* subsuming both categories, but some novel factor, which neither the eagle nor the *man of auctorite* can introduce, although their very ineffectiveness helps to spoil any ease of dialectic, and actually intimates a virgin novelty, perpetually offstage, in the story as told.

It is precisely the field of unconscious reference that Chaucer seems to have explicitly omitted, omitted in a way inviting notice, from the schema of the *House of Fame.* The life of unknown associates in the inmost mind is hinted by the narrator's fear, puzzlement, and doubt regarding the adequacy of what he does know, hear, and see. Unconscious mental life may be overheard in specific rhetorical moves: shifts and wrinkles in tone and imagery that show the verbal decor is only loosely tied to the consciously intended plan of the poem. The *Book of the Duchess* explores the caves of sleep and conversation which show the melancholic yet undetermined psyche that invents poetry, and the *House of Fame* picks up at the initiatory moment when the narrating mind, having thought itself, has as yet nothing to say, but has fantasized for the first time the possibility of saying something later. In this narrative, the poet takes the idea that he may be a poet out for a little experimental exercise, preparing with this fantasy action a space in his mind to receive his own emerging impulses towards actually writing about a subject. But his reluctance to tangle with any subject first requires a fable of its own. Only after setting out a history of this fantasy does Chaucer devote a work, the *Parliament,* which combines freely associated unconscious story with an avowedly artful and accomplished composition. Repression must be given its play to perform, lest the ambivalence that first motivates it turn, for lack of acknowledgment, into mindless defensiveness or cryptonomy.[6]

II. He Hides Things in Plain Sight

In the *House of Fame,* the superficial order of the narration, in the very process of falling apart, crowds the symbols, allusions, and devices that often key a poem's unconscious subtexts into the ornamental margins of the story.[7] While the lapse of narration into amplification busts the movement of the plot, the decampment to ornament draws our attention from the veneer of narrated causality (what Freud calls the secondary elaboration of a dream) to the excrescence of small oddities. In these, we might recognize unconscious motives in the poet's or our own verbal routines. To zero in on a possible content for this unconscious, we must ask at what point the narrative order splinters. But searching backwards through the poem for a plateau of figure to narrative relevance, one finds oneself at its beginning without ever having encountered some such keying alignment. The periphrastic catalogue of dreams, expressing and inviting doubt and confusion over the precise extent of the whole proposed discourse's referential talent, would seem to confirm the suspicion that Chaucer has set out to write a fragment from the start. (I don't mean that he plans the exact cut after the *man of auctorite,* but that he is writing narrative in a fragmentary state all along.) If the poem's flaw is to present mental experience rather than rework it, its advantage is to display literary process as intrinsically as tenuous and distracted in its references as our mind's life is in its associations. Our intentions in life or art are, as in Lacan's specular register, the mis-takings of others' desires for "our own," at just that moment in psychic development when we have no formed desires of our own, and thus are susceptible to the projections of those taking the formative care of us, in their necessary theft of its autonomy from a person who does not effectively exist yet.[8] The narrator, imagining for the first time the possibility of saying something later, must be possessed by the propositions of others in order to formulate this fantasy. With the plethora of ornament, the unreliability of Fame and Rumor, and the good-humored abuse of Vergil and Dante, the poem interrupts intentionality so as to offer the narrator some relief from his own project, and the reader a glance at unintended meaning. This intervention it cannot make by a mere show of irrelevance, but effects by a real conflation of the irrelevant and the significant, as in the exegemes that mix Providence with contrivance. Collectively, the exegemes supply an allusion to a set system of reference within a narrative devoted to unsettling such systems. Used ironically or casually, they run counter to their tradition, and thus give and take away right reference in one figure. With regard to the poet's fending off of meaning, the exegemes casually maintain the familiar truths, alarming or reassuring, which threaten either the poet's endurance or the risks he does manage to take within the poem by which he forestalls those truths. Truth as well as repression must be represented, first in order to stage the poet's whole psychic situation, and second to be put in its place, along with repression, as simply one more figure in the fable.

In creating a place of preparation for the narrator who may now say something later, the poem also affords a practice field for the readers who may now read anything as something else.[9] If Chaucer can keep our attention with the promises of meaning in ornament, fueling distraction with frills, the frills and promises being compromised in the same decorations, then he will have guaranteed that nobody whom he has drawn through the siren song seductions of the text's ambushing obstacle course will read anything else he might write later with any presumption of art or accident, or any privileging of declaration or evasion. Like Milton and Wordsworth, Chaucer is creating the reader for the poet he is inventing.

Exegetical allegory issues a special invitation to readers in search of inviolable truth to follow the aesthetic of the apparently arbitrary in deciding what meanings to assign to which motifs. Even the most traditional selection of divinely instituted *allegoriae in factis* refers the timing and choice of the applications to the reader's judgment as it is informed by the imaginative constructs of words.

The signal exegetical moment for the dreamer is his exclamation as he fears for his life in the eagle's claws: "Or what thing may this sygnifye? / I neyther am Ennok, ne Elye" (587–88). The prophets exemplify the confounding cases of people who do not see death (Enoch) or who revive the dead (Elias). The dreamer is afraid not so much of being carried upwards as of dying in a way he does not understand: hence his use of "signifye." The dreamer's quick citation of these scriptural prophets, whose authority only highlights his own confusion and fear, suggests that the prospect of understanding what is happening to him both allures and appalls him. In this instance, to supplant mastery with an invention that recognizes while it refigures authority, Chaucer deploys exegesis to imply and to avert the text of truth of the New Testament, replacing with Old

Testament figures the Paul to whom Dante alludes in the model for this exclamation: "Io non Enea, io non Paulo sono" (*Inferno* 2.32).[10] Yet: exegesis does customarily draw new perceptions from just those Old Testament persons, and it may be Dante's Paul who is intruding on the interpretative search for more truth. In fact, Chaucer is simply deferring his own allusion to Paul later in lines 780–82. Chaucer's initial expression of that exemplary visionary, whose special force derives from his having witnessed Christ without ever having met Him, returns to the poet with interest when, after some four hundred lines of the eagle's instruction, he qualifies himself as a rapt witness of some truth he knows he has not heard. In the Chaucerian version of the Pauline vision, the scales fall from one's eyes when one is safe from unmediated, or at least from physical and historical, contact with the sublime image of a godly truth.

He has been similarly perplexed upon emerging from the Temple of Venus into the desert at the end of the first book. Having just reveled in the image of Vergil's history, he is overcome with fear of untoward images, which might be closely related to a profane Venus, in the noonday desert of temptation. In Vergil's case, he conflates the pagan temple and Christian worship:

> "A, Lord!" thoughte I, "that madest us,
> Yet sawgh I never such noblesse
> Of ymages, ne such richesse,
> As I saugh graven in this chirche" (470–73)

He underscores both the visionary experience and his residual confusion when he adds, "But not wot I whoo did hem wirche, / Ne where I am" (747–75). And his confusion is followed not by a Pauline ravishment but by the sight of the barren desert, whose potential images evoke from him the fresh cry:

> "O Christ! thoughte I, "that art in blysse
> Fro fantome and illusion
> Me save!" (492–94)

Images do come *in bono* and *in malo*. The eagle's service to the dreamer's need for tiding argues his advocacy of images as equals of unmediated experience; indeed, the life of tidings in Fame and Rumor is so brisk that one comes to ask whether experience is made up of images in the first place, the life of the imagination preceding the life of perception. Winnicott might remind us that the infant's fantasy of action, provisionally dramatized for it by the mother's bodily action, precedes the infant's perception of its own or its mother's autonomy. Lacan might observe that the infant's image of another person's unspoken ideas preceded and inform the infant's perception of itself.[11] In either case, should Christ really shield the dreamer from such apparitions, if they are giving him apprehensiveness about one other than his own impulses? His own liveliness? Or is the dreamer insightfully, if unwittingly, suggesting that the exegemes themselves (Enoch, Elias, church decor) are among the noonday phantoms that lead the mind back into its detours from convention? Again, the moments participate in figurative life as well as in the certain path of substantive reference: "For, be Cryste, lo, thus yt fareth: / 'Hyt is not al gold that glareth' " (271–72).

The images in both Fame and Rumor are unstable in their link to meanings, and so it is provocative that Saint Peter makes his appearance at the threshold of both their houses. The sound emanating from the Palace of Fame is "Peter! lyk betynge of the see, / Quod y, "ayen the roches holowe" (1034–35). Here, Peter is the fisherman afraid to trust a savior in a storm (Matt. 8:23–27; Mark 4:36–41). Later, after his long initial gaze at the Mill of Rumor, the dreamer asks the eagle to stay to help him learn some tiding here, and now the eagle avers, "Petre! that is myn entente" (2000). Peter is now invoked as the keeper of the gate into the true heaven, where things take on their full and final guise. Placing him at the thresholds of deceptive settings ironically emphasizes how hollow both these rocks and Peter "the rock" may be. Does the allusion, however, also suggest a value in that hollowness? Does the founding Peter retain the fearful one? Does the erosion of substance reveal the volume of mind?

The confusion lies not just in the arbitrariness of Fame's significations, or in the random survival of signifiers in the frozen north facade and disappearance of signifiers in the melting south face. The primary gloss on Fame is Rumor, and if in the Palace of Fame the signifier-signified path was more often than not skewed, in the House of Rumor the path of reference runs from signifier to signifier, as tiding multiplies tiding and teller relays teller, leading to no discernible signified that does not immediately revert to being a signifier by virtue of bearing the full imprint of rumor's distortions and elaborations.[12] No signifier is posited as independent of the re-signifiers of explication. As a gloss on Fame, Rumor brings the need for glossing, and deferral of the signified, back into the palace of the famous subjects of poetic matter. Rumor's reaction upon Fame leads one to ask whether the poets have a matter whose import lies more in the invitation to commentary, regardless of whether it elicits evasive or incisive interpretation, than in their ostensible themes. Rumor here is less the simple chaos of incremental messages and games of telephone than the factor of not-yet-decided meaning in the fabric of literary language. Not even the poet can figure out all that has been figured into the work. His fantasy of what his mental life would be if he were a poet has become the idiomatic primal scene whence he must avert his eyes, even as he alone can draw the veil from off its presence. And, because it is a veil of his own design, it has already shaped the presence of which it is the incuse print.

III. He Fantasizes Saying Something

The narrator's unconscious is evident in his hedging report of his purpose in visiting Rumor:

> The cause why y stonde here:
> Somme newe tydynges for to lere,
> Some newe thinges, y not what,
> Tydynges, other this or that,
> Of love, or suche thynges glade. (1885–89)

His sketchy optatives and negatives suggest plenty of unconscious motivation in his visit. He says he wants something new, unknown, and possibly gladsome (as in Stevens' injunctions that "It Must Be Abstract;" "It Must Change;" and "It Must Give Pleasure" in the section titles of *Notes Towards a Supreme Fiction*). Yet the only tidings he will perceive, much less understand, are old, familiar ones that return him, albeit by way of upsetting, uncanny forms, to his initial avoidance of decision. The exegetical moments play a part in this disorientation. Their unconscious import here is the poet's wish for certainty, for tidings that are real subjects, subjects of which one may predicate facts one can master, and for firmness of reference, all of which he has renounced as a mature poet but for which he still longs.

Or rather, Chaucer is taking a desire of which he is quite conscious, but which he feels more strongly or more often than he wants to, and representing it as unconscious, and displaced from tropes about topics to tropes of interpretation, in order to register accurately the *force* of a desire that would motivate such deflections of statement. He knows that any desire of which he is conscious is the tip of an iceberg of unacknowledged longing that haunts the rough estimates of representation. (Note that the desire for certainty and tidings implies ambivalence towards those desiderata. Certainty would foreclose Chaucer's imaginative life. In the *Parliament,* he will defer the "certeyn thing" he looks for into one of those impossibly extended reading lists with which we are all familiar from our own fantasies of bibliographical diversion.) This forestalling of foreclosure is why I say the narrator fantasizes saying something before he fantasizes having something to say. Not only does verbal activity precede verbal significance, developmentally and philosophically, but also a fantasy of the tiding itself would overwhelm the fantasy of speaking with the coercions of its own coherence and relations to other topics.

Uncertain of the content of the unconscious (the object of his desire), and unsure of how much of it he wishes to represent, Chaucer simply represents a space for the unconscious, and its specific representation is ornament. Committed to write of poetry and desire rather than of things that would ground his personal subject, Chaucer in effect "restores" the matrix of his matter by *adding* to the scene a thick and serviceable encrustation of decor. In the parure of the poem, he and his reader can imagine truth and conviction without, however, ever thinking they have found them. The layering of ornaments preserves the mechanism of reference while deferring any one referent or act of reference. Restoration by addition—analepsis—prolongs (in a spirit of honesty) the precariousness of representing truth, and saves us (in a spirit of defense) from the conviction of confronting truth. The final reality of meaning, mind, and body is safely pocketed in an invisible bubble of amber: *safe* from being either fraudulently represented or catastrophically retrieved in all its plenitude and betrayal; and *invisible* because it cannot be distinguished from the airy hypotheses and distorted names in whose company it appears. Somewhere in the *House of Fame* we have *already* touched the core of a rhetorically and psychologically well-represented self, but we do not know at what turn this touch occurred. The exegetical images, in an intermittent but explicit way, describe interpretation under these elusive circumstances, as the act of discerning a deeper meaning in each detail, regardless of whether it is a major or minor signal.[13] The exegete's generous disregard for relative importance among symbols effectively circumvents the entire question of knowing which detail is candid and which indirect, which is amplifying and which gratuitous. Although this generosity may not serve as a means for evaluating the merits of a text, it is invaluable in validating the reader's fantasy of finding meaning in the body of the text.

It is part of the envisioned reader's experience, first, to be uncertain about meaning and unable to report it, and second, to realize that some of what one learns defies common notions of sanctioned or sensible discourse. At the height of the heavens in the eagle's claws, the poet displays to the reader a narrator who feels such a visionary confusion as Paul had:

> "Y wot wel y am here;
> But wher in body or in gost
> I not, ywys; but God, thou wost!" (980–82)

alluding to 2 Corinthians 12:3–4: "And I knew such a man, (whether in the body, or out of the body, I cannot tell: God knoweth;) [nescio Deus scit] / How that he was caught up [raptus est] into paradise, and heard unspeakable words [verba arcana], which it is not lawful for a man to utter [quae non licet homini loqui]." Here is the claim to Pauline vision, deferred from line 588, partly to allow the Dantean and Chaucerian versions of it to disentangle; partly to allow the Chaucerian to supersede the Dantean (as the New Testament the Old) and present itself as deriving from Paul's text without mediation; and then again, partly to derive from a text rather than from a person, and to convert visionary experience from a transcendent aim to a verbal response (to the eagle's syllabus), a recollection (of the literary tradition of visions), or a representation (of the still delayed, still apprehended revelations to be made in fantasy in Fame and Rumor). Paul's tale of the unspeakable becomes the matter of the poet's text. And since it is an artifice, Chaucer can choose when and whether to regard his language as primary material (words as the experiential stuff of poetry) or as derivative (words as the representation of other experiences).

The Palace of Fame also bears a partly skeptical and partly impressive valence, with its walls of beryl that magnify everything indiscriminately (1288–91), and gold and gems (1341–63) that refer to the Lapidary (1352) instead of the Bible. The expected reference of all this precious material to the heavenly city in Revelation is deferred and oblique. An activated Apocalypse must not be allowed to impinge on the initiatory gestures of the poet and reader in training. There is no reminder that beryl, believed to collect the sun's heat and burn the hand, emblemizes the apostles bringing the heat of Christ to their listeners. Nor are we asked to recall that the ruby can signify the word of God illuminating us through preaching.[14] These ideas are available but unaccented. At first, the dreamer simply claims that there were so many heralds for

Fame that one could have used their coats of arms to make "a bible / Twenty foot thykke" (1335): the key text positioned as an ornamental hyperbole. At the end of the description of Fame's abode, Chaucer uses the same tactic, referring to Revelation in the angle of a comparison:

> For as feele eyen hadde she
> As fetheres upon foules be
> Or weren on the bestes foure
> That Goddis trone gunne honoure
> As John writ in th'Apocalips.
> Hir heer, that oundy was and crips. . . . (1381–86)

Thus things divine rhyme off into Fame's curly hair, endowed with its own pagan, medusan resonances. Does the diffused allusion to Revelation ennoble the text, or at least supply some meaning to it, or does the allusion's diffuseness, and the context of Fame's incongruities, demean the scriptural figures?

> 5. And out of the throne proceeded lightnings and thunderings and voices:
>
> 6. . . . and round about the throne, were four beasts full of eyes before and behind.
>
> 7. And the first beast was like a lion, and the second beast like a calf, and the third beast has a face of a man, and the fourth beast was like a flying eagle.
>
> 8. . . . and they were full of eyes within. (Rev. 4:5–8)

The serious significance lent by this allusion is the nature and status of four other writers, the evangelists symbolized by the four animals, with eyes before and behind, on the Old and New Testaments, and with eyes within, of spiritual insight. Bede interprets that

> The animals moreover signify now the Evangelists and now the whole Church. . . . "full of eyes around and within," etc. Holy Church pays vigilant heed to both God and men. Or otherwise: whether one attends to the letter or seeks the allegory, one will always find light from the Gospel. Another translation has it thus: "full of eyes before and behind." For the light of the Gospel shines in the symbols of the law, and pours the light of new grace out to the world.[15]

The four animals send Bede to the four Evangelists, and their writing brings to his mind the double context of reading (law and grace), and its double method (literal and allegorical). Words that radiate the glory do not do so simply. The immediate implication of Chaucer's comparison might be that Fame has as much scope and diversity in her numerous eyes as the Evangelists have. The inverse implication would be that the gospel writers have as much scope and diversification as does Fame. Yet one can hardly press earnest reading much farther than this, for Fame's random dealings have little in common with the veracity of the four saints and the Holy Spirit. Or should we, at this point, go ahead and think of the disparities among the Gospels? Perhaps the allusion's parodic aspect points not so much against Fame's arbitrariness as towards the complexities of discourse imbued ever and especially with truth. If the Gospel writers have as many eyes as Fame, they presumably have as many approaches and insights into their subject. In the theology of linguistic incarnation, divinity can be expressed only by the figurations of allegory and the space they make for our understandings of God as amplified through a collection of individually limited images, and Deity conceived of as a subject can be diffused only over the fictive digressions of language and thought. God must live in the gossiping house of Rumor, if not in the treacherous precincts of Fame. The ineffability of God makes this a simple necessity, of which the parodic exegeme is a usefully surprising expression.

An earlier moment has hinted at the implication of tidings in figurative language: celebrating his splendid exposition of the mechanism of tidings on their way to Fame, the eagle soars higher and exclaims, "Be seynt Jame, / Now will we speken al of game!" (885–86). The eagle adduces the apostle most concerned with the right governance of speech precisely in the shift from serious to entertaining discourse. In chapter three of his epistle, we read:

5. Even so the tongue is a little member, and boasteth great things. Behold, how great a matter a little kindleth! [magnam silvam incendit]

6. And the tongue is a fire, a world of iniquity: so is the tongue among our members, that it defileth [maculat] the whole body . . .

7. For every kind of beasts . . . hath been tamed of mankind:

8. But the tongue can no man tame [linguam autem nullus hominum domare potest]; it is an unruly evil, full of deadly poison . . .

10. Out of the same mouth proceedeth blessing and cursing. My brethren, these things ought not so to be. (James 3:5–10)

Yet so they are.

An acknowledgment of the *House of Fame* as a busted poem is the first step not towards dismissing it but towards appreciating its mediation between subtle exposition and free-hearted play in a fantasy of exploring what is left of mind and art as sense and structure are by degrees erased. Between things and nothing lies a gloss. The poet's apparent erasure of the signifying relationship between words and things proves to be a displacement of both signified and signifier by commentary. He redraws Lacan's bar between signified and signifier as a dotted line. In the solution of commentary, the link between signified and signifier is not destroyed, but blurred, and thereby arguably all the more guaranteed in being given so many different possible structures to take up.

That the *House of Fame* signifies *something*, we may each be severally persuaded by our own reception of its illustrious dazzle detail, so suggestive of potential unconscious meaning.[16] The *House of Fame* gives to each its own, and employs its brushes with exegesis to invite us to claim it for our own, as well we may in the wake of Chaucer's tacit relocation of "auctorite." Exegesis without authority is possible, even in the absence (or inascertainability, or readerly ignorance) of the signified it customarily animates. Exegesis without authority may indeed be the needful tiding, the word from the narrator's fantasy, that measures out and tides the poem over, in between signifiers, from lack to insight, from failure to adequacy, from bust to boom. With respect to the undefined, unrecognized terms of language and theme, the *House of Fame* is busted by virtue of its neglect or mismanagement of both, its almost willful ineptitude; meanwhile, it is busted to the effect of discovering to us (and perhaps to Chaucer) the rich treasury of free-floating signs that move the heart of writer and reader to endite and interpret, without fear of annihilation, and apart from every economic, social, aesthetic, and emotional agenda clamoring for the "Fame" our attention might give it.

> Exegesye, though noon auctoritee
> Were in this world, is right ynogh for me
> To speke of joye that is in poesye.

We are taught to read for the excess of *jouissance* instead of the end zone of climax.

The program of the exegetical material lies in the context of the whole poem's character as a quest for *a way to* tidings, the effort to qualify the invited tidings by rerouting them through figurative representations and tropes that secure a known place for one's unknown mind: a way, so to speak, to entertain an angel unawares. The *House of Fame* is the dream of a rhetorician in which the manifest content is the poet's quest for thematic material, while the latent content (that which is unconsciously displaced in the Freudian dream, and figuratively implied in the artistic composition) is the poetic material of troping. The poetic tropes can be limited or repressed by an author's or reader's impulse to control its range of reference. In the *House of Fame,* troping appears in the jungle of "marginal" ornament encroaching on the dreamer's quest for a topic, encroaching, that is, on any impulse to mastery that might be suppressing his impulse to invent. Neither that quest nor its proximate goals of theme constitute the poem's plot, but rather the sequence of tropes themselves: from allusion and abbreviation in Book I, through exposition, dialogue, and parody in Book II, to description, catalogue, and amplification in Book III. This tropical plot is as complete when the poem breaks as the emotional tour is at the ending of Sterne's *Sentimental Journey:* "So that when I stretched out my hand, I caught hold of the fille de chambre's—." In Chaucer's rhetorical vision, the equivalent to the maid's blank dash is the aposiopesis on *auctorite.* As the form gives implicit space to the overflowing of fancy, the latter brakes the race of signifiers in their skid towards invention's apocalypse. For a moment, all possible meanings are accessible; then, uncertainty or indecision overthrows the structures drawn up for meaning, and the impulse to signify must shift from the writer to the reader. The advantage to readers is the opportunity to rehearse the poetic process in their work of interpretation; the advantage to the poet is the foreclosure of foreclosure, gained by his proposal of an idea of meaningfulness in the context of a withdrawal from specifying meaning. Chaucer flirts with the sublime moment of articulation, and leaves her. He moves in his own persona from the writer to the reader, looking for more ways of looking at the page, "Tyl fully daswed ys [his] look" (658). This is the poet who invokes the great god of poetry to lead the text not into revelation or mastery of the *ars poetica,* but to a pleasing of the reader, who will then complaisantly allow for flaws in the verse (flaws being indistinguishable from figures), and in the end accept as "sentence" the poet's "descryving":

> O God of science and of lyght,
> Appollo, thurgh thy grete myght,

> This lytel laste bok thou gye!
> Nat that I wilne, for maistrye,
> Here art poetical be shewed;
> But for the rym ys lyght and lewed,
> Yit make hyt sumwhat agreable,
> Though som vers fayle in a sillable;
> And that I do no diligence
> To shewe craft, but o sentence . . .
> Loo, that is for to menen this,
> The Hous of Fame for to descryve. (1091–1100, 1104–1105)

The ultimate rhetorical rejoicing is to fall short in midflight as one is nearing a revelation that would undo one's conscious power to represent.[17] The close calls of this unsafe middle flight is the syntax that exegesis maps as it reads-out-from difficult figures their associated meanings, straight or strange. Exegesis, with its genealogy of glossing generations, invites us into language as variable reference; by its analeptic work of providing for revelation with a fantasy of restoration, it playfully supplies meaning apparently made to order as if by a mothering text. Chaucer has made the toy or transitional object into the parent that provides it. Beyond the prophet, he finds the procreator. He goes behind Dante and Paul, to Vergil and Enoch, and further back to Aeneas and Christ, thence to Anchises and the Creator, and on to Venus and Theotokos, or Apollo and the Spirit, or Daphne and the leaf of the letter.

Let us, in turn, recall a restorative modern remembrance of the semiotic and temporal shimmer beating from the divided heart of medieval images. To read their optative garments is to spread such rumors about them, as will please the interpreting reader with finding the newest treasures of one's mind in the work of one's author, will please the reader of the interpreter with an increase of power and light to be found in that subjected author, and will by hypothesis please as well the author, with the credit given afresh to his invention, and the belief leapt to in the uncertain life of his language:

> Medieval pageantry
>   is human and we enjoy
>   the rumor of it,
>   as in our world we enjoy
>   the reading of Chaucer,
>   likewise
>   a priest's raiment
>   (or that of a savage chieftain).

It is all
a celebration of the light.

—William Carlos Williams,
Asphodel, That Greeny Flower, "Coda"

Notes

1. The way texts change at the advent of a reader evokes not only the Heisenberg uncertainty principle but a Derridean question of "la structure classiquement déterminée du signe" that reads signs as deferring and deferring to truths endowed with "une présence originelle." In texts already changing and mechanisms apart from, and thus subversive of, their traditional referents and their quality of presence. The word symbols in Fame's House and the poem about it reveal in themselves "quelque chose comme une différance originaire," which disputes the derivative status of signs, and further "met en question l'autorité de la présence ou de son simple contraire symétrique, l'absence ou le manque" (Derrida 9–10).

2. Carruthers' description of the mnemonics of the poem reminds us that Chaucer's visit to the mural of the *Aeneid,* in rehearsing Aeneas' visit to the mural of the fall of Troy in Carthage, is a memory of a memory (187). This compromises the idea of an original experience prior to memory, and sorts with Derrida's dismantling of presence and critique of the binary of presence and absence. Carruthers' detailing of the memorial architecture brings the poem's structural and logical antinomies, susceptible to deconstruction, into alignments with the psychic life, represented by memory. Her picture of "intercolumnar" spaces (188) in Fame's Palace implies the poem is structured as alternation: between surface and depth, or again between surface and gloss, and also between sight (recollection) and interruption (evasion, resistance, repression). Artful memory also bespeaks a reluctance to remember something clearly.

3. "Cum ex alieno scripto intelligitur aliquid veri, cum hoc ille qui scripsit non intellexerit. In quo genere [inplex error legentium] non parum est utilitatis, imo si diligentius consideres, totus legendi fructus est integer" (Augustine 4.10; *PL* 42.72).

4. This view of exegesis breathes fresh life into pious exegesis, whose reputation has suffered from the narrow results obtained by its puritan revisers Robertson and Huppé, whose exegesis of Chaucer's dream-visions in *Fruyt and Chaf* does not take on the *House of Fame.*

5. Chaucer's response to authority, and the kind of authority he creates, have successfully evoked commentary that suggests more self-revelation than objective comprehension (it is probably one of his points to move unintended self-revelation over to the register of conscious insight into the role projection plays in motivating interpretation). Howard reads Chaucer's hesitations in the *House of Fame* as signaling depression rather than psychic resistance (254), equating "inner discontent" with "lack of purpose" (252). Insisting on an anxious oedipal model for Chaucer's place in tradition, but confronted with a writer interested in but not dependent on either emulating or repressing predecessors, Howard must decide that "it was the *lack* of a mentor or model that caused him anxiety" (255). Spearing does better in taking Chaucer's uneasiness as part of a "portrait of himself as a poet whose timidity makes him positively resistant to inspiration," whose work, although

"deeply indebted to literary tradition yet generates a strong sense of the occasionally uneasy working out of a personal problem." He speculates that Chaucer cannot complete this poem "because it had too painful a point, in its exploration of
problems concerning Chaucer's own life as a poet," problems which, though insol-
uble, constitute "bearable pain" rather than *"Angst"* (*Dream Poetry* 87–88). As a
fable of resistance, the poem relieves its own pressures by representing a resistance
whose object is by virtue of that resistance unascertainable, not depressive. The
subtler account posits not an embedded obstacle that must be dissolved (Howard
256) but a difficulty in and with which to live and write (Spearing 88).

My reading tries to move one minim past Spearing's tact, in seeing the poem as
narrating Chaucer's first inner fantasy of saying something, without demanding
from myself or Chaucer a definition of what is to be said, for the tiding cannot
impinge on the growth of the poet's mind until after that mind has played with the
possibility of a tiding long enough to create a psychic place that can receive such
a tiding without being appropriated. Howard can call the poem's "surprising
glimpse into a poet's inner world of thought" a "lucky accident" only by comparing it, in a dismally predictable substitution of an Italian Renaissance for the English Middle Ages, to Petrarch, whom Howard, but not Chaucer, privileges for
nothing but the "sheer volume" of his epistolary self-reflections (252). The idea
that Chaucer cannot or will not match Italian authority/sublimity resurfaces in
Spearing's later characterization, from the perspective of an idea of the Renaissance, of the *House of Fame* as repeating Dante's enraptured vision as uneasy
comedy (*Renaissance* 23), an experience that for the narrator is "no more than a
disturbing and unsatisfying holiday from his normal work in the custom-house"
(27). I would suggest that Chaucer feels uneasy at just that point when his poetry
does take him beyond initial ambitions. The perception of humor's link to unconscious desire takes him straight into the abiding profundity in comedy which by
comedy he pretends to avert. Spearing felicitously also observes that "it is always
an important part of Chaucer's skill to make his difficulties into matter for amusement" (24). This trope of relief is, if anything, more incisive and more apprehen-
sive of sublimity than a trope of grandeur. It is helpful that an Italian critic whose
formation by I Tre Grandi might have rendered him incapable of esteeming comedy, sees Chaucer's evasion of the Dantean sublime as a "witty modesty," in a
poem whose lack of resolution signals that "[i]n the *House of Fame* Chaucer is
interested rather in exploring the world of art, without constructing systems" (Boitano *Chaucer* 165). The contrast between, for one instance, Boccaccio's anxiety
and Chaucer's tolerance for vicissitude is set out in sociohistorical context by
Ganim.

6. In "cryptonomy," I refer to the process of "preservative repression," which
creates traumatic events "as if they had never occurred" by incorporating them
asymptomatically into the psyche, which Abraham and Torok have discovered and
theorized in contrast to the "dynamic repression," discovered by Freud, which
leaves a trace distortion in mind or action by which the repressed material may be
recovered through an adequately figurative reading. Chaucer's preference for styles
of ambivalence, waffling, and tantalizing suggest he does not write in cryptonyms.
The multilingual cryptonomy Abraham and Torok find in the case of the Wolf
Man, however, does suggest that one could look for secret material, whose repression has itself been repressed, in the trilingual literary formation of authors in later
medieval England.

7. In this promotion of ornament, Chaucer's text exemplifies two key mechanisms in Freud's account of the "dream work:" displacement, by which disturbing

ideas are rendered as minor elements and weaker ideas as major elements in a dream narrative (Freud VI:B "The Work of Displacement"), and secondary revision, by which the congeries of distorting images generated by the dream-work is given a gloss of pseudo-logical connections and explanations that further defend the disturbing dream thoughts from detection (VI:I "Secondary Revision"). The result of these two mechanisms working together is that "A direct derivative of what occupies a dominating position in the dream-thoughts can often only be discovered precisely in some transitory element of the dream which is quite overshadowed by more powerful images" (VI:C "The Means of Representation"). (I have used the text reprinted from the Hogarth Press edition for the Pelican Freud Library, vol. 4., ed. Angela Richards, Harmondsworth: Penguin, 1967.)

8. I am adducing Lacan's account of self-awareness of ego as a *méconnaissance* in "The Mirror Stage as Formative of the Function of the I as Revealed in Psychoanalytic Experience," of which a brief review is never useless:

> the infant recognizes itself in its image, reflected in mirrors of mothers' faces, in a process of identification with that image: This jubilant assumption of his specular image by the child at the *infans* stage, still sunk in his motor incapacity and nursling dependence, would seem to exhibit in an exemplary situation the symbolic matrix in which the *I* is precipitated in a primordial form. . . . this form situates the agency of the ego, before its social determination, in a fictional direction . . . which will only rejoin the coming-into-being of the subject asymptomatically. (Lacan 2)

The poet still in search of tidings has the status of *infans,* Latin for not-yet-speaking, and writes a poetry whose reluctant relationship to meaning enacts a verbal analogue to the fictive self-image's asymptomatic approach to the hypothetical axis of its subject's supposed identity.

9. The poem as textual object that only manipulates readers but can still, if loosely written enough, be manipulated *by* its readers would seem to constitute the kind of uncommitted "potential space" described by Winnicott as "The Location of Cultural Experience": "The place where cultural experience is located is in the *potential space* between the individual and the environment (originally the object)" (100). Of particular relevance to literature is Winnicott's suggestion that "The interplay between originality and the acceptance of tradition as the basis for inventiveness [is] one more example, and a very exciting one, of the interplay between separateness and union" (99). We can read Chaucer as playing with either traditional authors or traditional meanings.

In response to his play with authorities, Ruffolo suggests that as he toys with the oedipal story, the only " 'anxiety of influence' that concerns Chaucer is his influence on his readership" (339). Winnicott's transitional object supports Ruffolo's perception of the pleasure Chaucer takes in his freewheeling creation. Unlike the Horatian poetic of instruction and delight, "the lists of the *House of Fame* assert that the value of poetry can rely upon delight alone, in their enjoyment of the verbal activity involved in hearing and spreading 'tydynges' " (326). Winnicott and Lacan differ, in that the Englishman believes a sensation of some duration of real wholeness (in the form of full connection to the mother) lives in the past of each person, while the Frenchman proposes that this never occurred and lives on only as a ghost. The metaphor or example both use, however, and which indicates the point of their theories' solution, is that of verbal fiction; as a fiction of fiction the *House of Fame* especially embodies and illuminates the way in which a verbally precocious person formulates the subject of a physically premature human being. Or, in literary terms, "One purpose of the dream-framework is no doubt to define an area within which the poem, as it were, 'has permission to exist', . . . within this area the medieval reader or listener was not necessarily called on to suspend his disbelief. The use of the dream-framework is frequently to evade the whole question of authenticity, of belief or disbelief" (Spearing *Dream Poetry* 75).

10. Ruffolo proposes this angle persuasively:

> The most important texts and writers for a Christian seeking authority, the New Testament and the Fathers, are absent from the *House of Fame*. The Old Testament figures in the poem, such as Enoch and Elijah, come from a work whose truth has been superseded by the New Testament. Chaucer's claim that "I neyther am Ennok, ne Elye" (588) imitates Dante's claim to be neither Aeneas nor Paul; by denying (at one remove) that he is Paul, Chaucer suppresses a New Testament parallel that some readers might spot in Geoffrey's visionary flight. (337)

Paul's appearance later in the poem argues that Chaucer may be proposing himself as the Christian Father equivalent. If Dante can play Messiah, Chaucer can play Apostle to the Gentiles.

11. Lacan 2; Winnicott 11–12 ("Transitional Objects and Transitional Phenomena"):

> at some theoretical point early in the development of every human individual an infant in a certain setting provided by the mother is capable of conceiving of the idea of something that would meet the growing need that arises out of instinctual tension. The infant cannot be said to know at first what is to be created. At this point in time the mother presents herself. In the ordinary way she gives her breast and her potential feeding urge. The mother's adaptation to the infant's needs, when good enough, gives the infant the *illusion* that there is an external reality that corresponds to the infant's own capacity to create.

Perhaps one does best to attribute the strange quality of care here to Chaucer's interest in confusing the reader's own recollection of maternal care, with some intent of inviting the reader to experiment with his poetry as a supplementing mother of imagination.

12. Fame and Rumor correspond in their structures of reference to the contrasting structures of metaphor and metonymy that Lacan posits as creating the effect of meaning in the unconscious. The hierarchical array of poets supporting heroes in Fame suggests the metaphoric structure, in which the progress from signifier to signified is effectively mimicked in a "progress" from one signifier to a substitute signifier. The whirl of Rumor suggests the metonymic structure, in which the existence of the signified is re-created as one's desire for a signified, the desire being expressed as a fugal quest that meanders from signifier to signifier (Lacan "Agency of the Letter in the Unconscious" 164). In metonymy, the bar to knowledge occurs in the person's relations to objects, whereas in metaphor it occurs in the acceptance of a comprehensible object as a substitute for an elusive one. Metonymic process is psychically earlier than the metaphoric and Chaucer's vision of rhetoric is thus regressing to earlier states of the person:word relationship in order to re-create the scene of initial tiding or signified in the mind's earliest apprehension of its possibility.

13. This aligns with Freud's methodological observation that

> It is decidedly more difficult to get hold of "involuntary ideas." Anyone who seeks to do so must . . . endeavour during the work [of interpretation] to refrain from any criticism, any *parti pris*, and any emotional or intellectual bias. He must bear in mind Claude Bernard's advice to experimenters in a physiological laboratory: "travailler comme une

bête"—he must work, that is, with as much persistence as an animal and with as much disregard of the result. (Freud VII.A "The Forgetting of Dreams")

One may also see Freud, in the *Studies on Hysteria,* repeatedly asking his patients to free-associate without regard for any embarrassing or nonsensical elements.

Piero Boitano sees in the *House of Fame* a "Chaucerian free association of themes and images found in tradition" (166), by which "[t]hough he exploits the suggestions provided by tradition, Chaucer creates his own *imaginaire* for concepts he refuses to pin down" (164). Chaucer is able to avoid the demands of reason for sense and logic in the linking of ideas, to which his most devoted readers are all too liable. Ruffolo, however, responds to the poem's diffused elements in the spirit of Freudian free association, remarking how its diverse and frequent lists suggest we should try "locating authority . . . in the limbs rather than in the head" of this apparently acephalic body of words, much as Freud insists one can interpret a dream only by pursuing the independent associations of individual elements, not the plot or scene as a whole.

14. Drawn from patristic tradition, especially Isidore and Bede, the conventional symbolism of these stones (beryl, the eighth course in the foundation of the walls of the Heavenly Jerusalem, Revelation 21:20; both stones in Aaron's breastplate, Exodus 28:17–20) was widely disseminated in vernacular lapidaries translated from French or Latin:

Berill. . . . When the sonne shyneth þervppon, hit takeþ feruent heete; hit signifieth þe first precheurs of holy chirche . . . oure lorde commanded twelue stones of berill to þe likenes & significacoun of þe twelue apostles þat first precheden þe cristendome. And also þe auctorites seyn þat who-so berith berill nere his flesche ayeins þe sonne, þat þe fire þat cometh oute cacheth þe flesche; þat signifieth thoo þat arne assembled & speken with holy men. (*English Medieval Lapidaries* 28)

When ye son smyttes appon a berel, & he be cutt, it betokenes ye first prechour of holy kyrke yt preched ye baptym of Ihesu criste. (48; also 72, 125)

Berillus est praedicantium perfecta operatio. Ut enim aqua sole percussa refulget: qui non aliter nisi septangula politur forma, quia ex angulorum percussione splendor acuitur. Aqua sensum hominis significat; splendor solis, divinam sapientiam, qua amplius fulget; sed non perfecte divina vel humana sapientia, nisi operibus consummetur. (Anselm Landunensis, *PL* 162.1579–1580)

(Beryl is the process of preaching perfected. For it gleams like water struck by the sun: and should not be cut except in sevenfold facets, since its splendor is sharpened by the striking of these angles. Water signifies human sensation; splendor of the sun signifies divine wisdom, which gleams more broadly; but neither divine or human wisdom is perfectly consummated except by works.)

This variation on the theme should be compared with Bede's diffuser account in his *Explanatio Apocalypsis,* 3.21, *PL* 93.200.

15. *Animalia* autem, nunc totam significant Ecclesiam . . . *Et in circuitu et intus plena sunt oculis,* etc. Sancta Ecclesia et coram Deo et coram hominibus se attendit. . . . Aliter. Sive litteram attendas, sive allegoriam quaeras, lucem semper ex Evangelio reperies. Alia translatio sic habet: *Plena oculis ante se et retro.* Quia lux Evangeli in aenigmata legis irradiat, et novae gratiae mundo fulgorem infundit. (Bede 1.4; *PL* 93.144)

16. Ehrenzweig describes "dazzle detail" with reference to the detective mystery, whose

technique could be called one of deliberate ambiguity. The author never allows the clues to narrow down so as to point definitely to a single culprit . . . [To conclude the story, a] few odds and bits which have been carefully tucked away under a dazzling camouflage of insignificant details are triumphantly dragged to the surface and displayed as the logical fundament of the story. . . . The reader . . . follows the unfolding of the whole intentionally incoherent and ambiguous story in a state of diffuse attention with one or the other possibility dimly flickering and extinguishing again, but never attracting attention exclusively. . . . If for real enjoyment one is to be kept in a continuous state of diffuse attention (so different from the rational method of thinking) then we understand why crime stories act as an indispensable sleeping-draught for some of their readers. (43–44)

Chaucer turns the human pleasure of avoiding foreclosure to the readerly skills of diffuse attention and suspended interpretation.

17. Boitano's readings picture a text that signals accomplishment as relinquishment: " 'Auctorite' can be taken as the sign of Chaucer's impotence and of his triumph. In all his works he will fail the moment he succeeds" (208). When Chaucer leaves the poem unfinished, he has not castrated the man of authority, but rather apprehended on the horizon of this plot the possibility of another one, and sent the figures of his authority on to fresh woods and pastures new. He does not visit castration on authorities, but displacement, with a pre-climactic flight like the serial key modulations of music.

Works Consulted

Abraham, Nicolas, and Maria Torok. *The Shell and the Kernal: Renewals of Psychoanalysis.* Vol. 1. Tr. Nicholas R. Rand. Chicago: University of Chicago Press, 1994.

———. *The Wolf Man's Magic Word: A Cryptonomy.* Tr. Nicholas T. Rand. Preface Jacques Derrida. Minneapolis: University of Minnesota Press, 1986.

Anselm Landunensis. *Enarrationes in Apocalypsin. PL* 162.1499–1586.

Augustine. *De Utilitate Credendi. PL* 42.65–92.

Bede. *Explanatio Apocalypsis. PL* 93.129–206.

Berger, Harry. *The Allegorical Temper: Vision and Reality in Book Two of Spenser's* "Faerie Queene". New Haven: Yale University Press, 1957.

Bible. *King James Authorized Version.*

Biblia Sacra iuxta Vulgatam Versionem. Ed. Robert Weber, OSB, et al. 3rd emended ed. Ed. Boniface Fischer, OSB. Stuttgart: Deutsche Bibelgesellschaft, 1983.

Boitano, Piero. *Chaucer and the Imaginary World of Fame.* Cambridge: Brewer, 1984.

———. *English Medieval Narrative in the Thirteenth and Fourteenth Centuries.* Tr. Joan K. Hall. Cambridge: University of Cambridge Press, 1983.

Carruthers, Mary. "Italy, *Ars Memorativa,* and Fame's House." *SAC Proceedings* 2 (1986): 179–188.

Chaucer, Geoffrey. *Complete Works.* 2nd ed. Ed. F.N. Robinson. Boston: Houghton Mifflin, 1957.

Derrida, Jacques. "La différance" (1968). In: *Marges de la philosophie.* Paris: 1972: 1–29.

Elton, Oliver. *The English Muse: A Sketch.* London: 1950.

English Mediaeval Lapidaries. Eds. Joan Evans and Mary S. Serjeantson. EETS 190. London: n.p., 1933.

Ehrenzweig, Anton. *The Psychoanalysis of Artistic Vision and Hearing: An Introduction to a Theory of Unconscious Perception.* 3rd ed. London: Sheldon Press, 1975.

Freud, Sigmund. *The Interpretation of Dreams.* Tr. James Strachey. Standard ed. Vols. 4 and 5. London: Hogarth Press, 1953; rpt. Pelican Freud Library Vol. 4. Ed. Angela Richards, Harmondsworth: Penguin, 1976.

Ganim, John. "Chaucer, Boccaccio, and the Anxiety of Popularity." *Assays* 4 (1987):51–66.

Howard, Donald R. *Chaucer: His Life, His Works, His World.* New York: Dutton, 1987.

Lacan, Jacques. *Ecrits: A Selection.* Tr. Alan Sheridan. London and New York: Tavistock, 1977. Includes "The Mirror Stage as Formative of the Function of the I as Revealed in Psychoanalytic Experience" (1949): 1–7; and "The Agency of the Letter in the Unconscious or Reason since Freud" (1957): 146–78.

Robertson, D.W. and Bernard F. Huppé. *Fruyt and Chaf: Studies in Chaucer's Allegories.* Princeton: Princeton University Press, 1963.

Ruffolo, Lara. "Literary Authority and the Lists of Chaucer's *House of Fame:* Destruction and Definition Through Proliferation." *Chaucer Review* 27:4 (1993): 325–41.

Scott, Sir Walter. Journal. Vol. I. 1825–1826. Ed. J. G. Tait. Edinburgh: 1939.

Spearing, A.C. *Medieval Dream Poetry.* Cambridge: University of Cambridge Press, 1976.

———. *Medieval to Renaissance in English Poetry.* Cambridge: Cambridge University Press, 1985.

Winnicott, D.W. *Playing and Reality.* London: Tavistock, 1971. Includes "Transitional Objects and Transitional Phenomena" (1953): 1–25; and "The Location of Cultural Experience" (1967): 95–103.

Chaucer's "Bad Art:" The Interrupted Tales[1]

MARTIN STEVENS

AT LEAST TWICE, AND DEPENDING ON THE EXPERTS WE READ, POSSIBLY three times in the *Canterbury Tales,* storytellers are interrupted *in medias res* with either the implication or a direct accusation that the tedium of the tale they were telling had overpowered their listeners. I wish, in this paper, to examine the nature of these interruptions, the problems that they pose for the reader, and the purposes that they might serve in our interpretation of the *Canterbury Tales.*

First and foremost, I must define the two key terms in my title. What is "an interrupted text," and what do I mean by "bad art"? In the *Canterbury Tales,* an interrupted text is a story that one of the leading pilgrims brings to an abrupt stop in the midst of its telling and one that is not intended to be resumed. The interrupter stops the tale because he has become impatient with its tedium and he wants a fresh beginning into something more entertaining from the next tale to be told. There are two stories in the collection that have been deliberately brought to an abrupt end. The first, ironically, is Chaucer's own *Tale of Sir Thopas,* which is rudely interrupted by Harry Bailly with the following words:

> "Namoore of this, for Goddes dignitee,"
> Quod oure Hooste, "for thou makest me
> So wery of thy verray lewednesse
> That also wisly God my soule blesse,
> Myne eres aken of thy drasty speche.
> Now swich a rym the devel I biteche!
> This may wel be rym dogerel," quod he.
> (VII.919–25)[2]

Here, whether or not we agree with the Host, a story is brought to an end because it has been deemed *drasty,* which according to the *Middle English Dictionary* means "crude," "ignorant," "inartistic," or even "trashy,"[3] and Chaucer is instructed to "tellen . . . in geeste" or "in prose" something "in which ther be som murthe or som doctryne" (VII.933–35), that is, some entertainment or in-

130

struction. The implication is that the worthless *Tale of Sir Thopas* contained neither game nor earnest, a favorite opposition offered frequently for the reader's deconstruction by Chaucer.

The second interruption in the *Canterbury Tales* occurs after the Monk has rehearsed his seventeenth tragedy, of which he had "an hundred in [his] celle" (VII.1972)—an instance in which the Ellesmere MS highlights the intrusion in rubrics with the words: "Heere stynteth the Knyght the Monk of his tale." The words of the Knight are much the same as those used previously by the Host: "Hoo! . . . good sire, namoore of this!" (VII.2767; cf. VII.906). The Knight has had enough of heavy tales; he says, ". . . litel hevynesse is right ynough to muche folk" (VII.2769–70). He does not like to hear of sudden falls (and probably of death) and would prefer to hear of "joye and greet solaas" (VII.2774).

The third tale is not as simple. Here, there is wide-ranging disagreement as to the nature of the incompleteness. I speak of *The Squire's Tale.* There are three possibilities:

1. The tale was left incomplete but not interrupted; Chaucer intended at some point to finish it.
2. The original manuscript contained the completed tale, but because of an accident in transmission, the missing part was lost or destroyed.
3. The tale is incomplete but interrupted (and therefore ended) because, like the other two manifestly interrupted tales, Chaucer used one of his pilgrims to put an end to it.[4]

What causes the interpretive dilemma is the absence of an indisputable sign of cessation. It is true that the Ellesmere MS abruptly ends the story just as the Squire has completed the first couplet of *pars tercia,* and it follows this uncertain closure with the explanation, "Heere folwen the wordes of the Frankeleyn to the Squier, and the wordes of the Hoost to the Frankeleyn." This format might suggest that we are to read the ending as an interruption; yet, the Ellesmere text stops in the middle of the page, and the rubrics announcing the Franklin's words might have been added by the Ellesmere scribe because he expected to fill the space (as he did the incomplete *Cook's Tale*) with the missing text if it should reappear. The case against the interrupted text lies mainly in the nature and the tone of the Franklin's remarks:

> "In feith Squier, thow hast thee wel yquit
> and gentilly. I preise wel thy wit . . .

> . . . consyderynge thy yowthe,
> So feelyngly thou spekest, sire. I allow the!
> As to my doom, ther is noon that is heere
> Of eloquence that shal be thy peere . . .
>   (V.673–74)

It has been argued quite persuasively that these words are just as fitting for the conclusion of a completed tale as one that is interrupted and that therefore they cannot be used to clinch the case that the Franklin used them to stop the Squire (see Seaman 12–18). On the other hand, one could argue just as plausibly, and many of our most astute interpreters have,[5] that the Franklin, out of respect for the Squire's (and perhaps his father's) rank and in observance of the ideal of *gentilesse,* which dominates the attention of the Franklin in his own tale, had no other means by which to end diplomatically and effectively the Squire's hopelessly incompetent tale. The argument widens on this last point. There have been those who have read the *Squire's Tale* with appreciation for its narrative art— Edmund Spenser and John Milton were among the earliest[6]—and who see not a scintilla of evidence that Chaucer meant the reader to respond to this tale as he clearly did the other two which were indisputably interrupted. The problem is a difficult one, for which I certainly promise nothing more than critical conjecture. For this reason, I shall save it for relatively cursory treatment at the end, with the hope that I shall find occasion to expand my thoughts at some future time. My intent, however, will be to read the Squire in the context of the interrupted tales and to see what, if anything, they might suggest to help solve the dilemma.

Let us now turn to a discussion of the undisputed interruptions of the *Canterbury Tales.* Interestingly, both are treated as if, indeed, they had come to an end *in medias res.* Thus, while the game of the framework insists we have heard only a part of a tale—the logic of play tells us that the Monk was quite ready to give us all one hundred of his tragedies—the reader is treated by Chaucer in both instances to a story that has indeed come to abrupt and unexpected closure. The interrupted stories, thus, are not fragments.[7] In this sense, they differ radically from the one other genuine incomplete story we have not yet mentioned, the tale of the Cook. In the absence of any kind of end link, no one has ever suggested that this apparently aborted story was either deliberately interrupted or that Chaucer gave evidence he would complete it at a later time. Indeed, many scribes filled the lacuna by inserting the quite unrelated tale of Gamelyn, and some few even tried to complete it with a version of their own. The *Cook's Tale* is clearly a fragment, and should therefore not concern us further here. One of the landmark manuscripts, the Hengwrt, is explicit in its rubrics on the point: "Of this Cokes tale maked Chaucer na moore."[8] In the broadest sense, it could finally be said that the tale of the Miller is an interruption. It does radically change the tone and the nature of the tale-telling, but if it is an interruption, it is such because it initiates a new discourse—as to some extent do all the tales. We recall that the Miller intrudes at the point where Harry Bailly, upon the Knight's conclusion, asks the Monk to tell his tale. That would have been the proper hierarchical succession of storytellers—each in turn according to his estate—and thus the Miller's intrusion is indeed the point at which the *Canterbury Tales* takes a significant swing into a new narrative itinerary. As Lee Patterson has noted, when the Miller "quites" the Knight with his fabliau, "The tale-telling game . . . becomes itself a fabliau and is apparently henceforth to be governed by the fabliau principle—explicitly announced by the Reeve—of *ars ut artem falleret*" (L. Patterson 245). Also, Alfred David extends beyond this interpretation by noting that the placement and effect of *"The Miller's Tale"* implies that "the whole pilgrimage had to be invented for the sake of the fabliaux" (David 106). But, for our purposes, this interruption begins a narrative strategy; it does not end one. The intrusion is into the plan itself, not a tale. The stories we are concerned with, that is the interrupted tales, represent a self-reflexive moment of closure, in which the nature of closure itself is being tested.

I have chosen the term "bad art" to describe the interrupted tales. As already noted, each tale is abruptly stopped because, for one reason or another, it failed to please a critical listener, who, we assume, was speaking for the entire company of pilgrims, though, as I shall show, not for the poet. The popular determination that dismisses a story as "drasty" raises a number of problems for the reader of the *Canterbury Tales*. First and foremost, it forces an exercise in deconstruction: if the story really was "drasty," if the Host and Knight, with their blunt responses, expressed a view that was also held by the poet (who, after all, has control over his manuscript), why did the poet not simply delete these stories and substitute others for them that pleased him, and in turn his "constructed" readers, more fully? Does not the interruption imply that what Host and Knight found unbearable is, in the mind of the poet Chaucer, really intended to be given critical attention, and at some more remote level intellectual approval by the reader, who is the ultimate judge? Is "bad art," then, actually a smokescreen for "good art,"

an ironic twist that invites the reader's silent dissent, his deconstruction of the objections raised in the text? Does not the act of
reversal in judgment that the poet invites provide the reader with
an extraordinary glimpse into "auctorial intent?" We do not know,
as we have seen, that Chaucer would have kept the fragmentary tale
of the Cook and possibly of the Squire in his final manuscript (if,
indeed, there was to be one). But we do know that in the final
version of the *Canterbury Tales* that has come down to us, he did
intend to keep the stories of *Sir Thopas* and the Monk, because he
made them integral parts of their narrative fabric. Is it not, then, an
especially daring maneuver on his part to flaunt a tale as "drasty"
when, in effect, he and we must consider it worthy of inclusion?
Does it not lead us to reflect on the nature and the properties of
"drastiness?" What, in fact, is a "good" story?

The "bad art" of the interrupted tales can well lend support to an
entire agenda of what I would consider a misreading of the *Canterbury Tales*. As is widely recognized, it was once fashionable to find
roadside drama as a basic structural feature in Chaucer's poem. The
point of reading the tales was to use them to create a character or
even to settle an extended argument among tellers, such as the now
largely abandoned "Marriage Controversy." It mattered less what
a story said than the comment it made about its teller. Since Chaucer did take enormous interest in constructing the personalities of
some of his tellers—notably, of course, the Wife of Bath and the
Pardoner—the argument goes that he must have wanted us to imagine the personalities of the others, most of whom he says little
about. Using this interpretive strategy, we could thus construct our
own tellers even when we know little or nothing about them. Thus,
for example, the Nun's Priest who, in the General Prologue, represents only the third part of a prepositional phrase (he is one of
"preestes thre," I.164), who is simply characterized in his own prologue as "This sweete preest, this goodly man sir John" (VII.2820)
and who is later playfully described for his muscles, his long
"nekke" and his "large breest" (VII.3455–56) by Harry Bailly—
actually, this very Nun's Priest is, in the eyes of one critic, a real-
life projection of Chaunticleer, who is the "hen-pecked" subject of
the Prioress (his boss), and who, consequently, must lead us to read
the *Nun's Priest Tale* as a projection of his repressed self, as well
as his veiled hostility toward his superior (Broes 156–62). To clarify this point in relation to strategies of reading, I need to return for
a moment to the *Squire's Tale*. For one reader, who would take that
tale as interrupted (and therefore inept), the dramatic approach has

"rescued" the tale from actual "drastiness." Here is how that argument proceeds:

> The faults in the Squier's Tale are elementary: too many motifs are introduced when the strange knight enters. . . . then, though more than enough had been introduced, Pars Secunda turns to a totally different topic—the lament of the falcon. At 1.401, the narrator acknowledges that the story is going badly. And the conclusion reads like notes a writer makes to himself about how he plans to continue.

> Why did one as conscious of technique and audience reaction as Chaucer include such a piece . . . ? Perhaps because its very deficiency was intended to make a dramatic contribution. (*Complete Poetry* 186–87)

Translated into roadside-drama logic, this statement says that Chaucer probably included an obviously deficient tale (1) to characterize the Squire as a genteel but incompetent storyteller (perhaps in line with his portrayal as something of a tyro in the General Prologue— one who has learned the drawing-room conventions but who has not yet assumed a serious role in life); (2) to comment on the Franklin's standards of judgment both of people and of literature. The problem with this logic is that it has forced us to sit through a lengthy, rambling tale (if such it is) with little profit. Ultimately, such logic will allow the reader to ignore an incompetent tale and to come to the same functional conclusion, whether a story is brilliant or dull. Thus, Chaucer is "off the hook" even when he has written a story that may be proclaimed deficient.

My point is that the interrupted tales are not deficient. Chaucer's deliberate "bad art" is invariably a highly polished parody. The act of reading that it promotes is for the sentient reader to discover the cleverness with which it deconstructs its target text. I would contend that what Mel Brooks' now classic film "Blazing Saddles," with all its "drastiness," does to the Western, Sir Thopas does to the metrical minstrel romance, a form that probably occupied the same place of popular entertainment in its time as the Western did until recently in our time (one assumes with a similarly charged political message underneath its apparently innocuous narration).

Before I proceed with a reexamination of the interrupted tales, I need to make a general declaration concerning my overall approach to the *Canterbury Tales*. For me, this culminating work of Geoffrey Chaucer concerns one general topic: the writing of narrative poetry at a time when the world was in flux. The late fourteenth century was an era of extraordinary change. It was the time when English was emerging not only as the primary language of the land, but when it was beginning to take shape as a standard written medium. It was a time when urban society spawned a powerful commercial middle class; a time when England took its place as one of the leading market economies of northern Europe; a time when land tenancy gave way to enclosure; a time that was recovering from the decimation of the Black Death, and consequently a time when the laboring man, then in short supply, rose against the empowered; a time that saw the papacy divided and that experienced the moral abasement of both the secular and the regular church. It was a time, moreover, in the midst of a one-hundred-year cold war that flashed into moments of heat, notably at Crécy and Poitiers; a time of an unstable monarchy (which later fueled the second historical cycle of William Shakespeare); a time when leading scholars in the universities took issue with universals and contributed an era of intellectual skepticism, which, in its force and influence, is not wholly unlike the social and philosophical revisionary ideology of the later twentieth century.

For a narrative poet, writing in English, this time of cumulative change spelled an enormous challenge. Geoffrey Chaucer was himself one of the "new men," a member of the aspiring middle class in public service, for whom such critics as Paul Strohm and Anne Middleton have given us a whole new historical appraisal (see Strohm; and Middleton, 15–56). When, therefore, Chaucer writes about the conflict between *experience* and *auctorite* (the Wife of Bath, we remember opens her prologue with the observation, "Experience, though noon auctorite, were in this world, is right ynogh for me . . .")—he writes essentially about life in its late-fourteenth-century pulse beat as against the authority that had been passed down, often uncritically, from the past in books. *The Canterbury Tales* is the first English poem whose setting is contemporary society and whose language is the heteroglossia of its culture. Chaucer is the poet of that heteroglossia; in consequence, he gives us, throughout his works but most notably in the *Canterbury Tales* a *poetria nova* of his own. Has any poet, before or since, invented a line as potent or as flexible or as enduring as the decasyllabic line of his open couplet? Has any poet contributed a unit of poetry more contained yet more conversational than his rhyme royal stanza? The poetry of Geoffrey Chaucer is an invention created out of the indigenous English language of the late fourteenth century. It carries the intonation, the stress, the basic syntax, and the rhythm of the living language of our own time.

It is within the context of this technical accomplishment—the creation of a whole new poetic language—and of the emerging new social dialectic of his time (to say nothing of the institutions that had entered their death throes), that Chaucer's poetry must be read. Was it his intention to write a self-reflexive metanarrative[9] when he undertook this final task that he set himself and, which, though yet unfinished, took up a quarter of his lifetime? This is a question for which we have no answer. It is never pure of the reader's meaning or of the transformations the text has undergone under stubbornly austere, sloppy, or imaginative editors. Chaucer's meaning has been reinvented by each age that has read him, and his text is still in such editorial disarray that even the experts have failed to agree on the best manuscript source for the *Canterbury Tales.* When, therefore, I propose a self-reflexive reading in which Chaucer's poetry is in constant dialectic with its own premises, I probably do no more than view the work in the mirror of our times.

I do, however, offer here a reliable glimpse into auctorial intent—and that is the subject that will buttress this essay. There are few times when an author comes out of his protective shell to tell us what he really meant to say in his writings. When he does, we are rightfully suspicious that either artifice or ignorance has shielded him from spilling the whole truth, and there is no writer more elusive than Chaucer when he does undertake to tell us, *in propria persona,* exactly what he really meant. We have—or should I say, E. Talbot Donaldson has?—in consequence constructed Chaucer the Pilgrim and Chaucer the Poet (Donaldson 1–12). Chaucer the Pilgrim is the simpleton: the narrator who begs us not to impute to his villainy that he will speak rudely and liberally: he is a mere observer-reporter, whose task it is to record reality exactly as it happened. Behind him stands that masked and indescernible figure, on whom we call for authentication every time that we read more into a passage than the simpleton tells us. Mr. Donaldson's "Poet" may therefore not be Robert O. Payne's or Donald Howard's, or Carolyn Dinshaw's, or Derek Pearsall's. He is the elusive absence whose unwritten dialogic constitutes the Chaucerian presence. Perhaps the only time he speaks to us directly is in his Retraction, and if he means part of what he says there, we might as well throw out all but the pious tales, those that do not "sownen unto synne." More likely, however, Chaucer has created his Retraction as a way of opening an interpretive gap, a creative space that, in Peter Travis's incisive words, "is a test of our ability to define our own space inside the *Canterbury Tales*" (see Travis 148).

This space, I believe, is given special significance in Sir Thopas; for here, more than anywhere else in the *Canterbury Tales,* is manifested an authorized reading. It is in the intertext between the surface and the deep structure—that is, in the gap between the parodic and the target text—that the poet's traditional absence is replaced by a presence. In my reading of the *Canterbury Tales,* Sir Thopas stands at the creative center of the poem. Here at last, the elvish Pilgrim gets his chance to *perform* rather than to report. As we launch into Chaucer's own tale, we are treated to what Harry Bailly justly characterizes as *rime dogerel* (VII.935), which, for the pilgrim audience, is a new, strange, uncharacteristic "Chaucerian" meter—the bounce of the metrical tail rhyme stanza with its rhythmic alliterative bobs and its oral formulaic tags. For years, the Tale's hermeneutics—or, to put it in another word, its intentions—lay sealed: not until after Bishop Percy published his *Reliques of Ancient English Poetry* in the mid-eighteenth century when the model popular romances were uncovered for the reading public did anyone realize that Sir Thopas indeed was a put-on—a parody of the minstrels' songs that had dulled the wits of hundreds of audiences in fourteenth-century England:

> Men speken of romances of prys,
> Of Horn child and of Ypotys,
> Of Beves and sir Gy,
> Of sir Lybeux and Pleyndamour, —
> But sir Thopas, he bereth the flour
> Of roial chivalry.

It was Thomas Warton, in his *History of English Poetry* in 1774, who first unsealed the tale's hermeneutics:

> "Genuine Humour," he wrote, "the concomitant of true taste, consists in discerning improprieties in books as well as characters. We therefore must remark under this class another tale of Chaucer, which till lately has been looked upon as a grave heroic narrative. I mean the Rime of Sir Thopas" (see Warton 433).

The fact is that only certain "initiated" readers know the subtext that will unravel Chaucer's narrative intention in *Sir Thopas.* Chaucer deliberately, it seems, provides us with no such fictional readers; we have only Harry Bailly's vehement assertion, "Namoore of this for Goddes dignitee" as the built-in reader response to the Tale. Harry is the incarnation of the common reader; he wants either a tale of mirth to entertain him or a tale of *sentence* to edify him. No tale can really do both for him, because, like so many travelers in the airport bookstore of our day, he either looks for the latest potboiler or for the edification of self-help (for him the "Tale of Melibee" is an instructional manual to teach his wife Goodelief the virtue of patience). It is the absent informed reader acquainted with the practice and the mode of the tail-rhyme romance who knows Chaucer's intent. For the present-day reader, much help in the decoding of Chaucer's deep structure is available; it takes only a scansion of the annotations in the *Riverside* edition for the reader to realize how much Chaucer relied on still extant minstrel romances (Perhaps even a whole manuscript like the Auchinleck now in the National Library at Edinburgh) to cobble together his originary subtext.[10] In our day (as possibly in Chaucer's) the "insider" jokes abound: what English graduate student in a Chaucer class does not know that the knight who pricks along the field (with all the vulgar connotations of the phrase) is an artful transformation of the romance lady (with a face "white as pandemayn," lips "as rede as rose," a "semely nose," a scent as sweet as the "bremble flour")? Who does not recognize him as a member of the decaying, bankrupt aristocracy whose values actually are middle class (he is a wrestler, he wears leather shoes, he fights with the "launcegay"—an innocuous short lance)? Sir Thopas, as his name implies, is a semi-precious jewel (the sexual connotation is not innocent), who rides out on the typical quest of the metrical romance into a literary landscape that provides us with wonderfully semi-authentic catalogues of spices and birds (especially woodpeckers and woodpigeons), and with the land of Fairye, where no wife or child will stand in his way to fight the burly "Sir Elephant" for the hand of the Fairy Queen? One look at the romance of *Bevis of Hampton* or *Guy of Warwick,* and the initiated reader recognizes the put on. The *Tale of Sir Thopas* is, in a phrase, the key to Chaucer's "ineptitude topos."

   The Tale of Sir Thopas must be understood as the "navel of unravelment" in the *Canterbury Tales.*[11] It frees the reader to find a deep structure, for it provides the one genuine moment of sustained parodic exposure in the poem as a whole. Chaucer's subject here is one kind of "authority" that stands behind the poetry of his time—in this case, not the old authors but the new minstrels—and he constructs in his exercise of accomplished imitation the perfect parodic surface text which converts the source text into the brilliant satire of "dogerell." This exercise teaches us that we must potentially respond to all of his tales with an eye open to what Talbot Donaldson called "dark readings" or what Hans Robert Jauss would call "readings against the grain." *Sir Thopas* is our tip-off that the "ineptitude topos"—which prominently features such rhetorical figures as *diminutio* (the narrator's self-deprecation) and *occupatio* (his long-winded dismissal of alleged irrelevancies)—can

be taken as critical apparatus for finding the discourse targets that
may not yet have been accessed for us by the discovery of subtexts
by the Bishop Percys of our own day. How, for example, do we
respond to the self-professed bumbler, the Man of Law, who pro-
nounces that there really are no more good stories to tell because
Chaucer has told them all already? Who confesses that "I were
right now of tales desolate"? Throughout his tale he reminds us
that he must not ramble *(diminutio)*, that he is deficient in recall
(diminutio), and that he tells a tale that must not be excessive *(occupatio)* when, in his words,

> The fruyt of every tale is for to seye;
> They ete, and drynke, and daunce, and synge,
> and pleye.   (II.706–8)

The Man of Law, in fact, makes clear that the rhetorical figures of
diminutio and *occupatio* are central to the critical self-reflexivity of
Chaucerian narrative. *The Tale of Sir Thopas* authorizes our metacritical reading of the Man of Law's tale of Constance. It asks us to
find the discursive targets—maybe the merchant tellers, maybe the
long-winded chroniclers of Chaucer's time—in an effort to bring
narrative competence into the practice of late-fourteenth-century
poetry.

    We all know that, throughout his works, Chaucer as poet ad-
dresses the authority of his so-called sources. It is the dialogic of
the source text and its Chaucerian reinscription that produces what
Bakhtin calls "double-voicing," an effect that is perhaps more immediately evident in *Sir Thopas* than anywhere else in the *Canterbury Tales.* Linda Hutcheon observes that

> parody is one of the techniques of self-referentiality by which art re-
> veals its awareness of the context-dependent nature of meaning, of the
> importance of signification of the circumstances surrounding any utter-
> ance. But any discursive situation, not just a parodic one, includes an
> enunciating addresser and encoder as well as a receiver of the text (*The-
> ory* 85)

I argue that virtually every line Chaucer wrote is context-dependent
in the broadest sense by which we can apply the term "parody." It
is for this reason that Chaucer's self-attribution of his most obvious
parody serves as the centerpiece of his metacritical fiction. As the
encoder of his "double-voiced" text, the parodist reveals an intention—one which, in this instance, makes a statement about the presence of the author which is transferable to other parts of the

Canterbury Tales.[12] Although the voice of the encoder is not always as clearly established as it is in *Sir Thopas,* I believe that the act of decoding is authorized by this central parody. In discussing the *Monk's Tale,* I propose to decode, without the manifest presence of the encoder, what I regard as a parodic text.

In the *Monk's Tale,* we have a situation somewhat different from that of Chaucer's own interrupted tale. Instead of targeting the new art of the oral minstrel or of other contemporary storytellers (although these are not necessarily excluded), the *Monk's Tale* presents us with an overabundance of sources: the Hebrew Bible, the New Testament, Vincent of Beauvais's *Speculm Maius,* Boethius' *Consolation,* Ovid's *Metamorphoses* and *Heroides,* the *Roman de la Rose,* Dante's *Inferno,* Valerius Maximus's *Factorum et dictorum memorabilium libri novem* (Jankin's favorite source), and, arguably, Boccaccio's *De casibus virorum illustrium* as well as the *De claris mulieribus* and Machaut's *Prise de Alexandrie.* Where once it might have been possible to find a single text of which *Sir Thopas* could have been a parody, the *Monk's Tale* is clearly an assemblage of texts, a literary anthology, so to speak. If *Sir Thopas* offends because it is too ignorant, the Monk offends because he is too tediously learned. This time, it is not the Host but the much more even-tempered Knight who interrupts with just a bit more grace but almost the same words: "Hoo . . . good sire, namoore of this!" The reason for the interruption is simply: "ye han seyd right ynough, ywis / And muchel moore; for litel hevynesse / is right ynough to muche folk, I gesse" (VII.2769–71). We recall, moreover, that the Monk has complicated his own case by announcing that he will tell a hundred "tragedies," an unrelieved agenda of morbidity, especially if he will give us tales that will deliver examples of his own definition:

> Tragedie is to seyn a certeyn storie,
> As olde bookes maken us memorie,
> Of hym that stood in greet prosperitee,
> And is yfallen out of heigh degree
> Into Myserie, and endeth wrecchedly.
> (VII 1973–77)

Here we have a clearly defined "horizon of expectations," by one of the few speakers in the *Canterbury Tales* who chooses to give his hearers a literary prolegomenon (the Clerk and the Pardoner are two others). Interestingly, he is incapable of the organizational discipline his introduction would lead us to expect. Quite apart from the fact that not all of his stories end in wretchedness for their principal figures, there is no chronological, narrative, or moral order to the Monk's recitation of woeful stories. While this is not the place to elaborate on these failings, a few examples may show the way: Nebuchadnezzar does not die an ignominious death at the hands of Fortune; Sampson is not misled by Fortune but by his trust in Delilah; and Fortune and God's vengeance are not, in the end, clearly differentiated. The Monk himself is aware of his lack of discipline, as he makes clear at the outset:

> But first I yow biseeke in this mateere,
> Though I by ordre telle nat thise thynges,
> Be it of popes, emperours, or kynges,
> After his ages, as men writen fynde,
> But tellen hem som before and som bihynde,
> As it now comth unto my remembraunce,
> Have me excused of myn ignoraunce.
> (VII. 1984–90)

He also prepares us in one singular instance for a tale that mercifully he never tells, the "lyf of Seint Edward" (V.1970), perhaps because he was cut off before he could get to it. Here, then, is a storyteller with an agenda, but who does not know what to make of it.

The observation we have made about *Sir Thopas* applies equally to the *Monk:* we are treated to a literary genre which exhausts itself before our eyes. At least 15 of the 51 manuscripts which contain the *Monk's Tale* label it as *De casibus virorum illustrium,* either in the *incipit* or the *explicit.*[13] Although this attribution may be editorial, there is nevertheless reason to believe that Chaucer's earliest readers, his redactors, associated the tale with Boccacio's work. In the sense, however, that the *Monk's Tale* is a literary composite of many source texts, it resembles *Sir Thopas,* and though it does not disfigure these texts with travesty, it does comment on a genre, the success of which the interruption clearly questions. The very incompetence of the teller—that is, his failure to present a collection of neatly ordered narrative sketches, as well as the confusions that prevail in his presentation of moral agency—rescues the composite tale from the tedium that it might otherwise have imposed on its readers. The poem presents a critical challenge which exerts the reader to discover the layers of ineptitude that its enumerations prompt. What, then, might be the point of this whole literary scenario invoked by Chaucer? That is, what caused him to introduce a speaker with such a weighty and unimaginative agenda, to let him go on and tell a sizeable number that "anoyeth al this compaignye?" Is this not yet another instance of making the reader endure a story for the sake of dramatizing a quarrel between two of the pilgrims?

My answer, as in the first instance, is "no." Here in the *Monk's Tale,* we have what may well be the most self-reflexive metacritical narrative moment in the *Canterbury Tales.* The Monk, after all, tells a tale that resembles the structure of the larger whole of which it is a part. If I am right, Chaucer planted the *Monk's Tale,* and even interrupted it, to highlight in a negative mode the qualities that a "collection" of stories requires to be artistically successful. *The Canterbury Tales* succeed as a collection because they have, in the language of M. M. Bakhtin, dialogized their speakers. The text is finally a collection of voices, some of which clash or supplement and complicate the discourse. Others speak inside narrowly defined frames or entirely outside their frames. The poet Chaucer is a great ventriloquist, a dissembler par excellence. He has given us a polyphony of the social, political, economic, religious, courtly, popular, sexual, philosophical, poetical, and dialectal heteroglossia of his time. The Monk in severe and obvious contrast presents us with a ponderously monologized text. There is but one voice here to present us with an unrelievedly weighty and monotonously reiterative discourse. As such, his stories make up the kernel countertext, and in the very contrast they give us between the univocal and the heteroglossic, they are the ultimate parody of the large text that encloses them. When we look at the Monk's thumbnail tragedies in this light, they ironically become dialogized for us. For then, consciously or subversively, we read their collected text as a voice in dialogue with its frame. Here is the moment when the ventriloquist shows us how he has manipulated his dummy. The thing finally does not have a voice apart from its teller—thank God. Whereas *Sir Thopas* gives us a glimpse into the deep structure of the *Canterbury Tales,* the *Monk's Tale* gives critical insight into the construction of its margins. Read as the countertexts they are, they show us that the interrupted tales lie at the heart of the work as a whole. They make clear that the *Canterbury Tales* at their core are concerned, first and foremost, with their own narratological competence.

As we now turn to the last of the three tales, the problematic *Squire's Tale,* I am, as I have said, not prepared here to review the historical response to the nature of its ending. It is worth noting that the tale itself, which was generally not read as a satire or even as "bad art" until the mid-twentieth-century (Lawton 112), is in many respects a proper target for self-reflexive reading. As Helen Cooper points out, "More than any other of the tales—more even than the Knight's—the *Squire's Tale* concentrates on the processes of telling rather than the advancement of the story" (Cooper 227). I will infer from several analogues that the *Squire's Tale,* which its curious narrative break from *pars prima* to *pars secunda,* is probably designed to be a failed interlaced romance. The first part lays out the devices by which a riveting set of adventures can be recounted:

> In at the halle dore al sodeynly
> Ther cam a knyght upon a steede of bras,
> And in his hand a brood mirour of glas.
> Upon his thombe he hadde of gold a ryng,
> And by his syde a naked swerd hangyng;
> And up he rideth to the heighe bord.
>
> (V.80–85)

The steed, as we all know, can take its rider, with the proper driving instructions, to any place within the compass of twenty-four hours. The mirror will identify for its viewer who is his friend and who his enemy. The ring will allow its bearer to communicate with any bird under the heavens in its own language. The sword can miraculously pierce any armor and kill one's enemy, but if reapplied to the same wound can make the enemy whole again. Now is this not a wonderful bag of tricks? And can one not envisage a whole variety of ingeniously intertwined tales to be told with these implements at the center of its adventures? We have a lot to look forward to, and, indeed, we are treated in *pars secunda* to the first of these adventures, when Canacee, the daughter of King Cambyuskan, uses the magic mirror and the ring to become involved in the sad story of a jilted peregrine falcon, whom she comforts and takes home to her chamber.

We never find out what other adventures lie in store for us, though we are certainly prepared to hear about the whole bag of tricks in a variety of interlaced adventures. The method of interlace is certainly made part of the plan. Here is how the Squire prepares us for the continuation of the falcon's story:

> Thus lete I Canacee hir hauk kepyng;
> *I wol namoore as now speke* of hir ryng,
> Til it come eft to purpose for to seyn
> How that this faucon gat hire love ageyn . . .
> But hennes forth I wol my proces holde

> To speken of adventures and of batailles,
> That nevere yet was herd so gret mervailles.
> (VII.651–60; italics added)

Imagine—if Chaucer had not pulled in the reins, how long would the Squire have gone on? But even if, as in the case of the Monk, the entire story had been brought to its distant end, and thus caused its readers and listeners to fall into paralysis, that is not, in my view, the metacritical point that the *Tale* highlights. Rather, whereas the poetic verse and its minstrelcy was the point of critical interest in *Sir Thopas,* and where the narrative frame was the object for our contemplation in the *Monk's Tale,* it is the pointed disjunction between the incompetent teller and the competence of his story that is in focus here. I hasten to add that, although I reject dramatic readings if their objective is to characterize the teller, I do take in general the portraits of the *General Prologue* as intricately related to the discourse of the tales. We have ample evidence of the interrelations of tale and teller in the *Wife of Bath's Tale*. In the case of the Squire, "a lovyere and a lusty bacheler" (I.80), we have the aristocratic novice whose whole life is organized around the fashions of the court. If, indeed, he could "wel endite," we may have a premature judgment of just how seriously to take his skills.

Just how competent a storyteller is he? If we take his own word, we come to doubt his self-confidence as a singer and *enditer*. Describing the dancing of Canacee and the strange knight, the Squire confides:

> Heere is the revel and the jolitee
> That is nat able a dul man to devyse.
> He moste han knowen love and his servyse,
> And been a feestlych man as fresh as May,
> That sholden you devysen swich array.
> (V.278–82)

Of course, it is precisely "the feestlych man as fresh as May" whom we encountered in the General Prologue ("He was as fressh as is the month of May" I.92), and therefore we set up to expect exactly the skill that the Squire abjures. The fact is that here and elsewhere throughout this narrative adventure, we are treated to the "ineptitude topos" inside the very rhetorical voice that is used to enhance by disparagement, within the rhetorical figure of *diminutio*. Here, there is a direct moment of heteroglossic showcasing: the voice of the narrator clashes with the voice of the rhetor, and the story creates for us an adventure in discursive practices. It dazzles with its invention, but it casts doubts on the style and order (the *elecutio* and *dispositio*) of the rhetoric that is rendering it. For me, the metacritical target in the *Squire's Tale* is the clash between teller and tale—that very fabric that has created the moments of high *solas* in the *Canterbury Tales*.

My point has been that the interrupted tales provide us with an index to Chaucer's self-conscious act of narration. They render various complicated signs of auctorial intention that help to uncover the deep structure of the poem. And, in the end, they also demonstrate the hermeneutics of endings. If one of the great concerns over the centuries has been the absence of endings in so many of Chaucer's texts, here we are supplied with an absence that, in fact, is a presence. Texts can be complete, Chaucer shows us, even when they are incomplete. Closure, which is a process, does not stand in opposition to ending, which is a product. The act of closure is itself and ending. To the extent that this is indeed the case, we can learn from these instances that the closure of the *Canterbury Tales* with its overarching "Retraction" is, in fact, an ending. "The man of great auctorite" has interrupted himself.

Notes

1. An earlier version of this essay was presented as the 1992 Rossell Hope Robbins Memorial Lecture before the Medieval Club of New York. My colleague, Robert O. Payne, was in the audience on that occasion. I now dedicate the essay to him, and in so doing, express my abiding admiration for his Chaucer criticism and especially his trend-setting book, *The Key of Remembrance: A Study of Chaucer's Poetics*.

2. All citations are to *The Riverside Chaucer*. Quotations are cited parenthetically within the text by fragment and line numbers.

3. See *Middle English Dictionary*, s.v. *drasti*, adj. (c).

4. The most complete overview of the critical reception of the *Squire's Tale* may be found in Lawton (106–129). Lawton believes that "at one stage Chaucer designed a complete plot for what was left as an unfinished fragment" (117). He divides the critical reception into four periods: (1) the prevailing view of the Renaissance (including, of course, the allusions by Spenser and Milton) which saw the tale as "half-told;" (2) the late Augustan and Romantic view which prized the first part of the romance but deprecated the second; (3) the late-nineteenth- and early twentieth-century approach which searched for sources; and (4) the criticism of the last forty years, which gives the poem a dramatic reading. It is the latter approach that he most vehemently rejects: "the Squire's Tale's stocks have fallen as dramatic readings have grown strong" (112).

5. For a comprehensive list of critics who take the passage as an interruption, see Seaman (13).

6. See John Milton:

Or call up him that left half told
The story of Cambuscan bold,
Of Camball and of Algarsife,
And who had Canacee to wife,
That owned the virtuous ring and glass,
And of the wondrous horse of brass,
On which that Tartar king did ride . . .
(*Il Penseroso* 109–105)

For Spenser's treatment of the story, see *The Faerie Queene* Book IV, esp. Canto iii.

7. Burrow (54–58) argues that "Sir Thopas" is, in fact, written in three fits (a term used by Chaucer himself in VII.888), each beginning with a "silencing topos" ("listeth," "holdeth your mouth") and marked by the occurrence of a large capital in the Ellesmere MS. The three fits, according to Burrow's interesting observation, are reduced by half. Thus, Fit 1 has 18 stanzas, Fit 2 has 9 stanzas, and Fit 3 four and a half stanzas. According to Burrow "the poems seems to narrow away, section by section, towards nothingness . . ." with a ratio of depletion of 4:2:1 (57). The consequent structural argument supports the view that Chaucer designed a complete self-deconstructed poem. The *Riverside* edition, unlike all others, provides a three-fit division.

8. None of the manuscripts suggests that Chaucer meant to interrupt the Cook's tale; all see it as having been abridged. In 21 MSS, no space is left after the *Cook's Tale*, and the *Man of Law's Tale* follows immediately without explanation of the interruption. Others simply brought the tale to a close with an added verse. Still others inserted the *Tale of Gamelyn*, where the *Cook's Tale* breaks off, usually with the couplet,

But hereof I wol passe as now
And of yong Gamelyn I wole telle yow.

For a complete account of the ending of the *Cook's Tale*, see *The Text of the Canterbury Tales*, 2.169–72.

9. In a recent essay, Robert Jordan discusses "Metafiction and Chaucer's *Troilus*." He defines metafiction as a "text calling attention to itself as form" (136); it foregrounds textuality, and, unlike realist fiction (which is in essence the mode prompted by roadside drama), it denies the illusion of textlessness. See also Waugh and Hutcheon, *Narcissistic*.

10. The best discussion of Chaucer's parodic debt is still the excellent chapter by Laura Hibbard Loomis on "Sir Thopas" in Bryan and Dempster (486–559).

11. In light of the program undertaken by *The Canterbury Tales*, it is in *Sir Thopas* where we can apply "the text's moment of transgressing the laws it apparently sets up for itself, and thus unravel—deconstruct—the very text." I borrow the phrase from Gayatri Spivack's restating of Derrida's response to Freud's concept of the unravelment of dreams ("Preface" xlvi).

12. Writing about Shakespeare, Annabel Patterson observes: "It is disingenuous, at best, to substitute for the concept 'Shakespeare' someone who certainly existed . . . the concept of 'the text'. . . ." I would make the same argument for Chaucer and, in that spirit, I similarly posit Chaucer "as a writer whose intentions, if never fully recoverable, are certainly worth debating" (4–5).

13. See Robert K. Root, "The Monk's Tale" (Bryan and Dempster 615–16).

Works Cited

Benson, Larry D., ed. *The Riverside Chaucer.* 3rd ed. Boston: Houghton Mifflin, 1987.

Broes, Arthur T. "Chaucer's Disgruntled Cleric." *PMLA* 78 (1963):156–62.

Bryan, W. F. and Germaine Dempster, eds. *Sources and Analogues of Chaucer's Canterbury Tales.* New York: Humanities Press, 1958.

Burrow, J. A. "Sir Thopas: An Agony in Three Fits." *RES* n.s. 22 (1971): 54–58.

Chaucer, Geoffrey. The Text of *'The Canterbury Tales'.* 8 vols. Ed. John M. Manly and Edith Rickert. Chicago: University of Chicago Press, 1940.

———. *The Complete Poetry and Prose of Geoffrey Chaucer.* 2nd ed. Ed. John H. Fisher. New York: Holt, Rinehart & Winston, 1989.

Cooper, Helen. *The Oxford Guides to Chaucer: The Canterbury Tales.* Oxford: Oxford University Press, 1989.

David, Alfred. *The Strumpet Muse: Art and Morals in Chaucer's Poetry.* Bloomington: Indiana University Press, 1976.

Donaldson, E. Talbot. "Chaucer the Pilgrim." *Speaking of Chaucer.* London: Athlone Press, 1970. 1–12.

Hutcheon, Linda. *Narcissistic Narrative: The Metafictional Paradox.* New York: n.p., 1984.

———. *A Theory of Parody.* New York: Methuen, 1985.

Jordan, Robert M. "Metafiction and Chaucer's Troilus." *Chaucer Yearbook* 1 (1992):135–55.

Lawton, David. *Chaucer's Narrators,* Cambridge: D.S. Brewer, 1985.

Middleton, Anne. "Chaucer's 'New Men' and the Good of Poetry." *Literature and Society.* Ed. Edward Said. Baltimore: Johns Hopkins University Press, 1980. 15–56.

Patterson, Annabel. *Shakespeare and the Popular Voice.* Cambridge: Basil Blackwell, 1989.

Patterson, Lee. *Chaucer and the Subject of History.* Madison: University of Wisconsin Press, 1991.

Seaman, David M. " 'The Wordes of the Frankeleyn to the Squier': An Interruption?" *ELN* 24(1986):12–18.

Spivack, Gayatri, tr. Preface to *Of Grammatology by Jacques Derrida.* Baltimore: Johns Hopkins University Press, 1974.

Strohm, Paul. *Social Chaucer.* Cambridge, MA: Harvard University Press, 1989.

Travis, Peter W. "Deconstructing Chaucer's Retraction." *Exemplaria* 3 (1991): 135–58.

Warton, Thomas. *History of English Poetry* London: Dodsley, 1774.

Waugh, Patricia. *Metafiction: The Theory and Practice of Self-Conscious Fiction.* London: 1984.

"Me thynketh It a Thyng Impertinent": Inaugurating Dialogic Discourse in the Prologue to the *Clerk's Tale*

WILLIAM MCCLELLAN

TRADITIONALLY, THE PROLOGUES TO THE INDIVIDUAL TALES OF THE *Canterbury Tales* have been read as supplying information about the personalities of the tellers, and providing the means by which the tales are introduced into the frame of the larger work. While the Prologue to the *Clerk's Tale* inserts the tale into the textuality of the larger work, it does so in an unusual way, producing other effects, some of which are unique to the Clerk's. One effect, as Carolyn Dinshaw has pointed out (135), is provoked by the Host's interpellation of the Clerk, which, unlike his addresses to the other pilgrims, carries an added charge because it interrogates the Clerk's sexuality:

> "Sir Clerk of Oxenford," our Hooste sayde,
> "Ye ryde as coy and stille as dooth a mayde
> Were newe spoused . . . (E 1–3)[1]

Dinshaw perceptively comments that the host's challenge to his sexuality contributes to the decentering of the Clerk's gender, so that he reads "like a woman" (12). Yet, although I agree that the Host's statement can be read as destablizing the Clerk's subject position, there are other features about this Prologue that set it off from the others. As Anne Middleton has suggested, the "performance" of the Clerk is not a "dramatized interaction" like the Wife's and the Pardoner's, but more like Petrarch's, "a rarefied act of literary-critical wit . . . caught only in the act of writing" (148–49). The tale, she insists, is the most "textual" of any of the *Canterbury Tales*.

The tale's distinctive textuality is introduced and thematized in the Prologue through the Clerk's extended commentary on Petrarch, the tale's previous author, and his rhetorical style. As I argue

elsewhere, identifying Petrarch as the tale's authority not only establishes an explicit genealogy, but it emphasizes the tale's "literary" qualities, extending its intertextuality beyond the frame of the
Canterbury Tales, to the Italian humanist tradition of Latinity
("Consequences"). It also introduces and connects two critical issues, political power and writing, that are later collocated with the
major thematic of the tale: the subjugation of women. More important, the Prologue serves as a prelude to the double-voiced discourse of the tale: that of the Clerk against that of Petrarch.

The Clerk's polemical attitude toward Petrarch and "his werk"
can be glimpsed in his critique of Petrarch's rhetorical style, which
he makes toward the end of the Prologue. There, after noting that
Petrarch wrote his introduction in the high style, "I seye that first
with heigh stile he enditeth," the Clerk gives a paraphrase of the
"prohemye," which is a *descriptio* of the tale's locus: "Pemond
and of Saluces the contree . . . (E44). Following the summary, the
Clerk offers this criticism:

> The which a long thyng were to devyse.
> And trewely, as to my juggement,
> Me thynketh it a thyng impertinent,
> Save that he wole conveyen his mateere;
> (E54–55)

The Clerk states that the style is prolix, "a long thyng to devyse,"
and that it is "impertinent"; that is, inappropriate or irrelevant. In
this characterization of the high style, the Clerk appears to be agreeing with an earlier assessment of rhetorical discourse made by the
Host, who urges the Clerk: "Speketh so pleyn . . . / That we may
understonde what ye seyde." The Host equates rhetoric with obscu-
rantism and inaccessibility. The Clerk, however, qualifies his initial
statement with an exception: "Save that he wole conveyen his mateere" (E55). This seems to contradict his previous assertion, or, at
least, it creates an ambiguity, muting his earlier criticism. With the
qualification, the Clerk may be implying that such amplification
might be essential to create any meaningful discourse. Or he might
be suggesting that the "heigh style" is necessary for Petrarch to tell
his story because of the kind of story it is.

It is clear that the Clerk is criticizing Petrarch's rhetorical style
from a different angle than would the Host, who rejects such discourse outright, regarding rhetorical figuration as incommensurate
with understanding. I think the problem the Clerk has with Petrarch's "heigh stile" has more to do with "his mateere" than with

its supposed excessive prolixity; that is, the Clerk's difficulty with Petrarch's style has more to do with the allegorical moral that is conveyed by the style, and by Petrarch's ideological point of view, as a detailed examination of the Clerk's discussion in the Prologue will reveal.

Although the radically marked textuality of the Prologue noted by Middleton has also been noticed by others, no one has given more than a cursory examination of it.[2] There are a number of ways of illuminating these literary effects. One is suggested by the type of prologue developed in the fourteenth century that A. J. Minnis has called the "Aristotelian Prologue" (*Medieval Theory* 28–29).[3] Using his model as a template shows that only two of the four topics usually discussed in these traditional academic prologues are highlighted in the Clerk's Prologue: the author *(causa efficiens),* and the style in which it was written *(causa formalis).* The other two common to such prologues, the subject matter and the final intention, receive little explicit commentary. This emphasis on the previous author and his style of writing already suggests the polemical attitude the Clerk has toward Petrarch and his interpretation of the tale. While this paradigm of the academic prologue makes visible the features that are accentuated by this rhetorical structuring, I think Bakhtin's concept of dialogic discourse will help us more fully understand and interpret the effects generated by it.

There are three related concepts constituting Bakhtin's theory of dialogic discourse that can help elucidate an interpretation of the Prologue: double-voicedness, the prior word, and polemic.[4] For Bakhtin, most, if not all, discourse or utterances have more than one voicing or intentional force to them; that is, they are double-voiced. There are at least two intentions or inflections of meaning residing in a single utterance, which can be defined as a single sentence or word or as a complete tale, story, or poem. Sometimes the different intentions co-habiting in the utterance are very close to one another and in fact merge with each other. Bakhtin calls this kind of discourse, "monologic." This usually occurs when statements are so authoritative that they tend to exert an overriding control over any subsequent (re-)statement of them. Such is the case for sacred texts. This mono-logic is the kind of hierarchical logic governing, for the most part, Griselda's and Walter's statements; she conforms her will and words to his as absolutely as possible. For Bakhtin, however, the dominant tendency in discourse is toward double-voicing where the relationships between the multiplicity of meanings and accents contained in an utterance have greater parity.

Neither subsume or eliminate the various meanings residing in an utterance.

The double-voicedness of discourse is due, in part, to the fact that all utterances have a priorness to them; that is, someone else said them earlier. In that sense, there are no originary statements, no origin utterances; words and statements come to us used and loaded with meaning(s). For Bakhtin, this quality of utterances "having-already-been-said" reflects the inherent sociality of all utterances, that is, the meaning or meanings of the utterances always transcend the individual(s) who utter and hear, write, and read them. The locus for this transcendence is not metaphysical but is located in the historical, social, and contingent.

In addition to the inherent sociality of the word, a second factor Bakhtin sees as motivating double-voiced discourse is the primal urge by individuals to assert their autonomy and create meaning for themselves, and to communicate this meaning to others. New meaning and inflections are generated by re-inflecting and deflecting the old meanings that reside in utterances and inhere on objects. Bakhtin generates a typology to describe the possible ways writers and speakers contend with the already uttered word, which includes such strategies as stylization, narrator's narration, and parody. The necessity for an individual speaker or writer to project a meaning onto a previously uttered statement generates an acute awareness of the other's word. Seeing this as a general tendency of discourse, Bakhtin calls this perception and the attendant evaluative force that is brought to bear in the scrutiny of another's word, polemic. *Polemic* designates a fundamental tendency of all discourse and is Bakhtin's explanation for what motivates double-voicedness.

Turning to the Prologue, we see that the Clerk raises the issue of its previous authorship in an emphatic and unusual way. After reassuring the Host: "And therefore wol I do you obeisance" (E24), the Clerk states that the tale he is about to tell is another's: "I wol you telle a tale which that I / Lerned at Padowe of a worthy Clerk" (E26–27). What is remarkable is that the Clerk repeats this attribution two other times in the Prologue, with the third citation being its last line. The first and last comments the Clerk makes about the tale focus on the previous author, and emphasize that it is another's discourse, thereby granting it thematic importance. This can be seen as part of his strategy of reevaluation and Petrarch's treatment of the tale. Bakhtin regards such reorientation of another's speech as an essential and defining characteristic of all rhetorical speech:

> Rhetorical genres possess the most varied forms for transmitting another's speech, and for the most part these are intensely dialogized forms.

Rhetoric relies heavily on the vivid reaccentuating of the words it transmits (often to the point of distorting them completely) that is accomplished by the appropriate framing context (Dialogic Imagination 354).

A detailed examination of the Prologue will show us more exactly
how the Clerk promotes his limited polemic against Petrarch's style
and allegorical moral and lays the groundwork for his reinterpreta-
tion of the tale.

The first time the Clerk mentions the previous author of the tale,
in a section which is in *abbreviatio* of the material presented in the
prologue, he does so without naming him:

> I wol yow telle a tale which that I
> Lerned at Padowe of a worthy clerk,
> As preved by his wordes and his werk.
> He is now deed and nayled in his cheste;
> I prey to God so yeve his soule reste! (E26–30)

In addition to his status as "auctor," the Clerk specifies three qualities of the yet unnamed Petrarch. The first is that he is a "worthy
clerk," the second that this is "proved by his wordes," and the
last that he is "now deed." Focusing on the first two, we see, not
surprisingly, that the Clerk establishes a causal relationship between an ethical category and writing, which later will be specified
as the "heigh stile." The Clerk, by linking the hierarchy of value
with that of style, is explicitly conflating the two Aristotelian categories, the *causa efficiens* with the *causa formalis* and consequently
pointing to their intrinsic connection. I am not suggesting that his
was a novel or unusual connection. It was, in fact, a commonplace.
What is significant is that the Clerk makes this implicitly understood relationship between moral worth and rhetoric an explicit,
and therefore ideological, statement.

His point is reinforced in the next paragraph of the Prologue
which is an amplification of these lines:

> Fraunceys Petrak, the lauriat poete
> Highte this clerk, whose rhetoric sweete
> Enlumyed al Ytaille of poetrie,
> As Lynyan dide of philosophie,
> Or lawe, or oother art particuler;
> But deeth, that wol not suffre us dwellen heer,
> But as it were a twynklyng of an ye,
> Hem bothe hath slayn, and alle shul we dye.
>
> (E31–38)

The now named worthy clerk, "Fraunceys Petrak, the lauriat poet," is identified as a famous poet whose writing, "rhetoric sweet," has "enlumyed" all of Italy. Once again, the interconnection between the hierarchies of style and value is made in the several meaning of the word *enlumyed,* which can mean "to make famous" or "to enlighten" or "to describe or depict in a certain style, especially to adorn or embellish."[5] Amplification, the "high stile," is enlightenment. But just what is the inflection here? The figure with whom the Clerk compares Petrarch in this passage might give some specificity to the connection being made.

The other figure in the comparison is Giovanni de Lignano who, according to Albert Cook, was a famous fourteenth-century jurist and professor who taught in Bologna (353–56). Giovanni wrote books on virtually everything, from astrology and common law to theology, ethics and politics. He personally knew three popes and had established an international reputation on the basis of a legal brief he wrote defending the election of Urban VI entitled, *De Fletu Ecclesiae.* As John McCall pointed out, he was the one major apologist mentioned by name in the only schism dispute heard before Richard II (478). His reputation in England was comparable to Petrarch's and might have even been greater. However, more than just the reputation of the two men are being compared in this amplification.

I think that it is Petrarch's and Giovanni's methods of illumination that the Clerk is comparing here. Petrarch's "rhetoric sweet" parallels Giovanni's "philosophie / Or lawe or other art particuler" in an "as" clause of manner which operates on an inclusionary and complementary principle. The comparison of Petrarch with Giovanni de Lignano defines the enlightenment the Clerk is referring to as a kind of wisdom associated with moral philosophy. Although "philosophie" can mean learning or rational speculation in the most general sense, it also can have a narrower meaning of a specific discipline or body of knowledge. I suspect that the term here indicates moral philosophy and that the other two terms in this passage, "law or oother art particuler," represent ethics and political science.[6]

This conclusion is based on the reception and use of Aristotle's *Rhetorica,* some of the treatises Giovanni de Lignano was known to have written, the political language employed earlier in the prologue, and finally the fact that a major theme of the tale concerns the issue of sovereignty. We should remember that Chaucer notes that the Clerk was a serious student, "Of Aristotle and his philosophie" (A295). So, the manner in which the fourteenth-century scholastics employed the *Rhetorica* might provide a context for the Clerk's comparison. James Murphy points to the dominating manuscript collocation of Aristotle's *Rhetorica, Ethica,* and *Politica,* arguing that Aristotle's *Rhetorica* was "useful in the study of moral philosophy" (101). He also suggests that the treatise was associated with the *scientiae speciales (artes particulier)* dealing with human actions—politics and ethics. The fact that Giovanni wrote several works on moral and political philosophy, including two on Aristotle's *Politics* (Holland, xxiv), further strengthens the supposition that the Clerk is following a well-known collocation of Aristotle's work.

The language the Clerk employs earlier and the qualification the host adds with his request for a tale reenforce this contextual pattern as well. The host, when urging the Clerk to forgo the "heigh stile," alludes to this association between rhetorical style and politico-ethical import:

> Youre termes, youre colours, and youre figures,
> Keepe hem in stoor til so be that ye endite
> Heigh style, and whan that men to kynges write.
> Speketh so pleyn at this tyme, we yow preye,
> That we may understonde what ye seye. (E16–20)

The Host, by equating the high style with royal discourse, links the hierarchy of style with the socio-political order of late feudal society. Suggesting that while the high style may be the appropriate way to communicate with "kynges," he asks that the tale be told in a "pleyn" style in order that it be understandable by the common folk.

The Clerk employs terms of political discourse in his response to the Host, and his answer constitutes an *interpretatio* on political sovereignty, one of the tale's major themes:

> "Hooste," quod he, "I am under your yerde;
> Ye han of us as now the governance,
> And therfore wol I do yow obeisance,
> As fer as resoun axeth, hardily. (E22–25)

He first states that he is under the host's rule, or "yerde." In the following line he substitutes the term *governance* and extends its application from the singular "I" to the more general and universal "us." The third line is another variation of this and a statement of the consequence of the first two: "And therfore wol I do yow obeisance." However, the Clerk, good Aristotelian that he is, does not grant the Host absolute governance, but only, "As fer as resoun axeth."

It is significant that the first lines the Clerk speaks contain an *interpretatio* on sovereignty, which, if it doesn't give a full-fledged theory of governance, nevertheless presents a definite attitude about it. The repetition confers an emphatic quality on the Clerk's statements and allows for the insertion of an important qualification: "resoun" imposes limitations on the contract between ruler and governed. This perspective toward sovereignty is in sharp contrast to Walter's and Griselda's more absolutist understanding. The words *governance* and *obeisance* here foreshadow their use in the tale itself, as can be seen in this example, where Griselda reaffirms her complete obedience to Walter:

> She seyde, "Lord, al lyth in youre pleasaunce.
>   My child and I, with hertely obeisaunce,
> Been youres al, and ye owe save or spille
> Youre owene thyng, werketh after youre wille. (E501–4)

The Clerk's *interpretatio* on sovereignty suggests a standard by which to measure the events and statements in the tale itself. More immediately, his reprise to the Host reveals his attitude toward the host, and toward the tale he is about to tell.

As Minnis has pointed out, a conventional prologue often included a discussion of the place in the scheme of knowledge occupied by the art or science relevant to the text ("Influence" 368). By including statements on political theory and rhetoric, rather than theology and scriptural exegesis, the Clerk can be seen as claiming a greater pertinence for the tale of the practical and natural arts: philosophy, ethics, politics, and law. At first, this seems an unusual assertion about a story that is the vehicle of a moral allegory.

I think it is an early indication, a prelude of the dialogic reorientation the tale will take in the Clerk's narration of it. Such a reaccentuating of the tale initiates a movement toward viewing the tale in the context of ordinary human experience. The Clerk's comparison of Petrarch and Giovanni implies that the "particular" arts concerning human action and utterance, rhetoric and politics, are more immediately relevant for understanding the tale than those concerning ultimate or divine matters.

The *interpretatio* on sovereignty and the comparison of Petrarch and Giovanni also begin to delineate the worldview of the Clerk, which, if it is not exclusively constituted by the horizon of the human, places new emphasis on human experience and employs a rhetoric of pathos. The movement of pathos affirms the legitimacy of the natural world, which can be said to be one of the legacies of Aristotle for the late medieval world. In terms of the changes this generates in the tale, the shift in ideological perspective accounts for the increase in the mimetic elements in the Clerk's narration, such as the increase in dialogue, the emphatic portrayal of emotions, and other "realistic" details. This augmentation of mimesis, in turn, produces the ambiguous admixture of real and symbolic, high and middle rhetorical styles which many readers of the tale have noted. The Clerk's voice of pathos inaugurates an internal dialogization in the narration of the tale and produces an equivocation that infiltrates and changes the meaning of the *allegoresis*. It does so by granting a new status to the allegory's vehicle, that is, by introducing a new attitude toward Griselda and her suffering. The Clerk will dwell on the human dimension of her suffering, in contradistinction to Petrarch, who views her suffering as symbolic representation of a spiritual testing. This shift of attitude and perspective is initiated in the Prologue.

Such a radical rewriting of the tale, however, is not immediately apparent in the Prologue. What the comparison of Giovanni and Petrarch, and, concomitantly, the *artes* of rhetoric and politics signals is a repositioning of the narrative perspective from the infinite horizon of the divine to that of the earthly and human. It begins to dialogize the narrative, Petrarch's "wordes", by intimating another perspective. It also links different styles of writing with specific ideological formations, foregrounding the evaluative aspect of rhetorical discourse. This incremental rotation of narrative viewpoint to the horizon of human experience is reenforced by the presence of the third figure in this passage, Death.

As I have mentioned, the third attribute of Petrarch the Clerk alludes to is his death: "He is now deed and nayled in his cheste" (E29). In this short presentation of the previous author, the Clerk links his moral status, "worthy" with his poetry, "wordes," and both with his mortality. At first, the comment on Petrarch's death appears to be just one more fact in a series summarizing his life, but the following lines invest it with a thematic importance that goes beyond mere recitation:

> But deeth, that wol not suffre us dwellen heer,
> But as it were a twynklyng of an ye,
> Hem bothe hath slayn, and alle shul we dye.
>
> (E36–38)

These lines complete the initial movement of this passage introducing the "poet lauriat." The last line first refers to Giovanni, including him in the category of the also dead, "Hem bothe hath slayn," then moves to encompass us all: "all shul we dye." The report of an individual death expands to two and then moves to a general assertion about the universal human condition. The effects of this passage are several and complex.

Here, the personification of death brings a set of paradoxes to bear. By personifying death, the Clerk places the three figures metaphorically on the same plane, emphasizing the distance and difference between them and us. They are in an absolute beyond. In fact, Death is presented having an agency that both Giovanni and Petrarch lack. The simile "twynkyng of an ye," which alludes with grim irony to the Host's demand for a "murie" tale, presents Death as an active agent while emphasizing the brief and sudden force of it. Petrarch, on the other hand, is made to be, as it were, one more remove from us than death in the image, "nayled in his cheste." The effect is to monumentalize Petrarch, distancing him from us and diminishing possibilities of communication and exchange.

The Clerk's statement asserting the universality of death, which ends the passage, also confirms a commonality. The experience joins Petrarch, Giovanni, and potentially himself and ourselves in a common bond. It implies a *communis sensus,* thereby affirming the possibility of communication and the creation of meaning, while at the same time undercutting anyone's claim—namely, Petrarch's—to privileged status. Whereas the experience does not directly deny Petrarch's verbal power and moral wisdom, it places "his wordes and his werk" in the zone of the human, in the realm of the fallible and fungible word, and therefore makes it available to interpretation and revision.

Following his comparison of Giovanni and Petrarch, the Clerk returns to a discussion of Petrarch's "words" in the third and final paragraph of the Prologue, which begins in a repetition of the Clerk's initial collocation of writing with moral status:

> But forth to tellen of this worthy man
> That taughte me this tale, as I bigan,
> I seye that first with heigh stile he enditeth,
> Er he the body of his tale writeth
>
> (E39–42)

Again, the attribution, "worthy" is applied to Petrarch, and his "rhetoric sweet" is now specified as the "heigh stile." It is signifi-

cant that their intrinsic connection is pointed to just before the
Clerk critiques Petrarch's style. After a paraphrase of Petrarch's
"prohemye," the Clerk says:

> The which a long thyng were to devyse.
> And trewely, as to my juggement,
> Me thynketh it a thyng impertinent,
> Save that he wole conveyen his mateere;
> But this his tale, which that ye may heere.
> (E52–56)

The *contrarium* with which he states his criticism both qualifies his
statement and extends his polemical comment to "his mateere,"
that is, the content of Petrarch's story, as the analysis of the Clerk's
earlier discussion of Petrarch and "his werk" makes clear. His comparison of Petrarch with Giovanni follows up the Host's initial connection of the high style with political discourse and emphasizes
the idea that rhetoric constitutes a moral discourse, whose limits he
suggests by specifying those "particuler" *artes* that focus on
human behavior: philosophy, ethics, and politics. The Clerk's critical comment on Petrarch's literary style is, by extension, a critique
of his ideological viewpoint. By criticizing his style, the Clerk prepares to dialogically reorient the meaning and interpretation of Petrarch's tale from an abstract allegory of spiritual constancy to a
narrative that views Griselda's travail as the "real" suffering of a
patient wife.

However, the qualifying statement with which he extends his critique, "Save that he wole conveyen his mateere," contains a certain
ambiguity, one that is never completely resolved. As I have suggested, on the one hand, the Clerk seems to imply that rhetorical
amplification is necessary for projection of any meaning, which
mitigates his criticism of Petrarch's style. On the other, he is sharpening his critique by pointing to the ideological basis of the rhetorical style: the "heigh stile" is necessary to write this particular kind
of allegorical narrative. The ambiguity, created by the rhetorical
figure, *contrarium* (that is, statement, counterstatement) reveals a
fundamental feature of Clerk's rhetorical style and method of argument, and consequently his own ideological viewpoint. In addition
to using it here in his comment on Petrarch's style, he also employs
the same figure in his reply to the Host: "And therefore wol I do
yow obeisance, / As fer as resoun axeth, hardily" (E24; 25). A
general statement is subsequently qualified with a counterstatement, which is almost the complete opposite of it, so the limitation

the qualification imposes on the original statement is substantial. His praise of Petrarch is stated in the same format: Petrarch is "worthy" *but* "dead." It is a complementary style of argument that initially signals agreement but then redefines the terms of the consensus. It is a style of argument befitting the academic Clerk, for it allows him to make very fine distinctions.

In the tale proper, the Clerk pursues this rhetorical strategy with great finesse. Virtually every one of the dozen apostrophes constituting his extended commentary contains a *contrarium,* reflecting the limited polemic he conducts against the outrages of the Griselda story. Just as he grants "obeisance" to the Host within the limits of "resoun," so, too, he accepts Petrarch's narrative as a moral discourse, but tries dialogically to mimetize its allegorical universe and make it understandable in terms of human reason and experience. As we know, the effects of his dialogic intervention make the tale even more horrifying, not the least because the Clerk accepts the necessity of testing wives.

The ambiguity generated by his rhetorical style reveals other tensions in the discursive universe of the Clerk. He never rejects Petrarch's tale and moral outright, as does the nominally Chaucerian voice of grotesque parody in the tale's Envoy. He thus betrays, as Elaine Tuttle Hansen has pointed out, his ambivalent attitude toward women and his marginal position in the dominant culture (245). The Clerk's style of argumentation discloses an awareness of the authoritativeness of Petrarch's "words," and the relative weakness of his own ideological position. This defining limitation of the Clerk's subject position reflects, at least in part, the social and cultural status of humanism in late-fourteenth-century England. Humanism with its attendant valorization of this world, was an emergent ideological formation. It lacked the strength to contend openly with the ideology represented by the allegorical point of view, which subsumed all earthly concerns in the gaze of eternal and ultimate "thyngs." Consequently, the Clerk's voice displays an uncertainty in his polemical attitude toward Petrarch's narrative. Just as he does not directly challenge the hyper-masculinist view of Harry Bailey, he cannot unequivocally dispute the absolutist claims of Petrarch's authoritarian morality tale.

The authoritativeness of Petrarch's "words" limits the Clerk's ability to impose his own meaning in his appropriation of them. The prior teller's viewpoint is not erased but maintained and explicitly dialogized. The effect is to emphasize the multiple viewpoints constituting the tale's discursivity. In this instance, the dialogizing of Petrarch's words produces a movement away from a fully objectified, individuated persona of the Clerk narrator toward a scene of multi-vocality; that is, a splitting of the narrative voice into voices. However, although these voices are distinctly visible, they are not completely autonomous. Petrarch's and the Clerk's voicings are intertwined with each other; they still form a conceptual bond and together constitute the complementary and contradictory discourse of the tale.

The prologue to the *Clerk's Tale* thus produces a complex series of effects. First, it designates a narrator and in so doing inserts the tale into the performative scene of the Canterbury context. It also establishes a genealogy and intertextuality for the tale that extends beyond the Canterbury frame by naming the previous author, Petrarch. In the process of describing him, it introduces two of the tale's major issues, writing and political power, that are collocated with the tale's primary theme: the subjugation of women. Finally, the Prologue distinguishes the distinctive voicings of Petrarch and the Clerk through their different rhetorical styles and ideological viewpoints, and it inaugurates the tale's dialogic discourse, suggesting, with a series of *contrariones,* the subtlety and range of the ideological argument that motivates the narrative.

Notes

1. All quotes from Chaucer are from *The Riverside Chaucer.*
2. See, for example, David (160–61), Ferster (116–17), and Morse (72–74).
3. Minnis maintains that the form of this Prologue, which was inspired by the "four causes" of Aristotlean philosophy, was created by religious academics in the late thirteenth and early fourteenth centuries, and later adapted by secular academics and writers to provide introductions to their own work. The adaptation of Aristotle's "four causes" for use in these prologues can be briefly summarized: (1) *Causa efficiens:* the auctor or author; (2) *Causa materialis:* the material, subject, or book under discussion; (3) *Causa formalis:* the duplex form of the work, the *forma tractandi,* the mode or style, and the *forma tractatus,* the order or division of the work; and (4) *Causa finalis:* the intention or raison d'être of the work. Minnis argues that these prologues constituted literary criticism and that Chaucer was knowledgeable about them and the literary/technical terms employed in them. Among other examples, he cites Chaucer's frequent use of the term *mateere,* his extended discussion of "entente" in the *Prologue to the Legend of Good Women,* and his listing of Aristotle's four causes in the *Tale of Melibee.*
4. For discussions of dialogic discourse (double-voiced discourse) see esp. Bakhtin, *Problems,* chap. 5; and [Bakhtin and] Volosinov, *Marxism,* 83–98. For the prior word, *Dialogic Imagination* (280–94, 325–27), and again Volosinov (115–23). For polemic, *Dostoevsky,* chap. 5. I also have synoptic definitions of these concepts in "Bakhtin's Theory," and "Bakhtin and Otherness."
5. Although the MED assigned the tertiary meaning to the word *enlumyed* here, "to make famous or glorious," E. T. Donaldson's attribution, of the primary mean-

ings, "to shed light upon, to illuminate or to give spiritual insight, to enlighten," seems more appropriate (195). I am interested, not in eliminating meanings but in presenting a sense of the word's richness. Another meaning of "enlumyed" is as I have noted in the text is more closely related to rhetorical discourse "to describe or depict in a certain style, especially to adorn or embellish."

6. The primary meaning of "particuler" is "pertaining only to a part, partial, not general." The meaning the MED assigns Chaucer's usage here is "special, specialized" and for "art particuler" it specifies, "a particular science, a specialized branch of learning." In like manner, the second term of this series, "lawe," can carry a more specific meaning as well as a general one. It can mean a particular body of law, such as common law, or it can mean ethics. Thus, we can assume that, here, "philosophie" has a specific as opposed to a generalized meaning, or, at least, that it is associated with a specific branch of learning.

Works Cited

Bakhtin, Mikhail. *The Dialogic Imagination: Four Essays.* Tr. Caryl Emerson and Michael Holquist. Austin: University of Texas Press, 1981.

———. *The Problems of Dostoevsky's Poetics.* Tr. Caryl Emerson. Minneapolis: University of Minnesota Press, 1984.

[———] V.N. Volosinov. *Marxism and the Philosophy of Language.* Tr. Ladislav Matejka and I. R. Titunik. New York: Seminar Press, 1973.

Chaucer, Geoffrey. *The Riverside Chaucer.* Ed. Larry Benson. 3rd ed. Boston: Houghton Mifflin, 1987.

Cook, Albert S. "Chaucer's 'Linian.' " *Romanic Review* 8 (1917): 353–82.

David, Alfred. *The Strumpet Muse: Art and Morals in Chaucer's Poetry.* Bloomington: Indiana University Press, 1976.

Dinshaw, Carolyn. *Chaucer's Sexual Poetics.* Madison: University of Wisconsin Press, 1989.

Donaldson, E. T. *Chaucer's Poetry.* New York: Ronald Press, 1958.

Ferster, Judith. *Chaucer on Interpretation.* London: Cambridge University Press, 1985.

Hansen, Elaine Tuttle. "The Powers of Silence." *Women and Power in the Middle Ages.* Ed. M. Erler and M. Kowlaleski. Athens: University of Georgia Press, 1988.

Holland, Thomas E. "Introduction." *Tractatus: De Ballo, De Represaliis et De Duello.* Giovani da Legnano. Ed. T. E. Holland. Washington: Carnegie Institution, 1917.

McCall, John P. "Chaucer and John of Legnano." *Speculum* 40 (1965): 484–89.

McClellan, William. "The Consequences of 'Treuth:' Reading Two Versions of the *Clerk's Tale. Genre.* XXV (1992): 153–77.

———. "The Dialogic Other: Bakhtin's Theory of Rhetoric." *Discours social/ Social Discourse.* Ed. Robert Barsky and Michael Holquist 3 (1990): 233–50.

———. "Bakhtin's Theory of Dialogic Discourse, Medieval Rhetorical Theory and the Multi-Voiced Structure of the *Clerk's Tale.*" *Exemplaria* 1 (1989): 461–88.

Middleton, Anne. "The Clerk and His Tale: Some Literary Contexts." *SAC* 2 (1980): 121–50.

Minnis, A. J. *Medieval Theory of Authorship: Scholastic Literary Attitudes in the Later Middle Ages.* London: Scolar Press, 1984.

———. "The Influence of Academic Prologues on the Prologues and Literary Attitudes of Late-Medieval English Writers." *Medieval Studies* 43 (1981): 342–83.

Morse, Charlotte C. "The Exemplary Griselda." *SAC* 7 (1985): 51–86.

Murphy, James J. *Rhetoric in the Middle Ages: A History of Rhetorical Theory from Saint Augustine to the Renaissance.* Berkeley: University of California Press, 1974.

Sandrine's Fable: Courtly Discourse and Courtly Behavior

JOHANNA C. PRINS

THE MIDDLE DUTCH VAN HULTHEM MANUSCRIPT, DATED BETWEEN 1400 and 1410, contains more than 200 texts of various nature— prose and poetry, religious and secular, serious and comic. Among these pieces are four plays identified in their rubrics as *Abele Spelen, "Abel plays."*[1] The exact meaning of the word *Abel* is uncertain, with various editors giving "serious," "handsome," "ingenious," or "fine." They are serious, secular plays, and, although they are not necessarily by the same author, they are usually grouped together because of their common provenance and characteristics, although the significance of this provenance and these characteristics have been in dispute. The text specifies that each of the plays is to be seen together with the farce following it. These farces represent a different world from the *Abel* plays, a world where poor, simple men and women battle each other for a bit of food or pleasure.

Traditionally, critics have seen the *Abel* plays as courtly in mood and vocabulary, and have therefore assumed they were intended for a courtly audience. There are several problems with this view. One is that it leaves no place for the farces, and, not surprisingly, many editions leave out the farces, even though their connection to the serious plays is specifically stated. The rubric for the play of *Lancelot of Denmark,* for instance, states: "An *abel* play of Lancelot of Denmark, how he fell in love with a maiden who served his mother; and a farce to follow." At the end of the play, the speaker of the epilogue says:

> Nu biddic u allen dat ghi wilt swigen
> Ons voerspel dat es ghedaen
> Men sal u ene sotheid spelen gaen. (950–52)

> (Now I beg you to remain quiet;
> Our first play has ended
> And we will play you a farce.)

164

Stamping these plays as "courtly" also ignores the fact that they are by no means consistently so, and that their tone is often uneven. Idealistic, and idealized, statements alternate with practical, even pedestrian proverbs and *sententiae*. Furthermore, the concept of courtliness, and especially of "courtly love," has been subject to extensive critical debate and re-definition. Even apart from what courtly love meant in the twelfth century, when Andreas Capellanus wrote his much disputed treatise on love, *De Amore,* these ideas had surely been modified extensively by the fourteenth century, when the *Abel* plays originated.[2]

Situating the Van Hulthem manuscript with regard to its function and purpose is a problem of long standing. The manuscript contains 241 texts of the widest variety of genres and character (though probably all were copied together into this manuscript by the same hand). Geographically, a link with Brussels seems likely, because, among the texts, one or two show a connection to Brussels, such as a report on a miracle in that town, which occurred in 1399, very shortly before the manuscript was composed (Anrooij, "Bijdrage" 225–33, and Anrooij and Van Buuren," 's Levens felheid" 190–92). According to Vanhamme's historical study of Brussels (76), that city had, by the fourteenth century, about 40,000 inhabitants; it is likely that these were as varied as the texts in the Van Hulthem manuscript. Herman Pleij's studies of the culture (or cultures) of the towns have shown us large and teeming agglomerations of people that were, by the mid-fourteenth century, already moving towards greater coherence and a sense of identity among themselves, often by cultural means (Pleij, *Sneeuwpoppen* and *Op Belofte van Profijt.*) One new ideology occupied itself with a new model for relationships between men and women—no longer the courtly model presented in the twelfth- and thirteenth-century romances, nor the brutish behavior shown in songs about the peasants, but a new model suitable to the varied people of the towns. The *Abel* plays show us some—mostly positive—examples of the new relationships, and the farces show the reverse of the coin: how men and women should *not* relate. Locating the *Abel* plays in an urban situation, and seeing them as responding to specific urban problems, provides a useful approach to interpreting these plays, and the courtly and "urban" elements in *Lancelot of Denmark* illustrate the arrival of the new ideology.

Sir Lancelot of Denmark is in love with his mother's lady-in-waiting, Sandrine, and pursues her with his attentions. When she rejects him (because her inferior social station makes a marriage unlikely), he follows his mother's malevolent advice, rapes her and then (literally) turns his back on her. Sandrine flees into the woods, where she is approached by another knight out hunting. The hunter-knight listens to Sandrine's pleadings not to take advantage of her situation, and eventually proposes marriage. Sandrine accepts, though not without communicating by means of a fable what happened to her earlier. Lancelot, meanwhile, distressed by Sandrine's disappearance, sends his chamberlain, Reynold, to look for her and tell her that he wants to marry her; but she declines, pointing out that she is happily married and intends to remain so. Pressed for a "token" for Lancelot (to prove that Reynold actually has talked to her), she repeats the fable she already told the hunter. Reynold returns to Lancelot but, worried about unleashing a violent confrontation between Lancelot and Sandrine's husband likely to involve many relatives, he reports that she died when he gave her his message. When Lancelot refuses to believe him, Reynold repeats Sandrine's fable once more; Lancelot then recognizes the truth about his actions and dies of regret.

Sandrine's fable, then, told three times in all, is central to the play and to our understanding of the action and deserves a closer look:

> Nu ga wi dan in dese warande
> Her ridder spreken alluttelkijn
> Ende verstaet die redene mijn
> Dies biddic u hoghe geboren baroen
> Ane siet desen boem scone ende groen
> Hoe wel dat hi gebloyet staet
> Sine edelen roke hi doer gaet
> Al omme desen bogaert al
> Hi staet in soe soeten dal
> Dat hi van rechte bloyen moet
> Hi es soe edel ende soe soet
> Dat hi versiert al desen bogaert
> Quame nu een valcke van hogher aert
> Ghevloghen op desen boem ende daelde
> Ende ene bloeme daer af haelde
> Ende daer na nemmermeer neghene
> Noch noit en haelde meer dan ene
> Soudi den boem daer omme haten
> Ende te copene daer omme laten
> Dat biddic u dat ghi mi segt
> Ende die rechte waerheit sprect
> Edel ridder in hovescher tale. (484–505)
>
> (Let us go then into this garden
> Sir knight, to talk a bit

And mark well my words
I beg you this, noble baron:
Look at this handsome green tree
How full of blossoms it stands.
The perfume of it spreads around
Throughout this orchard.
In such a lovely valley it stands
That it just has to bloom.
It is so noble and sweet
It is an ornament to this orchard;
If a noble falcon were to come
Flying down onto this tree
To pick a flower from it
And never another thereafter,
And never more than that one,
Would you hate the tree for that reason?
And refuse to take it therefore?
I pray you: answer me that,
And tell me the full truth,
Noble knight, in courteous words.)

These are eloquent and affecting words. She had been equally eloquent in her attempt to explain her objections to Lancelot, but he was too absorbed in his own feelings to listen to her. The fact that she takes another chance to explain herself (to another man), as well as the form she chooses for her statement, are equally striking. The knight seems to realize this, because he communicates both his understanding of her message and his acceptance of her in any condition:

Scone wijf ic versta u wale
Ene bloeme dat en es niet
En esser nemmeer toe ghesciet
Daer omme en salic den boem niet haten
Noch te copene daer omme laten
Want hi es soe scone ghedaen
Ic sie daer op soe meneghe bloeme staen
Met groten hopen sonder ghetal
Daer edel vrucht af comen sal
Op dat god ghedoghen wille
Nu ewelijc hier af een ghestille
Ende comt met mi wel scone wijf. (506–17)

(Handsome woman, I understand you:
One blossom is as nothing;
If nothing more has happened

> I'll not hate the tree for that reason,
> Or refuse to take it therefore,
> For it is formed in beauty,
> And I see many blossoms on it
> Far more than can be counted.
> Noble fruit will come from that tree
> If God will grant it so.
> No further word about this,
> And come with me dear woman.)

Although the message of Sandrine's fable is immediately clear to us, as well as to the knight, it is useful to analyze the constituent elements of her fable more closely.

The falcon is an important bird in the courtly world, a symbol of the courtly life. Hunting in general was considered an appropriate activity for the nobility, with deer-hunting and falconry vying for position as the noblest pastime. Although Marcelle Thiébaux, in her book *The Stag of Love,* points out that the stag "is the quarry most often hunted in medieval epics and romances," in his *De arte venandi cum avibus,* the Emperor Frederick II of Hohenstaufen states that the art of falconry is "intrinsically an aristocratic sport; and one may once more add that it is nobler, more worthy than, and superior to other kinds of venery" (Thiébaux 19; Frederick II 6). Frederick II especially emphasizes the noble qualities, devoid of self-interest, that the ideal falconer should possess.

The terminology of falconry was frequently applied to the situation of courtly lovers. In the *Nibelungenlied,* Kriemhild dreams that she is training a strong, handsome falcon, who is then killed by two eagles. Her mother explains the falcon as a noble man, whom she will lose unless God prevents it (First adventure, stanza 13). The two eagles, of course, prefigure Gunther and Hagen, who kill Siegfried during the hunt. In Der von Kürenberg's "Falkenlied," the falcon is variously interpreted as being the lover, by Wapnewski, or a messenger between the two lovers by Hatto (Wapnewski 1–19; Hatto 20–23).

In the Low Countries, too, falconry was a favorite pastime, as the court records of the Hague court show by frequent references to fees for messengers going after lost falcons, or purchases of new ones in Brabant or Flanders (Oostrom 181). That the figurative use of the falcon occurred in medieval Dutch literature as well is shown in one of the other plays in the Van Hulthem manuscript, when the lady sees her lover-from-afar appear before the gate of her father's palace and says:

Dank hebbe mamet ende apolijn
Ic sie den valke van hogher aert
Neder dalen in minen bogaert. (*Gloriant* 617–18)

(Thanks be to Mohammed and Apollo,
I see the noble falcon appear
And descend into my garden.)

In some of the lyrics from the Hague Song Manuscript, the game
of love is portrayed as a hunt, with the traditional configuration of
the man as hunter and the lady as prey, but in one poem "a maiden
has spread a net to catch a hawk, planning to clip her prey's wings
and then keep him as a pet," which reads like a warning to prospec-
tive lovers.[3] This imagery, then, is common and open to different
interpretations. Although the falcon is a fierce predator, that quality
plays no role in the image of the falcon as a lover.

The language of hunting in general is often used for the pursuit
of the beloved, and although this may sound unpleasant to the modern ear, there is no indication that it could not be neutral in the time
of our play. The knight in the forest, who has been out hunting
without success when the finds Sandrine, uses hunting language to
express his appreciation:

Bi den here die mi ghewrochte
Ic sie ginder porren een wilt
Daer mijn herte op es ghestilt
Ic wane noit man op ghenen dach
Alsoe sconen wilt en sach (380–84)

. . . .

O scone maget nu staet al stille
Ghi moet mijn ghevanghen sijn
Ic hebbe u liever dan een everzwijn
Al waert van finen goude gewracht. (396–99)

(By the Lord who made me,
I see game running over there;
My heart is relieved now
I believe no man, any day,
Saw such beautiful game

. . . .

O lovely maiden, stand still now,
You must be my prisoner.
I'd have you rather than any boar,
Even were it made of find gold.)

This language does not seem to be objectionable in itself, and later
the knight is capable of moving his conversation from the formulaic

to the personal. But, even if we grant that the language of hunting as applied to courtship may be inherently neutral, this does not eliminate the possibility that the "game" feels hunted in an unfavorable sense. Thus it is that Sandrine herself uses a hunting term after the rape, saying that Lancelot's mother brought her to Lancelot "caught in a snare" (inden stric ghevaen, 328). Sandrine, aware of the traditional, courtly language used in courtship, is able to use it not just to gloss over certain unpleasant customs but to expose the more predatory actions as well.

Falconry and hunting, then, are traditional elements of the courtly discourse; this falcon is not hunting game, however, but picking a flower—hardly typical falcon behavior. The image suggests "defloration," but no comparable Latinate word exists in Middle Dutch, which uses "ontmaagden" just as classical Latin uses "devirginare." The word "deflorare" turns up only in the Patristic Period of Latin Literature and in Medieval Latin.[4] With the appearance of the word, the image of the flower for virginity becomes current and very soon, picking flowers ("bloemen lesen") is also used more generally for making love. This seems to be the meaning here, since in her fable Sandrine stresses that it occurred only once ("And never another [flower] thereafter, / And never more than that one" 499–500). In his response, the hunting knight picks up on that, noting that "One blossom is as nothing," and that many more are still on the tree, promising noble fruit (lines 506–515).

As we have seen, the elements of Sandrine's fable can be said to be firmly within the sphere of courtly discourse. Although the language may be coded, however, the fable itself is alive and flexible enough to be retold in slightly different form the second time. (When Lancelot's messenger Reynold comes searching for Sandrine to tell her that Lancelot wants to marry her, she retells the fable but adds a few lines to the ending in which the falcon returns to look for the blossom tree and, to his great sorrow, cannot find it.) In fact, the entire play shows a tendency to use coded language that alternates with breaks in the code, drawing attention to the discourse and turning it into a source of meaning on its own, just as courtly situations and courtly exchange, in a subtle way, suggest character and inner nobility.

The key words in the Middle Dutch courtly discourse are the adjectives *hovesch* ("belonging to the *hof,* the court") or its synonym, *noyael,* and their opposites, the adjective *dorperlike* and the nouns *dorpernie* and *dorperheit* ("the quality of the *dorper,* or peasant"). The force of these words is similar to that of *vilain* and *courtois,* as used in medieval French and discussed by Katherine Gravdal; originating in the contrast between behavior at the court and that of the peasants, the words *vilain* and *dorperlike* later came to denote lack of manners and lack of morality (Gravdal 12–19). In the play of *Lancelot of Denmark,* less than 1,000 lines long, *hovesch* or the adverb *hoveschelike* occur ten times, *dorper, dorpernie* or *dorperheit* eight times, indicating that at least part of the courtship takes place in rather formulaic terms. Lancelot approaches Sandrine with many phrases from the courtly register. He prays God to protect them from the gossip of the *niders,* the jealous spies of courtly lovers, who like to "sing evil tales" (58–63), but soon he forgets himself and promises her a jewel if she goes inside with him. Later, he begs her to come with him to "play in the green valley / where the little birds sing their songs / and the flowers stand in the green / . . . all without dorpherheit"—clearly a contradiction in terms. Sandrine points out that "many were tricked by believing too lightly," and that she would trust no one on earth not to take advantage of her if they went playing in the woods. Lancelot, however, refuses to listen to her and swears he loves her too much to dishonor her.

Sandrine leaves to avoid gossip, and Lancelot bemoans her resistance until his mother comes to scold him for loving below his rank. Here, Lancelot becomes ideological. He has "often heard it recited," he says, that love's power does not pay attention to riches and birth, but cares only for equality of the heart. These are noble words, but the reference to *recited* allows us to see them as part of a code, rather than a lived experience or sentiment. His mother disregards his courtly formulas and is brutally practical. She holds out the promise that he will have her at his *will.* This is often the word used for having someone in one's power, or for sexual possession, so that the suggestion of rape is clear.[5] Further down, the mother says: "Seldise hebben in uwer *ghewelt* . . ." 'When you have her in your power' (263). In her detailed instructions to Lancelot on how to behave when he has Sandrine in his room, the mother uses an even more ambiguous expression: "Als ghi . . . / Hebt ghedaen al u ghevoech." (238–39) "Sijn ghevoech doen" is used for the satisfaction of basic urges, ranging from "following one's desire" to "relieving oneself."[6] After he has "relieved himself," Lancelot is instructed to tell Sandrine that he is as fed up with her as if he ate seven sides of bacon, then to turn away from her and go to sleep. Lancelot fully recognizes the *dorpernie* (vileynie) of this behavior, but persuades himself that people often say things they do not mean. Just as he refused to really hear Sandrine's objections, so he now refuses to hear the crassness of his mother's proposal, persuading himself that Sandrine will understand his intentions rather than his words.

By contrast, the hunter-knight, though he starts off with the same verbal flourishes as Lancelot, is soon touched by Sandrine's words showing her inner nobility. At first, he had asked only if she was waiting to meet someone who "might be of such power / That it would be a danger to speak to you" (420–21), but he now declares his love and asks for her name. When she turns out to be of noble birth, he proposes marriage. There is a curious blend of idealism and practicality in this scene, which connects it with the urban class-consciousness of its audience: whereas Lancelot had expressed the fairy-tale notion that love conquers all (though responding to his baser urges without a qualm), the hunter-knight has more realistic ideas. His attraction to Sandrine is immediate, but the new information that she is the daughter of a squire is no less welcome, because it clearly makes marriage an even more acceptable option. Sandrine, too, is practical about marriage. She had acknowledged that Lancelot would not marry her, but, though she loved him, she would not be his or any man's mistress. The need to tell the knight about her rape arises from [medieval] society's double standard on sexual experience.

Historians generally state that whatever tolerance for the free expression of sexuality existed applied only to men: when men married, they married virgins; when married women were raped, the crime was more likely to be treated as adultery, which constituted theft in regard to the husband. In his *Tafel vanden Kersten Ghelove* (Table of the Christian Faith) Dirk of Delft, court chaplain of the Bavarian court in The Hague, emphasizes the seriousness of adultery, arguing that "adultery cries out [to Heaven] as murder does. Abel's blood cried for God's vengeance from the earth and all the adulterors' blood, which they pour into foreign vessels, calls for vengeance. Furthermore, adultery is theft and murder, for when our Lord God gave His commands to the Jews, written on stone tablets, He put the injunction against adultery in between theft and murder, as if [to say that] they all deserved the gallows or the wheel" (Summer piece XXXVII, 209–16).

Discussions of rape in archival records, as well as in literature, show a wide range of punishments for the crime. Both canon and secular law are strong in their condemnation: "The punishment for abduction or rape of a woman who called for help was beheading," quotes David Nicholas in his *Domestic Life of a Medieval City: Women, Children and the Family in Fourteenth Century Ghent*

(54). Nicholas, however, also shows that the lines between abduction, rape, and seduction (the word used most often is medieval Dutch *ontscaken,* meaning "to cause to lose chastity, to abduct") were extremely unclear, and that these actions "were far less severely punished in practice than the law prescribed" (59). In the rape of a virgin, the records repeatedly refer to the fact that loss of virginity ruins a girl's chance for a marriage, and this, presumably, frequently led to the arrangement of a marriage between the rapist and his victim, saving his life and her future.

If these circumstances led Sandrine to reveal her rape to the hunter-knight, why did she choose to do so in the genteel, courtly indirectness of her fable? As we saw, the courtship of Lancelot started in that same mode, although Lancelot did not always maintain it and did not behave in accordance with his words. This discrepancy between Lancelot's words and actions has been noted by other critics (Van Dijk 110–11). We might see Sandrine's courtly tone as a somewhat old-fashioned gesture. From the thirteenth- and fourteenth-century adaptations of courtly romances, we know that the town elites started out reading courtly literature for entertainment and role models, but that elements of a more bourgeois morality soon changed their tone and ideology. Sandrine rejects not just Lancelot but his whole world by leaving the court altogether, yet she still phrases her delicate tale in refined, courtly words, thus preserving the polite tone of her conversation with the hunter-knight (who remains without a name). In accepting his proposal, Sandrine notes several times that the knight has spoken *hoveschen woorden* (courteous words) and seems *hovesch van herten* (courteous in his heart), that is, that his courteousness is not just external but shows a fundamental decency. In his acceptance of her in spite of the rape, he acts from that decency rather than from older concepts of honor. Although the hunter-knight starts out in the courtly but also predatory style, representing lovemaking as a hunt, in the course of their conversation, he develops a more pragmatic approach. Later on, as Orlanda Lie has also pointed out, their marriage is described by one of the knight's retainers in terms that are much more in accordance with bourgeois ideals (Lie 200–16):

> Want si es hem soe ghetrouwe
> Ende ghehoersam ende onder daen. (674–75)

> (And she is so loyal to him
> Obedient and docile.)

But most striking is the change in Sandrine's own words when she responds to Reynold message from Lancelot that he wants to marry her, after all:

> Reinout vrient dat spel is uut
> Segt hem dat hi een ander beghinne
> Ic en gave niet om lanseloets minne
> Een gers dat uut ter eerden gaet. (726–29)

> (Reynold, that game is up!
> Tell him to start another.
> I don't care for Lancelot's love
> As much as a blade of grass.)

When Reynold tries to persuade her to change her mind, she responds:

> Reinout dat moet sijn een blijft
> Want ic ben eerlijc ende wale ghehout
> Ende hebbe enen edelen man ghetrout
> Dien ic minne boven alle die leven
> Hem en willic niet begheven
> Al ware lanseloet alsoe rike
> Dat hi ware hectors van troyen gelike
> Ende dat hi hadde van gode te lone
> Dat hi droeghe die selve crone
> Die die coninc alexander droech
> Soe en ware hi nochtan niet *mijn ghevoech*.
>   (744–54; emphasis mine)

> (Reynold, that's out of the question!
> I am wedded in good faith
> And have married a noble man,
> Whom I love above all men,
> And I do not want to forsake him.
> Even if Lancelot were so mighty
> As to be the equal of Hector of Troy;
> If he had, by God's grace,
> The very self-same crown
> That belonged to king Alexander,
> He would still not be to my taste.)

In accepting the "new" kind of marriage of the urban bourgeoisie, a marriage based on mutual respect rather than rigid rules on social rank (which prevented Lancelot from marrying her), she has adopted a direct, blunt, almost crude form of speech totally different from Lancelot's empty flourishes and her own veiled words in the fable. The words she uses, "ware hi . . . niet mijn *ghevoech*" (he would not be my taste, my lust), are exactly the offensive words used by Lancelot's mother (who told her son what to say after he had "relieved himself" (Hebt ghedaen al u ghevoech) (239). This is perhaps a bit extreme, but satisfies our sense of poetic justice as much as the end of the play itself. Lancelot dies of regret—though still blaming his mother rather than himself—and Sandrine lives happily ever after.[7]

Notes

1. This study uses the Louise van Kammen edition. Unless otherwise noted, translations are mine.
2. Walsh's introduction gives an excellent overview of the critical debate.
3. Poem 51, discussed by Oostrom (103–5).
4. Lewis and Short, s.v. deflorare; Niermeyer, s.v. deflorare.
5. Verwijs and Verdam, s.v. *wille* 5, 6, 7.
6. Verwijs and Verdam, s.v. *ghevoech*.
7. My studies of the *Abel* plays started during the 1991 NEH Summer Seminar for College Teachers, "Shakespeare and the Native Dramatic Tradition." I am grateful to the National Endowment for the Humanities for allowing me to participate in the Seminar, and to Professor Martin Stevens and the participants in the Seminar for many stimulating discussions. Dr. Mary-Jo Arn has made valuable editorial comments.

Works Cited

Abele Spelen (Abel plays). Ed. Louise van Kammen. Amsterdam: Athenaeum/ Polak & Van Gennep, 1968.

Andreas Capellanus: see Walsh.

Anrooij, W. van. "Bijdrage tot een geografische situering van het handschrift Van Hulthem" (Contribution to a Geographical Placement of the Van Hulthem Manuscript.) *Spiegel der Letteren* 28 (1986):225–33.

——— and A. M. J. van Buuren. " 's Levens felheid in een band: het Handschrift-Van Hulthem" (Life's Sharpness in One Volume: The Van Hulthem Manuscript). In *Op Belofte van Profit,* H. Pleij, ed., 184–99.

Dijk, Hans van. "*Lanseloet van Denemerken,* One of the *Abele Spelen* in the Hulthem Ms." In *Popular Drama in Northern Europe in the Later Middle Ages: A Symposium,* ed. Fleming G. Andersen et al. Odensee: Odensee University Press, 1986. 101–12.

Dirk van Delft. *Tafel vanden Kersten Ghelove* (Table of the Christian faith). 4 vols. Ed. Father L. M. Daniëls, O.P. Ons Geestelijk Erf Publications 4–7. Antwerp: Ons Geestelijk Erf, 1937–39.

Frederick II of Hohenstaufen. *The Art of Falconry* (De Arte Venandi cum Avibus).

Tr. Casey A. Wood and F. Marjorie Fyfe. Stanford: Stanford University Press, 1943.

Gloriant: see *Abele Spelen.*

Gravdal, Katherine. *Vilain and Courtois: Transgressive Parody in French Literature of the Twelfth and Thirteenth Century.* Lincoln: University of Nebraska Press, 1989.

Die Haager Liederhandschrift (Hague Song Manuscript). Ed. E. F. Kossmann. The Hague: Martinus Nijhoff, 1940.

Hatto, A. T. "Das Falkenlied des Kürenbergers" (The Falconsong of Der von Kürenberg). *Euphorion* 53 (1959):20–23.

Lewis, Charlton, and Charles Short. *A New Latin Dictionary.* New York: American Book Company, 1907.

Lie, Orlanda S. H. "Het abel spel van Lanseloet van Denemerken in het handschrift Van Hulthem: Hoofse tekst of stadsliteratuur?" (The Abel Play of Lancelot of Denmark: Courtly Text or Urban Literature?). In *Op Belofte van Profijt,* ed. H. Pleij. 200–216.

Das Nibelungenlied. 21st ed. Ed. Helmut de Boor after Karl Bartsch. Wiesbaden: Brockhaus, 1979.

Nicholas, David. *Domestic Life of a Medieval City: Women, Children and the Family in Fourteenth Century Ghent.* Lincoln and London: University of Nebraska Press, 1985.

Niermeyer, Jan Frederik. *Mediae Latinitatis lexicon minus.* Leiden: Brill, 1976.

Oostrom, Frits Pieter van. *Court and Culture: Dutch Literature, 1350–1450.* Tr. Arnold J. Pomerans. Berkeley: University of California Press, 1992.

Pleij, Herman. *De Sneeuwpoppen van 1511: Stadscultuur in de Late Middeleeuwen* (The Snowmen of 1511: Urban Culture in the Late Middle Ages). Amsterdam: Meulenhoff, 1988.

———, ed. *Op Belofte van Profijt: Stadsliteratuur en Burgermoraal in de Nederlandse Letterkunde van de Middeleeuwen* (On Promise of Profit: Urban Literature and Burgher Morality in the Dutch Literature of the Middle Ages). Amsterdam: Prometheus, 1991.

Thiébaux, Marcelle. *The Stag of Love: The Chase in Medieval Literature.* Ithaca and London: Cornell University Press, 1974.

Vanhamme, M. *Bruxelles: de Bourg Rural à Cité Mondiale.* (Brussels: From Rural Borough to Metropolis). Antwerp and Brussels: Mercurion, 1968.

Verwijs, E., and J. Verdam *Middelnederlandsch Woordenboek.* 11 vols. 's-Gravenhage: Nijhoff, 1885–1952.

Walsh, P. G., ed. *Andreas Capellamus on Love.* London: Duckworth, 1982.

Wapnewski, Peter. "Des Kürenbergers Falkenlied" (Der von Kürenberg's Falconsong) in *Eurphorion* 53 (1959):1–19.

Ockham, Chaucer, and the Emergence of Modern Poetics

BURT KIMMELMAN

WILLIAM OF OCKHAM'S CONTRIBUTION TO THE INTELLECTUAL LIFE OF fourteenth-century England can hardly be exaggerated. Indeed, a likely gauge of his impact on thinkers of his time is the influence he has enjoyed ever since. His "patience and remorseless" application of principles of logic to the nature of statements, as Ernest Moody has put it (413), led to the emergence of Newtonian science more than three hundred years later.[1] It is also fair to say that Ockham's dismantling of Aristotelianism, his "merciless criticism" of alleged proofs of theological beliefs (Moody 432), is vividly remembered by philosophy today. In large, Ockham nurtured a philosophical tendency that began as early as Anselm's recognition of any statement's intrinsic worth; in and of themselves, Anselm held, utterances possessed coherence, without having to signify objective reality.[2] This inquiry into the nature of language per se continued and deepened with the speculative grammarians, the terminists, *modistae* and *moderni*. Ockham's timing could not have been better—to take nothing away from his originality and tenacity—and he remains a pivotal figure in the histories of logic and epistemology.

Whatever the personal attributes that drew him to the notion of language, and to his intense engagement with the idea that language was a key measure of the universe, Ockham was to share this fascination with persons near to him in time other than theologians. Geoffrey Chaucer lived a generation later; his poetry—in its ideology not too distant from what Ockham had written—also anticipated the modern world. The *Canterbury Tales'* true-to-life portraits of pilgrims are remarkable for their roundness—the portraits are whole, the characterizations detailed and particularized. Legion claims that modern literary realism is invented in the *Tales* can only benefit from the acknowledgment of such invention as having been beholden to Chaucer's profoundly personal, philosophical, and theological views—views, perhaps surprisingly often,

177

in sympathy with Ockham's, and to be found throughout the Chaucer corpus, ever present and detectable as a kind of genetic code.

Chaucer's cosmology was that of a late-fourteenth-century man; yet we may understand it to have been unlike anything normally associated with the Middle Ages when it is located within the larger context of the nominalist-realist debate that had been rekindled by Ockham and cast in a contemporary light by others Chaucer knew or could have known, such as Robert Holcot, Ralph Strode, Thomas Bradwardine, and John Wyclif. In this light, it hardly seems coincidental that Ockham, the nominalist, and Chaucer, a fervent philosopher of language, place great emphasis on the importance to epistemology of experience. To be sure, Chaucer's poetry never asks absolutely Ockhamist questions, even though it was written during a time when people like Holcot were being strongly persuaded by what Ockham had had to say; and Chaucer's friend Strode, a realist and Ockham reactionary like his associate Wyclif, took up a number of anti-realist positions after 1375 (Jeffrey "Chaucer," 111; see also Bennett). But even when no philosophy is openly espoused, Chaucer's vocabulary clearly partakes of the nominalist controversy. There are to be found in his poems, of course, ubiquitous discussions concerning the nature and significance of experience—how its very force can present the hope of genuinely knowing, of genuinely *being* in the world. These discussions argue for situating Chaucer within the sphere of the controversy.[3]

Chaucer's discourse, moreover, furnishes us with a fundamental insight into his poetics. The degree of attention Chaucer paid to the question of experience, particularly firsthand experience as a conduit for arriving at truth, is of extraordinary importance in trying to understand his major literary innovation, the persona, especially as this persona developed from poem to poem; this development charts his experiments with and ultimate turn away from allegory, that medieval poesis par excellence. It is no accident that, in each successive poem, Chaucer's persona increasingly resides outside any allegorical framework.[4] Keeping Ockham's ideas in mind, what becomes strikingly clear is that Chaucer employs his persona to carry on an implicit criticism of allegory as both a poetic and an epistemological form.

Many studies of Chaucer's use of a persona to achieve a variety of literary ends have been carried out. None, however, has thoroughly analyzed the impact of contemporary intellectual theories precisely on his development of that memorable figure, Geffrey. This oversight is regrettable on two counts. The first has to do with our understanding of the persona's role in a poet's poetics. In Chaucer's poems, his persona maintains a markedly philosophical discussion. Either Geffrey or an anonymous narrator questions and offers opinions about how truth can be obtained—through direct experience, hearsay, or authority and books. This discussion, at least implicitly, interrogates the viability of one or another rhetorical form, at the same time as it is ultimately asking a singular, Ockhamist question: What constitutes direct experience? Second, as I have already suggested, the persona's role leads us to a consideration of Chaucer's use or progressive abandonment of allegory. The Chaucerian persona's protracted discussions of epistemology—considering that nominalists emphasize experience as a ground for making truth statements—reveal its author's attitudes toward allegory or, perhaps it would be more apt to say toward a modern poetics that we have come to know as literary (not philosophical) realism. Chaucer's realism requires the Ockhamist conditions for direct experience and therefore is in opposition to the essential impulse of allegory, for allegory asks readers to look beyond the significance of the immediate, the direct, to an other meaning.[6]

Here, we might usefully recall Walter Benjamin's dictum that "allegories are in the realm of thoughts, what ruins are in the realm of things" (Miller 362–63), a modern idea but one that is not completely alien to the sensibility Chaucer inherited. As Laurie Finke writes while drawing a connection between Benjamin and Augustine, an "unbridgeable" hiatus exists between words and things and likewise experience and its representation. Benjamin's

"ruinous" theory of allegory insinuates itself into Augustinian theory (and theology) by reminding us of allegory's difference from the "spirit" it purports to recover. The meaning and truth that allegory seeks to represent are, by the deferred nature of the representation, present only as fragments. . . . Allegory, as it tries to incarnate the absent signified that would authorize meaning and truth, testifies to their absence. The more language seeks to clarify (literally to illuminate or free from darkness and gloom) meaning, the more it reveals the void, the darkness of its own reflexivity. (Finke 56–57)[7]

Allowing for these two temporal, if not theoretical, poles—Benjamin and Augustine—which effectively bracket the fourteenth century, the question we need to ask is, how does Chaucer's persona mediate the problems presented by language generally and allegory specifically? To answer this question, we must first examine the persona as it functions structurally, since Chaucer's work exhibits an intimate relationship between what the persona says and how it is said.

As is true of any poet's, Chaucer's persona is a synechdoche. Evolving over the course of a poet's oeuvre, a poet's persona comes to represent all of the author's literary enterprise—not merely the particular poem in which that figure resides. Chaucer must have become acutely sensitive to this dynamic. In the Prologue to the *Legend of Good Women,* for example, surely we are being asked to evaluate Chaucer's persona in the context of his relationship to other elements of the poem, but also to all of Chaucer's other works that contain other versions of that persona. His defense against Cupid's attack on Chaucer's writings, as well, requires us to contemplate what Chaucer has attempted to do overall—that is, what Chaucer's theory of poetry has come to be. The persona, therefore, becomes the poet's essential gesture and the emblem of his or her vision.

Poets who begin to write with an eye toward a totality of their verse, beyond any immediate poem, will increasingly regard the formulation of the persona as that most crucial poetic gambit. In all likelihood, Chaucer's formulation owed a great deal to the early medieval tradition of the poetic debate. As Jon Whitman explains,

> [T]he adversaries [in a poetic debate] share a common frame of reference, that on some level they both contribute to a single continuity. Indeed, one of the salient features of the poetic debate is its effort to show contraries complementing, rather than simply opposing,[8] each other, a feature that leads many debates to end either without a clear "winner" or with some kind of reconciliation. . . . A more complex, cosmological approach to the strategy of interdependence, based on broader philosophic sources and principles, will develop by the twelfth century, but already in the poetic debate, there is a constant tendency to turn metaphoric figures into metonymic terms of a larger whole. (142)

The relationship between poem and poem's speaker becomes especially compelling when, as is true for Chaucer, the speaker contemplates the nature of knowledge, language, poetry, and even the writing of the very poem from which he or she speaks. Thus, we can say that Chaucer is involved in constructing a metapoetics.

This writerly strategy—the persona as a tool for achieving self-reference—represents a fully developed epistemological system, a system that originated at least as early as the troubadours and Chrétien; it was developed by Dante and was fully evolved by Chaucer's contemporary, Langland, whose representative figure not only bears his name, Will, but also that of its poem's theme, *voluntas* (see Kimmelman). Chaucer's version of this persona is unique, however, since he developed it in quite another direction, which is readily apparent in comparison with the Dante figure in the *Commedia*. Geffrey often has the responsibility thrust upon him of having to defend his author's achievements, the past poems Chaucer has written, even the very poem in which such a defense can take place—as occurs in the Prologue but elsewhere too. In effect, this persona is speaking out at us from the poem, speaking out about the nature of poetry, and more largely, about the nature of language itself. Chaucer is particularly teaching us how a poet's persona is that literary device which quintessentially stands for what is basic in a poet's body of work.

Indeed, rather than being a mere emblem, the persona can be fashioned into a theoretical voice that reveals its author's notions of the world. Chaucer's persona—in this instance, like Dante's figures, as well as the figures of others—is specifically constructed out of the tension between a supposedly true or rather real and an ostensibly fictional, that is, literary, self. Under such a condition, a reader might view the persona as the very sign of the poetry embodying it, or the reverse, of the poetry it embodies. And Chaucer is forcing a distinction between two selves—a distinction best appreciated in the context of Paul de Man's claim that trying to separate autobiography and fiction is ultimately a fruitless task (70)—for Geffrey both is and is not his *auctor*.

Chaucer's poetry is most memorable, arguably, because of the tension established therein between the elegance and reach of its ideas and the expression of them by a speaker whose reach apparently is limited and whose bumbling antics are at times quite comical. In contrast to de Man, Jacques Derrida has recently proposed the notion of a "fabulous invention"—which is useful in exploring Chaucer's poetic—apoeticizing that

> becomes the invention of truth, of its truth as fable, of the fable of truth, the truth of truth *as fable*. And of that which in the fable depends on language (*fari,* fable). It is the impossible mourning of truth: in and out through the word. For you have seen it well, if the mourning is not announced by the breaking of the mirror [i.e., the ostensibly fictionalized text that reflects actuality], but consists in the mirror, if it comes with specularization, well then, the mirror comes to be itself solely through the intercession of the word. It is an invention and an intervention of the word. . . . (332)

In Derrida's terms, Geffrey becomes Chaucer's imperfect mirror image of himself. And this persona does in fact speculate about truth—or rather, he often blindly stumbles over it in his attempts to find the true words he desires to describe his experiences; invariably these experiences are characterized by a contemplation of both the power and the futility of language. Chaucer's question, which was Augustine's, is: How can words comprehend truth? What question could be of greater interest to a poet? Chaucer's mode of inquiry can be excruciatingly funny, but we need to note how seriously busy Geffrey is, as he keenly reflects the dramatically intellectual changes of his time. These changes have everything to do with, poetry aside, a widening gulf between theology and philosophy.

The fourteenth century's conceptualization of the divine deepened with Ockham; however, it had also taken on new limits, and the same can be said for individual human potential. In Chaucer's time, the divine had become more awesome, but Ockham's form of nominalism had also set the individual adrift in his or her moral life, lacking any surety in absolute truths, with the assumption that the will and intelligence were finite and ultimately weak, and with the perplexity that is a given in such a circumstance; logically, for example, God could withhold grace from an individual despite the fact of his or her good works, or He could command a person to hate or to disobey Him.[9] This complex of beliefs gave rise to a wealth of great literati—Chaucer and Langland, the *Pearl* poet, and the author who composed the mystical "Cloud of Unknowing." The fact is that, in the face of what, for Ockham, became a severely limited mortal world, one in which God could do anything including withholding grace, the best a *viator* such as Geffrey or Langland's Will could do in striving for salvation was simply his best. Figures like Geffrey and Will deeply resonate their authors' beliefs—despite, perhaps, what these personae at times have to say. In any event, it is the poetic figure of the persona—in Chaucer's case, it is virtually a constant, predictable in its resemblance to him and in its depiction of weak will and weak wit—which provides a useful way of critically entering into and essentializing a body of poetry. This persona, employing the very lexis that comprises a set of beliefs both poetical and philosophical, will enunciate those beliefs either directly or indirectly. Ultimately, then, we can say that the persona, as the metasign that emerges from the poetry itself, is what a reader, after reflection, may most recall, may most vividly have been impressed by over time in the reading of a poet's oeuvre—and it is what leads that reader into the rich and problematic world of philosophy.

The connection between philosophy and poetry was abundant and provocative in Chaucer's time, as is typified by the development of the persona in fourteenth-century England, which could but only have been influenced by the Ockhamist debate. Thus, considered in terms of the nominalists' emphasis on experience and Geffrey's continual weighing of it against authority, it is fair to conclude that Chaucer was trying to tell us about the nature of allegory and his choice to form an alternative poetry,[10] as if he were saying that allegory was not a useful poetics. Geffrey may have said as much. But, whatever he may want to convey, what becomes obvious when looking through the Ockhamist lens is that this persona vitiates the potency of the allegorical form.[11] Of all literary strategies, Chaucer's employment of Geffrey—which was elaborate and serial from poem to poem—compellingly establishes a basis for comparison of fourteenth-century literature and philosophy or theology, and opens the door to the exploration of a possible relationship between poetic form and philosophical formulation. There are two loci for such comparison; both are central factors in the contemporary nominalism.

First is Ockham's critique of his received theology and philosophy, which focuses on the illogicality of postulates that accept the possibility of speaking about theological truths yet fail to demonstrate how such statements might be made; the ultimate criterion for ruling out this possibility is that of experience. Ockham and his followers never denied the existence of divine truth; for them, divine force(s) became richer and more powerful than had previously been thought. The Ockhamists did insist, however, that such truths were not demonstrable. Ockham had driven a wedge between mundane and divine knowledge by insisting on the validity of experience in order for there to be ontological plenitude. In its extreme, this insistence means that immanence, universals, and the like, cannot be said to exist—with the exception that there can be a faith that they do, unless they can be empirically shown through their actual experience or what Ockham called *intuitive knowledge*.

Second, Ockham defines his premise through an examination of the nature of linguistic terms and thereby through a rejection of the thirteenth century's and Aristotle's notion of species. It is one thing to know an object by experiencing it directly, by experiencing it sensually; it is another to know of it in its abstract sense. Ockham's ideas are a renovation of what had been proposed by Duns Scotus, who had introduced the theory of intuitive knowledge. Scotus allowed for abstract cognition based on the concept of separately existing entities that were likenesses of any directly apprehended object—what Aquinas, Bacon, Scotus, and others called *species*. Ockham, however, simply denied the notion of abstraction as dependent on species. Instead, he held that abstraction is a function of the object per se in an indirect form, which occurs when different acts of experience are repeated (*Quodlibeta septem* I q. 3). Ockham's "razor" did away with any entities that might have existed as separate from that which could be directly experienced, except when there was a memory of an object or act or otherwise a familiarity from a repetition *(habitus)* of an act—since abstract knowledge could not guarantee any evidence of an object or act. In short, he eliminated any intermediary entities between the intellect and the object of knowledge. Any sign, then (and, here, we should note in passing the importance to Chaucer of the sign), could but only be rememorative and was not needed for there to be knowledge, even as it reproduced knowledge, and, so, an "immediacy" of a "subject-object relationship [was] affirmed" (Tabarroni 209). Ockham makes this point in his examination of the difference between an object and its representation based on a priori sensual perception; in doing so, he throws the concept of species (for example, "secundum ponentes speciem" etc., below) into doubt:

> Item, repraesentatum debet esse prius cognitum: aliter repraesentans nunquam duceret in cognitionem repraesentati tanquam in simile. Exemplum: statua Herculis nunquam duceret me in cognitionem Herculis nisi prius vidissem Herculem; nec aliter possem scire utrum statua sit sibi similis aut non. Sed secundum ponentes speciem, species est aliquid praevium omni actui intellegendi obiectum, igitur non potest poni propter reraesentationem obiecti.

> (A representation [of an object] ought to exist prior to an acquaintanceship [with the object]: differently, representing would never lead to acquaintanceship as a representation unless through resemblance [between the object and its representation]. For example: a statue of Hercules would never lead me to a familiarity with Hercules unless I had seen Hercules first; neither could there be knowledge [of Hercules merely by seeing his statue] whether or not his image might be similar [to him]. And as for the positing of a species . . . a species [of an object] is other than prior to all acts of perceiving an object; indeed [species] can not be posited as prior to a representation of an object.) (*Reportatio* II qq. 12–13, p. 274, ll. 7–14).[12]

This treatment of Hercules' statue or image demonstrates Ockham's refusal, on the basis of an assiduous application of logic to his examination of language, to grant that names (or other representations) in and of themselves of entities were ontologically grounded. Ockham came to the conclusion that what can be known and spoken about is only the experiential entity, as a singular fact.

Ockham's epistemological construct is typified by the Chaucerian persona, a narrator who precisely wrestles with the question of experience and knowledge. Often a character, this fictional personage describes what he sees, hears, and feels. Geffrey is both witness and reporter of his experiences, and he is virtually obsessed by the question of whether experience—Ockham's *intuitive knowledge*—can adequately convey the truth of existence. Through Geffrey, in other words, Chaucer maintains an ongoing epistemological discussion, from one poem to the next, regarding the possibility of knowing what is real and true, and, too, of being able to speak and, importantly, to write about such truth. As if to make sure that the reader does not miss the philosophical point, Chaucer's persona is presented as being either mentally slow or reluctant to live at the center of the events he is reporting. As well, he often makes the claim that he is in fact "only" the rehearser of such events, that, in a sense, this is his fate, and that he doesn't necessarily understand the deeper nature of those events although he would like to if only there could be an ideal world in which such understanding might occur. These are Chaucer's Ockhamist underpinnings; they are profoundly serious undertones of a poetic discourse—which could have contributed to Chaucer's late medieval reputation, advanced by Thomas Usk and others, as being a philosophical poet.

Geffrey's attitudes and actions (or inactions), all the same, are underwritten by another crucial tenet of Ockhamism—the role of *voluntas* in the attempt to achieve salvation. The very credence Ockham placed in the structure and force of logic compelled him to conceive of a universe of radical contingency, which meant there had to be a division of the universe into two worlds, *potentia absoluta* and *potentia ordinata;* one was a world of God's potential power, the other of actuality. Thus, the central nominalist question became one of casuality—whether or not there could be a demonstrable causal relationship between these two worlds. Ockham wrote that the only way of establishing a causal connection between one thing and another is by observing that, when one thing takes place, another also takes place simultaneously in proximity to that first thing. But because God's enactment of miracles is logically possible, the furnishing of absolute proof of causal transactions becomes impossible (*Sententiae* II:8–5). Here, Ockham is once again relying on experience as the only sure, if limited, ruler for establishing truth. This criterion also allows him to speak of liberty of will and of an individual's capacity to exercise will (cf. *Sent.,* d. 38, q. 1;

Moody 434–35). That the will is free, though, cannot be reasonably demonstrated, "because every reason proving this assumes something equally unknown as is the conclusion, or less known." Nevertheless, this freedom is knowable evidentially, through experience, since "a man experiences the fact that however much his reason dictates some action, his will can will, or not will, this act" (*Quodlibeta* I, q. 16; Moody 434).

The recognition that there can be, evidently, freedom of individual will, again helps to explain Chaucer's Geffrey, who in terms of both intention and intelligence usually finds himself in circumstances that for him are overwhelming. Ockham and others viewed wit and will as virtually synonymous; Chaucer dramatizes this dyad. It is likely that he embraced the Ockhamist idea of the liberty of the will, which was nothing less than a moral ground where human dignity, goodness and responsibility could exist (cf. *Quod.* III, q. 13); therefore, the will was more important than thinking, even as wit and will were intimately intertwined. In a poem like *Troilus and Crysede* the narrator, not without sympathy for his tale, tells us that he "weeps" as he "writes" (cf. 17)[13] perhaps in part because he is merely "the sorwful instrument" (1.10) who wonders whether he will have both wit and will enough to carry out his task of rehearsing the lovers' tragedy.

Of all Chaucer's many other works (in passing, I must mention "Sir Thopas" and "Melibee" as poems where the persona is prominent), two especially set out a philosophical position bespoken by a textual representation of Chaucer himself: his "Retraction" to the *Tales,* and the Prologue. Each can be understood as an *ars poetica* that reflects back specifically on what Chaucer has written. Each considers the worth of his industry in a theological and philosophical light. Both texts address the issue of authorial intention, a motif echoing the Ockhamist position regarding free will and decisions. And both serve to foreground a meditation on the nature of fiction.

In the "Retraction," Chaucer repudiates those works that the modern world most prizes for the dynamic they present comprised of ostensible fiction and actual, experiential truth. Chaucer comments, significantly, that

> if ther be any thyng that displese [my readers], I prey hem also that they arrette it to the defaute of myn unkonnynge and nat to my wyl, that wolde ful fayn have seyd bettre if I hadde had konnynge. / For oure book seith, "All that is writen is writen for oure doctrine," and that is myn entente (1082–83).

In this passage we find the typical Chaucerian ploy of equivocation. Is this Chaucer speaking, or his persona? In the Prologue, the answer ultimately may be that both are speaking.[14] The Prologue is poetry and on its surface is meant to be taken as "playful." In this prose Retraction, reading carefully, we can detect the author's deepest concerns, those that will help construct a picture of the "real" Chaucer and will help us see below the surface of his verse. We should not underestimate the speaker's dependence on the explanation that, if he has sinned in what he has done, this is due to his "unkonnynge" and "nat to [his] wyl." Using the excuse of his "unkonnynge," Chaucer "retracts" several of his works, not least among them the *Canterbury Tales*. In the words of David Williams, Chaucer is taking back the work

> he is in the very act of disseminating. The paradox of an author denying what he is simultaneously saying, or unwriting what he is writing, suggests in the Chaucerian context a [literary] realist theory of fiction in which two intentions are operating at the same time—an intentional representation and a communicating one—the one put forward, the other withdrawn. But the relation of these directions is binary, like the ontological relation of universal to particular, and as poetics it suggests a theory of fiction, primarily representational, in which the intention to communicate is variously absent and present. (Williams 90–91)

Fiction merely represents. Inhering in the fictional text, a text of particulars, is the nominalist recognition that communication is limited and that the will is fallible, although one must exercise it as best as one can.

But what is it to say that fiction is "mere" representation? As pertinent as Williams's recognition is to the *Tales,* it is more so to the Prologue, where Chaucer deliberately sets out the parameters for a persona he had been working on for decades. The question of God's active presence in the palpable universe constitutes the Prologue's underlying philosophical dialogue as in all of Chaucer's dream poems. The dream poem genre is a more than likely arena for the testing of a doctrine that emphasizes the particulars of the world landscape but refuses to accept the possibility of a universal ordering of these "things" of the world, for the dream *visio* poses the aesthetic alternative to a wrestling with this dichotomy. The dream state's miraculous-like texture, if at times a sharpening force, may also blur or otherwise undermine differences between particularity and abstraction, time and eternity—the feasible as opposed to the supernatural. The dream vision poem returns to these distinctions, but from within the *visio* context, because this kind of poem must acknowledge a paradoxical and logically determinable truth, a truth that resides within the imaginative literary impulse—a truth that exists separately from the sensible, factual world. Thus, Chaucer will directly confront the conundrum of knowing through literature as opposed to firsthand, material experience (cf. Payne *Key,* 93 ff):

> But Goddes forbode but men shulde leve
> Wel more thyng than men han seyn with ye!
> Men shal nat wenen every thyng a lye
> For that he say it nat of yore ago.
> God wot a thyng is nevere the lesse so
> Thow every wyght ne may it nat yse.
> Bernard the monk ne say nat al, parde!
> Thanne mote we to bokes that we fynde,
> Thourgh whiche that olde thynges ben in mynde. . . .
> (Prologue "G" 10–18, cf. "F" 10–18)

The philosophical and problematical relationships between memory and the factual present, the *auctoritee* of books—history as well as imaginative literature—and experiential reality, eventually are resolved through a narrator's intuitive epiphany that a dream may allow: in the dream state alone, we are told, is humanity able to solve such riddles of nature as, for example, the possibility of communication, in the Prologue's case between man and beast. The marvelous qualities of dreams, and nature as well, will be celebrated through the joy readers find in the poem's persona when this character listens to and understands in his dream, as if with a new mind, the singing of birds:

> This song to herkenen I dide al myn entente,
> *For-why I mette I wiste what they* [the birds] *mente,*
> Tyl at the laste a larke song above:
> "I se," quod she, 'the myghty god of Love" [and so on].
> ("G" 139–42; my emphasis)

A reader bridges the real and surreal when witnessing the unfolding of events leading to the God of Love's comical indictment of the Chaucer figure, as well as Alceste's clever defense of his actions. Yet, to appreciate what transpires, the reader should remain aware throughout that Chaucer's narrator is dreaming, and the reader must participate in that dreaming. When partaking of the dream's fantasy, readers can then also intuit a sense of unity out of a contradictory actuality—that is, the experiential as well as the literary "reality."

Indeed, the introduction of gods, Cupid and Alceste, into an existential formula is announced by the fictive birds in the narrator's dream.[15] They are precisely like the birds he would encounter on his walks through the countryside in his worship of the daisy. And, after all, they are the same birds. One realizes this duplication in part because the settings and actions of visionary and waking states are closely aligned, although what the birds say and do are altered by dream consciousness. It is a wondrous and lovely scene. Nevertheless, and perhaps paradoxically, a more serious note is sounded at this juncture in the poem.

This same dream circumstance becomes the vehicle by which Chaucer's persona and the gods take up the problem of epistemology. It is because all that finally occurs in the Prologue happens within a *dream* framework that the very *real* problem of how *to know* by way of a cerebral process like literature may be discussed and synthesized. Literature enjoys a kinship with dream consciousness because, like dreaming, it is once removed from the experiential, physical, certainly objective reality that is its very "matter." So the problem of *matiere* becomes the *raison d'être,* if not necessarily the crux, of the God of Love's argument against what Chaucer has accomplished in his translations of poems that become the *Romaunt of the Rose* and *Troilus and Crysede:* Chaucer has "lat be" the "corn" and written the "chaff" of old "apreved storyes."

In Chaucer's poem, however, the answer the dream state allows will preclude philosophical dogma. Therefore the dream vision itself becomes emblematic of an imaginary, intuitive process that suggests the possible coherence as well as the complexity of "truth." Chaucer also understands that the dream vision represents language's idealized potential—a philosophically realist assumption—for which literature may strive because literature, like truth, is a complex affair, and if we try to make less of it than it is, if we try to simplify it, we will lose our way in what becomes meaningless language. Exactly and disjointedly so, the God of Love misreads Chaucer's translations; our narrator is accused of crimes against love. Confusion ensues, to be sorted out by Alceste who, like the daisy and rather than Cupid, is a symbol of love. Alceste becomes a figure, a poetic embodiment, the "apotheosis" of the dairy the persona was worshipping earlier in the poem (Payne 106); as part of his poet's revamping of the French *margerite* lyric genre, and as the deified flower, she also exists as an inscription, a symbol of intelligence.[16]

The God of Love perceives what Chaucer has written and, in fact, the phenomenon of *traductio* itself, through nominalist eyes. The irony in this circumstance is that he is a god who remains an icon for ideality in its interaction with the phenomenal world. To return to the larger philosophical problem this situation implies, by definition the God of Love is a contradiction in terms, for the nominalist question precludes ideality's capacity, paradoxically, to manifest itself. How, then, will the ideal be known through literature? In one sense, the poem's persona is being asked for the impossible when the God of Love misinterprets the *Troilus* and the *Romaunt of the Rose.* Even in a dream, this seems to be a bit much. Yet, for many thinkers of Chaucer's time, an awareness of the limitless ideal, the immortal, was still an actual possibility. Hugh of St. Victor, perpetuating a very old theme, had said that the whole sensible world is like a book written by the hand of God.[17] One need only "read" the book, an imaginative act Chaucer undertakes in his writing of the dream poems and the *Troilus.* Because the God of Love is incapable of *reading* Chaucer's translations correctly, however, he prefers them rewritten, to suit his own sensibility.

The method of knowing the world body in which writing itself becomes a form of "reading" the world is not an altogether new notion in the fourteenth century, although Chaucer occupies himself with it often enough. He begins the *Parlement of Foules,* for example, with an analogy that sees love as a truth to be attained through the struggle for craftsmanship, based on Horace's "ars longa, vita brevis:" (Everett 1 ff)

> The lyf so short, the craft so long to lerne,
> Th'assay so hard, so sharp the conquerynge,
> The dredful joye alwey that slit so yerne:
> Al this mene I by Love, . . . (1–4)

Like the skill in loving that helps define courtly love, Chaucer's "craft," or *makyng,* becomes the means by which he seeks a vital relationship with his environs, with the natural world and God. Thus, readers often encounter the perversion of *skyl* or craft—humanity out of synch with nature—a disorder such as occurs in the "Prologue" when a fowler is cursed by Spring's birds for betraying them:

> Now hadde th'atempre sonne al that releved,
> And clothed hym in grene al newe ageyn.
> The smale foules, of the seson fayn,

> That from the panter and the net ben skaped,
> Upon the foulere, that hem made awhaped
> In wynter, and distroyed hadde hire brod,
> In his dispit hem thoughte it dide hem good
> To synge of hym, and in here song despise
> The foule cherl that for his covetyse
> Hadde hem betrayed with his *sophistrye.*
> This was here song, "The foulere we defye" [. . .].
> (G 116–26; cf. F 128–38; my emphasis)

Although nominalist epistemology emphasizes the importance of the physical, the *potentia ordinata,* Chaucer might reasonably have included words as part of this natural, phenomenal world. Augustine's notion, to offer another example of miraculous thinking, is that words, perhaps even literature,[18] are signs indicating the knowledge of God, making truth pleasing, plain, and effective.[19] On the other hand, recalling the problem of abstraction or universals, "words" must also be the *names* for these things of the world and are therefore at variance from the physical universe. Chaucer surely had access to a branch of nominalism in the stoicism of Macrobius' commentary on the dream of Scipio Africanus, which asserts that "every word has a true meaning" (*Somnium* 20.1); this would mean that, for Chaucer, words may have possessed their ontological realities after all. Russell Peck writes that Chaucer

> is profoundly interested in the moral implications of nominalistic questions. Dorigen will gladly leave the fine points of disputation to the clerks [*viz.* her complaint to "Eterne God" in the *Franklin's Tale* 865–93, but especially 885–90]; after all, she has the conclusion. Chaucer, for the most part, is her opposite. He seems to prefer the questions and will leave the conclusions to the clerks (or rather, the clerks to their conclusions). Though he may not be interested in whether we can know with certitude only individual things, he is profoundly interested in how we know individual things. And though his concern may not be with the questions about whether universals exist in creation or only in our heads, he is always interested in those generalizations which fill people's heads and which exist there exclusively insofar as they matter to that individual. (745)

It is as if examinations of this same nominalist-versus-realist theme through characters and plots, in all of Chaucer's poetry, are to one degree or another thrown askew by his persona, thus producing what Diomede, in the *Troilus,* calls an "ambage" or, in this case, a wanted ambiguity: "That is to seyn, with double wordes slye, / Swiche as men clepen a word with two visages (5.898–99).

As quickly as a dignified consideration of philosophical issues can get underway in a poem, just then they will be undercut by none other than the narrator. This decompression is surprising and can be stunningly beautiful, as in Chaucer's Horace echo, "The lyf so short, the craft so long to lerne . . ." when appended by "Al this mene I by Love;" or the surprising undercutting can be riotously comical. Such choices represent, in sum, the "two visages" of language, and more to the point of poetry, which in the Prologue are what get Chaucer's persona into trouble with the God of Love, for this supernatural god can only understand literature in ideological—or allegorical, highly determined—terms. Yet the ambiguity is desirable because ultimately Chaucer's literary realism recognizes the irresolution of conflicting philosophical dogmas, which are themselves exegeses of human, fallible situations. Moreover, ambiguity operates even when the persona is merely one who may report events, albeit he cannot, he claims, understand them, as in the *Troilus* in which the narrator tells his tale of erotic love and betrayal even though, he dutifully reminds us, he has never experienced such a love for himself, and so he cannot judge the love events in his poem.

Chaucer's dreams actually are valued by modern readers (and were perhaps so by their prescient medieval counterparts) precisely because they have gone far in abandoning what can be viewed to be burdensome allegorical frames; allegory reduces the possibility of creating meaning in the sense of such meaning being an accurate reflection of the sensible, real, synthesized world—that is, of "reality." Angus Fletcher has pointed out that because they tend to be anatomical, or otherwise depend for their success on principles of enigma (that is, the inclusion of a formal obscurity that results from mysterious, so to speak, elements of a poem or plot [*Allegory . . . Symbolic Mode* 5 n. 9]), allegories tend to subvert the poet's capacity to create textures consonant with the more complicated reality of living, those actual complexities of life and love alluded to in the opening lines of the *Parlement of Foules* and elsewhere.

> The whole point of allegory is that it does not *need* to be read exegetically; it often has a literal level that makes good enough sense all by itself. But somehow this literal surface suggests a peculiar doubleness of intention, and while it can, as it were, get along without interpretation, it becomes richer and more interesting if given interpretation. Even the most deliberate fables, if read naïvely or carelessly, may seem mere stories, but what counts . . . is a structure that lends itself to a secondary reading, or rather, one that becomes stronger when given a secondary meaning as well as a primary meaning (*Allegory . . . Symbolic Mode* 7).

Although an allegory's virtue is its ability to sustain a consistent "secondary meaning," Fletcher's comment indicates that such a duplicity, almost by definition, will not readily lend itself to the mirror-like unity, the distillation of intellect and experience, which in fact constitutes aesthetic realism. As Kiser observes, the most significant shortcoming

> in the God of Love's reading of the *Troilus* is his failure to perceive the poem's complex expression of the relationship between pagan secular love and Christian *caritas*. . . . In short, his thought is dominated by a rather simple-minded conflation of pagan and Christian love, both of which he sees as the same virtue. (82)

Again, considering the comedy Chaucer creates, we might remind ourselves of the matter of the legends he resuscitates, which is particularly violent and uncharacteristic of an idealized courtly love the God of Love is supposed to, but does not, represent (Frank 26). The legend genre, however, is especially appropriate to assuage him because of its exemplary, allegorical nature. Kiser rightly notes, as well, that the

> *Legend* is also a poem about the difficulties inherent in Chaucer's role as a teller of others' tales, one who has obligations to his sources and also to the new and different audience [here, of course, the audience must include the God of Love] for whom these sources were to be adapted. To present his views on the uses of classical fiction, Chaucer finds it necessary to include several other issues in his poem [that is, in the *Legend of Good Women* entire] as well. He reacts to certain traditional theories of art, he comments on allegorization (one of the commonest ways in which medieval poets made classical texts confirm Christian truth), he reveals to us many fourteenth-century assumptions about literature's usefulness to everyday life, and he betrays his beliefs about the act and purpose of translation (26).

All the same, it is because the God of Love thinks in a simplistic, polemical fashion (as many fourteenth-century readers of religious sermons and other exemplary literature might have done), that he has misunderstood Chaucer's translations. Speaking of the *Troilus,* for instance, he asks, inflexibly, "Why noldest thow as wel [han] seyd goodnesse / Of wemen, as thow hast seyd wikednesse?" (268–69). Regardless of whether we can find any redeeming qualities in Crysede, obviously we are struck by the one-dimensional approach to literature this allegorical god adopts (he calls the Chaucer figure his "mortal fo" [248] because, on the one hand, he is an allegorical construct, and, on the other hand, he is a figure in a poem that ultimately attacks allegory):

> In the simplest terms, allegory says one thing and means another. It destroys the *normal expectation* we have about language, that our words "mean what they say." When we predicate quality *x* of person Y, Y really is what our predication says he is (or we assume so); but allegory would turn Y into something other *(allos)* than what the open and direct statement tells the reader. Pushed to an extreme, this ironic usage would subvert language itself, turning everything into an Orwellian newspeak. (Fletcher *Allegory . . . Symbolic Mode* 2; my emphasis)

Insofar as allegory "destroys" our "normal expectation" for discourse, we might conclude that the proclivity of dream visions is toward allegory in that they are indeed dreams, not real; yet they use reality's very space to establish something *other* out of it, some new meaning from this same ground. Ultimately, this is a problem of poetics. And it is indeed a problem. By modern standards, allegory is understood as a form of thought and/or expression that might naturally subvert reality, as it forsakes language's full semiotic power. Chaucer would have us condemn or praise by virtue of tensions he establishes between personalities and situations in his poems, which depend for their vitality on shaped meanings that avoid a one-to-one, "unreal" or fantastic deciphering of imagery on the part of the reader.

The dream vision that so readily—and here it is assumed "dangerously"—lends itself to an allegorical epistemology, may also achieve an effect of quite another order. As we have said, readers of the *visio* sequence of "events" eventually will be brought back to the realization that what occurs in the dream state is merely a fantasy, a dream. A reader cannot avoid this reflection, even in the Prologue. Yet, to know the miraculous—the dream—so might the logic run, means that, in fact, the dream sequence suggests a principal, unifying God-force behind an imperfect and sensible world: the dream is itself a psychological miracle implicating the fantastic, providing the participating reader with some helpful machinery in his or her exegetical search for the divine.

This sensible world, in and of itself incomplete, is best described by nominalism. Perhaps in some way Chaucer understood that the dreamscape provides a respite to the Ockhamist system's unrelieved doggedness. On the one hand, driven to its logical end, the absolutely nominalist system precludes the possibility of generalizations. On the other, the realist system allows transcendence. Realists, for example, accept the idea that a linguistic term like *father* connoted an entity called *fatherhood;* the implication, moreover, was that fatherhood inhered in the thing denoted by the term *father* (although Ockham did admit as absolute terms qualitative predicates like *white* and *whiteness* or *hot* and *heat*). But, while nominalism's strict adherence to logic seems to provide only a shallow, inert world, we must remember that Ockham envisioned the world as extraordinarily deep and full. "From a logical point of view," Moody notes,

> Ockham's analysis is a restriction of the domain of reference of terms, or of the domain of objects constituting possible values of the variable of quantification, to individual substances and singular (*not* common) sensible qualities. [However, in] thus impoverishing the domain of objects of reference, Ockham enriches the domain of truths to be known about these objects. The frequent charge that Ockham atomized the world by refusing to recognize relations as real entities distinct from substances and qualities fails to take account of the fact that the connotative terms relate the individuals by implying factual conditions by which the objects are tied together in an existential sense—something that cannot be done by treating relations as entities distinct from their relata and, in effect, as just another class of substances. From Ockham's point of view, it was the realists who atomized the world by treating all predicates as absolute names. (423–24)

In not denying the existence of the divine on the basis of faith, yet by insisting that the divine cannot be adequately spoken of, Ockham in effect enlarged the spiritual aspect of existence. In this sense, then, we might better interpret Chaucer's experiments with and without allegory, and in relation to his persona, within a nominalist, and not a realist, context.

The dream poem may be seen as a creation of the miraculous world by way of the hand and an almost Coleridgean imagining of the poet (and of course, the Prologue's focus is directly on the poet and his striving to "make" truth in his poetry).[20] The inclusion of the imaginary is readily perceptible in such poems as *Piers Plowman,* but this dynamic is more deeply embedded, and more powerful for its subtle presence, in a work like the Prologue. Chaucer the *makyr*'s meditation is based on the assumption that dreams, like words, have their ontological realities, even when words are names sequent to, instead of concomitant with, the things named (a sentiment he might have found expressed in Dante's *La Vita Nuova*: "nomina sunt consequentia rerum" [names are the consequence of the things {they name}]) (*Cap.* 13). By logical extension, imaginative and historical literature[21] seem also to be real, suggesting truth in themselves and beyond their own instances of being—beyond themselves as well.

What is interesting is that Chaucer may have arrived at this viewpoint through exposure to the nominalist emphasis on the singularity of experience. Not only can experience be unique; it must be so. Yet the unique need not be one-dimensional or inert. In other words, literature may partake of a protean nature—art as the product of the creative, intuitive impulse. Chaucer points to this phenomenon in his preoccupation with the viability of tradition and authority as epistemological keys. Set against such a construct of *knowledge* is the *real*, experiential world. Hence, the Prologue begins with this very discussion, finding in mind-sustained memory a unifying force:

> A thousand sythes have I herd men telle
> That there is joye in hevene and peyne in helle,
> And I acorde wel that it be so;
> But natheles, this wot I wel also,
> That ther ne is non that dwelleth in this contre
> That eyther hath in helle or hevene ybe,
> Ne may of it non other weyes witen
> But as he hath herd seyd or founde it writen;
> For by assay there may no man it preve.
> But Goddes forbode, but men shulde leve
> Wel more thyng than men han seyn with ye!
> Men shal nat wenen every thyng a lye
> For that he say it nat of yore ago.
> God wot a thyng is nevere the lesse so
> Thow every wyght ne may it nat yse.
> Bernard the monk ne say nat al, parde!
> Thanne mote we to bokes that we fynde,
> Thourgh whiche that olde thynges ben in mynde,
> And to the doctryne of these olde wyse
> Yeven credence, in every skylful wyse,
> And trowen on these olde approved storyes
> Of holynesse, of regnes, of victoryes,
> Of love, of hate, of othere sondry thynges,
> Of which I may nat make rehersynges.
> And if that olde bokes weren aweye,
> Yloren were of remembrance the keye. ("G" 1–26)[22]

The poem starts by outlining precisely its own and Chaucer's prevailing and very workable strategy: literature as a viable world force will be tried by present experience, even when that experience occurs within the poem-sustained dream frame. Furthermore, Chaucer's poetry will be put to a test by his own persona's artlessness (although we may easily concede Cupid's simpleminded reading of Chaucer's poetry; Alceste's defense does not invoke his poetry's fundamental virtues either).

The Prologue makes a claim for figuration and tropism, for the referential, truth functions of symbols and analogical thought, just as there is an understanding of psychological and philosophical necessity in the experiential present. The tension Chaucer establishes between these divergent viewpoints, in fact, unifies his poem. His meditation is humorous while it simultaneously considers serious linguistic and philosophical alternatives, using this double-edged sword hopefully to strike an aesthetic unity. In this, the dream state is akin to language when language is not limited; and in this, Chaucer departs from the merely allegorical, conventional dream *visio* mode. Chaucer's narrator in the dream poems, therefore, represents a pose, for the sake of the matter being presented by and through him, which depends on Diomede's *ambage*. As Peck writes, "the *ficta* of the mind have no independent reality outside the mind, [yet] they form the basis of man's deductions." This is a decidedly nominalist proposition that Chaucer finds appealing. The mind "manipulate[s] words and images." Indeed, the idea "that the mind and its knowledge are an ongoing imagistic-linguistic process" (747) forms the basis of his claim for the efficacy of literature vis-à-vis tradition. The mind provides the terms for what it apprehends.

Chaucer's contemporary Holcot noted that, despite humanity's double incapacity of weak intellect and weak will, we still can achieve our final end if we do what is in us to the best of our ability (Oberman 241–48). This sentiment echoes Ockham's belief that God cannot be known in Himself or as a single concept proper to Him, but only as in a concept that is predicable of Him (i.e., creation, especially the mortal mind) (see Peck 750). Chaucer's posturing through his obtuse persona reveals this philosophical and theological construct (in conjunction with a meditation on aesthetics) deeply embedded in the characters and in the actions of the poems themselves; the persona also establishes a relationship between the theologico-philosophical debate and poetics. Kiser points out that in the *Legend of Good Women,* Chaucer's aesthetical problem is brought under control through a contrast between his narrator and a God of Love who is equally obtuse, though this is manifested quite differently because he is a god and not a poet. Cupid's difficulty in separating "wheat" from "chaff" means he cannot distinguish between language, *traductio,* and the *matiere* that language treats—*auctoritee*. However, keeping Holcot's view of humanity's double incapacity in mind, it is because of Chaucer's

> characteristic refusal to be self-congratulatory [that] we do not get a "corrected" interpretation of the *Troilus* from the *Legend*'s narrator, even though he is given a chance to respond to the accusations of his deified (and reified) reader [Cupid]. Instead, the only remark we get from him is the reminder that authorial intent ought to be weighed in the literary Last Judgment over which the God of Love presides ["F" 471–74, "G" 461–64]. Neither articulate nor forceful, the intimidated narrator only weakly asserts his innocence in response to the charges brought against him. Finally, Alceste is left with the responsibility of defending him, which she does with shrewdness and skill. (Kiser 83–84)

Alceste as dream figure barely exists beyond an allegorical pale, yet she is not merely allegorical in intention because of, among other things, her striking resemblance to the real daisy. She resolves the discrepancy between ironic narration and a philosophico-aesthetical problem, embodied here in the indictment of what Chaucer has written (Cupid's ". . . in pleyn text, it nedeth nat to glose, / Thow hast translated [etc.]" ("G" 254–55); and, earlier, Chaucer's own remark: "For myn entent is, or I fro yow fare, / The naked text in English to declare / Of many a story") ("G" 85–87).[23] But note that she resolves the problem only within the context of her own figuration, at Chaucer's hand (as well as in Chaucer's dream), and therefore we view the indictment of translation by the God of Love, who is the representation of a simpleminded version of nominalism, from within the dream vision mode (in the point of view of Alceste) as well as in terms of the objectively real and experiential (the poem's narrator who relates to us both his dream *and* his feelings about how one may "know" the truth—either through books or through experience or, we are left to conjecture, through a combination of the two).

Chaucer as persona may therefore claim to be making no judgments on what he sees taking place around him in his poems,[24] but because he begs his own question, he prepares readers to pass judgment, to condemn or celebrate as if they are free to understand all of the implications of the poems' events and discussions. Readers feel this way, however, not because of the poem's allegorical structure, but exactly as a consequence of the poems' narrator putting them off their guard. Because they are told, and because they see the bungling narration of the persona, they tend to take what he says and does as false. Therefore, readers jump to conclusions of right and wrong based on a polarity the poems' persona has, in effect, established for them. Readers make decisions, that is, within the narrator's choice of context, although they often tend to forget this.

Recalling the opening to the *Parlement of Foules,* we can now say that Chaucer paraphrases Horace to bring together the strands of a complex discussion in the dream poems and in all of Chaucer's work; his is a progressively trenchant meditation on knowledge sustained in literature and in other life experience as well, knowledge that is to be measured against a religious and philosophical ideal. Rhetoric itself, then—or certainly the question of figuration in poetry, which for Chaucer perhaps underlies the concept of *translatio*—becomes *the* metaphor in a poetic search for a truth that may be viable in all spiritual, mental, and experiential states of being.

The world "text" Chaucer reads is composed of sensible "things," but as Hugh of St. Victor's remark intimates (that is, that the whole sensible world is like a book written by the hand of God), through the power of cognition the mysterious force that orders the palpable world body may also be known. Allegory reflects the presence of the mysterious through enigmatic duplicities of meanings, while it seeks to establish a context for logical thinking within an aesthetic mode. Interestingly, however, as this logic was elaborated to its ultimate ends by Ockham and others, the weaknesses of allegory were revealed. Of many aesthetic epistemologies, allegory is the form that attempts to reconcile the factual with the supernatural through a reinvention of a world experience often dismantled by philosophical attempts to "explain" such experience. Poetically framed inquiries, however, invoke the supernatural because, like language (and dreaming), logically the imagination must be God-induced, even if this contingency cannot be established empirically. Ockham understood this problem. As Andrea Tabarroni explains,

> for Ockham, intuitive knowledge does not necessarily require the presence of the object, but can also logically exist *(de potentia Dei absoluta)* in the absence, or even given the [postulated] non-existence, of the object. The difference between the two types of knowledge is therefore purely epistemological. Intuitive knowledge is the necessary and sufficient condition for an evident judgement of existence or nonexistence, and thus for all contingent propositions concerning the object in question, while abstractive knowledge does not guarantee any evidence.[25]

Logic such as Ockham's need not concede, due to its very nature, the existence of the less material, supernatural, dreamlike and often enough literary, world elements. This discrepancy is played out in the debate between Chaucer's narrator and the Prologue's God of Love. *Translatio* or *makyng*—the imaginative acts of "reading" the world or God's text—is questioned because they are interpretive, imaginative ways of being-in-the-world, performed in compliance with Jerome's translation principle, "non verbum de verbo, sed sensum de sensu exprimere" (*Epist.* 57). Likewise, dreaming is an interpretive act in *its* rendition of reality. Alceste, naturally, who finally is real *only* through her figuration in a dream, in a literary work, in the Prologue, "settles" the issue.

Smiling and mollified, the God of Love, also Chaucer's figure, concedes that, after all, Chaucer may restore the unified world, may reestablish order by writing the "wheat" and letting go of the "chaff" in the forthcoming legends of women true in love. We, as readers, know the connection between love and imagination; and *we* restore the unity by reading Chaucer's text of the buffoonery of dream-induced gods. This text is a reflection of the complex book of the world from which it derives—a book whose "narrative," as Jesse Gellrich states, "is the 'history' of mankind from creation to the ascent to the celestial city" (22, cf. 211).

The nominalistic idea that the "mind and its knowledge are an ongoing imagistic-linguistic process" (Peck 747, cf. above) forms the basis of Chaucer's meditation on the authority of literature within a nominalist world that had come to rely on experience alone. When we "read" the world landscape, however, we may also realize historical and imaginative dimensions beyond the physical present. Reading is, indeed, humanity's unique, ennobling epistemological virtue. Through the act itself, reading also becomes an experiential action. Thus, through the Prologue's comedy, our nobility is recalled in the various *mis*readings of the Chaucer corpus by the God of Love, by Alceste, and even by the Prologue's narrator. Chaucer's comedy serves a serious purpose. In Chaucer's hands, misreading, rather than reading, becomes the emblem for the efficacy of all artistic endeavor. Art may most authentically signify the truth, Chaucer seems to be saying, in its gesture toward that truth, a gesture that takes the form of human expression's ultimate failure at truth's transcription.

Notes

1. I am profoundly grateful for John M. Hill's patient suggestions about and incisive emendations of this essay.

2. See *De Veritate* esp. pp. 4–5.

3. Many scholars have done so. See, for example: Bloomfield, Boucher, Gardner 298ff, Jeffrey "Chaucer," Justman, Morse, Peck, Ruud, Shepherd, Steinmetz, Stepsis, Taylor, and Williams. Ruud esp. argues that Chaucer's attention to detail results from the influence of Ockham's emphasizing of experience or what he called *intuitive cognition* (211).

4. There may be some question as to the persona's fundamental role in Chaucer's earlier poems, when the distinction between allegory and a less determined sort of logico-rhetorical structure is not as subtle as it was eventually to become; but I believe that there can be no doubt of Chaucer's decision to move beyond a strictly ordered allegorical framework (as I shall define this below) in his late and monumental works, *Troilus and Crysede* and *The Canterbury Tales* (here, individual tales may be allegorical, but the frame of the tales surely is not), and, arguably, in the Prologue to the *Legend of Good Women*.

5. See, among others, Abshear-Seals; Baker; Bethurum; Fries; Greetham; Herzog; Jeffrey ("Sacred"); Kiser; Lawton; Payne (*Key*, "Late Medieval Images," and "Making His Own Myth"); Schricker; Stephens; and Waswo.

6. Fletcher, *Allegory*, 2, and esp. n. 1, as Fletcher's etymology makes evident: "*Allegory* from *allos* + *agoreuien* (*other* + *speak openly, speak in the assembly or market*). *Agoreuein* connotes public, open, declarative speech. This sense is inverted by the prefix *allos*. Thus allegory is often called 'inversion.' " Cf. Fletcher's remarks below.

7. Cf. *On Christian Doctrine:*

Have we spoken or announced anything worthy of God? Rather I feel that I have done nothing but wish to speak: if I have spoken, I have not said what I wished to say. Whence do I know this except because God is ineffable? If what I said were ineffable, it would not be said. And for this reason God should not be said to be ineffable, for when this is said something is said. And a contradiction in terms is created, since if that is ineffable which cannot be spoken, then that is not ineffable which can be called ineffable. This contradiction is to be passed over in silence rather than resolved verbally. (10–11; in Finke 52)

8. Again, witness Chaucer and Cupid in the Prologue.

9. *Commentary on the Sentences* III, q. 8 in Ockham: *Philosophical Writings;* in Moody, 435–36.

10. This turn away from allegory has long been noted by critics, starting at least as early as Malone (96).

11. Fletcher has noted that the "symbolic mentality" of the Middle Ages denied

the more immediate puzzles presented by the senses. The flight [via allegory] from the limited toward the infinity of the Divine Being kept its balance only, if at all, by asserting that man's world was closed and finite. Ockham's principle of parsimony was invented, it seems, to stem this iconographic tide, since scholastic thought, at first rationalizing, ends by absorbing the medieval compulsion to turn relations into icons. ("Allegory," I:46)

For his part, Chaucer must have been acutely sensitive to the essential dynamic of allegory, for by its very nature (as stated above) allegory urges a reader to interpret a second meaning from a story, a story that is the "vehicle" (à la Richards) of the trope or rather we can say that the story is the trope's "experience," an experience reported to the reader by a persona.

12. I am grateful to Andrew Tomko, Robert E. Lynch, and Dennis Donahue for their various and helpful comments regarding this translation.

13. This and all further citations of Chaucer's work are from *The Riverside Chaucer.*

14. As de Man would have it (cf. above).

15. My discussion throughout this essay focuses on Chaucer's "G" text, which I consider to be the later, revised version of the Prologue. The birds in the "F" text do not introduce Cupid and Alceste.

16. On the etymology of *margerite* and the connection, in English, between "pearl" and "daisy" (from the French and Latin) and the religious associations between the daisy and the Virgin Mary, see Dronke, and Payne.

17. "The entire sensible world is, so to speak, a book written by the hand of God [. . .]. All visible things, visibly presented to us by a symbolic instruction, that is, figured, are proposed for the declaring and signifying of things invisible" (*Didascalion PL* CLXXVI.814). Hugh of St. Victor died in 1141; nevertheless, his thinking influenced others in the fourteenth century. See Gellrich. See Jesse M. Gellrich, *Idea of the Book.*

18. Taylor writes that "Augustine, in *Soliloquia* 2.16, explains that the feigning of art is pleasing rather than deceiving. . . . In *De mendacio* Augustine lists eight categories of lies; but in *Soliloquia* 2.18 he distinguishes between those who will to be false and those who are capable of being true. He excludes from opprobrium the artist's will to imitate truth" (315–16 nn. and 325 n).

19. *De Doctrina Christiana* 4.11.26. Earlier in *De Doctrina Christiana* Augustine writes: "Rerum autem ignorantia facit obscuras figuratas locutiones" (2.16.24). Hence words, as being the beginning of any potential figuration, figuration's Urforms, would seem to be contingent upon at least one's knowing the "things" of the world, which are the source, it appears to be here, of knowledge.

20. See Payne 93ff. This passage, of course, is a reflection of the philosophical debate being carried on by Ockham, Holcot, Bradwardine, and others. *Skill,* however, suggests also the technical virtuosity such as we might find in the poet's art, just as it resonates the deceit implicit in the bird trapper's *sophistry* in the Prologue; here it is the "artifice" of nature: so that the poet must seek, in some way, to mirror the experiential, paradigm of *kynde* in his verse. His words must possess or adhere to the force of an intuitional, pre-Gallilean gravity (the notion that all elements in the world have their proper place) as much as would any natural event; cf. Robinson *Chaucer* 783.

21. In my argument I am, of course, presuming the medieval world's confusion in which imaginative literature is, to a degree, taken to be synonymous with written history.

22. Note Chaucer's verbal echo of Ockham in his phrase, "For by assay there may no man it preve." Ockham—and, here, Chaucer—allow that there is a heaven and hell, that is, that there is a divine order; both men also realize the futility of speaking seriously, in the sense that there words could be ontologically full, about such divine existence. Without experience, without intuitive cognition, there can be no proof (see above, and Tabarroni).

23. My reading of the poem, here, is emphasizing the leitmotif of Cupid's displeasure with the act of *traductio* itself. This I understand to be a decidedly nominalist view of all art and, underlying this attitude, a distrust of language itself.

24. "For, as to me, is lefer non, ne lother" ("G" 66–75). The narrator's analogy between "corn" and "chaff," and flower and leaf, makes clear his valuation within a larger discussion, in the poem entire, of the value of both *auctoritee* and *traductio.* He would of course prefer the "corn"—in other words, the matter of the old approved stories that should be brought to life, once again, in English. This problem of the matter of old stories is, as has been discussed, the substance in part of Cupid's indictment.

Nevertheless—to return to the original point—beyond the persona's adherence to one symbol or figure (such as the daisy, or the "corn") over another, he does not take sides in the larger philosophical debate (that has more to do with the phenomenon of translating than it does with that of the matter to be translated).

25. Tabarroni 208; cf. *Ord., prologus,* q. 1, vol. I, pp. 31–33, and *Rep.* II, qq. 12–13, pp. 256ff.

Works Cited

Augustine. *De Doctrina Christiana. PL.* 32–46.

———. *On Christian Doctrine.* Tr. D. W. Robertson. Indianapolis: Bobbs-Merrill, 1958.

Abshear-Seals, Lisa. "Boccaccio's Criseida and Chaucer's Cryseyde." *Spectrum* 27:25–32.

Anselm. *Opera Omnia.* Ed. F. S. Schmitt. Edinburgh: T. Nelson, 1946–61.

Baker, Donald. "Dreamer and Critic: The Poet in the *Legend of Good Women." University of Colorado Studies in Language and Literature* 9 (1963):4–18.

Bennett, J. A. W. *Chaucer at Oxford and at Cambridge.* Oxford: Oxford University Press / Clarendon Press, 1974.

Bethurum, Dorothy. "Chaucer's Point of View as Narrator in the Love Poems." *PMLA* 74 (1959):511–20.

Bloomfield, Morton W. "Fourteenth-Century England: Realism and Rationalism in Wycliff and Chaucer." *English Studies in Africa* 16 (1973):59–70.

Boucher, Holly Wallace. "Nominalism: The Difference for Chaucer and Boccaccio," *Chaucer Review* 20:3 (1986):213–20.

Dante Alighieri. *Le Opere di Dante.* Ed. Michele Barbi. Florence: R. Bemporad, 1960.

Derrida, Jacques. "From Psyche." *Acts of Literature.* Ed. Derek Attridge. New York and London: Routledge, 1992.

Chaucer, Geoffrey. *The Riverside Chaucer.* Ed. Larry D. Benson. Boston: Houghton Mifflin, 1987.

———. *The Works of Geoffrey Chaucer.* Ed. F. N. Robinson. 2d ed. Boston: Houghton Mifflin, 1957.

Dronke, Peter. *Medieval Latin Literature and the Rise of the European Love-Lyric.* 2 vols. London: Oxford-Clarendon, 1968.

Everett, Dorothy. "Some Reflections on Chaucer's 'Art Poetical.' " Oxford: Oxford University Press, 1950; rpt. *Proceedings of the British Academy of London.* 36 (1956):131–54.

Fletcher, Angus. "Allegory in Literary History." *Dictionary of the History of Ideas.* Vol. I. Ed. Philip P. Wiener. New York: Charles Scribner's Sons, 1973.

———. *Allegory: The Theory of a Symbolic Mode.* Ithaca: Cornell University Press, 1964.

Frank, Robert Worth, Jr. *Chaucer and the Legend of Good Women.* Cambridge, MA: Harvard University Press, 1972.

Fries, Maureen. "The 'Other' Voice: Woman's Song, Its Satire and Its Transcendence in Late Medieval British Literature." *Studies in Medieval Culture* 15 (1981):155–78.

Gardner, John. *The Poetry of Chaucer.* Carbondale and Edwardsville: Southern Illinois University Press, 1977.

Gellrich, Jesse M. *The Idea of the Book in the Middle Ages: Language, Theory, Mythology, and Fiction.* Ithaca and London: Cornell University Press, 1985.

Greetham, David C. "Self-Referential Artifacts: Hoccleve's Persona as a Literary Device," *Modern Philology* 86:3 (1989):242–51.

Herzog, Michael B. "The *Book of the Duchess:* The Vision of the Artist as a Young Dreamer." *Chaucer Review* 22:4 (1988):269–81.

Hugh of St. Victor. *Didascalion. Patrologia Latina* CLXXVI.

Jeffrey, David Lyle. "Chaucer and Wyclif: Biblical Hermeneutic and Literary Theory in the XIVth Century." *Chaucer and the Scriptural Tradition.* Ed. David Lyle Jeffrey. Ottowa: University of Ottawa Press, 1984. 109–42.

———. "Sacred and Secular Scripture: Authority and Interpretation in the House of Fame," *Chaucer and the Scriptural Tradition.* Ed. David Lyle Jeffrey. Ottowa, University of Ottawa Press, 1984. 207–28.

Jerome. *Epistola. PL.* 22.571.

Justman, Stewart. "Literal and Symbolic in the *Canterbury Tales.*" *Chaucer Review* 14 (1980): 199–214.

Kimmelman, Burt. *The Poetics of Authorship in the Latter Middle Ages.* New York: Peter Lang, 1996.

Kiser, Lisa J. *Telling Classical Tales: Chaucer and the* Legend of Good Women. Ithaca and London: Cornell University Press, 1983.

Lawton, David. *Chaucer's Narrators.* Cambridge: Brewer, 1985.

Macrobius. *Macrobius'* Commentary on the *Dream of Scipio.* Ed. and tr. William Harris Stahl. New York: Columbia University Press, 1966.

Malone, Kemp. *Chapters on Chaucer.* Baltimore: Johns Hopkins University Press, 1951.

Man, Paul de. "Autobiography as De-Facement." *The Rhetoric of Romanticism.* New York: Columbia University Press, 1984.

Miller, J. Hillis. "The Two Allegories." *Allegory, Myth and Symbol.* Ed. Morton Bloomfield. Cambridge: Harvard University Press, 1981.

Moody, Ernest A. "William of Ockham." *Studies in Medieval Philosophy, Science, and Logic.* Berkeley: University of California Press, 1975. 409–40.

Morse, J. Mitchell. "The Philosophy of the Clerk of Oxenford." *Modern Language Quarterly* 19 (1958):3–20.

Oberman, Heiko. *The Harvest of Medieval Theology: Gabriel Biel and Late Medieval Nominalism.* Cambridge, MA: Harvard University Press, 1963.

Ockham. *Ockham: Philosophical Writings.* Ed. P. Boehner. Edinburgh: n.p., 1957.

———. *Quodlibeta septem.* Opera Theologica 9. Ed. J.C. Wey. St. Bonaventure, NY: St. Bonaventure University, 1980.

Payne, Robert O. *The Key of Remembrance.* New Haven: Yale University Press, 1963.

———. "Late Medieval Images and Self-Image of the Poet: Chaucer, Gower, Lydgate, Henryson, Dunbar." *Vernacular Poetics in the Middle Ages.* Ed. Lois Ebin. Kalamazoo, MI: Medieval Institute Publications, 1984. 249–61.

———. "Making His Own Myth: The Prologue to Chaucer's *Legend of Good Women.*" *Chaucer Review* 9 (1975):197–211.

Peck, Russell. "Chaucer and the Nominalist Questions." *Speculum* 53 (1978): 745–60.

Ruud, Jay. "Chaucer and Nominalism: The 'Envoy to Bukton'." *Mediaevalia* 10 (1984):199–212.

Schricker, Gale C. "On the Relation of Fact and Fiction in Chaucer's Poetic Endings," *Philological Quarterly* 60 (1981):13–27.

Shepherd, Geoffrey. "Religion and Philosophy in Chaucer." *Geoffrey Chaucer.* Ed. Derek Brewer. London: n.p., 1974. 262–89.

Steinmetz, David C. "Late Medieval Nominalism and the 'Clerk's Tale'." *Chaucer Review* 12 (1977):38–54.

Stephens, John. "The Uses of Personae and the Art of Obliqueness in Some Chaucer Lyries." Part I. *Chaucer Review* 21:3 (1987):360–73; part II. *Chaucer Review* 21:4 (1987):459–68; Part III. *Chaucer Review* 22:1 (1987):41–52.

Stepsis, Robert. "*Potentia Absoluta* and the 'Clerk's Tale.' " *Chaucer Review* 10:2 (1975–76):129–46.

Tabarroni, Andrea. "Mental Signs and the Theory of Representation in Ockham" *On the Medieval Theory of Signs.* Ed. Umberto Eco and Costantino Marmo. Amsterdam and Philadelphia: John Benjamins, 1989.

Taylor, P. B. "Chaucer's 'Cosyn to the Dede.' " *Speculum* 57:2 (1982):315–27.

Williams, David. "From Grammar's Pan to Logic's Fire: Intentionality and Chaucer's 'Friar's Tale.' " *Literature and Ethics: Essays Presented to A. E. Malloch.* Ed. Gary Wihl and David Williams. Kingston and Montreal: McGill-Queen's University Press, 1988. 77–95.

Waswo, Richard. "The Narrator of *Troilus and Criseyde*." *English Literary History* 50 (1983):1–25.

Whitman, Jon. *Allegory: The Dynamics of an Ancient and Medieval Technique.* Cambridge, MA: Harvard University Press, 1987.

Text as Arena: Lament and Gnome in *The Wanderer*

SEALY GILLES

THE LITERATE POETS AND SCRIBES OF ANGLO-SAXON ENGLAND WORKED to preserve the oral traditions that preceded them and which still endured in many of their institutions (Clanchy 232–33). However, the very incarnation of the word in the text meant that traditional modes or genres would be transformed even as they were enshrined. In her study of traces of orality in Old English vernacular manuscripts, Katherine O'Brien O'Keeffe argues that

> the power to preserve is gained at the cost of the intimacy of words. Through writing, words, divorced from oral source and substance, are conveyed by silence and absence. Writing becomes a technology of alienation. (O'Keeffe 52)

Divorce and alienation, however, always carry within them the memory of loss, and in the Old English exile poems the separation of speech from performer, audience, and context seems to compel articulation of what has been lost. In poetry, which dwells in the intersection of the oral and the literate, the kinds of analysis and introspection noted by Walter Ong as characteristics of textualization (105) are complicated by the felt absence of speaker and audience. In turn, this absence allows generic shifts and hybridizations in inherited oral forms. Such instability is particularly evident in the Old English elegies.

In Old English elegiac poems, two forms with pretextual histories—the gnome, out of an age-old wisdom tradition, and the lament, a direct, ostensibly unmediated response to personal or cultural loss—offer competing interpretations of one central experience. Their juxtaposition in *The Wanderer* and its fellow laments creates an intense critical pressure from which neither mode escapes unscathed. I will be looking at *The Wanderer* in particular as representative of a group of five elegiac poems. This group includes *The Seafarer, The Wife's Lament, Deor,* and *Resignation B.*[1]

I argue that *The Wanderer* has as its central generic feature the juxtaposition of two competing voices, lament and gnome, and that the dialectic between these genres, their dual voicing, is made possible by their location in a text. Moreover, I find that both gnomic pronouncement and the lyric *cri de coeur* associated with lament are compromised by their absorption into the insistent voice of the fictional *anhaga*. The text, as the site for their mutual impingement, makes possible the synchronic juxtaposition of the two modes, but it also presses for their conciliation. Within the poem each repeatedly tests and modifies the other. I shall not pretend to resolve that confusion, but rather I shall try, first, to explain it by placing the poems in the context of a marginally literate society whose literature was indebted to a powerful oral tradition, and, second, to explore the unstable hybrid that results from the convergence of disparate forms with irreconcilable rhetorical strategies.

My study of the poem as a textual locus for the interplay of wisdom and complaint has been made possible by work in orality and literacy, especially that of Walter Ong, Brian Stock, and Jeff Opland. In the last several decades, the tendency among students of preliterate cultures to see an oral tradition as monolithic, as producing one highly integrated genre of performed poetry, which is primarily epic and narrative, has given way to a more complex understanding of oral cultures and their products. Jeff Opland and Ruth Finnegan have helped us see that various forms are possible within one tradition, even though one may be favored over the others (Opland *Anglo-Saxon,* 19ff; Finnegan, chs. 4–10). Thus, in the Xhosa tradition, poetry may be eulogistic, autobiographical, narrative, political, or ritualistic (Opland *Xhosa,* 32–52). Moreover, these types need not be exclusive: narrative kernels may surface in eulogy; gnomes, in praise poems. Students of multiple literacies have also reminded us that orality and literacy function along a continuum rather than at two distinct and distant poles. This view is reinforced by historians of orality such as John Miles Foley, who argues for abandoning the "Great Divide" (Ruth Finnegan's term) between oral and written camps to study in full "the unique phenomonology of a text that nonetheless has deep (and nourishing) oral roots" (Foley 35). *The Wanderer* is just such a text.

A literate poet creating a text in a semi-literate culture is writing out of a wealth of inherited forms and venerable rhetorical ploys. More important, he or she can also draw on techniques for improvising, combining, and adapting those forms to new situations and contexts. The text, however, can itself create a problem. Whereas the performance situation, out of mnemonic necessity and audience expectations, demands a certain conservatism, the text operates under few such constraints (Ong 39–41, 101–2). Once created, however, it is fixed and responds to its audience only in subsequent versions, if at all. These possibilities and dilemmas are especially evident in the Old English elegiac laments, in which traditional modes are combined anew, often with disconcertingly little coherence.

Although most studies of oral poetry focus on narrative poems, I believe that less linear works can suggest a great deal about oral forms in a literate context. It may be that the texts Opland has called "stative" ("Plenary") are most open to a generic multivocality, and most vulnerable to the chaos it can induce because they have no strong controlling linear mode. *The Wanderer, The Seafarer, The Wife's Lament, Deor,* and *Resignation B* are not narrative, although they may contain narrative moments. They juxtapose conflicting voices within nonlinear, cyclical structures. The contest between these generic voices shapes these poems and their impact. The polyphonic nature of a text such as *The Wanderer* generates both self-commentary and meta-commentary; through this reflexive discourse the poem serves as a mirror for the culture that produced it, a culture in the throes of its own struggle with tradition and invasion.

The relationship between an oral performance and its tradition has been described as a "dialogue" (Parks 57). Parks argues that a performance has a diachronic relationship with other performances—remembered performances—rather than a synchronic relationship such as exists between texts. He calls this relationship a "dialogue of memories" and, with Plato, sees texts as the enemy of memory. Nevertheless, he argues that, in displacing memory, the text also serves as a mnemonic:

> From an oral culture's standpoint, the written text could be defined as memory concretized, memory torn out from its native soil in human experience but in the process fixed in durable form that frees it, apparently, from the effects of time. (58)

I don't find these Old English texts to be as disembodied as this implies, and I believe oral performance is more durable than we can imagine. However, Parks' use of dialogue as a way to describe the performance's relationship with other performances and the text's relationship with other texts is useful. I would like to collapse his model and posit a dialogue that takes place within a work between inserted or integrated traditions (or citations from such traditions). Bakhtin argues that such multivocality—in which the "voices" of characters, contexts, and traditions speak to, over, and under each other—becomes possible only with the novel or its predecessors (Bakhtin *Dialogic* 278), and that "the poet must assume a complete, single-personed hegemony over his language" (297). This view of poetry as homogeneous and univocal overlooks the cacophony created when the persona's voice, forged in experience, must quote maxims inherited from another time, derived from other realities. The Old English elegiac poem, a type for which we have no adequate name, may give us a compressed version of the dialogism and heteroglossia that Bakhtin finds only in the plenitude of the novel.[2]

As we begin more specific discussion of *The Wanderer,* some brief definitions and a related pitfall should be noted. The danger is that some of the following discussion may essentialize the gnome and the lyric and imply that in the Old English elegy these forms spring from sealed compartments and encounter each other inviolate and for the first time. Other literatures and other poets combine the two, and, of course, echoes of other genres and other forms reverberate in these poems. The argument here is simply that, by identifying lines in the elegies as primarily gnomic or primarily lyric, and by listening to the nature of their interactions, we may begin to hear these texts as not simply laments for lost ideals or injunctive instructions to *eorls* but as complex explorations of a society in flux.[3]

The two crucial definitions are of *gnome* and *lament.* The gnome, as I define it, is a short, sententious generalization. Deeply rooted in a wisdom tradition of social commentary and control, it is often heard in the *speculum principis* and survives in some of the world's oldest texts, the Egyptian *Instructions of Amen-em-ope,* for example. The gnome's most complete manifestation in Old English is in the catalogic poems of *Maxims I* and *II;* it can also be found in various listing poems that draw on the tradition to delineate such topics as the "fates of men" or the "gifts of men."[4] In its broad generalizations and lack of temporal or spatial specificity, the gnome eschews the texture and resonance of an individual voice while insisting on the power accorded the collective voice of culture and tradition. *Maxims IA* tells us:

> Ðing sceal gehegan
> frod wiþ frodne;   biþ hyra ferð gelic,
> hi a sace semaþ,   sibbe gelæraþ,
> þa ær wonsælge   awegen habbaþ

> (They must meet,
> the wise with the wise; their mind is alike,
> they ever settle disputes, teach peace,
> which before the wretched have carried away.) (*Maxims IA* 18b–21)[5]

When the lament's persona uses a gnome, it is in the nature of a citation or incorporation. Often it is made clear that the utterance is not original with the speaker (see lines 11b–12 of *The Wanderer,* cited below). The force of the gnome depends on its having originated in something larger and of greater significance than the immediate situation. Thus the persona will often refer to a gnome as objectified, as coming from without.

A crucial gnome in *The Wanderer* is the injunction to control one's emotions (lines 11b–14) which also appears in the sapiential collections:

> Hyge sceal gehealden,   hond gewealden,
> seo sceal in eagan,   snyttro in breostum,
> þær bið þæs monnes   modgeþoncas

> (The heart must be restrained, the hand controlled,
> a pupil must be in the eye, wisdom in the breast,
> where man's heart-thoughts are.) (*Maxims IB* 121–23)

This mandated stoicism is aimed precisely at the voice which forms our second mode in the Old English exile poems. This is the lament or complaint, which is presented as arising out of personal experience and which opposes gnomic wisdom in both form and tone. It either narrates, or reflects narrative; it is descriptive, not prescriptive. It speaks out of misery, fueled by reverie, and constantly compares past and present. Whereas gnomic lines may well travel almost intact from one text to another and derive much of their potency from that universality, the lament is potent in direct proportion to its topicality. It adheres to a persona, an experience, a concrete loss.

Lament in many of these poems is introduced almost immediately as the "self-song" commonly announced in their first few lines:

> Mæg ic be me sylfum   soðgied wrecan,
> siþas secgan

> (I can concerning myself utter a true song,
> speak of journeys) (*The Seafarer* 1–2a)

As it continues, this strain tells, in the first person, of the hardships of exile and a journey undergone alone. In *The Wanderer,* the persona uses it to express his longing for vanished companions and a beloved lord, now dead. It violates, again and again, the gnomic injunction to silence.

Both gnome and lament have histories of oral performance, if we believe the evidence of poets in England and Iceland. In *Beowulf,* gnomes are part of Hrothgar's delivery in the hall (Fit XXIV) and the *scop*'s tale of Finn and Hnæf (Fit XVI). In *The Poetic Edda,* we hear Odin's advice to Loddfáfnir in the *Hávamál* (st. 111–37). Lament has a less clear-cut formal presence, but is just as ubiquitous. In Old English, simple, seemingly unadulterated laments are referred to more often quoted. Thus, we are told that Hildeburh mourned the death of brother and son (Fit XVI), and that Beowulf was mourned, first by an unnamed woman, then by twelve eorls, brave in battle. In Old Icelandic, directly quoted monologue in *The Lay of Guthrun* tells of Sigurth's death and Guthrun's grief (*Poetic Edda* 269ff). In all these instances, the gnomic and the sorrowful, the predominant form is clearly defined for us. We know that Hrothgar is imparting wisdom. We are warned that Guthrun will "rehearse her sorrows."

In the Old English exile laments, on the other hand, neither form predominates, and labels fail us. Both lament and gnome may reside in the voice of the persona itself. Moreover, the persona becomes congruent with the poem, lightly framed if framed at all, no longer a discrete type. In crafting his speaker out of two divergent traditions, and in allowing that persona's voice to become the poem, the poet renders our own position, as audience, uncertain. Are we looking at the survivor, or through his eyes? Does he speak to us, or for us?

In both the narrative tradition and the wisdom collections, the lamenting persona serves more as an example than a character. In *Beowulf,* he speaks as the lone survivor, the last of his race (Fit XXXII), or as a father bereft of his son and unable to exact vengeance (XXXIV). In the gnomic poetry, we see him as if from afar and do not hear him speak. We know from *Maxims IC* that the lone exile was a type useful to the sage who wished to emphasize the value of community. He serves as a negative exemplum by showing us the price men pay when they move beyond the pale.

> Wineleas, wonsælig mon genimeð him wulfas to geferan,
> felafæcne deor. Ful oft hine se gefera sliteð.

> (The friendless, wretched one takes wolves as companions,
> very treacherous beasts. Full often his companion rends
> him.) (*Maxims IC* 146–47)

He proves by his plight that brotherhood is of elemental importance:

> Earm biþ se þe sceal ana lifgan,
> wineleas wunian   hafaþ him wyrd geteod;
> betre him wære þæt he broþor ahte,

> (Wretched is he who shall live alone;
> to dwell friendless fate has granted to him.
> Better it would be for him if he had a brother) (*Maxims IC* 172–174a)

In *The Wanderer,* the nexus of lament, born of experience, and gnome, derived from authority, yields a kind of *amplificatio* on this shadowy type, this *anhaga.* Through a blend of lyric and narrative the gnomic kernel is amplified, given breath, a face, a history.

The elegiac laments take the gnomes, which use the exile primarily as an exemplum of what *not* to be, and give their subject voice. They take what has been a marginal figure, beyond the pale of social interaction, and therefore inarticulate, and make it central to their poetic:

> Oft him anhaga   are gebideð,
> metudes miltse,   þeah þe he modcearig
> geond lagulade   longe sceolde
> hreran mid hondum   hrimcealde sæ,
> wadan wræclastas.   Wyrd bið ful aræd.

> (Often the anhaga awaits favor for himself,
> the Ruler's mercy, though he, anxious at heart,
> through the sea waves, for a long time, had
> to stir with his hand the frost chilled sea,
> follow the steps of an exile. Wyrd is entirely
> determined.) (*Wanderer* 1–5)

Here, the plight of the lone one, or *anhaga,* is finalized by the ancient gnome which tells us that fate is determined, set, inalterable. Not even the mention of the mercy of a Christian god can override the closure of that gnomic verse which delineates the final perimeter of the *anhaga*'s world. This is the centripetal movement identified by Bakhtin as characteristic of univocal texts (Bakhtin

Dialogic, 272, 286). The waiting, the need, the physical conditions, and formulaic account of exile all coalesce. The unitary language of these initial lines, however, fails once the narrator of the frame (lines 1–7) is displaced by his subject, a witness to both experience and tradition, a speaker who is able to apply one to the other and find them both wanting.[6] In *The Wanderer,* even as the *anhaga* cites gnomes mandating a stoical silence in the face of adversity, he reminds us that there is no one to hear the complaint bursting forth from the unlocked "breostocofan":

> Oft ic sceolde ana   uhtna gehwylce
> mine ceare cwiþan.   Nis nu cwicra nan
> þe ic him modsefan   minne durre
> sweotule asecgan.

> (Often I alone, every night before daybreak,
> had to speak my sorrow. Nor is there now any one living
> to whom I dare speak my mind clearly.) (8–11)

Even as he quotes from a public poetic, the *anhaga* weaves in a private sorrowing. Within his voice coexist the authoritative gnome and the bitter fruits of exile. He uses the wisdom tradition as a source for his own type, but he goes much further than citation. The fictive amplification of the gnomic kernel, which both cites and decontextualizes the exile of *Maxims I,* perforce gives that exile his own voice, which he then uses to violate traditional injunctions to be silent. The lament is made more powerful, and more problematic, by this fiction of the self-song, in which the *anhaga* is heard directly, speaking to no one. The early conflation of singer and exile gives the persona the authority of a witness, whose accounts of loss and hardship compromise the traditional detached authority of the gnome.

The dialogue between genres in *The Wanderer* also has significant implications for the text's rhetorical strategies. The personalizing, and compromising, of the gnome is vividly embodied early in the poem through a form beloved of oral poets, the variation. Some years ago, Arthur Brodeur used this term to discuss recursive elements in *Beowulf,* and it has been subsequently employed by Stanley Greenfield and others. Indeed, Greenfield calls it "probably the most distinctive as well as pervasive stylistic feature in Old English poetry" (*Interpretation* 60). Brodeur defines variation as "a double or multiple statement of the same concept or idea in different words, with a more or less perceptible shift in stress" (*Art of Beo-*

wulf 40). As a mnemonic and formulaic technique, variation allows an oral poet and his audience both to retain and to develop crucial nuggets of theme and character; it satisfies the need for repetition and for movement. In Brodeur's analysis of *Beowulf,* and in Greenfield's account of the names of exile ("Formulaic Expression"), variation operates as a kind of *repetitio,* in which meaning is maintained and emphasized; the stress is on retention of content. I would argue that, in *The Wanderer,* variation diverges from this definition in two ways. First, Brodeur's "concept or idea" becomes a more complex entity. Second, variants may act to undermine and displace meaning rather than reinforce it. In one sequence early in the poem, the injunction to silence moves through a series of three repetitive statements, each more personal than the last:

> Ic to soþ wat
> þæt biþ in eorle   indryhten þeaw,
> þæt he his ferðlocan   fæste binde,
> healde his hordcofan,   hycge swa he wille.

> (I in truth know
> that it is a noble habit in an eorl
> that he his soul's chamber bind fast;
> guard his treasure, feel what he will.)
> (11b–14)

> Forðon domgeorne   dreorigne oft
> in hyra breostcofan   bindað fæste;

> (Just as those eager for praise often
> bind sorrow fast in their heart's chamber.) (17–18)

> swa ic modsefan   minne sceolde,
> oft earmcearig,   eðle bidæled,
> freomægum feor   feterum sælan

> (so I, wretchedly sorrowful,
> deprived of homeland, far from kinsmen,
> had to confine my spirit in fetters) (19–21)

This sequence provides us with incremental instances of utterance and suppression of utterance which stand at the heart of the text's incorporation of oral modes. Both Brodeur and Greenfield see variation as the repetition of a particular. I would argue that the above passages represent variation also, but, in these lines of *The Wanderer,* the thing being repeated is not a discrete nominal but, rather, a full sentence in which the elements are: first, the *eorl* as actor (in the nominative case), second, (in the Old English word order) the self or heart as object, and third, the verbal idea "must bind" or "must confine." Thus, the persona says three times that he knows that an eorl, *dreorigne,* that is himself, must bind, or bind fast, or confine in fetters his soul-chamber, or treasure-house, or spirit. Yet, in the very act of repeating this injunction, the *anhaga* subverts it. For, the more specific the injunction becomes, the closer it comes to actual complaint. The *anhaga* first cites it as something he knows "to soþe." In the next varians, the eorl becomes "domgeorne" (eager for praise), and we hear that he has sorrow (more specific than "feel what he will"). Then, with a simple "swa," he takes the first person plunge, and abandoning mediation, expands the eorl who feels what he will, and the virtuous one who is often sad into "I, wretchedly sorrowful, deprived of homeland, far from kinsmen." The subjectification of the gnome is followed quickly by a narrative vignette amplifying the *anhaga*'s sorrow and moving the poem, for the moment, out of the gnomic insistence on stoicism and restrained speech and into the narrative lament that violates those precepts:

> siþþan geara iu   goldwine minne
> hrusan heolstre biwrah,   ond ic hean þonan
> wod wintercearig   ofer waþema gebind,
> sohte sele dreorig   sinces bryttan
>
> (since, long ago, I buried
> my gold-friend under concealing earth. Humbled then
> mad with wintersorrow, over a flood-binding,
> I sought the glorious hall, bright treasure)
>
> (22–25)

Here, the insistence on self-control has opened the gates of memory and given occasion for renewed grief.

If *The Wanderer* stopped there, we would have good reason to characterize it merely as supplanting an outworn ethic with a new, if disenfranchised, voice. Verse 29b, however, represents a shift back into the wisdom tradition. First-person, past-tense narration gives way to a third-person, present-tense reassertion of the gnomic mode:

> Wat se þe cunnað,
> hu sliþen bið   sorg to geferan,
> þam þe him lyt hafað   leofra geholena.

> (Wise is he who knows
> how dire is the sorrow of a comrade
> who has to himself few beloved protectors.)
> (29b–31)

Now, however, the accrual of wisdom has become a matter of out-lasting desolation and deprivation, of rejecting reverie and accept-ing the destruction of the very world crafted and governed by the gnome:

> Cearo bið geniwad
> þam þe sendan sceal   swiþe geneahhe
> ofer waþema gebind   werigne sefan.

> (Care is renewed
> for him who must send so very often
> a weary spirit over waves bound in ice.)
> (55b–57)

Moreover, the gnomic exemplum, the single and isolated example of one who stands (or sails) beyond the pale, who is, by virtue of his or her singularity, weary and without legitimate voice, is about to be reversed. In lines 58ff, the single, anonymous, lamenting "I" is given the heuristic powers once attributed to the collective or the authoritative persona:

> Forþon ic geþencan ne mæg   geond þas woruld
> for hwan modsefa   min ne gesweorce,
> þonne ic eorla lif   eal geondþence,
> hu hi færlice   flet ofgeafon
> modge maguþegnas.

> (Thus I cannot think concerning this world
> why my spirit does not darken
> when I think on all the life of eorls—
> how they with grace relinguished the hall,
> noble retainers)   (58–62)

Here, the poet returns to the first person, not as a narrator but as a contemplative. The lament's individual reverie on the misfortunes of one man has been broadened to embrace the fate of all *eorls,* a generalizing foreshadowed by the use of the gnomic type in preced-ing passages. But the central element of this passage is its query, "for hwan modsefa min ne gesweorc . . ." and its central dynamic is the individual's anguished contemplation of the fate of humankind, rather than a collective acknowledgment of an individual, if generic, end that satisfies a law, that fulfills expectations. The *anhaga*'s fate has not been altered, but the lens through which we see it has shifted, and with that shift new questions arise.

How is the spirit able to receive the terrible knowledge of human fate and not descend forever into darkness? To answer this heart-rending query, the *anhaga* relies heavily on a diverse body of inherited wisdom, wisdom which nevertheless stands compromised by the extremity of his experience. Even as he acknowledges the necessity for fortitude, for moderation, and for knowledge and control of the self (65b–72), he also insists on an uncompromisingly brutal account of the destruction of a beloved world—by weather, battle, and finally the creator himself. The lament, begun as a self-song, is now broadened to address the tragedy of a culture, a beloved community, destroyed.

In this poem, gnome and lament do not simply coexist. Rather, the jussive force of gnomic citations from a collective cultural ethic is expended against the insistent motif of lament, which includes complaint, reverie, and narrative allusion, all circling around a fictive personal history, a tragedy remembered, alluded to, continuing. Elaine Tuttle Hansen notes the "apparent contradiction in Old English wisdom poems between the joys of speaking and the need for discretion and restraint in speech." She identifies this as a "cross-cultural motif" indebted to the Near-Eastern tradition, in which "speech is a two edged sword, so pre-eminently the vehicle and the sign of wisdom, so synonymous with access to power and hence at once so precious and so dangerous that it must be controlled in order to be exercised and enjoyed" (Hansen 6). Speech that partakes of power, however, is not the speech of the exile, and no one is mandating silence for Hroðgar. The speech of the powerless—the widow, the exile, the lone survivor—often is referred to in larger texts without quotation. The Old English gnomic laments cannot bring back the dead or restore the homeland; but they can, through textuality, enshrine their loss.

The elegiac lament in Old English is characterized by the shifting, and sometimes uneasy, interplay between the collective voice of gnomic wisdom and a very personal and ostensibly individual response to experience. In the most successful of the elegies, the individual and the collective voices exert increasing pressure on each other. As the voice of the *anhaga* deepens and matures, it increasingly calls into question the usefulness of the venerable values it had earlier cited uncritically through the maxim. As the tone of the lament converges with that of its inherited gnomes, its substance becomes more and more subversive of them. This is not the aggregative, empathetic work once thought to be typical of the oral poet (Ong 38–39, 45–46); instead, it is analytical, critical, even isolating. Finally, the private world of the fictional persona encloses the public ethos:

> Swa cwæð snottor on mode,   gesaet him sundor æt rune.
> Til biþ se þe his treowe gehealdeþ   ne sceal næfre
>   his torne to rycene
> beorn of breostum acyþan,   nemþe he ær þa bote cunne,
> eorl mid elne gefremman.

> (Thus spoke the wise man in his mind; he sat alone,
>   apart in solitary counsel
> Blessed is he who keeps his vow. Never must the eorl
>   make known
> his grief, child of his heart, too readily, unless he
>   can first zealously
> enact a cure)

$$(111–14a)$$

These lines distill the complex relationship between poet, *snottor,* and *anhaga.* The injunction to be silent is modified for the *eorl* who can effect his own cure.

There is no cure for exile, however, and the Christian formula in lines 114b–115 offers only conventional closure. Nor is there an easy resolution to the generic contradictions that drive this poem. In *The Wanderer,* the authoritative tradition of the maxim is challenged by the exilic experience lying behind the lament. In its turn, the lament is circumscribed, stifled by gnomic pronouncement. In this poem, as in its fellows, the gnome is revealed as inadequate in the context of violent change and severe isolation, and the lament is seen to be limited, blinkered, in the face of the need for vision and wisdom.

Notes

1. In spite of Anne Klinck's arguments *("Resignation"),* I follow Bliss and Franzten's division of *Resignation* into two quite different poems.
2. Even in regard to the epic, Bakhtin's conclusions about early literatures are suspect. See Niles 81 n.3.
3. For a concise discussion of the state of tenth- and eleventh-century England and its impact on the poetry being produced at the time, see Niles.

4. See Hansen for a comprehensive discussion of the wisdom tradition in Old English; see also Shippey.

5. Old English quotations are taken from *The Exeter Book,* vol. 3 of *The Anglo-Saxon Poetic Records.* Translations are my own.

6. Leslie and Dunning-Bliss see lines 1–5 as part of the *anhaga*'s monologue. I follow Krapp and Dobbie in part because I hear lines 1–5 as a citation of the exilic type, rather than the voice of the exile himself.

Works Cited

Bakhtin, M. M. *The Dialogic Imagination: Four Essays.* Ed. Michael Holquist. Trans. Caryl Emerson and Michael Holquist. Austin: University of Texas Press, 1981.

———. *Speech Genres and Other Late Essays.* Ed. Caryl Emerson and Michael Holquist. Trans. Vern W. McGee. Austin: University of Texas Press, 1985.

Bauml, Franz H. "Varieties and Consequences of Medieval Literacy and Illiteracy." *Speculum* 55 (1980):237–65.

Beowulf and the Fight at Finnsbug. Ed. Friedrich Klaeber. 3rd ed. Boston: D.C. Heath, 1950.

Bliss, Alan and Allen J. Frantzen. "The Integrity of *Resignation.*" *Review of English Studies* ns 27 (1976): 385–402.

Brodeur, Arthur. *The Art of Beowulf.* Berkeley: University of California Press, 1959.

Clanchy, M. T. *From Memory to Written Record: England, 1066–1307.* London: Edward Arnold, 1979.

Dunning, T. P., and Alan J. Bliss, eds. *The Wanderer.* London: n.p., 1969.

The Exeter Book. Ed. George Philip Krapp and Elliott Van Kirk Dobbie. Vol. 3 of *The Anglo-Saxon Poetic Records.* New York: Columbia University Press, 1936.

Finnegan, Ruth. *Oral Literature in Africa.* Oxford: Clarendon Press, 1970.

Foley, John Miles. "Orality, Textuality, and Interpretation." *Vox Intexta: Orality and Textuality in the Middle Ages.* Ed. A. N. Doane and Carol Braun Pasternack. Madison: University of Wisconsin Press, 1991. 34–45.

Greenfield, Stanley. "The Formulaic Expression of the Theme of 'Exile' in Anglo-Saxon Poetry." *Speculum* 30 (1955):200–6.

———. *The Interpretation of Old English Poems.* Boston: Routledge & Kegan Paul, 1972.

Hansen, Elaine Tuttle. *The Solomon Complex: Reading Wisdom in Old English Poetry.* Toronto: University of Toronto Press, 1988.

Havelock, Eric A. *The Muse Learns to Write: Reflections on Orality and Literacy from Antiquity to the Present.* New Haven: Yale University Press, 1986.

Klinck, Anne L. *The Old English Elegies: A Critical Edition and Genre Study.* Montreal: McGill-Queen's University Press, 1992.

———. "*Resignation:* Exile's Lament or Penitent's Prayer?" *Neophilologus* 71 (1987): 423–430.

Leslie, Roy F., ed. *The Wanderer.* Manchester: n.p., 1966.

Niles, John D. "Locating *Beowulf* in History." *Exemplaria* 5 (1993):79–110.

O'Keefe, Katherine O'Brien. *Visible Song: Transitional Literacy in Old English Verse.* Cambridge Studies in Anglo-Saxon England 4. Cambridge: Cambridge University Press, 1990.

Ong, Walter J. *Orality and Literacy: The Technologizing of the Word.* New York: Methuen, 1982.

Opland, Jeff. *Anglo-Saxon Oral Poetry.* New Haven: Yale University Press, 1980.

————. Plenary Address. Barnard Medieval and Renaissance Conference on Literacy and Orality. November 1988.

————. *Xhosa Oral Poetry: Aspects of a Black South African Tradition.* Cambridge: Cambridge University Press, 1983.

Parks, Ward. "The Textualization of Orality in Literary Criticism." *Vox Intexta: Orality and Textuality in the Middle Ages.* Ed. A. N. Doane and Carol Braun Pasternack. Madison: University of Wisconsin Press, 1991. 46–61.

Peabody, Berkeley. *The Winged Word: A Study in the Technique of Ancient Greek Oral Composition as Seen Principally Through Hesiod's Works and Days.* Albany: S.U.N.Y. Press, 1975.

The Poetic Edda. Tr. Lee M. Hollander. Austin: University of Texas Press, 1962.

Shippey, T. A. *Poems of Wisdom and Learning in Old English.* Cambridge: D. S. Brewer, 1976.

Stock, Brian. *The Implications of Literacy.* Princeton: Princeton University Press, 1983.

The Alba Lady, Sex-Roles, and Social Roles: "Who peyntede the leon, tel me who?"

GALE SIGAL

THE ELOQUENT AND DRAMATIC VOICE OF THE ALBA LADY HAS BROUGHT this lesser-studied medieval lyric genre to the attention of literary and social critics for the light it may shed on medieval women's roles in poetry and in twelfth-century society. These scholars have determined that the alba lady shares the qualities attributed to women by almost all the literary traditions known to the Middle Ages; there is nothing new in "her passion, her exclusive concern with love, her upholding of erotic values above all others, and her violent opposition to reality. . . ." (Saville 155). Characterized by these critics as an abandoned, wailing woman, the alba lady, like Dido, is degraded by her lover and deserted by Love. She becomes merely a link in the long chain of powerless, passive females; the genre is notorious for illustrating "the otherness of woman in medieval lyric by positing her ultimate desertion by her lover, as well as her exclusion from the male community of action" (Fries 158).

By fitting the alba lady so neatly into existing categories, these critics fail to see her singularity. Far from reiterating the role of the passive, victimized female, she is neither ignored nor rejected by her lover; rather than being destroyed by love, she gains strength. She sings to an audience of presumed sympathizers, and even though her illicit activities are to be kept secret, she serenades us so ardently about them that we become willing accessories to her "crime." Her dignity, her active control over her love life, her implicit defiance of her traditional role, and her poignant expression of feeling are as unprecedented as they are persuasive.

If "courtly literature of the twelfth century is the first secular medieval literature in which women play an important role" (Ferrante 67), in the alba they have the starring part. Although most, if not all, medieval erotic albas were composed by male poets, the troubadours' use of the female voice, rather than being a misogynistic usurpation (as it is in medieval Latin verse), is empathic.[1] The alba allies itself with female passion, unites male and female experience, and poet, characters, and audience are swept up in the intensity of the emotions. The alba lady celebrates consummated, reciprocal love even as she laments its disruption. The lady of the genre, unlike her literary predecessors, is an eloquent spokeswoman for fulfilling mutual love.

The alba presents a new feminine paradigm: unlike her contemporaries—the female characters created for other medieval vernacular lyric genres—the alba lady is not mediated through the eyes of a male narrator or lover (like the pastourelle shepherdess or canso lady) even though she is, like her lyric sisters, created by a male poet. In her reciprocity and outspokenness, the alba lady implicitly critiques the frustrated posturings of the unrequited canso lover and the silence of its iconic lady. The alba lady is similarly reducible neither to Ovidian influences nor allegorical representations (akin to Dante's later Beatrice).[2]

The stylized courtly *domna* springs to life in the alba poet's shaping hand. She is humanized into a lively, forthright, and spontaneous woman. Rather than being wedded to conventional, oppressive conceptions of women or promoting female subordination, alba poets are concerned with depicting, investigating, and anatomizing the anarchic emotions and equalizing alchemy of sexual love. They tacitly criticize the stultifying gender roles and societal expectations that their alba lovers heroically decry and that the love they portray or create seeks to transcend. Within the courtly corpus, the alba provides an outlet for subversion.

When one reads through the alba corpus, rather than finding conventional roles for lady or lover, one discovers a more expansive and liberating view of traditional gender roles. The illicit alba lovers are, if anything, anti-conventional, and the lady's role is significantly less confining than her canso counterpart, forced as the latter is into majestic silence. Moreover, in her varied and artful voices, in her adoption of diverse roles, and in what could be called her exchanges—rather than reversals—of roles with her lover, the alba lady escapes the confinements of traditional female roles both social and literary. She fully indulges in the creative expression promoted by the liberating, though secret, love she pursues. Her freedom and self-indulgence reveal a shedding of conventional roles rather than a substituting of one set of roles for its opposite (the sex-role reversal).

Rather than recognizing the fundamentally anti-conventional (and anti-social) nature of the alba, however, critics have sought to show that the genre upholds conventional sex-roles. But sex-role theory is a dangerous interpretive tool: many of the assumptions that lie behind our perceptions of the differences between male and female roles are so deeply ingrained and automatic that those who are most bound by them are often the least conscious of their presence. Because our most powerful impulses frequently turn out to be those we have most deeply repressed, it is difficult to be fully aware of our own perspective, hence, our own biases. Assessments of male and female roles are particularly vulnerable to such subjective treatment, for gender-based assumptions are intertwined with our most fundamental understandings of our culture (Gilbert 33). Consequently, in researching gender-related subjects, we must be especially careful not to allow our own conceptions of sex-roles to cloud our view. Numerous errors of perception have been made by past researchers; in many disciplines, feminist scholars have taken the lead in correcting the record.

In *Female Strategies,* a fascinating exposé of past omissions and errors of biological researchers, biologists Evelyn Shaw and Joan Darling conclude that "the feminine stereotype is so tightly etched in scientific thought that a female [animal] who is brightly colored, promiscuous and a gadabout is described as showing 'sex role reversal'—in other words, taking the expected masculine role. . . . [M]any scientists are reluctant to relinquish their cherished image of the male's monopoly on courtship behavior and sexual drive" (11–12).[3] Researchers who record data that conflict with their notions of appropriate or expected behavior designate such behavior "sex-role reversal." As we are only too well aware, scientists are not the sole culprits of such flawed perceptions. As scholars, we must be very wary of imposing personal views of sex-roles onto literary characters or narrative voices, since such designations reveal more about our own preconceptions of masculinity and femininity than about the poetry our studies intend to elucidate.

Robert Kaske first introduced the idea that alba lovers consistently illustrate specified sex-roles. In his well-known article, "The Aube in Chaucer's *Troilus*" (1961), he posits not only that there are definitive sex-roles in albas, but that Chaucer intentionally reverses those roles in his masterful alba in Book III:

In particular, Chaucer seems to have bestowed on Troilus several speeches usually assigned to the lady in an aube, and on Criseyde certain speeches usually assigned to the lover, thus enriching a theme sometimes detected in other parts of the poem: the reversal of the roles of man and woman as they are popularly or romantically conceived. (171)

To assess how sex-roles are "popularly or romantically conceived" even today is no simple matter; to speculate about how they were conceived in the Middle Ages in general, or in a particular genre of lyric, would seem nigh impossible. Although Kaske qualified his interpretation with a proviso that it was inconclusive, that the number of his examples is "suspiciously slight," and that exceptions to his patterns are present "[i]n every instance" (176), his cautions have not been heeded. Since the extant corpus of albas is small to begin with (and that corpus possibly only a fraction of what was composed and popularly known), one should, at the least, hesitate to make large generalizations about its male and female roles, especially when there are many exceptions to the posited "norms," as Kaske carefully acknowledges.

Yet, Kaske's interpretation has never been challenged; instead, it has been accepted and elaborated. Consequently, sex-role analysis and its corollary, the sex-role reversal theory, have engendered a view of the alba that has become not only more entrenched with time but also increasingly distorted. Rather than examine the albas themselves to corroborate Kaske's initial impressions, subsequent critics have relied on Kaske's hypothesis *as a closed case.*

Kaske's quest for consistency in sex-role presentation reveals his own concern with prescribed gender roles far more than it illuminates the medieval genre. The continuing preoccupation with this line of inquiry by subsequent scholars reflects not medieval but modern cultural anxiety about the proper roles of male and female and about the catastrophic consequences of not conforming to these roles. Hence, Kaske's hypothesized "sex-role reversal" between Troilus and Criseyde may conveniently be used to explain the disasters that inevitably follow.

Unlike critics who have relied on Kaske's knowledge of the genre, Jonathan Saville displays a comprehensive knowledge of the genre; nonetheless, he applies sex-role theory to it. In characterizing alba males and females, Saville invokes the sex-role reversal theory:

> . . . while the knight is usually the first to give in and accept reality, the lady usually accepts it only grudgingly, if at all, and only when the man is already taking his leave. In a few albas the lady is much concerned with the knight's safety, and seconds the watchman's urgings that he leave. But this is so unusual a state of affairs that we are probably justified in considering it a conscious reversal (on the part of the poet) of the norm. (154)

Saville further describes the alba lady as "much more passionate than the knight; and much more eloquent in her expression of feeling" (153). Although the genre's artistry often resides in the lady's eloquent lament—the song's *raison d'être* and centerpiece—and although albas are sung more often by the lady than any other character, the careful reader finds that whenever alba men (be they watchmen or lovers) address the lady or the audience, their voices are intense and ardent—complementary to, rather than competitive with, the lady's.

The idea that because the alba lady is passionate and eloquent, her lover cannot be so as well may likewise be a modern bias. Theatrically minded or psychologically aware critics bring to their view of lovers in dramatic poetry the idea that they are competing for external recognition (that is, from either the inscribed or the extra-diagetic audience), a contest more relevant to siblings competing for parental attention or actors vying with one another for the spotlight or the audience's acclaim than to parting lovers. No such rivalry is evident between alba lovers. In other lyric genres, male and female are inherently unequal: in the pastourelle, the peasant shepherdess is accosted by an aristocratic knight-errant; in the canso, the exalted lady is worshipped by one who feels (and may be) inferior.[4] But the alba never postulates one lover's or gender's superiority over the other. Indeed, this equality is one of the most significant and touching innovations of the genre.

Ironically, while Kaske and Saville have sought to distinguish gender-defined behavior, as well as significant divergences from a posited set of "norms" in the alba, they have overlooked the much more pervasive and obvious similarities between the sexes. Interpretations based on sex-role stereotypes expose the critics' limited recognition, not only of the genre's variety but of its major concerns. Equality and reciprocity, not difference or indifference, are at the heart of the alba. Kaske twice notes, offhandedly, the free assignment of roles in the alba, ignoring the definitive value of such fluid role-adoption: "Criseyde's wish for longer night (1427–28) is a commonplace, freely assigned to either of the lovers in an aube. . . . This commitment of the loved one to God's care is a frequent motif in the aube, where it is freely assigned to either the lover or the lady" (172, 174).

Disregarding the active, aggressive role the alba lady regularly takes as initiator and participant-celebrant of the love affair, Fries considers the alba lady an exemplification of the philocentric, passive, and impotent female desperate to retain her lover within her narrow world: "The woman speaker is absorbed in the experience of the beloved's presence in or absence from her arms, a passive experience as opposed to that world of male activity which occupies most of his life . . . she may be rhetorically dominant but is actually powerless in her attempts to confine her man within the bounds of her feminine world, as most dramatically illustrated in the *alba*" (159). Fries disregards the alba male's equal obsession with his lady; and in contrasting the lady's presumed passivity to an opposing "world of male activity," Fries presumes that the lady's experience is personal and passive ("her feminine world," that is, domestic and stultifying), as opposed to male experience, which is in and of "the world"—public, active, free. These loaded terms illuminate Fries's (and typically modern) biases more than they do the alba.

Before we turn to the lyrics that contradict such sex-role analyses, let us note in passing that the "world of male activity" is so remote from the alba landscape as to render it irrelevant to the lovers' laments. The exclusion of the outside world is an essential generic attribute: alba love strives for a self-enclosed autonomy that shuts out external forces. *Both* lovers long to escape from that "world of male activity," which for them is synonymous with the despised authoritarian obstruction to their love, self-expression, and freedom. That the lovers try so hard to shut the world out of their nocturnal tryst is testimony to its pervasive, tyrannical presence in their daily lives.

Examination of individual albas reveals that either lover can be passive or aggressive, but both are powerless—and equally desperate—to change their situation. They both desire to perpetuate night. The male lover, like his lady, is completely absorbed in the love experience, rather than any other activity. In the Old Provençal alba, "Ab la gensor que sia," the male lover longingly recounts an idyllic tryst with his lady. He recollects how, after their joyful play, he fell asleep beside his beloved until dawn:

> Ab la gensor que sia
> et ab la mielhs aibia
> mi colgei l'autre dia
> tan solamen
> jogan rizen
> m'adormi tro al dia. (1–6)

> (By the noblest Lady
> and the fairest
> I lay me down the other day
> so alone
> playing, laughing
> I slept the night away.)

Passively receptive to his lady's actions, the lover reminisces as longingly as any alba lady:

> Mentre qu'ieu mi jazia
> En sobinas dormia,
> Un dous bais mi tendia
>   Tan plazenmen,
>   Qu'enquer lo·m sen
> E farai a ma via. (7–12)

> (While I lay
> Supine, sleeping,
> A sweet kiss she tendered me
>   So pleasingly
>   That I feel it still
> And all my life I will.

The lady in this dreamlike sequence appears as the more active partner, while the lover paints himself as passive, reclining, sleeping, responding—a self-portrait that might tempt some readers to characterize him as "feminine," especially because he presents himself as the object of another's desire. But to so "type" him would be distorting. In the remainder of the lyric, he angrily threatens the watchman and the *gilos* (the "jealous one," presumably her husband). His aggressive side is revealed in strophe three:

> Gaita, s'ieu ti tenia,
> De mas t'auciria,
> Ja res pro no·t tenria,
>   Aur ni argen
>   Ni hom viven
> Ni res que e·l mon sia.

> (Watchman, if I held you,
> In my hands, I'd kill you,
> Nothing would ever help you at all
>   Neither gold nor silver
>   Nor living man,
> Nor anything in the world.)

He calls down curses on the watchman: "Gaita, dieus ti maldia."

The contrast between his loving affection for his lady and his verbal (and potentially physical) aggression toward the watchman reveals his complexity and emotional range, his humanity. Ironically, *he* resembles Fries's "rhetorically dominant but . . . actually powerless" lady. At the same time, the reader who, bound by sex-role stereotypes, evaluates the lover's initial self-presentation as "feminine," would now be forced to reappraise him in light of his subsequent "masculine" behavior.

In fact, all alba lovers, male and female, are "rhetorically dominant but . . . actually powerless" to alter their circumstances. The power of rhetorical dominance, especially as expressed by a gifted poet or singer, should not be underestimated. That the poet gives his lovers license to cry out against their pain is an empowering recognition, even a legitimation of it. Loud complaint may signify powerlessness and desperation, but in the literary or performance context, it is the rhetorically dominant voice that is heard and endures. The more authoritarian forces of husband or society are excluded from the lyric; they are silenced.

Although the poet endows the lover with particular behavioral traits, he nowhere suggests that they are gendered. The lover of "Ab la gensor que sia" behaves with discrimination: he is gentle and passionate toward his lady but not toward the *gilos,* or watchman. He adjusts his emotions according to their object, demonstrating an elasticity of response, a capacity for making distinctions within a range of possible reactions. For all his range, however, he resists reality as much as any alba lady.

If this lover reminisces longingly, so too does the lady of the Old French "Entre moi et mon amin." She recalls a tryst in which she and her lover were also "playing" *(juwant)* one moonlit night until dawn. Like the male lover of the previously cited lyric, she then relates her lover's actions:

> Adont ce trait pres de mi,
> Et je ne fu pas anfriune;
> Bien trois fois me baixait il,
> Ainsi fix je lui plus d'une,
> >K'ainz ne m'anoiait.
> >Adonc vocexiens nus lai
> >Ke celle nut durest sant. (13–19)

> (Then he drew himself to me
> And I did not hold back
> Three times at least he kissed me
> More than once I kissed him back
> >For that did not bore me.
> >Then how glad we should have been
> >Had that night lasted one hundred.)

The activities in which these two alba couples engage are almost identical. In the first poem, the male recalls his lady's actions; in this one, the lady remembers her lover's. Both narrators recount their reciprocating responses. These parallel portrayals cannot lead us to conclude that one of the two poets is consciously reversing a norm, for we cannot establish a norm in the first place. What we can perceive is that lady and lover can be active or passive, and sometimes both active and passive.

The knight of the alba "Us cavaliers si jazia" tells his beloved of his great desire for her—so strong that living without her would kill him: "Que ses vos vida non ai" (For without you I have no life). Pledging to return quickly, he like many an alba lady, bewails the emptiness of life without his beloved. These sentiments do not "feminize" him any more than strong emotions "masculinize" a lady; rather, we learn that the male alba lover is as obsessed, declares his devotion as forcefully, sorrows as poignantly, and loves as intensely as his lady.

Mutuality is the most essential and distinctive aspect of alba love. Alba lovers address one another as "friend" or are described literally as "friend with friend" (amic d'amia ["Us cavaliers si jazia"]), friend being a synonym (or euphemism) for "lover" in many languages, including Old Occitan, Old French, Middle High German, and English. The great poet Wolfram von Eschenbach[5] tells us the lovers form a "fellowship" *(gesilleschaft)* or lie together companionably *(geselleclîchen als si lâgen* ["Sîne Klâwen", "Den morgenblic"]), making ironic allusions to the knightly bonding he so cherishes elsewhere in his oeuvre. While such companionship is, first and foremost, sexual, and the words *friend* and *companionship* euphemistic, these terms nonetheless manifest a specific aspect of their intimacy: the lovers share confidences and provide mutual emotional gratification and affection. Alba love is not solely sexual gratification.

The lover of either sex anticipates a sympathetic hearing from his/her paramour. If the male lover of Walther von der Vogelweide's "Friuntlîchen lac" asks for his lady's thoughts: "Now tell me in our brief moments all that you wish" (nû rede in kurzen zîten allez daz dû wil [19]), the lady of Cadenet's "S'anc fui belha ni prezada" declares that her lover is one in whom she freely confides:

> E murria
> S'ieu fin amic non avia
> Cuy disses mo marrimen. (5–7)

(And I would die
Had I not my true love by
To whom to tell my sorrows.)

Sharing secrets typifies alba lovers, making it a measure of their companionship and closeness.

If "[i]t is almost a commonplace to say that the couple as we know it was invented in twelfth-century France" (Duby 144), that concept derives much of its refinement from the intimacies portrayed in the alba. The portrait of lady and lover laterally conjoined that opens one of the most famous Old Provençal albas sets generic expectations: "En un vergier sotz fuella d'albespi, / tenc la dompna son amic costa si" (in a park under the leaves of the hawthorne, / the lady holds her lover at her side). The motif of attachment is further marked by the juxtapositioning of the words "tenc la dompna son amic costa si," which accentuates the lovers' conjoinment (literally, "holds the lady her lover at her side"). The lady of "Cant voi l'aube dou jor venir" laments that she misses the presence "encoste mi" (at my side) of her lover's body. The "breast-to-breast" embrace referred to in the tageliet, echoes the Romance poets' use of the word *costa,* which etymologically derives from "rib." If the lovers' side-by-side position is evoked by a mere phrase, such as "ab son amic," or "pres de mi" in the Romance alba, in the tageliet, the identical position is referred to in the phrase "bi mir." These references to specific body parts emphasize the physicality, corporeality, and intimacy of the attachment. Because these body parts are already doubled (that is, an individual has two breasts; a ribcage, two symmetrical halves), the poet magnifies how the lovers mirror each other. Attachment is so essential a component, it becomes a motif in itself.

Furthermore, the continual, almost obsessive references to the lovers' side-by-side and reclining postures literally portray the lovers on an equal plane; their relationship is horizontal rather than hierarchical. Speaking of his tryst with an unidentified but superlative lady, the lover of "Ab la gensor que sia" begins by describing his position:

Ab la gensor que sia
et ab la mielhs aibia
mi colgei l'autre dia.

(1–3)

(By the noblest who could be
and the fairest
I lay me down the other day.)

At the beginning of the second strophe, he again refers to his reclining position:

Mentre qu'ieu mi jazia
e·n sobinas dormia.
(7–8)

(While I was lying
and supine, asleep.)

Although vague about the mundane details of place, the poem twice carefully specifies the lover's reclining posture. Twice also in "Gaite de la tor," the lovers' recumbent position is referred to, first by the watchman: "cortois ameor, / qui a sejor / gisez on chambre coie" ("courteous lovers, / who lie at rest / in the quiet room" [44–46]), and later by the lover himself: "Pou ai geü / En la chambre de joie" (Too briefly have I lain / in the chamber of joy [62–63]). The opening lines of Walther's "Friuntlîchen lac" portray the knight reclining:

Friuntlîchen lac
ein rîter vil gemeit
an einer frowen arme.
(1–3)

(Companionably lay
a splendid knight
in the arms of a lady.)

Later, the lady asks her lover to lie there longer: "nû lige eht eine wîle: sô getaet dû nie sô wol" (now just lie awhile: you could never do so well [40]).

In many of these examples, the lover's supine posture is mentioned at the very opening of the poem, as though it in itself gives a sense of place to the poems. In "Dieus, aydatz," the lover's posture is withheld until the conclusion, when the lady speaks of her lover, "qu'e mon bratz / jauzen jatz" (who in my arms / joyful lies [53–54]).

The emphasis on this horizontal positioning, which coincides with other aspects of mutuality and equality, appears with such prevalence that it becomes in itself a motif or generic signifier; no similar phrasing or posturing appears in other genres. Such posturing is not mentioned in poems where the lady speaks about her relationship with her husband, despite the fact that there may be physical intimacy between them. In the marriage scenario, the husband is (metaphorically) on top, in contrast to alba lovers who are companionably side by side. The linguistic formula I refer to—present in Old Provençal, Old French, and Middle High German versions of the dawn-song—is too consistent to be accidental or insignificant. The poet's continual reference to the lovers' being together side by side emphasizes the importance of the detail to the relationship. The side-by-side formula is but one of several descriptive phrases indicative of the lovers' equality and mutuality.

Despite its idyllic reciprocality, the alba is elegiac, a song of loss and separation. When Fries claims that the alba posits the lady's desertion by her lover, as well as her exclusion from the male community (158), she fails to see that the loss is felt by both lovers, not by the lady alone. To see the alba as solely about the desertion of women by men is reductive and one-sided. Such a view creates a distorted portrait of the alba lady as abandoned and victimized by the one person she has freely chosen and with whom she shares her most intimate moments and feelings. The enforced leave-taking does not constitute desertion; in fact, the lovers might meet every night and yet sing an alba when they part. The fact that more albas are narrated by the lady than by her lover does not indicate that she is more often deserted or that the man's plight (even when it goes unspoken) should be lightly dismissed. When the male lover has a singing role, he expresses sorrows similar to those of his lady.

Fries's observation is representative of a general critical myopia: even when a man does express his sorrows or fears, it is all too easily overlooked. If it is noticed, he is considered an "exception," and the sex-role reversal theory is put into operation. In this way, critics relegate extremities of emotion—the heights of passion and desire, the depths of sorrow, dread, and fear—to the female domain. Hence, we can persuade ourselves (or be persuaded) that intense emotions and their eloquent renderings in song are—or should be—alien to the masculine "norm." Alba poets portray loving and suffering men who never signify that they may be violating a masculine code. And in writing the alba, the male poet identifies with the anguish of love-parting, whether that sorrow is voiced by the male or female lover.

The lover of "Us cavaliers si jazia," after expressing his great desire (cited above), goes on to relate the unparalleled anguish he feels about parting:

> Doussa res, que qu'om vos dia,
> No cre que tals dolars sia
> Cum qui part amic d'amia
> Qu'ieu per me mezeys o sai.
>
> (20–24)

> (Gentle one, whatever they say,
> Never believe there could be such dismay
> Like that which parts lover from lover,
> For I myself have proved it.)

The lover of "Gaita be" suffers as well:

> mays enics sui de l'alba
> e·l destrics que·l jorn nos fai
>   mi desplai
> plus que l'alba, l'alba, oc l'alba!
>
> (10–14)

> (but grievous to me is the thought of dawn
> and the distress wrought by morn
> displeases me
> more than the dawn, the dawn, yes the dawn!)

Tageliet men are no less sorrowful. The narrator of Wolfram's "Von der zinnen" laments: "allen mannen / trûren nie sô gar zerstôrte ir vroiden vunt" (Sadness never so utterly destroyed the fund of happiness of any man). Why pass over or turn these expressions into sex-role reversals except to minimize such emotions or deny their appropriateness for male behavior?

The lady of Wolfram's "Ez ist nu tac" sings of the sorrow she and her lover share, never doubting that he feels it as deeply as she: "Ich weiz vil wol, daz ist ouch ime" (I know full well that it is the same with him). Her intuition is corroborated when, like his lady, the lover cries out: "jô erkande ich nie / kein trûric scheiden alsô snel" (I never knew such a sad and sudden parting). The narrator does not neglect to recount the sharing of pleasures as well as sorrows: "Si beide luste daz er kuste si genouc / . . . Ir ougen naz dô wurden baz, och twanc in klage" (that he kissed her enough they both liked it well / . . . Her wet eyes then grew wetter, sorrow also oppressed him). Wolfram binds together their joys and their sorrows in the same line. In his "Den morgenblic," the lady's tears "moistened the cheeks of both" lovers (diu beguzzen / ir beider wangel). With this image, Wolfram portrays how close the lovers are physically and emotionally.

Wolfram surpasses his poetic rivals in showing how fluid the roles can be by portraying the turns his lovers take in embracing each other. He twice depicts the lovers' embrace. First the lady, and next the lover, initiates the embrace: "Daz guote wîp ir friundes lîp vast umbevie / .... an sîne bruste druhte er sie" (the good woman her friend's body fast embraced / .... He drew her to his breast ["Ez ist nu tac"]). Wolfram's portrayal of their reciprocity ensures that the audience will understand how mutual and equal alba love is. Under these circumstances, it is disheartening to come across critical appraisals that make gender distinctions where none exist in the poetry. Paden, for example, declares that in the alba "the lover has enjoyed the lady's favors from the start" ("Troubadour's Lady" 158), assuming a power relationship in which only men enjoy ladies' "favors" and failing to recognize that love, in the alba, means that both sexes share, love, and enjoy.

Although Fries claims that the alba is about the desertion of women by men, no consistent pattern can be found in the lyrics. If the lady of the Old French "Cant voi l'aube dou jor venir" asks her lover to remember her, it is the male partner who begs for remembrance in "Us cavaliers si jazia." The lady of "Cant voi l'aube dou jor venir" warns her lover:

> Biaus dous amis, vos en ireis,
> A Deu soit vos cors comandeis.
> Por Deu vos pri, ne m'obleis.
> Je n'ain nulle rien tant com vos.
>
> (19–22)

> (Fair gentle friend, be off,
> To God may your body be commended.
> In God's name, I beg you, never forget me.
> I do not love anything as much as you.)

The lover of "Us cavaliers si jazia" begs his lady:

> Per Dieu, no m'oblidetz mia
> Que·l cor del cors reman sai
> Ni de vos mais no·m partria.
>
> (33–35)

> (In God's name, don't ever forget me
> For the heart of my body remains here
> And from you shall I never part.)

On either side of the gender fence, lovers invoke God when imploring the beloved's remembrance. The lover of "Us cavaliers si jazia" speaks of his "cors," playing with the same association between heart and body as the lady of "Cant voi l'aube dou jor venir." Whereas the lady of "Cant voi l'aube dou jor venir" commends her lover's body into God's keeping, the lover of "Us cavaliers si jazia" pledges his heart to his mistress, leaving it in his lady's keeping. Kaske, too, indicated that the commitment of the loved one to God's care is freely assigned to either sex, as already noted (174).

Furthermore, despite Fries's assumption, it is not only the male who is capable of abandoning. Indeed, if we consider the most famous of all medieval alba scenarios, and the only extant example in which the secret love affair is worked out in some narrative detail, we find that the desertion is perpetrated by the lady—Criseyde—not by ever-faithful Troilus. The fact that Criseyde, rather than Troilus, is unfaithful does not, however, justify Kaske's conclusion that a "sex-role reversal," which can be traced through the alba, has taken place. Kaske contrasts Troilus's "hesitant request for assurance (III, 1485–91) and Criseyde's long answering promise of faithfulness" (III, 1492–1518) with the "prevailing pattern" of the medieval alba: "Though there are strong exceptions, its prevailing pattern seems to be that in which the lady introduces the question of faithfulness, and the lover replies with an elaborate pledge in what might be described as the superlative mood" (173). We have seen, however, that the interchange between lady and lover takes a variety of forms, that both speak of their faithfulness and both make pledges. Indeed, the poets may have known each other's lyrics and may have been experimenting with "role-playing" and with responding to one another's motifs long before Chaucer would have been able to discern "prevailing patterns."

Kaske further observes of the alba in general that it is the male who is "more nearly resigned to the necessity of parting, while the lady emotionally opposes or laments his departure and begs for his quick return" (173). Although examples of this type certainly exist, there are also albas that contradict these "patterns." Such "strong exceptions" (as Kaske calls them) within so small a corpus suggest that the theory does not hold. In fact, the absence of sex-roles, rather than their establishment and subsequent reversal, is at the very heart of the alba.

My conclusions suggest not that Chaucer was intentionally planting a sex-role reversal between Troilus and Criseyde, but rather that alba poets championed a much less rigid conception of sex-roles than do modern critics. There is no sex-role reversal from the early alba to Chaucer's dawn-song in *Troilus and Criseyde* because sex-roles are not assigned in the alba in the first place. Indeed, this lack of sex-role differentiation is one of the miraculous aspects of the alba; for alba poets, it is also a truth about love itself.

Chaucer uses Troilus and Criseyde's alba to highlight the very real differences between his characters; yet, crucial as these differences are for the denouement of Chaucer's narrative, these "character" differences are not the product of an intentional sex-role reversal on Chaucer's part. Like their alba forerunners, Troilus and Criseyde transcend their differences with joyful abandon during moments of mutual bliss. Chaucer captures the reciprocal love they enjoy their first night together in the image of the twining honeysuckle:

> And as aboute a tree with many a twiste
> Bytrent and writhe the swote wodebynde,
> Gan ech of hem in armes other wynde.
> (III, 1230–32)

Regardless of the behind-the-scene machinations required to bring about their union, this honeysuckle image reveals the symbiosis of love operative throughout the alba genre. For a brief time, Troilus and Criseyde relax their personal boundaries; they merge together. The romantic situation Chaucer plays out is embedded in all albas: the idealized and distant lady, warmed to responsiveness, is not diminished by returning her wooer's affections, nor is love destroyed when she reciprocates. On the contrary, love deepens and intensifies.

But, while his alba predecessors take the similarity, mutuality, and symbiosis of alba lovers as their subject, Chaucer portrays love as having only a temporary power to obliterate personal boundaries. Dawn's light reimposes Troilus and Criseyde's individual personalities, each addressing a different aspect of dawn at sunrise. When Chaucer replaces the image of dawn with night and day in Troilus and Criseyde's dawn-song, he simultaneously discards the symbolic fusion of alba lovers in favor of fragmentation and difference.

Troilus and Criseyde each abide by a different aspect of the Janus-faced dawn. When she begins her lament, Criseyde turns toward night, pleading for delay in its flight; Troilus addresses day, the dreaded future. That Chaucer bestows on Troilus and Criseyde very different personalities, needs, and motives does not mean, however, that he was intentionally planting a sex-role reversal between them that destroyed their potential happiness. Their laments highlight temperamental tendencies that, in the course of the poem, receive fuller development. The differing response each has to the necessity of parting paints in broad strokes the contrasting personalities of the lovers. The lovers' individual responses prefigure their separate, though intertwined, fates.

Chaucer's bifurcation of the alban dawn into night and day is innovative; but this poetic dichotomization of dawn also expresses a pessimistic attitude toward love not manifest by his generic predecessors. When Chaucer moves alba love from a Christian into a pagan world, he can represent it as a transient, unenlightened experience, however precious and worthy, that leads, finally, to a tragic demise.[6]

Chaucer's greater interest in the idiosyncracies of personalities within the couple rather than in the sharing and attachment between them demonstrates his, and possibly his later age's, new way of problematizing individuality as it encounters erotic love. For Chaucer, the differences within the couple are more dominant and enduring than the intimacy the lovers share; and these differences, in combination with potent external forces, direct the downward spiraling of the love affair.

The sex-linked roles of male and female may be enacted after dawn, once alba lovers separate. But when they are together, there is no outside world. Any thought of the future—or "reality"—is purposely evaded in the alba. Sex-role differentiation is enforced by the very social codes the lovers seek to escape. The alba depicts lover and lady while they are together, and at that time they are portrayed as equals, as friends. It is the mutuality and liberating qualities of their love, rather than a set of separate, prescribed roles, that the alba portrays. Its receptivity to the intimacy, generosity, and androgyny of love not only gives the alba its marvelous appeal but makes it truly avant-garde.

In the alba, the troubadours were launching a new vision of love that valued reciprocity and equality. Even if, like most other medieval literary female creations, the alba lady is a male-constructed ideal, she reveals something about the poets' aspirations and dreams. She is a more humane and humanized woman than the ladies of antiquity or of medieval epic; she is more responsive than the canso *domna* and far more dignified than the pastourelle *vilana*.

In creating women who adopt a variety of roles, whose voices are fluent, artful, and independent, alba poets provide metaphors as well as vehicles for their own creativity. They sympathize with lovers who desire to transcend the limitations of confining, conventional roles just as the poets themselves may have desired to transcend the confinements of established poetic codes. That alba poets were able to convey the lovers' voices so movingly speaks an eloquent tribute to their own desire to represent some human truths that, at least in their eyes, transcend gender altogether.

Those who view the lady as victimized by her lover, and by the social conventions that (they believe) endow him with superior status to hers, distort the genre. They underestimate the lady's strength and independence, and they polarize the lovers' ungendered actions into male and female roles; in so doing, they miss the poets' most momentous innovation. Far from being a recapitulation of literary and social conventions, the alba puts forth a subtle, understated, but nonetheless revolutionary critique of the social order. In the alba, lady and lover construct a space apart from the sordid conventions that place the sexes in disequilibrium.

Rather than view the male partner as more powerful or free than the lady, we should acknowledge that in the alban love triangle, it is the lady's husband who is on top, at the apex. Lady and lover are equal but disenfranchised, and both remain at the triangle's base; that is, unless they can convince us, through their eloquent lament, that their ennobling love can turn the triangle upside down.[7]

Notes

1. Although we cannot rule out the possibility that, in the cases where we do not know the authorship, anonymous was a woman, scholars find no evidence to suggest that a significant number of anonymous medieval lyrics were composed by women. Anonymous medieval Latin lyrics, as Schotter has shown, "constitute a projection of women's erotic experience" in which Latin is used to "express antifeminism with impunity" ("Woman's Song in Medieval Latin" 19). In contrast to vernacular verse, the medieval Latin love lyric "was written not only by men but for men, to be performed before a male clerical audience" (19). There are Ovidian infiltrations in these lyrics—from those antifeminist works of Ovid (unlike his *Heroides*) that celebrate the deception and seduction of women. Schotter observes that these works present love for women as an experience whose invariable unhappiness meets with their approval: "The genre as a whole is, in a sense, an extended use of prosopopoeia, in that it is an attribution of thought and feeling to a group which was historically mute. . . . The majority of woman's songs, however, are cynical, showing approval of the woman's abandonment" (30). The use of Latin simultaneously served the misogynistic aim of excluding women while expressing a sympathy with men that revealed contempt for women.

2. The sympathetic portrayals of female experience that Ovid creates in the *Heroides,* noble and full of pathos as they are, are also formal, stilted, and rhetorically flamboyant. They possess none of the spontaneity, immediacy and directness of the alba lady.

3. Only in the past twenty–five years have researchers actively undertaken serious study of the female in the sciences and the humanities. For example, newer

research in female biology, including physiology and behavioral traits, shows that the female frequently plays an aggressive role in courtship and mating and that her role in animal societies is pivotal in ways that were previously overlooked (Shaw and Darling 3).

4. This inferiority may be of either social rank or moral character.

5. Author of four highly regarded tagelieder (the Middle High German version of the dawn-song), one "anti-tageliet," and the narrative masterpiece *Parzival,* among other notable works.

6. See Sigal, "Dawn and the Dual Negativity of Love in Chaucer's *Troilus.*"

7. While this essay was in press, a longer analysis of the sex roles in the dawn-song appeared as part of chapter one of my book, *Erotic Dawn-songs of the Middle Ages: Voicing the Lyric Lady.* Gainesville: University Press of Florida, 1996.

Works Cited

All the dawn-songs referred to here are published, along with English translations, in Arthur T. Hatto's readily accessible *Eos: An Enquiry into the Theme of Lovers' Meetings and Partings at Dawn in Poetry.* However, where one exists, I have taken the text of the lyric from the most recent scholarly edition rather than from *Eos.* Most citations of tagelieder are taken from *Des Minnesangs Frühling,* ed. Karl Lachmann, Moriz Haupt, Friedrich Vogt, and Carl von Kraus, bearbeitet von Hugo Moser and Helmut Tervooren (Stuttgart: S. Hirzel-Verlag, 1977; referred to henceforth as *MF*).

Brulé, Gace. "Cant voi l'aube dou jor venir." *The Lyrics and Melodies of Gace Brulé.* Ed. Rosenberg and Danon. New York and London: Garland Publishing, 1985. 266–69.

Chaucer, Geoffrey. *Geoffrey Chaucer: Troilus & Criseyde. A New Edition of 'The Book of Troilus'.* Ed. Barry Windeatt. London & New York: Longman, 1984.

Raimbaut de Vaqueiras. "Gaita be." *The Poems of the Troubadour Raimbaut de Vaqueiras.* Ed. Joseph Linskill. The Hague: Mouton & Co., 1964. 25:261–63; Hatto, 365–66.

Wolfram von Eschenbach. "Den morgenblic." *MF.* 436–37; Hatto, 450.

———. "Ez ist nu tac." *MF.* 445–47; Hatto, 448–49.

———. "Sîne klâwen." *MF.* 437–39; Hatto, 451–52.

———. "Von der zinnen." *MF.* 442–43; Hatto, 453.

Walther von der Vogelweide. "Friuntlîchen lac." *Die Gedichte Walthers von der Vogelweide.* Eds. Karl Lachmann and Carl von Kraus. Berlin, n.p., 1936. 88–89. Hatto, 455–56.

Duby, Georges, ed. *The History of Private Life.* Vol. 2. Tr. Arthur Goldhammer. Cambridge, MA: Belknap Press of Harvard University Press, 1987.

Ferrante, Joan. "Male Fantasy and Female Reality in Courtly Literature." *Women's Studies* 11 (1984):67–97.

Fries, Maureen. "The 'Other' Voice: Woman's Song, Its Satire and Its Transcendence in Late Medieval British Literature." *Vox Feminae: Studies in Medieval Woman's Song.* Ed. John F. Plummer. Kalamazoo: Medieval Institute, 1981. 155–78.

Gilbert, Sandra M. "What Do Feminist Critics Want? A Postcard from the Volcano." *The New Feminist Criticism: Essays on Women, Literature, and Theory.* Ed. Elaine Showalter. New York: Pantheon Books, 1985. 29–45.

Kaske, Robert E. "The Aube in Chaucer's *Troilus.*" *Chaucer Criticism II.* Ed. Richard J. Schoeck and Jerome Taylor. Notre Dame: University of Notre Dame Press, 1961: 167–79.

Paden, William D. "The Troubadour's Lady: Her Marital Status and Social Rank." *Studies in Philogy* 72 (1975): 28–50.

Saville, Jonathan. *The Medieval Erotic Alba: Structure as Meaning.* New York: Columbia University Press, 1972.

Schotter, Anne Howland. "Woman's Song in Medieval Latin." *Vox Feminae: Studies in Medieval Woman's Song.* Ed. John Plummer. Kalamazoo, MI: Medieval Institute, 1981: 19–34.

Shaw, Evelyn, and Joan Darling. *Female Strategies.* New York: Walker & Co., 1985.

Sigal, Gale. "Benighted Love in Troy: Dawn and the Dual Negativity of Love in Chaucer's *Troilus.*" *Voices in Translation: The Authority of "Olde Bookes" in Medieval Literature. Essays in Honor of Helaine Newstead.* Ed. Gale Sigal and Deborah Sinnreich. New York: A.M.S. Press, 1992. 191–206.

The Veil and the Knot: Petrarch's Humanist Poetic

DIANE R. MARKS

" . . . And call the man a liar who says I wrote
All that I wrote in love for love of art."
— from *A Plea to Boys and Girls* by Robert Graves

ALTHOUGH NOTHING WAS DEARER TO PETRARCH THAN THE LAUREL crown of the poet, it burdened him with certain problems, in particular with regard to the veracity of his vernacular poetry. Petrarch's persistently fragmentary description of Laura draws attention to different concepts of the body which are mirrored in two metaphors, the veil and the knot. The veil is a commonplace metaphor for flesh, the matter that houses the soul; the knot, an image peculiar to Petrarch, represents the body, the intricate combination of the complementary elements of flesh and spirit. This image of the knot radically alters the traditional relationship between flesh and spirit. But the veil is also a traditional metaphor for rhetoric, and the equation of flesh and rhetoric suggests an analogy between the body and poetry. In reconceptualizing the body in the metaphor of the knot, Petrarch proposes a theory of poetry that redeems it from suspicion and scorn and gives greater status and significance to the poet at the same time it elevates its secular subject matter.

The suspicion that poets are liars is an ancient prejudice, and Petrarch did not escape its irksome burden. The very premise of Petrarch's poems has been called into question: the entire corpus of his vernacular poetry is dedicated to one lady, Laura, about whom there have been centuries of speculation. Her existence has been doubted, her identity variously discovered and disproved, and the strength, nature, and sincerity of the poet's feelings for her debated even in the poet's own time: Giacomo Colonna doubted her reality (*Fam.* II, 9), and Boccaccio thought she should be understood allegorically (Scaglione 119, 205 n. 36).

241

The body of the beloved is a natural topic for the love poet of any epoch, but perhaps even more so for a humanist like Petrarch. It is at once first cause, means, and end of the erotic impulse, both creating desire in the lover and satisfying it. Laura's elusiveness, as Nancy Vickers has observed, is due in part to Petrarch's refusal to describe her physically in a coherent and comprehensive verbal portrait. He chooses to ignore the elaborate medieval rhetorical tradition of head-to-toe description, concentrating, instead, on the part rather than the whole. Eyes, hair, hands, and feet are praised, but not the ensemble. Furthermore, Petrarch "avoids those structures that would mask fragmentation. . . . When more than one part figures in a single poem, a sequential inclusive ordering is never stressed" (Vickers 96). As a result, Laura remains a disembodied presence, her corporeal being dissected and scattered throughout the poems, while her name and spirit are continuously invoked.

Rather than demonstrating a defensive desire to neutralize the threatening beloved (Vickers 103), Petrarch's discrete attention to Laura's body may reflect an attempt to reconstitute her within an erotic tradition that includes the sensual desire and delight of classical pagan literature, as well as the moral direction afforded by far-away princesses and angelic ladies. The re-membered Laura is a source of emotional inspiration and spiritual guidance at the same time that she is the object of fleshy desires.

In addition, Petrarch's analytical treatment of Laura's body may be understood as synecdochic: the part may be seen as representative of different aspects of the whole. Also, Petrarch's method often is parenthetical; that is, it brackets the body and, by referring to extremes (hair and feet), suggests inclusiveness without providing it: a head *and* toe description substituting for a head-*to*-toe description. His descriptive technique, then, operates like his favorite devices of oxymoron and antithesis, embracing extremes in order to include all variations between them.

Thus, Petrarch's piecemeal corporal descriptions may be seen as efforts to integrate into a more inclusive whole diverse aspects of the beloved and of the literary tradition. However, the extremities of the body—hair and feet—also serve to illustrate an important distinction for the poet: the difference between mere flesh and flesh inhabited by a soul, animated by spirit—a complex, interdependent combination of material and spiritual, which we will call the body.

Flesh and the Body

Flesh is simply matter, inanimate and neutral, but its beauty may seduce and corrupt the soul. We can see the attractions of the flesh in Petrarch's treatment of Laura's hair, an ornament of the body, inert matter emanating from the secret interior of it, at once public and intimate, often confined and controlled, and either hidden or decorated. It flagrantly exhibits lustrous, colorful, textural qualities, like the stone and metal which often describe Laura (Vickers 96; Frecerro "Fig Tree" 39); like these materials, it resists change and decay. Petrarch's early graying distressed him (Sen. VIII, 1) and while his own changing hair signals his aging and the passage of time (83, 195, 264, 316, 319, 362),[1] Laura's hair is eternally golden, immutable matter, like no nymph ever had (159). Petrarch describes the hair in various states: in 90, "Erano i capei d'oro a l'aura sparsi che'n mille dolci nodi gli avolgea . . ." (her golden hair was loosened to the breeze which turned it in a thousand sweet knots); in 196, her golden locks, formerly loosed and gathered again so that the lover trembles to remember it, are now twisted with pearls and gems; and in 198, Laura's braids are golden knots on her shoulders which have bound him. Fettered or free, Laura's hair exercises a dangerous, irresistible attraction on the lover. For "le chiome bionde e'l crespo laccio che si soavemente lega et stringe l'alma" (the blond locks and the curling snare that so softly binds tight my soul) (197) trap him like an animal.[2] And he is pleased by the prospect of captivity and death, for in poem 270, the poet tells Love:

> . . . e i tuoi lacci nascondi
> fra i capei crespi et biondi,
> che 'l mio volere altrove non s'invesca;
> spargi co le tue man le chiome al vento,
> ivi mi lega, et puo mi far contento.

> (hide your snares
> among her curling blond hair
> for my desire is enlimed nowhere else;
> with your own hand spread her locks to the wind,
> there bind me, and you can content me.)

The sheer material beauty of Laura's hair, knotted naturally in curls or artificially in braids, binds the lover to her, both body and soul. It is a paradox of human nature that matter and the senses which perceive it are often agents that move the spirit, but which may arouse it or lull it, work with the spirit or against it. In this instance, a purely aesthetic and sensual response, a pagan pleasure in a material stimulus, reduces the lover to the level of a tame animal, with neither reason nor will, contentedly captive to sensual delight.

At the other extreme of the body are the feet, material, like hair, but directed by the spirit. The feet are perhaps the most humble, utilitarian, unaesthetic part of our anatomy, and Petrarch here reverses the tradition that assigns greater respect and spirituality to parts of the body above the waist than below. For even so lowly a part of Laura is superior to the entire world, which was unworthy to be touched by her holy feet (268), although flowers beg her foot to press them (192); and Petrarch says, "Qualunque erba o fior colgo, credo che nel terreno aggia radice ov ella ebbe in costume gir" (Whatever grass or flower I gather, I believe that it is rooted in the ground where she was wont to walk) (125). These "generative footsteps" which miraculously cause flowers to spring up are a source of inspiration and virtue for the poet (Villas 168). Unlike the hair, the feet are not described beyond the epithet *bel,* nor are they valued for their beauty, but rather they are praised for their spiritual significance and marvelous effects.

Even Laura's footprint deserves praise. It is paradoxical evidence of, at the same time, existence and absence; for, while it announces "I am," at the same time it says, "I am not here." There is no footprint until the foot that made it is removed. Physical absence, however, can still provide spiritual presence and guidance through the footprint. The first stanza of sonnet 162 is devoted to the ground that receives the impression of Laura's foot:

> Lieti fiori et felici, et ben nate erbe
> che madonna pensando premer sole,
> piaggia ch'ascolti sue dolci parole
> et del bel piede alcun vestigio serbe
>
> (Happy and fortunate flowers and well born grass,
> whereon my lady is wont to walk in thought,
> shore that listen to her sweet words
> and keep some print of her lovely foot.)

The footprint is both souvenir and signpost. Laura's footprints sign the grass (243), recording not only her former presence, like a signature, but, like a sign, marking the direction she took. If walking is "an incarnation of the act of choice" (Freccero "Firm Foot" 42), footprints are manifestations of moral decisions, and they are venerated because they guide the poet-lover to safety and salvation (204);[3] for the appeal to the senses of Laura's physical beauty is associated with the temptations of paganism, but the wisdom of her chaste spirit expressed through her flesh provides a Christian remedy for them. While her hair ensnares the lover with its material beauty and makes of him a captive beast, her flowering footsteps guide him to a godly destiny, immortality. In poem 306, Petrarch searches through all the regions where he saw Laura in life; he does not find her, but ". . . suoi santi vestigi tutti rivolti a la superna strada veggio lunge da' laghi averni et stigi" (her holy footprints all turned toward the road to Heaven, far from the Avernian and the Stygian lakes). For celebrating her beauty, Petrarch receives from Laura the pagan equivalent of immortality, fame; but for acknowledging her spiritual value, he receives its Christian counterpart—redemption and eternal life. She has been such a powerful example of virtue that Petrarch is compelled to praise Laura and only her, for his feet know no other road (97).

Thus, in his deliberately fragmentary representation of the body, Petrarch acknowledges the power and attractions of materiality; yet he distinguishes flesh—spiritless matter with its sensual appeal, epitomized by hair—from the body—flesh animated and directed by spirit, represented by the feet. Laura's hair is purely flesh, decorative and seductive, and traps and binds the poet. Her feet, though equally material, are controlled and directed by spirit, guiding the poet from a sensual response to beauty to one that transcends the physical to include the moral. What Laura looked like was unimportant; what Laura meant to Petrarch, as the source of his physical and psychic pain and delight, is made abundantly clear. In the body the diverse aspects that constitute the human—fleshly and spiritual—are united. Petrarch makes a similar distinction between the metaphors of the veil and the knot.

The Veil and the Knot

Petrarch calls the flesh a veil to the soul (77), a garment to clothe the invisible spirit. This traditional image of a dualistic philosophy emphasizes the difference between matter and spirit, their essential separateness and merely temporary alliance. It implies preference for spirit over matter, for the thing that is hidden or ornamented rather than the ornament itself, and opposition between the two. The notion of covering inherent in the metaphor also suggests the discrepancy between appearance and reality, and the possibility of deception. Petrarch characterizes his own body as a heavy veil (122), a burden of noisome flesh he longs to discard (331). This fleshly veil weighs him down, obscures his vision, and impedes the powers of his spirit (264). Therefore, he longs to be free of it: "Cosi disciolto dal mortal mio velo, ch'a forza mi tien qui foss'io con loro fuor de' sospir, fra l'anime beate" (Would that I, alas, freed from my mortal veil, which keeps me here by force, were with them beyond sighs, among the blessed souls) (313).

Laura's flesh, however, has only the most favorable connotations. Her veil is an analog to her spiritual beauty. It does not disguise her soul but, being in harmony with it, ornaments it. After her death, Petrarch speaks to Laura, "lasciasti in terra, et quel soave velo che per alto destin ti venne in sorte" (left in the earth with that soft veil that was allotted to you by destiny) (352). She expresses regret rather than joy at being relieved of her flesh. In poem 302, Laura herself says, "te solo aspetto, et quel che tanto amasti et la giuso et rimaso, il mio bel velo" (I only wait for you and for that which you loved so much and which remained down there, my lovely veil). Although the flesh is beautiful, the spirit is even more so: "Ma la forma miglior che vive ancora et vivra sempre su ne l'alto cielo di sue bellezze ogni or piu m'innamora" (But her better form, which still lives up in the highest heaven, makes me ever more in love with her beauties) (319). Despite the beauty of her flesh and its harmony with her spirit, it is mortal and inevitably suffers the depredations of age, childbearing, and disease. In poem 268, Petrarch says, "l' invisibil sua forma e in Paradiso, disciolta di quel velo che qui fece ombra al fior degli anni suoi" (her invisible form is in paradise, set free from the veil that here shadowed the flower of her years). This veil, mutable and earthbound, is both corruptible and corrupting. In poem 292, Petrarch acknowledges the noxious effect and ultimate end of Laura's diverting beauties: her eyes, arms, hands, feet, face, curling locks, and smile, "che m'avean si da me stesso divisio et fatto singular da altra gente . . . poca polvere son che nulla sente" (that had so estranged me from myself and isolated me from other people . . . all are a bit of dust that feels nothing) (292).

The veil represents the flesh, matter which during life shrouds the spirit. It is put on at birth and shrugged off at death. The explicitly superficial nature of the metaphor creates ambiguity and ambivalence. The fleshly veil is opaque, not transparent, and is valued for its materiality, its appeal to the senses; however, while it may manifest and ornament the spirit within, it can also conceal the spirit or disguise it, cover it or cover it up. To counter the distrust and devaluation of the flesh inherent in this dualist notion, Petrarch offers us an alternative metaphor: the knot.

The knot represents the body as the quintessentially human union of flesh and spirit which produces animate intelligent beings capable of judgment and action. This knot is composed of two distinct, discrete, and complementary strands, intertwined during life and separated only at death. Thus, when the metaphorical knot, the body, is dissolved in Laura's death, Petrarch bewails the years that "sol due parte d'ogni mio ben farsi, l'una nel Cielo et l'altra in terra starsi" (turned all my wealth into two parts only; one is in heaven, the other in the ground) (298). Not only does the knot join these disparate elements but, formed entirely of them, it creates a new entity. The bodily knot gives form, shape, and dimension to the immaterial and provides animation and intelligence to the material—gives each what the other is not. The intermingling of matter and spirit enables the invisible to be manifested and to be perceived by us mortals who depend on our sensory apparatus for knowledge. Thus, Laura's virtue is embodied in her beauty and the poet praises both the flesh and the spirit of his beloved; in poem 305, he speaks of the "Anima bella, da quel nodo sciolta che piu bel mai non seppe ordir Natura" (Beautiful soul, freed from that knot more beautiful than any Nature ever made). Flesh also permits the spirit to be an agent in the world; in poem 283, the poet addresses Death: "spirito piu acceso di vertuti ardenti del piu leggiadro et piu bel nodo ai sciolto" (you have loosed the spirit most on fire with ardent virtues from the most charming and beautiful bodily knot). These virtues can be known only through their physical manifestations, like footsteps. Not only does spirit require a mingling with matter so it can act and be perceived, but the purely spiritual is ineffable. Only when the soul is allied with flesh is it within the poet's power to describe it. In poem 307, Petrarch declares: "I pensava assai destro esser su l'ale per gir cantando a quel bel nodo eguale onde Morte m'assolve, Amor mi lega" (I thought I was skillful enough in flight . . . to sing worthily of that lovely knot from which Death looses me but Love binds me); but in 308, he confesses that he cannot depict her divine part.

This knot not only unites Laura's fleshly beauty and spiritual valor, it binds the lover to her as well. Irresistible and unique, once the knot is dissolved by Laura's death, the lover never again fears temptation. In poem 270, he taunts Love:

> Ma me sol ad un nodo
> legar potei . . .
> Ma poi che Morte e stata si superba
> che spozzo il nodo ond'io temea scampare
> ne trovar poi . . .
> di che ordischi 'l secondo . . .
> Morte m'a sciolto, Amor d'ogni tua legge . . .

> (Me you have been able to bind
> in only one knot . . .
> but since Death has been so proud
> to shatter the knot from which I feared to escape
> and since you cannot find . . .
> one to tie a second knot . . .
> Death has freed me Love from all your laws.)

During life, the flesh and spirit that form the knot are inextricable. The spirit's love for the flesh binds us to life. Only death can separate them and thus release the lover from his bond. This does not mean that flesh and spirit exist without conflict. On the contrary, the knot is formed by each end pulling against the other, and tension and friction keep the knot tied. Despite this lack of resolution, Petrarch presents the knot as positive. It is the appropriate middle ground of the human, between the beastly and the divine. Flesh and spirit belong joined together. From the union of opposites, each gains: flesh becomes animate, the spirit efficacious. In the lyrics set after Laura's death, both the bereaved lover and the departed beloved look forward to the time when flesh and spirit will be rejoined, but this doctrine is even more forcefully illustrated in the *Trionfi*.

The *Trionfi,* along with the *Canzoniere,* comprise Petrarch's entire body of vernacular poetry. Like the *Canzoniere,* it is inspired by Laura and extends the implied narrative of love from the lyric's perpetual present into the prophetic infinite future. Although the *Canzoniere* begins with a palinode regretting youthful error and claiming that the poet is now another man from what he was, the *Trionfi* recapitulate the same history of infatuation, frustration, longing, and loss, but from the more objective perspective of eternal omniscience. Still, the very last lines of the "Triumph of Eternity," the culmination of the entire vernacular oeuvre, predict a beatific vision of Laura re-veiled, her flesh reunited with her soul in her glorified body. This return to the beginning, the vision of the beloved of sonnet 3, reaffirms the value of the body, the human, the knot.

Rhetoric and Poetry

The veil is a favorite and venerable metaphor for rhetoric or poetic language as well as for the flesh. The exegetical tradition, harking back to the biblical description of Moses' veiled radiance after his confrontation with God (Exodus 34:29–35), equated the veil with allegory or poetic fiction which both hides what should not be seen by the profane and reveals the ineffable, what cannot be expressed directly.[4] In time, the veil came to represent any deviation from the literal—be it fiction, allegory, or metaphor—that provides a peculiarly suitable obscurity, one which both clarifies and affords pleasure to those capable of understanding. All language, however, particularly that of poetry, whether it actually transforms the literal or merely emphasizes the sensual aspects of language with sound, is a veil that clothes thought in pleasing and persuasive style. Rhetoric, the artful use of language, expresses ideas in language that distracts the rational faculty as it simultaneously attracts the senses. It competes with ideas for attention and provides aesthetic pleasure as it informs.

According to Howard Bloch, the veil—both literal, as an item of feminine apparel, and figurative, as rhetoric—was an object of the early Church fathers' concern and criticism. These remnants of antique pagan culture could apply artificial beauty to conceal error and falsehood, exalt the base as easily as the worthy, and, as a result, seduce the unwary, unsophisticated Christian. Tertullian, in particular, inveighed against veils and other articles of feminine attire. Ironically, "it is not the flesh that Tertullian denounces. On the contrary it is the draping of the flesh with dress and ornament that is the equivalent of seduction" (Bloch 12). For the Church fathers, nakedness would have been preferable to ornament, for the completely revealed is less of a danger than the artfully concealed or disguised. Just as a woman could hide her flaws and increase her charms with ornament, so could the popular stories, poems, and philosophy of the pagans disguise their triviality with the arts of rhetoric, long practiced and refined in the classical world. Therefore, the naked truth of Christian revelation was to be preferred to the seductive ornaments of literature. Although the attack against the literal veils worn by women continued unabated, a defense of the allegorical veil of rhetoric was undertaken by Augustine, whose success permitted the development of a religious and secular literature throughout the Middle Ages.

Both flesh and rhetoric, then, traditionally were equated with the ambiguous, ambivalent veil, so that by the thirteenth century, veiled and ornamented women were synonymous with poetics (Bloch 17). The veil metaphor stresses the primacy of spirit and thought, as well as the superfluous and decorative qualities of flesh and language. It also cautions us about the possibility of deceit. For the veil may conceal a multitude of sins and seduce us, or reveal a panoply of virtues and inspire us. It may arouse desires and passions, not all of which are virtuous, but it also may manifest the beauty of the ineffable and make spiritual things perceptible. The versatile veil, either of flesh or of rhetoric, transmits ideas through the senses to affect the soul, sometimes for good, sometimes for ill. The knot is a more obscure, idiosyncratic symbol than the veil. Traditionally, it has been understood as a negative influence, a barrier to the free passage of the soul from the body, taboo at childbirths and at deathbeds (Frazer 321). The knot is often identified with a tangle, an undesirable complication in matter, an obstacle, like the Gordian knot. Or it may be a complex and decorative but nonfunctional construction like Solomon's knot, also known as the endless knot or the pentangle. Although it suggests unity, complexity and infinity, this mysterious symbol is endlessly recursive and isolated, unable to escape from or transcend itself.[5] Thus, it comes as no surprise when Augustine speaks of figurative action in the Bible as a knot to be united in order to be understood (25), and Boccaccio credits Dante with untying the hard knots of theology (Osgood 53). But the most provocative and pertinent use of the word *knot* in the context of poetry occurs in *Purgatorio* XXIV, where the pilgrim Dante explains to Bonagiunta the simple task of a poet of the sweet new style: to note the inspiration of love. Love dictates, the poet speaks and shapes. To this simple and humble formula Bonagiunta replies:

> "O frate, issa veggio," diss'elli, "il nodo
> che'l Notaro, e Guittone e me ritenne
> di qua dal dolce stil novo ch'i' odo." (55–57)

> ("O brother, now I see," he said, "the knot
> that kept the Notary, Guittone, and me
> short of the sweet new manner that I hear.")

Here, as elsewhere in Dante, *knot* has the traditional connotation of impediment, and clearly refers to Bonagiunta's attachment to the flesh and the senses, to the earthly things he celebrates. His concept of poetry places him and this most sustained discourse on poetics in Purgatory amidst the gluttons, as Mazzotta points out, to pay for excessive nourishment of the fleshly part and insufficient attention to the spiritual (Dante 201). For Bonagiunta has not, like Dante, subordinated the pleasure of poetry to the divine will and transcended the delights of the senses.

This discussion on poetry among the gluttons associates flesh with rhetoric, Bonagiunta's sensual concept of poetry, both traditionally represented by the veil but here symbolized by the knot to indicate the limitations of this attitude. Petrarch's use of the knot, however, rejects this negative connotation. When used as a metaphor for the body, *knot* is almost always accompanied by favorable connotations, in particular, the word *bel*.[6] The bodily knot, beautiful and complex, emblem of the human, thoroughly integrates its two constituent elements in a useful union associated with moral action. Petrarch's knot holds together, not back. Although Petrarch never explicitly uses the idea of the knot in relation to poetry, the alternative image of the veil is so strongly and traditionally associated with both the flesh and rhetoric that we are led to complete the analogy: the flesh and rhetoric are equated with the veil, just as the body and poetry are equated with the knot. The veil is an equivocal symbol of an impartial materiality ready to be put to the service of any goal. The knot, however, with its mixture of elements, contains both spirit and matter and includes a moral dimension.

Through the knot metaphor, Petrarch's conception of the body acknowledges the value of the flesh, of the sensually perceptible and appealing. The flesh expresses the spirit and receives sense impressions for the spirit to interpret. Similarly, Petrarch's idea of poetry accepts the necessity of rhetoric—language in all its ornamental and sensual aspects—to make an impression on the flesh and ultimately to advise the spirit. The spirit, however, must guide the flesh and make determinations on information received from the senses; it must inhabit the flesh to constitute the body. In the same fashion, rhetoric must be guided and put in the service of truth, the spirit of poetry, to animate and convert rhetoric, an empty form, into poetry. Just as the body is an intricate combination of flesh and spirit, so is poetry a combination of rhetoric and truth. The idea of the knot redeems both flesh and rhetoric from their negative associations with pagan culture and sensuality, superficiality, and deception. The requirement of truth in poetry as the equivalent of the soul in the body defends poetry against those charges leveled against it since ancient times—that poetry is a beautiful lie, an untruth made believable and attractive by the skillful use of language. Nowhere is the artistic use of language in the service of truth better exemplified than in poem 206 of the *Canzoniere*.

This canzone, one of the most ornate and obsessive poems in the collection, is the denial of a lie. Neither the circumstances that occasioned the poem nor its meaning are entirely clear, but troubadour songs in which the slanders of the *losengiers* are a frequent topic provide literary precedent. Many Provençal poems descry the

discord caused by the tale-bearers' wicked tongues in several lines
or stanzas, but no poem in its entirety is devoted to refuting their
lies. Two-thirds of Petrarch's poem catalog the miseries the poet-
lover should suffer if he had ever said what he was accused of
saying; in the final third, the poet defends himself and denies the
charge. The thematic simplicity of the poem contrasts with its structural complexity of phonic and syntactic constraints and its allusive
adornment.

There are six nine-line stanzas in the poem: the first five lines
have fourteen syllables, the next three short lines have seven, and
the final line reverts to fourteen. In a total of fifty-nine lines, there
are only three rhymes: -ella, -ei and -ia. The rhyme scheme is ab-
baacca x 2, bccbbaaab x 2, caaccbbbc x 2; the tornada is cbbac. In
addition to this tight, restrictive rhyme scheme, the poem is even
further controlled by the syntactic anaphora or parallelism beginning lines one, three, and five of the first four stanzas, a subordinate
conditional clause, s'i 'l dissi, (if I said it), repeated twelve times
and demanding twelve corresponding subjunctive clauses of result.
If the poet ever uttered the unspecified statement, may he suffer all
sorts of misfortunes: may his beloved hate him, his days be few
and miserable, and every star be against him; may fear and jealousy
be his companions and his enemy ever more cruel and beautiful.
The second stanza follows the model of the first but focuses on
hardships in love the poet-lover would endure were the accusation
true: Love with his gold and leaden arrows, the gods and men, and
his beloved are called on to mete out his punishment. Metaphors of
voyage and exile—the road, straying, stormy weather—dominate
the third stanza, at the end of which the poet-lover wishes to suffer
like Pharaoh did when he pursued the Jews into the Red Sea, should
he be guilty as charged. The fourth stanza resurrects courtly allegory: let pity and courtesy be dead for him and his lady's gentle
speech become harsh; or let him be hated by the one he is willing
to contemplate alone in a dark cell for all his days. But this idea is
so attractive that he reconsiders the crime for the sake of the punishment. In the fifth stanza where the refutation begins, "ma s'io nol
dissi" (but if I did not say it) is not repeated in that stanza and the
voyage metaphor returns with an entirely different context. Instead
of the wanderings of exile, the poet-lover has a destination and direction: if he did not say it, may his beloved guide his ship with the
tiller of mercy as she did before. The sixth and final stanza before
the tornada abandons the conditional mood completely and turns to
emphatic denial: "I' nol dissi giamai" (I never said it). These last
two stanzas are linked together by negation and identical rhyme

schemes and by their lack of syntactic repetition. In the sixth stanza, the denial is categorical, and personification allegory and chivalric metaphor return:

> I nol dissi giamai, ne dir poria
> per oro o per cittadi o per castella;
> vinca'l ver dunque e si rimagna in sella
> et vinta a terra caggia la bugia!
>
> (I never said it, nor could I say it
> for gold or for cities or for castles;
> let the truth conquer, therefore, and remain in the saddle,
> and let falsehood fall vanquished to earth!)

Myth and meteorology, astrology and allegory, chivalry, navigation, Ovid, and the Bible are all brought to bear in this poem. Particularly notable are three biblical allusions. At the end of the third stanza, Petrarch, maintaining his innocence, contrasts himself with Pharoah, who received a terrible but just punishment. At the end of the poem, in the tornada, Petrarch compares himself with Jacob, who was deceived by Laban and unjustly forced into seven extra years of servitude for his bride. Finally, so strongly does Petrarch protest the accusation that he would even risk departing with his beloved in Elijah's terrible fiery chariot. Here, Petrarch relies on the authority of Old Testament stories of retribution, injustice, and baneful reward to testify to the truth of his position.

The clearest indication of the occasion of the poem occurs here at the very end:

> Per Rachel o servita e non per Lia,
> ne con altra saprei
> viver; e sosterrei,
> quando 'l ciel ne rapella,
> girmen con ella in sul carro de Elia.
>
> (For Rachel I have served and not for Leah,
> nor could I live with another;
> and I would endure, if heaven called us,
> going off with her on the chariot of Elijah.)

Robert Durling suggests that Petrarch has been accused of denying his love for Laura, of using her like a veil to disguise his love for another. The charges occasion a vehement response culminating in the story of Rachel and Leah. The reference recalls a number of points the poet has made about his beloved in the course of the poems. First, the beloved is not mere flesh: if she were, then one woman could substitute for another; and if she were just spirit, she could be neither desired nor possessed. But the beloved is a knot, an image of human integrity, that mixture of flesh and spirit which is uniquely human. Further, because the beloved is unique, no replacement is possible, and the lover will endure any hardship for her. However, what applies to the beloved applies to poetry as well. This obsessive poem is not merely Petrarch's response to complaints about his erotic decorum but a defense of his professional ethics. Like the beloved, poetry is a knot: not mere words nor pure truth but a union of the two. In order to defend truth, Petrarch marshals all the techniques of rhetoric into a complex, ornate, and allusive poem. Rhetoric, suspect when represented by the veil, becomes an ally to the truth, its vehicle, in the image of the knot.

As well as being an elaboration of a Provençal motif and a traditional protestation of a lover's fidelity, this poem is a statement about the nature of poetry and the responsibility of the poet. Leah and Rachel represent women on a literal level. On the symbolic level, they stand for attitudes: the active and the contemplative, the temporal and the eternal. Even the great schism of Petrarch's time between Avignon and Rome is reflected in this opposing pair. Petrarch's use of the story of Jacob unequivocally states that appearance cannot substitute for reality, deception must not be accepted in place of truth. Poetry serves the true and authentic, not the convenient, and it is the poet's responsibility to distinguish them.

Petrarch's most profound defense of poetry is embedded in his poems. The tradition he inherited was consciously ambivalent, for since the time of Plato, rhetoric had been recognized as double-edged. Rhetoric works on the senses as well as on the mind, and appeals to both the irrational appetites and reason. Its power to arouse the emotions, play on them, overcome the rational faculties, and stir men to action can be directed toward any end. It can obscure and distort as well as depict, seduce to evil as easily as inspire to good. It can even sway the audience in unexpected directions. Only the character and principles of the rhetor determine its use. The poet engaged in inventing fictions aggravates the already precarious situation. To this general distrust and disbelief of poetry, the early Church fathers added their own disdain for any literature other than the sacred scriptures.

The metaphor of the veil, which applies to both flesh and rhetoric, embodies this epistemological ambivalence. The image posits an outside separate from the inside. The outside covers, protects, hides or adorns but has itself no value; what is hidden inside is what is important, and covering and covered have only a tangential and temporary relationship. The veil appeals to the senses and makes what it conceals attractive—regardless of what is concealed.

The metaphor of the knot revises these conceptions of flesh and poetry. Unlike the veil, the knot has no clear inside and outside. Inside is sometimes outside, outside sometimes in. The two elements of the knot constitute an integrated whole of mutually dependent and equally important parts. This is not to say that they coexist without tension; it is, after all, tension that forms the knot and friction that keeps it binding. But one element is not subordinate to another. And, because the parts are both inside and outside, they are both visible: one does not conceal the other, so the danger of deception is eliminated. The knot is a metaphor drawn from the realm of utility, suggesting a structural relationship between elements; the veil suggests decoration and only a surface relationship. Therefore, the knot defies our separating one element from the other, while the veil invites it. The image of the knot reevaluates the contributions of flesh and rhetoric. They are not to be despised or discarded. The body is not just flesh, nor is poetry just rhetoric. Flesh provides the material for the spirit to inhabit in that crowning achievement of God's creation, the human body. So does rhetoric provide the medium for the expression of truth in man's greatest creation—poetry.

The use of the metaphor of the knot for poetry gives rhetoric a value and importance it did not have previously. Rhetoric without truth, like the flesh without its animating soul, is corrupt, but truth without rhetoric is incommunicable except among pure spirits. Rhetoric, the vehicle, is necessary for effective action in the world, just as the body is the effective agent of the soul. The idea of the knot thoroughly integrates its two elements, so that the unity and integrity of poetry, the interdependence of thought and the words that express it, of form and of content, are foregrounded in this image. The knot also conveys the complexity and difficulty of both reading and writing poetry, and reflects, better than the veil, Petrarch's relentless revision. It acknowledges the difficulty of suiting the word to the thought, of finding the exact, appropriate language to express an idea.

By identifying truth as the necessary animating spirit of poetry, Petrarch elevates poetry from the status of suspect entertainment and social pastime to a source of wisdom and guidance, a rival of scripture. The poet rises with his art, from minstrel to scholar, court jester to sage, as poetry becomes worthy of serious effort and attention. The concept of poetry represented by the knot justifies the study of poetry. It becomes the highest achievement of mankind, aligning the most profound thought with refined sensual pleasure, necessary to all men who hope to live above the level of the beast. Hence is born the humanist idea of education through the study of literature, especially the ancient classics. As the metaphor of the veil equates rhetoric with flesh, the metaphor of the knot suggests an analogy between poetry and the body. In reconceiving the body, Petrarch found a notion of poetry that was more satisfactory than the traditional one, one that brought seriousness and importance to what previously was a marginal and suspect activity.[7]

Notes

1. References to poems by number, as well as quotations and translations of Petrarch's lyrics, are taken from *Petrarch's Lyric Poems,* edited and translated by Robert M. Durling.

2. As Mazzotta has pointed out, poem 90 more closely resembles Ovid's description of Diana than, as been frequently stated, Vergil's Venus ("The Canzoniere" 277). It is appropriate (yet perverse) that Laura should be associated with Diana, sister of Apollo, goddess of chastity and the hunt, who haunts woods and wild places, and that she manufactures snares—that, in fact, her body produces them.

3. Freccero's study of the firm foot in the *Inferno* explains the history of the traditional analogy between the feet of the body and the wings of the soul.

4. The metaphor of the veil occurs in Macrobius, Augustine, Isidore, and Vincent of Beauvais before Dante employs it and both Boccaccio and Petrarch use it in their defenses of poetry. On this topos, see Osgood (157 n. 8).

5. Mazzotta equates the knot with the pentangle, symbol of natural perfection, "the condition of human existence sundered from the perception of God" (Dante 202). Shoaf discusses this image and associates it with poetry. He suggests that it may represent arcane obscurity or needless complexity, closed off to all but one interpretation (88 n. 13). I thank Daniel Rubey for pointing out Shaof's note to me, and Professor Shoaf for discussing it with me.

6. *Bel* is also applied frequently to the foot and the eyes, both of which have moral dimensions and guide the poet.

7. I am grateful to Giuseppe Mazzotta, R. A. Shoaf, and Nancy Vickers for their aid and encouragement, and to Walter Stiller for a patient ear. I am also indebted to the National Endowment for the Humanities Petrarch Institute at Yale University in the summer of 1989, where much of the research for this essay was done.

Works Cited

Augustine. *On Christian Doctrine.* Tr. D. W. Robertson, Jr. Indianapolis: Bobbs-Merrill, 1958.

Bloch, R. Howard. "Medieval Misogyny." *Representations* 20 (1987):1–24.

Dante. *Purgatorio.* Tr. Allen Mandelbaum. New York: Bantam, 1982, 1984.

Frazer, James George. *The Golden Bough: A Study in Magic and Religion.* Abr. ed. London: Macmillan, 1957.

Freccero, John. "The Fig Tree and the Laurel: Petrarch's Poetics." *Diacritics* 15:1 (Spring 1975):34–40.

———. "The Firm Foot on a Journey Without a Guide." *Dante: The Poetics of Conversion.* Ed. Rachel Jacoff. Cambridge, MA: Harvard University Press, 1986.

Mazzotta, Giuseppe. "The Canzoniere and the Language of the Self." *Studies in Philology* 75 (1978):271–97.

———. *Dante, Poet of the Desert.* Princeton: Princeton University Press, 1979.

Osgoood, Charles G. *Boccaccio on Poetry.* 2nd ed. Indianapolis: Bobbs-Merrill, 1956.

Petrarch, Francis. *Letters from Petrarch.* Tr. Morris Bishop. Bloomington: Indiana University Press, 1966.

———. *Petrarch's Lyric Poems.* Ed. and tr. Robert M. Durling. Cambridge, MA: Harvard University Press, 1976.

———. *Rerum Familiarium libri I-VIII.* Tr. Aldo S. Bernardo. Albany: S.U.N.Y. Press, 1975.

Scaglione, Aldo. *Nature and Love in the Late Middle Ages.* Berkeley: University of California Press, 1963.

Shoaf, R. A. *The Poem as Green Girdle.* Gainesville: University Presses of Florida, 1984.

Vickers, Nancy. "Diana Described: Scattered Woman and Scattered Rhymes." *Writing and Sexual Difference.* Ed. Elizabeth Abel. Chicago: Chicago University Press, 1982. 95–109.

Villas, James. "The Petrarchan Topos Bel Piede: Generative Footsteps." *Romance Notes* 11 (1969):167–73.

The Role of the Feminine in Dante's Model of Literary Influence

ANNE HOWLAND SCHOTTER

ALTHOUGH FEMINIST CRITICS HAVE FINALLY BEGUN TO TURN THEIR AT-
tention to medieval literature, surprisingly, they have—with the exception of one book, an important chapter, and a handful of
articles—avoided Dante.[1] The role of the feminine in the *Divine
Comedy,* however, is a major one, and in this paper I would like to
explore in particular the feminist implications in Dante's medita-
tions on literary influence. I shall first suggest that there is a structural analogy between the way both Dante and women writers of
the past two centuries view their precursors as generous and nurturing, rather than as rivalrous and overwhelming, as in the model of
influence developed by Harold Bloom. The thorough analysis,
which feminist critics have made of the inadequacy of this model
in accounting for literary relations among women contains, I think,
important insights for our understanding of Dante. Second, I shall
argue that, despite his gender, Dante achieves what recent feminist
theorists have called an "inscription of the feminine"[2] in showing
an attitude of gratitude rather than rivalry toward his most revered
precursors—particularly in *Purgatorio* XXI-XXVI, which constitutes an extended encounter with them.[3] In doing so, he uses imagery of generation and nurturing which, although often paternal in
the traditional patriarchal manner—showing the poet as insemina-
tor—is also occasionally maternal—showing the poet as mother
bringing forth the text and suckling other poets. In either case, the
imagery compares poetic creativity to the creation of life, rather
than to its destruction.[4]

Such a model of influence contrasts strikingly with Harold
Bloom's oedipal one, in which "strong" poets struggle against their
major precursors, like sons against overwhelming fathers,[5] a model
which has recently been applied to Dante. I believe that feminist
criticism of the gender-bound nature of Bloom's theory throws
light on Dante's complex use of sexual imagery to describe literary

influence. The most extensive critique of Bloom's model from a feminist perspective has been by Sandra M. Gilbert and Susan Gubar, in *The Madwoman in the Attic: The Woman Writer and the Nineteenth-century Literary Imagination.* They find Bloom's view "intensely (even exclusively) male, and necessarily patriarchal," because it fails to account for the situation of the woman writer, who, rather than struggling against a precursor of either sex, is likely to select female precursors to give her courage, a sense of legitimacy in writing at all (47). In fact, they argue, literary influence among women tends to be characterized by a search for female precursors rather than by a rivalry with male ones (49).[6]

Gilbert and Gubar, furthermore, find in Bloom's theory of influence as oedipal struggle two related patriarchal assumptions, the first expressed by the "metaphor of literary paternity" (6)—the "notion that the writer 'fathers' his text just as God fathered" the world[7]—and the second by the metaphor of the female muse as a mother/lover for whose favors the poet competes with his male precursors (Bloom 60–62). While most feminist critics object to this literary use of Freudian concepts on the grounds that they leave no role for woman as creator, my objections to their application to Dante are somewhat more complicated. It is true that on occasion he expresses sentiments of literary rivalry and uses the traditional patriarchal literary metaphors of poets begetting texts and invoking the female muses. Dante's portrayal of the generosity of poets toward precursors, however, is more dramatic than his portrayals of rivalry, and his use of maternal imagery for male poets is unusual in the Western patriarchal tradition, although this is partly explicable by certain developments in twelfth-century mystical thought.

In arguing for an attitude of generosity in Dante, I differ not so much with Bloom (who excludes pre-Enlightenment poets from his model and explicitly comments on Dante's love of Vergil),[8] but with those critics who, extending the model to medieval poets, argue that Dante is active and even aggressive toward his precursors. Giuseppe Mazzotta employs Bloom's general concepts of literary paternity and revisionism in his chapter on *Purgatorio* XXI–XXVI (194–226); Winthrop Wetherbee explicitly calls "Dante's engagement with Virgil . . . a unique instance of a medieval poet responding to what Harold Bloom . . . would call a 'strong' poetic ancestor" (146); and Teodolinda Barolini, while conceding Dante's generous relation to Vergil, points out that his treatment of relatively minor contemporary poets is often competitive and even petty (175). In accepting Bloom's psychological model, if not his exclusion of Dante from it, all these critics, I believe, err in seeing the poet's literary relations in entirely masculine terms. For, although it is true that Dante shows an aggressive attitude toward some precursors, particularly in his slighting treatment of two notable influences from the classical and vernacular traditions—Ovid and Guido Cavalcante[9]—his generosity toward the others is more noteworthy.

One might ask where Dante got a view so at odds with traditional Western attitudes toward literary creation. The answer may lie in the new emphasis on the feminine in twelfth-century religious thought, which the historian Caroline Walker Bynum has so well explored in *Jesus as Mother*. She argues that a new sense of God which emphasized his creative power and love encouraged a portrayal of male figures with feminine imagery—imagery of "child-bearing, nursing, [and] female sexual surrender or ecstasy" (136). Saint Bernard, more than any of his contemporaries, applied maternal imagery to males, using " 'mother' to describe Jesus, Moses, Peter, Paul, prelates in general, and, more frequently, himself as abbott." The aspect of motherhood he stresses, interestingly, is not birth, but nurturing and, in particular, suckling (Bynum 115).

Such a concept is most likely behind Dante's portrayal of his precursors as nurturing rather than rivalrous, as well as his use of maternal imagery to describe them. He presents his most prominent influence, Vergil, not only as "dolce padre," but also as mother, once comparing him to an instinctively protective mother rescuing her child from fire.[10] Dante's use of such dramatic expressions of tenderness throughout the first two *cantiche* sharpens our sense of his structural and intertextual echoes of the *Aeneid* and is, I believe, related to his memorable homage to Vergil when the two poets first meet in *Inferno* I. Reassured, in his moment of despair, by seeing the Roman poet, Dante addresses him,

> "O de li altri poeti onore e lume,
> vagliami 'l lungo studio e 'l grande amore
> che m'ha fatto cercar lo tuo volume.
> Tu se' lo mio maestro e'l mio autore,
> te se' solo colui da cu' io tolsi
> lo bello stilo che m'ha fatt onore." (82–87)[11]

(O glory and light of other poets, may the long study and the great love that have made me search your volume avail me! You are my master and my author. You alone are he from whom I took the fair style that has done me honor.)

Whereas this expression of literary gratitude does not use the imagery of a child's relation to its parent, Statius' homage to Vergil in *Purgatorio* XXI–XXII does.[12] For the first-century Roman poet describes Vergil's influence on his epics, the *Thebaid* and the *Achilleid,* as being like that of a mother nursing her child:

> "Cantai di Tebe, e poi del grande Achille;
> ma caddi in via con la seconda soma.
> Al mio ardor fuor seme le faville,
> che mi scaldar, de la divina fiamma
> onde sono allumati piu di mille;
> de l'Eneïda dico, la qual mamma
> fummi, e fummi nutrice, poetando:
> sanz' essa non fermai peso di dramma.
> E per esser vivuto di là quando
> visse Virgilio, assentirei un sole
> piu che non deggio al mio uscir di bando."
> (*Purg* XXI:92–102)

(I sang of Thebes, and then of the great Achilles, but I fell on the way with my second burden. The sparks which warmed me from the divine flame whereby more than a thousand have been kindled were the seeds of my poetic fire: I mean the *Aeneid,* which in poetry was both mother and nurse to me—without it I had achieved little of worth; and to have lived yonder when Virgil lived I would consent to one sun more than I owe to my coming forth from exile.)

Calling a precursor text—and by extension, a precursor poet— *"mamma"* and *"nutrice"* (97, 98) invokes the feminine in presenting precursors as aids, rather than rivals, to be struggled against and overcome. Rachel Jacoff has suggested that the choice of Statius at this juncture is particularly appropriate not only because of the homage to Vergil with which he actually ends the *Thebaid,* but also because of that poem's departure from the *Aeneid* in privileging the role of mother (Jacoff 166).[13]

In the next canto, which continues to deal with literary influence and adds a specifically theological dimension to it, Dante also uses maternal imagery. First, he uses the topos of the suckling muses, which, though retaining the traditional gender roles with respect to poetic creativity, nevertheless privileges the feminine in presenting that creativity as generative and nurturing rather than agonistic. To Statius' question about the other Roman poets, Vergil replies that they, like him, are in Limbo with Homer, "whom the Muses suckled more than any other" ('che le Muse lattar piu ch'altri mai" [*Purg.* XXII:102]), and often talk of Parnassus, the mountain "that has our nurses ever with it" (che sempre ha le nutrice nostre seco

[*Purg*. XXII:104–5]). It is likely that this imagery enriches the classical tradition of the muses with the Christian concept of the nursing Virgin or the nursing God which Bynum has pointed out (115).[14] Earlier in the canto, Dante had implicitly used the imagery of the suckling muses in the context of Vergil's dual poetic and religious influence. Having invented for Statius a Christian conversion through reading Vergil which grants him a salvation Vergil paradoxically was denied (per te poeta fui, per te cristiano [73]), Dante has Statius say to his precursor, "You it was who first sent me toward Parnassus to drink of its caves" (Tu prima m'invïasti / verso Parnaso a ber ne le sue grotte [*Purg*. XXII:64–65]), an implicit reference to the nourishment of the muses' milk.[15] Finally, in describing the influence of Christian rhetoric on the growth of Christianity in ancient times, Statius uses the imagery of insemination and fetal development. Reading Vergil's fourth eclogue, whose account of a new race descending from heaven he and others took as a prophecy of Christ's birth, at a moment when the world was already "pregno / de la vera credenza seminata / per li messaggi de l'etterno regno" (big with the true faith, sown by the messengers of the eternal realm [*Purg*. XXII:76–78]), he was converted by seeing the consonance of Vergil's words with scripture. Verbal influence, both literary and religious, has consistently been portrayed with generative imagery in this canto.

In canto XXV of *Purgatorio* is a passage on human embryology, which though apparently a digression, has, because of its imagery of insemination and parturition, come to be regarded as central to the discussion of poetry which surrounds it. Giuseppe Mazzotta first argued that this canto establishes an Incarnational model for Dante's theological poetry (194),[16] and Sylvia Huot, adopting his view, sees the passage as a source of female imagery—the creation of a human being as a figure for the creation of a poem—which might in the next century have given Christine de Pizan a more positive model for a woman writer than the prevailing patriarchal one of "pen as phallus" (365). Although such interpretations would support my contention that Dante uses female imagery to convey a view of literary influence as generative and nurturing in this section, I fear that the passage does not sustain them, given the passive role it assigns the female in reproduction. For, following Aristotle and Aquinas, Dante has Statius explain that in conception the semen

> "geme
> sovr' altrui sangue in natural vasello.
> Ivi s'accoglie l'uno e l'altro insieme,
> 'un disposto a patire, e l'altro a fare." (*Purg*. XXV:44–47)

(drops upon other's blood, in natural vessel. There the one is mingled with the other, one designed to be passive, the other active.)

That is, as Bruno Nardi explains, the semen is the active force which shapes the embryo, and the menstrual blood contains only the passive fetal matter: "The one furnishes the matter of the genetic process, the other the form."[17] Not only is this account of conception an inappropriate model for a woman writer, since it renders the male as active and the female as passive, it also is a weak analogy to the Incarnation, for its subordination of the female role to the male subordinates the flesh entirely to the Word. But, if Mazzotta's and Huot's readings do not demonstrate the privileging of female imagery in this part of the poem, they at least call attention to an image of generation which, however patriarchal, contributes to a portrayal of literary influence as more like procreation than warfare.

Furthermore, if Dante denigrates the female role in procreation in *Purgatorio* XXV, he grants it much more prominence in other parts of the *Commedia*. For he was influenced not only by the Aristotelian/Thomistic view of reproduction described above—the dominant one in the Middle Ages—but also by a more mystical view associated with Saint Bonaventure and Saint Bernard. Joan Ferrante has shown that the latter was more open to the feminine than the former, and she specifically contrasts Aquinas' antifeminism with Bonaventure's "identification with women and women's role," which derives from his mystic's emphasis on an erotic union with God. Unlike Saint Thomas, Bonaventure wrote that the Virgin played an active role in the conception of Christ (Ferrante 105). Even in *Purgatorio* XXV, Dante alludes to the Virgin's role in the Incarnation, in the souls' singing " '*virum non cognosco*' " (128), but his most reverent treatment of it, of course, is in Saint Bernard's prayer to her at the end of *Paradiso*:

"Vergine Madre, figlia del tuo figlio,
umile e alta piu che creatura,
termine fisso d'etterno consiglio,
tu se' colei che l'umana natura
nobilitasti si, che 'l suo fattore
non disdegno di farsi sua fattura.
Nel ventre tuo si racesse l'amore,
per lo cui caldo ne l'etterna pace
cosi e germinato questi fiore."

(XXXIII:1–9)

(Virgin mother, daughter of thy Son, humble and exalted more than any creature, fixed goal of the eternal counsel, thou art she who didst so enoble human nature that its Maker did not disdain to become its creature. In thy womb was rekindled the Love under whose warmth this flower in the eternal peace has thus unfolded.)

Such a description of the Virgin as a woman in whose *"ventre"* Christ the flower was *"germinato"* privileges the feminine much more than the account of the disembodied *"vasello"* of *Purgatorio* XXV, showing an attitude more characteristic of the mystical *Paradiso* than of the previous *cantica*.

This discussion of male and female roles in procreation is relevant to the further treatment of literary influence in this section of *Purgatorio*. Balancing the discussion of Vergil's nurturing influence on Statius in cantos XXI and XXII is a discussion of literary influence among vernacular love poets and by them on Dante himself, in cantos XXIV and XXVI. Here we find maternal and procreative imagery—presenting poets sometimes as mothers bringing forth poems, sometimes as fathers encouraging sons—which supports an interpretation of Dante's view of literary influence as nurturing rather than agonistic.

In *Purgatory* XXIV, whose cryptic definition of the *"dolce stil novo"* (57) has inspired much commentary,[18] Dante implies that the creating poetry is like giving birth, when the poet Bonagiunta asks the pilgrim whether he is the one "who brought forth the new rhymes beginning, 'Ladies that have understanding of love' " (che fore / trasse le nove rime cominciando, / *'Donne ch'avete intelletto d'amore'* [49–50]). Dante's modest reply, "I am one who, when Love inspires me, takes note, and goes setting it forth after the fashion which he dictates within me" (I' mi son un che, quando / Amor mi spira, noto, e a quel modo / ch'e ditta dentro vo significando [52–54]), suggests an image of poet as female vessel receiving inspiration from the male god, Amor. This image anticipates the one with which Dante presents himself at the beginning of *Paradiso*, where, rejecting the muses as inadequate, he invokes Apollo's aid in describing this realm: "for this last labor make me such a vessel of your worth as you require for granting your beloved laurel" (a l'ultimo lavoro / fammi del tuo valor si fatto vaso, / come dimandi a dar l'amato alloro [13–15]). That is, no longer figuring himself as male poet asking for the muses' milk, he presents himself in this mystical *cantica* as resembling a female poet asking for inspiration and fulfillment from a male god.

Dante goes on in *Purgatorio* XXVI to describe a meeting with vernacular love poets Guido Guinizzelli and Arnaut Daniel with the imagery of fathers and sons which, despite its masculine nature, shows a relation among poets which is nurturing rather than competitive. In a sense, this passage is the vernacular counterpart to the portrayal of gratitude in the meeting of Vergil and Statius. Dante expresses great joy at hearing the voice of Guido Guinizzelli, "the father of me and others my betters who ever used sweet and gracious rhymes of love" (il padre / mio e de li altri miei miglior che mai / rime d'amor usar dolci e leggiadre [97–99]). In a gesture that recalls his earlier homage to Vergil, he offers his service to Guinizzelli, explaining "Your sweet verses, which so long as modern use shall last, will make dear their very ink" (Li dolci detti vostri, / che, quanto durera l'uso moderno, / faranno cari ancora i loro incostri [112–14]). Although Dante has addressed Guinizzelli as a father (of benign rather than overwhelming influence), the poet disclaims that honor, addressing him as not son, but "brother" and pointing out Arnaut Daniel as "a better craftsman of the mother tongue" (miglior fabbro del parlar materno [115, 117]). He thus portrays himself, Dante, and Arnaut as brother poets nurtured by the maternal vernacular. Although the image continues to be the patriarchal one of male as active poet, the literary attitudes are generous rather than competitive: both Dante and Guinizzelli acknowledge the existence of poets better than they.[19]

Thus, although Dante expresses a number of different attitudes toward precursors, in the section of *Purgatorio* we examined, gratitude is especially prominent. He frequently uses imagery of generation and nursing to convey the nurturing relations between poets and between poets and texts, and, while this imagery puts the poet in the male role as often as in the female, it generally portrays the writing of poetry as being more like germination and growth than strife and warfare.[20] The result is a view of influence which has striking similarities to the model recently proposed by feminist critics as characteristic of women writers. By suggesting that it is as timebound as it is gender-bound, these similarities help call into question the universality of the agonistic model of literary influence.

Notes

1. See Shapiro, Ferrante (129–52), Spivak, Dronke, and Huot.
2. For a summary of work in this vein, see Jones (80–112).
3. Mazzotta points out the imagery of generation and seminality in these pas-

sages (192–226) but is not concerned with the patriarchal nature of this imagery or with questions of gender.

4. I am indebted in this paper to Rachel Jacoff, not only for her article, "Models of Literary Influence . . ." but also for her lectures and conversation at the Dartmouth Dante Institute, sponsored by the NEH, summer 1986.

5. See Bloom's *The Anxiety of Influence*.

6. A feminist critic who questions Bloom's model from a psychoanalytic point of view, based on object relations rather than Freudian theory, is Elizabeth Abel, who sees female writers as having a "willingness to absorb literary influence instead of defending the poetic self from it" the way many male writers do (433). Other critics who see literary influence among women as more nurturing than competitive are Moers, *passim,* and Auerbach (91–93).

7. They also link the idea to the anxiety of influence (46). See also Gubar " 'The Blank Page' and the Issues of Female Creativity."

8. Bloom (8, 122). Jacoff (159–60) cites Greene's similar treatment of Dante's marginality to a tradition of literary imitation based on a model of strife (45).

9. On Dante's complex relationship to Ovid, see Hawkins, "Virtuosity and Virtue . . ." and "Transfiguring the Text . . . ;" see also, Barkan, *The Gods Made Flesh.* On Dante's slighting of Guido Cavalcante's contribution, see Barolini (122–29, 178–79).

10. *Inf.* XXIII:38–42; see also, *Purg.* XXX:40–81, where Dante, turning toward Vergil like a frightened child toward his mother, finds that he has been replaced by a stern Beatrice. The portrayal of Vergil as mother has been pointed out by Shapiro (138–46), Ball (75), and Jacoff (166).

11. All subsequent citations to Dante are to the Singleton edition. On Dante's treatment of influence here and in *Inf.* II, see Wetherbee.

12. This passage has attracted much attention recently from critics concerned with literary influence; see Hawkins, "Resurrecting the Word," Stephany, Mazzotta (217–23), and Wetherbee. Jacoff stresses the nurturing aspects of the passage (165–67).

13. For the *Thebaid's* homage to Vergil, see Singleton, note to *Purg.* XXI:94–96.

14. See also Warner (192–97). For general background on Dante's use of the muses, see Hollander.

15. For a similar reference to the muses' milk, see Dante's confession of his inability to describe Beatrice's smile in Paradise: "Though all those tongues which Polyhymnia and her sisters made most rich with their sweetest milk should sound now to aid me, it would not come to a thousandth part of the truth" (Se mo sonasser tutte quelle lingue / che Polimnia con le suore fero / del latte dolcissimo piu pingue, / per aiutarmi, al millesmo del vero / non verria [*Par.* XXIII:55–59]).

16. Mazzotta also connects the passage with the use of reproductive metaphors for literary creation and filiation in *Purg.* XXI–XXV (216–17), but makes no distinction about gender roles.

17. Singleton, note to 47. Nardi calls the "virtute informativa" (informing power [41]) which, according to Dante, the semen gives to the body "an active virtue derived from the principle agent, the father" (note to 40–41), and Dante further stresses the active role of the male in the lines, "Anima fatta la virtute attiva" (the active virtue having become the soul [52]) and "la virtue ch'e dal cor del generante" (the virtue which precedes from the begetter" [59]).

18. See, for instance, Mazzotta (192 and note 1).

19. Mazzotta (217) discusses some of this reproductive imagery in terms of the "seminality of literature," but makes no distinctions about sex roles in its use.

20. Jacoff has suggested that Dante's treatment of influence corresponds to a typology described in Longinus' *On the Sublime,* so that he moves from seeing precursors as rivals in the *Inferno,* to guides in the *Purgatorio,* to (in the form of scripture only) "empowering source" in the *Paradiso* (175–76).

Works Cited

Abel, Elizabeth. "[E]Merging Identities: The Dynamics of Female Friendship in Contemporary Fiction by Women." *Signs 6* (1981):433.

Auerbach, Nina. *Communities of Women: An Idea in Fiction.* Cambridge, MA: Harvard University Press, 1978.

Ball, Robert. "Theological Semantics: Virgil's *Pietas* and Dante's *Pietà.*" *Stanford Italian Review* 2 (1981):59–80.

Barkan, Leonard. *The Gods Made Flesh: Metamorphosis and the Pursuit of Paganism.* New Haven: Yale University Press, 1986.

Barolini, Teodolina. *Dante's Poets: Textuality and Truth in the Comedy.* Princeton: Princeton University Press, 1984.

Bloom, Harold. *The Anxiety of Influence.* New York: Oxford University Press, 1973.

Bynum, Caroline Walker. *Jesus as Mother.* Berkeley: University of California Press, 1982.

Dante Alighieri. *The Divine Comedy.* Tr. Charles S. Singleton. Princeton: Princeton University Press, 1970–75.

Dronke, Peter. "Francesca and Heloise." *Comparative Literature* 27 (1975):113–25.

Ferrante, Joan. *Woman as Image in Medieval Literature from the Twelfth Century to Dante.* New York: Columbia University Press, 1975.

Gilbert, Sandra M., and Susan Gubar. *The Madwoman in the Attic: The Woman Writer and the Nineteenth-Century Literary Imagination.* New Haven: Yale University Press, 1979.

Greene, Thomas. *The Light in Troy: Imitation and Discovery in the Renaissance.* New Haven: Yale University Press, 1982.

Gubar, Susan. " 'The Blank Page' and the Issues of Female Creativity." *Critical Inquiry* 8 (1981):243–63.

Hawkins, Peter S. "Resurrecting the Word: Dante and the Bible." *Religion and Literature* 16 (1984):59–71.

———. "Transfiguring the Text: Ovid, Scripture, and Dante's Dynamics of Allusion." *Stanford Italian Review* 5 (1985):115–39.

———. "Virtuosity and Virute: Poetic Self-Reflection in the *Comedia.*" *Dante Studies* 98 (1980):1–18.

Hollander, Robert. "The Invocations of the *Commedia.*" *Yearbook of Italian Studies* (1973–75):235–40.

Huot, Sylvia. "Seduction and Sublimation: Christine de Pizan, Jean de Meun, and Dante." *Romance Notes* 25 (1985):361–73.

Jacoff, Rachel. "Models of Literary Influence in the *Commedia.*" *Medieval Texts and Contemporary Readers.* Ed. Laurie Finke and Martin B. Schichtman. Ithaca: Cornell University Press, 1987.

Jones, Ann Rosalind. "Inscribing Femininity: French Theories of the Feminine." *Making a Difference: Feminist Literary Criticism.* Ed. Gayle Greene and Coppelia Kahn. New York: Methuen, 1985. 80–112.

Mazzotta, Giuseppe. *Dante, Poet of the Desert: History and Allegory in the Divine Comedy.* Princeton: Princeton University Press, 1979.

Moers, Ellen. *Literary Women.* Garden City, NY: Doubleday, 1977.

Shapiro, Marianne. *Woman Earthly and Divine in the Comedy of Dante.* Lexington: University of Kentucky Press, 1975.

Spivak, Gayatri Chakravorty. "Finding Feminist Reading: Dante-Yeats." *American Criticism in the Poststructuralist Age.* Ed. Ira Kongisberg. Ann Arbor: University of Michigan Press, 1981. 42–65.

Stephany, William. "Biblical Allusions to Conversion in *Purgatorio* XXI." *Stanford Italian Review* 3 (1983):141—62.

Warner, Marina. *Alone of All Her Sex: The Myth and Cult of the Virgin Mary.* New York: Simon & Schuster, 1976.

Wetherbee, Winthrop. "*Poeta che mi guidi:* Dante, Lucan, and Virgil." *Canons.* Ed. Robert von Hallberg. Chicago: University of Chicago Press, 1984. 131–48.

The Body of/as Evidence:
Desire, Eloquence, and the Construction of Society in *Decameron* 7.8

ROBERT W. HANNING

Two of the most noteworthy characteristics of the *Decameron* are its appropriation and reworking (often parodic) of antecedent narrative forms—fabliaux or comic tales, Greek romances, visions of the other world, eremitic saints' lives, travel narratives, deathbed confessions, miracles at the tomb of saints, religious or moral exempla, and so on—and its infusing them with characters, situations, and tensions drawn from the social, political, religious, and commercial life of thirteenth- and fourteenth-century Italy (especially, but by no means exclusively, Tuscany).[1]

A fuller understanding of the relationship between the construction of fictions and the construction of society in the *Decameron* seems a goal worth pursuing, and with such a goal in mind, the following pages undertake to examine in one novella—the eighth of the seventh day—a feature of the *Decameron's* narrative technique which, I believe, can shed considerable light on that relationship—namely, Boccaccio's exploitation of forensic (judicial) rhetoric, the verbal techniques of analysis and persuasion developed in classical antiquity to decide those legal disputes where, in the absence of definitive proof, the determination of innocence or guilt depends on the establishment of probable facts and circumstances—what happened and why?[2]

Forensic rhetoric, as adapted by Boccaccio, offers clues to his program in the *Decameron* because of its heavy emphasis on the construction of plausible narratives (or probable fictions) which, to be convincing, must respond to and manipulate the cultural or social assumptions on which its "audiences" (judges or juries) base their construction of society and its members, and thus their judgments of right and wrong, or innocence and guilt, in a particular legal case. In a few *Decameron* novelle, Boccaccio creates what I shall call para-forensic occasions—ones in which, without overt recourse to judges, trials, or other formal legal procedures, a protagonist must rely on a ready tongue, fueled by a ready wit, to establish his/her own innocence or someone else's guilt. It is my thesis—which I will attempt to support with evidence drawn from my reading of 7.8—that this playful deployment of techniques recalling classical forensic practice embodies and signals the point of intersection between broadly based human impulses to construct fictions, on the one hand, and society, on the other—precisely the impulses strikingly present throughout the *Decameron.* Hence, the forensic dimension of 7.8 establishes Boccaccio's vernacular masterpiece, not just as an exercise in storytelling but as a microcosm or perhaps a metonymy of socialized human activity in general, so much of which involves constructing, adhering to, and/or challenging powerful, authoritative cultural fictions.[3]

Under Dioneo's kingship, the stories of the *Decameron's* seventh day are to be "about the tricks which, either out of love or for their own self-preservation, wives have played on their husbands, whether those tricks were discovered or not" (410–11).[4] Neifile's story of Arriguccio and Sismonda hews to this theme in recounting how a wife outrageously deceives her husband in order to save herself from physical abuse and disgrace. Boccaccio's achievement in this novella lies in taking a preexistent comic tale and doubly adapting it: on the one hand, by giving it a Florentine setting and evoking various cultural tensions indigenous to that setting; on the other, by making of its narrative climax the occasion for a brilliant and problematic display of forensic rhetorical techniques.

By contrast, although 7.8's closest known antecedent, the thirteenth-century French fabliau, *Des tresces,*[5] evokes, in passing, a cynical construction of social rank—a noble *dame* abuses representatives of the lower nobility and bourgeoisie, controlling one by her wit, the other by her wealth—its dominant theme is the mysogynistic commonplace that women are wily tricksters who can always win out over men, even (or especially) when they are in the wrong. To support this contention, the last scene of *Des tresces* suggests a parallel between the activities of the devil, the trickster and beguiler par excellence, and those of a wily wife.

The wife is placed in jeopardy one night when her lover, while entering her connubial bed, awakens her husband, a worthy *chevalier,* and escapes with his life only through her quick thinking and trickery. Banished from her home by the furious husband, she sends another woman—a neighboring *borgeoise*—to impersonate her and feign repentance, but the performance only prompts the knight to beat the surrogate savagely (thinking her to be his spouse) and cut off her hair (a traditional Germanic punishment for an adultress).[6] After generously rewarding the *borgeoise,* the *dame* returns to her bedroom and sets the stage for the fabliau's climactic scene by substituting, for the shorn tresses in her sleeping husband's pillow, the tail of his favorite charger, amputated by her for the occasion.

Once the husband awakens, his wife (adducing her unmarred body and the horse's tail to corroborate her argument) easily convinces him that she is innocent, even though she is guilty, and that his recollection of the preceding evening's events is wrong, even though it is, in fact, correct. The key to these reversals is, of course, the wife's substitution of another woman to receive the beating and haircutting intended for herself—what we might call her tampering with the body of evidence—which sets up both her own "truthful lie" and her husband's "correct incorrectness," and results as well, by the tale's end, in his apologizing to her for his offenses, instead of the other way round. Indeed, the principle has been established that in future disagreements she will *always* be right, and he mistaken:

> Le chevaliers chose ne dist,
> Se la dame le contredist,
> Qu'il ne cuidast ce fust menonge
> Ou qu'il l'eust trouvé en songe.
> (423–26)

The assimilation of the wife's brazen self-exculpation to devilish trickery is carefully established. In her first denial of her husband's assertion that he caught her with her lover, the dame broaches the theme of diabolic possession, exhorting him,

> Reclamez Dieu, si vos seignez.
> Ge crieng que en vos se soit mis
> Ou fantosmes ou enemis
> Qui ainsi vos ait desvoié
> (308–11)

Having astonished the knight by revealing the perfect state of her body and her hair, she returns to the idea of enchantment, suggesting that if his faulty vision is not due to gout or vertigo, it must be the result of

> fantosme qui vient
> As genz por ax faire muser

Et por ax folement user,
Et por faire foler la gent.
(364–67)

Finally, the tale makes its bias unmistakably clear: the bewildered husband is miserable "que il cuide estre anfantosmez, / Et si est il, n'en doutez mie" (396–97); not by the devil's guile, however, but by his wife's (321, 330), as embodied in her stratagems, which the text describes, using another Old French term for diabolic activity, as "un tel engig [= engin] . . . / Ja mes n'orroiz parler de tel" (160–61).[7]

In fact, the last scene of *Des tresces* not only equates women and the devil as tricksters; it even suggests women's superiority on at least three grounds. First, while diabolical guile can sometimes be counteracted by prayer, spells, or pilgrimages, feminine guile cannot. (This point is made unmistakably clear when the husband crosses himself to ward off the Devil, but his wife remains free of any sign of the beating he thinks he has given her [375–77].) Second, women are able to appropriate and manipulate to their own ends both popular lore about devils and popular remedies against them. And finally, women are so guileful that they can tell the truth and lie at same time—a feat beyond what the Devil, as mere father of lies, can accomplish.

Neifile's version of the tale of the cut/uncut hair follows the plot line of *Des tresces* (with a few small but important variants to be discussed later) through the point where the husband—Arriguccio Berlinghieri, a wealthy Florentine merchant—administers a sound thrashing to a woman he believes to be his adulterous wife, the aristocratic Donna Sismonda (but who is in fact her *fante,* or maid-servant, substituted for herself by Sismonda in the darkened bed-room). At which point, instead of expelling his errant spouse, Arriguccio, intent upon repudiating her, storms off, shorn tresses in hand, to enlist the support of Sismonda's brothers in chastising her, and returns with them (and her mother), only to find her unscathed and—having paid off and hidden the battered *fante*—acting as if nothing had happened earlier.

It is the last section of the novella that shows Boccaccio brilliantly creating what I have called a para-forensic occasion, involving a series of dramatic reversals: (1) of the narrative situation as it has unfolded thus far; (2) of the (perceived) respective culpability of its principals; and (3) of the relative authority of male and female eloquence founded on competing sets of social or cultural constructions.

The process of reversal is based on two acts of rhetorical virtuosity: first, Sismonda calmly and completely demolishes Arriguccio's account of earlier events and counterproposes her own version, a brilliant and highly effective portrayal of herself as the innocent, long-suffering victim of a neglectful, depraved, drunken husband. Then her mother, completely accepting this description of the marriage because she has been convinced all along of her daughter's impeccable virtue, extravagantly denounces both Arriguccio—for his lowborn vulgarity as well as his abuse of her beloved Sismonda—and her sons, for their stupidity in having trapped their exemplary sister in such a degrading marriage.

The novella ends with the brothers as furious at Arriguccio as they were earlier at Sismonda—they threaten him with severe reprisals for any future transgressions against their sister—and Arriguccio completely confused, "not knowing himself whether what he had done he had actually done or if he had been dreaming" (457); as for the clever wife, "not only did she avoid an impending disaster, but she also opened the way to fulfilling her every pleasure in the future, without ever having to fear her husband again" (458).

In order fully to explore and problematize both the specifically forensic dimension of Sismonda's fiction-making eloquence and the familial and social structures within which that eloquence must be exercised, *Dec.* 7.8 transforms the concluding section of tale told in *Des tresces* from a purely domestic debate between husband and wife in the privacy of their bedroom into Arriguccio's formal accusation of Sismonda to her male kin—as part of his action of repudiating her—thereby inviting her family to play a role (albeit not the role Arriguccio has in mind) in the denouement of the marital drama.[8] One other difference between Boccaccio's story and its French antecedent requires mention: 7.8 lacks (or suppresses) the substitution of the horse's tail for the shorn tresses, which instead remain in the husband's possession throughout. Consequently, Sismonda, instead of refuting Arriguccio's accusation of adultery on the grounds of his enchantment (using the tail/tresses as "proof"), must employ a less supernaturally oriented defense strategy that both exculpates her of his complaint to her kin and provides a satisfactory, alternative explanation of the "evidence" with which he supports it.

Taken together, these two changes shape the climax of *Dec.* 7.8 as a courtroom drama and Sismonda's performance within it as a triumph of forensic rhetoric.

The novella's para-forensic thrust begins when, to support his accusation of infidelity against his wife, Arriguccio offers to her brothers a circumstantial account of her transgression—"beginning with the string which he had found tied to the toe of Monna Sismonda's foot [as a signaling device to her lover] . . . [including] everything he had discovered and all that he had done up to that point"—complete with supporting evidence: "to provide them with conclusive proof of what she had done, he handed over to them the hair which he thought he had cut off his wife's head . . ." (454). In terms of classical forensic rhetoric, Arriguccio becomes a prosecuting lawyer offering to the judges (or jury) a *narratio expositionis causae* (a narrative expounding the events of the case; see *De inv.* I.xx.28), buttressed by a *signum,* "something apprehended by one of the senses and indicating something that seems to follow logically as a result of it" (*De inv.* I.xxx.48, which offers as examples of *signa* "blood, flight, pallor, dust, and the like").[9]

In fact, however, the evidence Arriguccio offers only supports his description of his own behavior toward Sismonda, not of hers toward him. The implicit result is a patently false syllogism: a wife who cuckolds her husband deserves a beating; I have beaten my wife; therefore she cuckolded me. Or, to put it in semiotic terms, since a transgressive female body should be punished, a punished female body is an accurate sign of its transgression.

Notwithstanding its logical shortcomings, Sismonda's brothers accept Arriguccio's representation of the facts: "[believing] every word of the story, [they] were furious over what they had heard, and full of anger at [Sismonda] . . . [they] set out with Arriguccio for his home with the intention of severely punishing their sister." (The reasons for their ready acceptance of their brother-in-law's accusation will shortly come under scrutiny.) Her mother, on the other hand, sees the flaw in Arriguccio's argument, and as she tearfully follows her sons to his house, "begging [them] not to be too hasty in believing these things without first seeing more evidence or learning more about the circumstances," she offers her own interpretation (in rhetorical terms, a color)[10] which (anticipating her daughter's strategy) impugns both Arriguccio's veracity and his motives: "her husband might well have become angry with her for some other reason and treated her badly, and he could be blaming her in order to excuse himself" (454).

Arriguccio's attempt to prosecute his wife, based on his possessing her supposed tresses, sets the stage for a complex para-forensic proceeding, combining elements of *constitutio conjecturalis* and *constitutio generalis* (cf. *De inv.* I.viii.10), that is, one in which both facts and motivation become subject to contestation between the contending parties. Sismonda's brothers function as a court or jury—Cicero's *auditores*—evaluating conflicting testimony, and her mother continues to be Sismonda's advocate, in the process launching a devastating attack on her daughter's husband which effectively neutralizes her sons' initial partisanship toward him.

Ultimately, Sismonda succeeds in defending her actions and discrediting her husband, first by undermining the *signum*—the shorn tresses—on which he rests his case,[11] then by using her formidable skill at constructing fictions to offer an alternative account of the night's events and the motives behind them. She buttresses her argument by appeals to character (her own and her husband's), and by manipulating her family's strong feelings, especially their aristocratic disapproval of upward mobility, a key element of their class-based construction of society. (These three dimensions of Sismonda's defense—*logos, ethos,* and *pathos*—constitute the "classic" elements of verbal persuasion [Greek *pisteis*] at least since Aristotle.)[12]

When Arriguccio brings Sismonda's kin back to his house, he expects to find her in her nightclothes, her hair cut off, "all beaten up and crying her eyes out" (454). That the would-be-avengers of male honor are greeted instead by a fully dressed, domestically occupied, visibly intact, and apparently calm mistress of the house—in Marga Cottino-Jones's words, "the physical contradiction of the accusations Arriguccio makes against her to her family"—has an immediate and marked impact on the dynamic of the scene.[13] Arriguccio is stunned by the contrast between expectation and observation, and "when her brothers saw her sitting there sewing, not a visible mark of a beating on her face though Arriguccio claimed to have given her a sound thrashing, they were at first surprised, and their anger began to cool a bit. Then they asked her for an explanation of the affair Arriguccio was accusing her of, threatening her severely if she did not tell them the whole story" (455). That is, they announce the defining *quaestio*—what happened earlier that evening? Did Sismonda do what she is accused of doing?—of what has suddenly become a *constitutio conjecturalis.*

The language of this passage, by its repeated recourse to the vocabulary of sight (*veduta, vista, vedendola, vedeva),* emphasises the crucial importance of a signum, "something apprehended by one of the senses"—here, Sismonda's beaten body—to Arriguccio's case; Sismonda's defense brilliantly exploits his misguided, though understandable (if not inevitable) reliance on evidentiary claims she has put herself in a position to deny.[14]

After hearing from her brothers the charges against her, Sismonda links a denial of Arriguccio's having beaten her (a denial already supported by her healthy appearance) with a denial that he was in bed (or even at home) with her that night. This tactic lures him into a series of self-defeating counterquestions—"What, you wicked woman, did we not go to bed together? Did I not return here after chasing your lover away? Did I not give you a good beating and cut off your hair?"—which offer her the perfect opportunity to reveal dramatically that her hair, hidden under her "veli di testa" (ironically a sumptuary symbol of matronly modesty) is as intact as her body.[15]

Sismonda's gesture is doubly effective: as a hermeneutic symbol, it enacts her lifting the veil of inaccuracy and confusion created by Arriguccio, in order to expose the clear, incontestable truth of the matter.[16] And forensically, as a conclusive refutation of the *signum* on which Arriguccio has built his case, it damages his overall credibility, and conversely increases her own, with her adjudicating brothers (*De inv.* I.xliii.81: "therefore in the refutation it will be shown . . . that [the *signum*] favours one's own side rather than the opponents' . . .", cf. note 9, above).

Before removing her headdress, Sismonda repeats but then shrewdly offers to strike her testimony that Arriguccio has not slept at home that evening: "but let us forget that, since I cannot provide you with any proof of this except my own true words . . ." (455). In the light of her spectacular disclosure of her tresses, this ostensible disclaimer functions as a signal to her "judges" that, unlike her opponent, she knows and respects the difference between assertions that can be proven (or dis-proven) by recourse to evidence—does she have hair or not?—and those which cannot—did her husband sleep at home last night or not?

But Sismonda's very acknowledgment of this distinction is part of her skillful attempt to persuade her *auditores* to violate it by deducing from the *irrefutable* proof that her tresses have not been shorn the following false conclusions: (1) since Arriguccio's recourse to tangible evidence is clearly incorrect, all his other contentions are probably false; (2) hence, Sismonda's counterstatement probably is true, all the more so as she forthrightly admits that she cannot prove it.[17]

In short, Sismonda implicitly is making the case that her testimony is likely to be what she says it is—"vere parole"—because, unlike Arriguccio's evidence-based testimony, it cannot be proven false; the collapse of his argument creates the powerful (albeit entirely illogical and unwarranted) presumption that hers, the only one left in the case, must therefore be true. Hence, Boccaccio's version of the cut/uncut hair tale throws into particularly high relief the problematic relationship, on which the tale is built, between "facts" and "truth": the circumstances and motives governing the revelation of a particular fact will determine whether, and how much, it contributes to the discovery of a larger truth.[18] In this instance, Sismonda is able to conceal the larger truth about her behavior by suppressing what we may call the middle term—the beaten *fante*—between Arriguccio's violence and the body (her own) at which it was aimed.

The response of Sismonda's kindred to her exposure of her unshorn locks confirms that she has reversed the momentum of her "trial": "When her brothers and mother saw and heard these things, they turned to Arriguccio, saying 'what does this mean, Arriguccio? This does not fit the story you came to tell us, and we do not know how you will prove the rest of it" (translation altered). And Arriguccio, unaccountably denied his "body of evidence"—the mutilated, because transgressive, body of his wife—is left without a forensic strategy: " . . . seeing that what he thought he could prove was not the case, he made no attempt to say anything" (456).

The way is now clear for Sismonda to offer her own (completely fictional) *narratio* of her innocence—and, as important, of Arriguccio's guilt—combining strategies of *logos, ethos,* and pathos. Having, in effect, destroyed Arriguccio's argument, she now resurrects it and, by applying a new color to it, turns it against him. The events he described did take place, she argues, but not to her. "I am sure that when he was good and drunk he went to bed with one of his sorry whores and when he woke up, he found the string on her foot, and then proceeded to perform the brave deeds he recounted, and finally turning against her, he beat her and cut off her hair; and not quite having come to his senses yet, he believed, and I am sure he still does believe, that he did all those things to me."

Sismonda has prepared some circumstantial evidence in support of her contention that Arriguccio was out all night: the made bed, her fully dressed state. The tresses, clearly not her own, constitute circumstantial evidence as well: they must have come from someone, so why not the harlot with whom he spent the night? Finally, in support of her charge that Arriguccio was drunk, and thus confused his whore with his wife when he beat and mutilated her, Sismonda suggests that the "judges" examine him for evidence of continued inebriation: "if you take a good look at his face, you can see he's still half-drunk." (This last detail apparently seeks to capitalize on, by offering a self-serving color for, Arriguccio's state

278 THE RHETORICAL POETICS OF THE MIDDLE AGES

of shock—"he stood there as though in a trance"—at the annihilation of his case against his wife [456].)

The construction of character, her own and Arriguccio's, is an element of Sismonda's self-defense throughout the climactic scene of 7.8. When Arriguccio and her kin arrive at her door, they encounter a persuasive image of the good wife, seated quietly and engaged in the archetypally female domestic activity of sewing. Furthermore, Sismonda's immediate response to her brother's recapitulation of Arriguccio's complaint against her builds on this carefully created first impression. "Turning to Arriguccio, the lady exclaimed, 'Oh, husband, what is this I hear? Why, to your own great shame, do you make me out to be such a wicked woman, when I am not, and yourself to be such a wicked and cruel man, when it is not so?' " (455). Far from evincing merely a selfish desire to defend herself, these heartfelt words express her wish to defend him against the imputation of being "malvagio uomo e crudele" which (she implies) follows from his claim to have beaten her. Indeed, she is such a good wife that she is as upset at the "gran vergogna" that accrues to him if she is a "rea femina" as she is at the accusation itself.

By establishing herself as a loyal and devoted wife, Sismonda can pretend that her depiction of Arriguccio as a terrible husband is being drawn from her against her will and almost in spite of herself. Her first hint that he has been out all night whoring and drinking comes in the form of a question, ostensibly forced from her by his account of finding first the string on her toe in bed, and then her lover lurking outside the house: who says you were even at home last night, never mind in bed with me? Only after the exposure of her hair has "proven" the unfoundedness (and thus the scandalousness) of Arriguccio's claims against her does Sismonda, still protesting unwillingness, go over to the attack: "Well, my brothers, I see now that he is asking for it; he is forcing me to let you in on a secret I would never have revealed concerning his miserable and wicked way of life, and I shall tell you about it" (456).

Thus Sismonda carefully creates an idealized version of her own character—as Cottino-Jones puts it (128), she "endows herself with the virtues of humility, patience, and modesty"—before she undertakes to destroy Arriguccio's, thereby heading off imputations of vengeance or malice on her part; and by suggesting her reluctance to air his misdeeds, makes her situation seem all the more desperate (and his behavior all the more heinous) when she finally does so.

Sismonda's representation of her own character thus complements her disproof of Arriguccio's claimed evidence; her soul is, in effect, as unblemished as her body. Taken together, these two parts of her case render credible the almost parodically denigratory picture of Arriguccio as a hypocrite and wastrel that she goes on to create:

> this worthy man to whom in my most unfortunate hour you [her brothers] gave me in marriage, a man who calls himself a merchant and wishes to be respected as such, who would like to be thought of as being more temperate than a monk and more virtuous than a maiden—this man comes home drunk from the taverns most evenings, playing around now with one whore and now with another, and I have to stay up until midnight, and sometimes until morning, waiting for him just the way you found me now (456).[19]

(Sismonda cleverly recycles the corroborative detail of her kin having found her sitting up fully dressed at an early hour of the morning: originally it supported her claim that he hadn't been home at all that night; now it argues that he never comes home until dawn—a heinous trait in a husband.)

In addition to her evocation of ethos to undergird the plausibility of her fabricated story concerning the events of the preceding hours, Sismonda also relies on a direct appeal to the emotion of her familial "judges." As she destroys her husband's character, she reminds her brothers that they are responsible for having married her to Arriguccio, "nella mia mala ora." And by bringing up her husband's status as a merchant and suggesting that he is a hypocrite—"dovrebbe esser più temperato che uno religioso e più onesto che una donzella"—she takes aim at what we will soon discover to be her mother's strong opposition to, and deep resentment of, her wonderful, gently-born daughter's being forced into a misalliance with a parvenu tradesman. (All of this conforms, though in a more diffuse manner, to the *indignatio*—"a passage which results in arousing great hatred against some person" [*De inv.* I.liii.100]—which forms part of the peroration, or concluding section, of a forensic *narratio*.)

Sismonda's appeal to the emotions of her kin aims, above all, to activate their class-determined construction of Florentine society (and of its members). Her goal is to counterbalance or neutralize Arriguccio's analogous attempt to exploit her brother's emotional investment in gender construction. And it is by drawing on such class and gender constructs that Boccaccio transforms 7.8 from a traditional misogynistic tale into a para-forensic occasion grounded in Florentine social assumptions and tensions.

On the one hand, the status of Sismonda's brothers as men with responsibilities for and authority over their female relatives, combined with widespread mysogynistic notions about female sexuality, shamelessness, and lack of self-control—notions fostered by a male-dominated culture in order to justify its exercise of preponderant power over women—would lead them to sympathize with a fellow male whose authority and honor—and hence, theirs—have been threatened by the behavior of his wife; their *pathos* would automatically, as it were, support Arriguccio's *logos*.[20] Conversely, Sismonda's mother, appropriately for a woman, distrusts her son-in-law's accusations from the beginning while defending Sismonda as "the best and most virtuous daughter in Florence" (457).

But the mother's partisanship concerning (and therefore faulty judgment of) the daughter is rooted at least as deeply in socially prompted notions about class as in gender solidarity: when Sismonda asks her kin to follow her in forgiving, as the behavior of a drunk, Arriguccio's neglect, depravity, and false accusations, her mother volubly dissents, insisting "we shall do nothing of the kind; on the contrary, we ought to murder this pesty dog of a nobody . . .," and thereupon launching into a brilliant exhibition of billingsgate, directed against not only Arriguccio—an "insignificant trader in donkey dung" and a "twerp of a two-bit merchant"— but all upwardly mobile peasants like him, who come to town from the countryside "with their short baggy stockings and their quill pens sticking out of their asses," prosper through trade, and "as soon as they've gotten a few cents in their pockets, they want the daughters of noble men and worthy ladies for their wives. . . ." Her sons, she fulminates, could have made an honorable match for their sister had they followed her advice, instead of giving her to "this fine jewel of a fellow" who accuses her in the middle of the night of being a whore, "as if we didn't know you" (457).

It is clear from this hyperbolic performance—Cottino-Jones, for example, calls it "a heated commentary on fourteenth-century Florentine class struggles" (129)—that the outcome of *Dec.* 7.8, whatever it says about female trickery, exemplifies the forensic effectiveness of the argument from (and to) ideologically generated emotion. From the beginning, the most profound reason for the mother's skepticism about Arriguccio's story is evidently her deepseated, Florentine gentlefolk's prejudice against *nouveau riche,* social-climbing merchants.[21] Hence, she, and perhaps also her sons, are eminently susceptible to the analogously hyperbolic verbal picture of drunken, whoring Arriguccio painted by Sismonda, a fact the clever wife is doubly counting on: first to win acceptance for her version of the night's events, and second, to have her kin reject her appeal that they simply pardon the offending husband.

Nor is she disappointed. After the mother has finished her tirade, the brothers, though they let Arriguccio go unharmed this time "because you were drunk," revile him, "calling him the worst names ever called a criminal," and warn him that if they hear of his causing similar trouble in the future, they will punish him doubly, for then and now (457).[22] Clearly, their earlier solidarity with Arriguccio on the basis of gender construction—a solidarity that recognizes the male need to discipline (and if necessary repudiate) the transgressive female body—has been overcome by their sister's appeal to more profound imperatives of class solidarity and construction.

By her eloquence and ingenuity, Sismonda is able to turn the paraforensic occasion in *Dec.* 7.8 entirely to her advantage; by the end of the novella, she is, in Natalie Zeman Davis's term, the woman on top.[23] From one perspective, injustice and the tricky woman have triumphed in Neifile's novella, as in the fabliau *Des tresces*. Are we, then, to find in the former as misogynistic an attack on women as we have in the latter, even without the earlier work's diabolizing imagery to guide us? Put differently, is *Dec.* 7.8 simply an instance of Boccaccio's *aggiornamento* of an inherited fictional type?

The major difference between *Des tresces* and the Boccaccian novella lies in the latter's stress on coherent motivation of characters and events. In contrast to the rather casual and "paratactic" plotting of the fabliau, Neifile's tale integrates character and social setting to provide tight, as it were hypotactic, motivation that controls the unfolding of the narrative to its conclusion. Arriguccio is a rich merchant who marries above his rank, thereby courting disaster. Since, like all merchants, he is often away from home, Sismonda takes Ruberto as her lover; the implication is that this is not an act of mere feminine lasciviousness but the almost expectable consequence of a social mismatch and an absent husband.

Neifile professes uncertainty—"either because he heard rumors of the affair or for some other reason"—as to why Arriguccio suddenly becomes "the most jealous man in the world" and puts Sismonda under such close observation that she can no longer meet with Ruberto (451). (In fact, merchants in medieval comic tales are almost always depicted as jealously possessive of their wives—as a metaphor for their stereotypical characteristics of greed and retentiveness—even [or especially] when they can least adequately discharge the sexual obligations of a husband—in keeping with another stereotype, that merchants devote all their energy and de-

sire to making and keeping money.[24] In any case, the real importance of Arriguccio's jealousy is that it motivates Sismonda to
develop the first really distinctive element of the novella: the device
of the string tied to her toe and extending into the street, whereby
her lover can signal his arrival outside her house in the middle of
the night, and she can signal back whether he is to leave (because
Arriguccio is awake) or come to the door to be let in for lovemaking
(because Arriguccio is asleep).

That Arriguccio should eventually discover the string stretches
credibility less than that Sismonda should employ it in the first
place. But the aim of the pattern of motivation I have sketched is
not, I think, credibility (or incredibility) per se. Rather, it exists to
show two things: the cleverness of Sismonda, and the social circumstances beyond her control which stimulate, challenge, and im-
peril that cleverness—above all, her unchosen marriage to a
merchant whose too frequent absences create the relationship that
appears, in turn, to motivate his subsequent, too frequent presence.
The extraordinary stratagems to which Sismonda must resort after
Arriguccio discovers the string, and Ruberto, are thus both consistent with what she has accomplished before the moment of crisis
(namely, the string device), and grounded in her clear sense of how
she can exploit to her advantage her husband's social rank—and
more particularly, the class-based ambivalence about that rank
which she knows her kinfolk harbor.

Sismonda's established cleverness at reconstructing unsatisfac-
tory situations in accord with her desires—emblematized by the
string which establishes a "plot line" between her body and her
lover's (or between the restricted, patriarchally controlled household and the possibilities for pleasure in the world outside it)—[25] is
refigured in the novella's climactic para-forensic episode as the
more elemental and crucial skill of surviving a perilous situation
by transforming it to her advantage through fiction-making that persuades its audience to accept it as "true." Indeed, she already displays marked forensic abilities in her response to Arriguccio's
discovery of the stratagem of the string: "When Arriguccio opened
the bedroom door, the lady awakened to find that the string had
been cut from her toe, and she knew at once that her trick had been
discovered; hearing Arriguccio running after Ruberto, she quickly
got out of bed, and, realizing what was likely to happen, called her
maid-servant . . ." (453). Sismonda's deductive skills allow her to
draw from the "evidence" of the present—the noise outside, the
string gone—a correct interpretation of the past and a probable scenario for the future. Like a logician, she can work out causes and

effects; like a good lawyer she can put together a narrative of a case from bits of evidence; like a good storyteller, she can carry a plot forward.

But the fiction that simultaneously exonerates her and convicts Arriguccio succeeds only because it responds to, and builds on, the social construction to which the other players in the drama contribute their energies and imaginations. Arriguccio partakes of a construct of upward social mobility. The aim of his cohort, as understood alike by Sismonda's mother and many twentieth-century social historians, is to use his wealth to gain social status as well as material success. As the mother puts it, such men marry into genteel families, "and they make up a coat of arms, and then they claim, 'I'm one of the so-and-so family' or 'The people in my family do such-and-such'" (457).

Sismonda's kin, on the other hand, even if they cooperate in such constructed careers, remain wholly or partially committed to a construction of society in which blood tells, divisions of rank are immutable, and virtue is the possession of a specific class (not surprisingly, their own).[26] If Sismonda did not understand such social constructions, and could not make them serve her personal needs, she would be much less successful in forensic competition than she is in 7.8.

We must also note that the skills we are attributing to Sismonda—constructing effective plots and probable fictions, and manipulating social constructions to her advantage—are precisely those that distinguish Neifile as novellista of 7.8. (It is no mere coincidence, I think, that Sismonda's brothers warn Arriguccio at the end of the novella that henceforth they do not want to hear any more stories—"simili novelle'—about him; we, on the other hand, are delighted at the prospect of another twenty-plus "simile novelle" before the brigata's storytelling has run its course.) The difference in motivation between *Des tresces* and Nefile's version of the same story is that the latter is more coherent, its constituent episodes more understandably, even inevitably—which is not the same thing as verisimilarly—linked; where *Des tresces* is a comic exemplum of feminine guile, 7.8, like Sismonda's forensic display within it, is a well-made argument.

Like the Sismondan microcosm, the Neifilean macrocosm depends for its effect on recognizing and manipulating social construction as part of its construction of an effective fiction. It is Neifile who contributes to her inherited story of the truthful lie and the simultaneously amputated and unamputated tresses the social matrix of the unequal marriage which, as she presents it, is itself sufficient to motivate all that follows and to provide Sismonda (and, behind her, Neifile) with the occasion to demonstrate their fiction-making gifts: "You should know, then, that in our city there once lived a very wealthy merchant named Arriguccio Berlinghieri, who quite foolishly . . . thought that he could enoble himself by marrying into an aristocratic family, and he chose a young noblewoman very badly suited to him, whose name was Monna Sismonda." "Scioccamente; . . . male a lui convenientesi"; Neifile's words sound an alarm as clear as fire bells in the night.

Neifile, however, is not simply talking about a Florence of the past; Arriguccio marries inappropriately, she says, "as we still see merchants doing today" (451). In other words, the social construction of Neifile's fiction is also that of her "reality" (cf. note 26). Nonetheless, her fiction manages in various ways to suggest that the social construct it enshrines—one that exalts inherited gentility at the expense of mercantile upward mobility—is itself a fiction erected on the "pathetic" foundation of classist prejudice.

Most flagrantly, the mother's angry denunciation of parvenu merchants deploys an abusive, "lower body"-oriented discourse more suggestive of popular excess than of genteel refinement.[27] In this, her rhetoric contrasts greatly with (and perhaps calls into question?) that of the tale-telling *brigata* (a group whose status presumably approximates hers), who speak among themselves with unfailing elegance, even when making off-color remarks. Furthermore, the representatives of the genteel class in 7.8 show themselves to be either significantly capable of perpetrating deceptions (Sismonda) or significantly susceptible to believing them, because blinded by class antagonism (the mother and, ultimately, the brothers). And, of course, at the very heart of the novella is a "body of evidence" that challenges the construction of society as depicted both in 7.8 and in the *Decameron* cornice: the mauled and shorn body of the *fante* whom Sismonda orders (and subsequently pays, with money from her husband's mercantile successes) to take her place in bed and bear the brunt of her husband's fury. The resulting paradigm—the aristocracy robs the merchant classes to pay off the servant classes for the hardships it inflicts on them—cannot be said to flatter the upper class. (The servants of the brigata, who accompany them on their escape from plague-devastated Florence, are not required to receive beatings intended for their "betters," but the text makes it clear they do the work that enables the young "gentils" to lead lives of leisure and pleasure *in villeggiatura*.)[28]

At this point, the binary, fiction/social reality, breaks down; each is a process of construction, and each is imbricated in the other.

Fiction-making is always already present, playing a vital role in the construction of any social order, and social construction is always already in place (whether or not overtly) as a conditioning factor of the fictions offered for the amusement of "brigate" in every time and place. Indeed, one might argue that the string connecting Sismonda to Ruberto, her bedroom to the urban street outside, is also an adequate emblem of the necessary, if not always easily discovered, connection between the abstract ability to construct fictions and the social exegencies that must be understood and appropriated if fiction-making is to be successful in a particular milieu.

What, finally, does the *Decameron*'s staging of interactions between fictional and social constructs tell us about the place of the para-forensic occasion in the work's overall scheme? One possible response to 7.8 is to read it as an ironic tribute to the power of forensic rhetoric, which allows falsehood to triumph over truth, fiction over fact. (A further irony of Sismonda's forensic mastery over Arriguccio would not be lost on Boccaccio's original Florentine audience—namely, the fact that

> Florentine law created a clear distinction between [the] respective legal capabilities [of men and women]. Women were always under the control of men. In Florence the law established that a woman, married or not, was in need of a guardian in order to take part in legal transactions. She had to have a *mundualdus,* who could be any designated male; although, in the case of a married woman, her husband [!] could be assumed to be her *mundualdus.*

Furthermore, for judicial proceedings, "a woman needed more than a *mundualdus;* she needed a *procurator.* . . . The role [of *procurator*] was generally filled by notaries, who were versed in the law and could argue in court on behalf of their clients. . . .") (Kuehn 204, 214).[29]

This is not, I think, the novella's primary intent, although it does problematize the application of forensic techniques to legal or para-legal fact-finding situations, but only in the larger context of problematizing both the human skills that underlie effective argumentation—and, thus, effective fiction-making—and the social structures within which those skills are, of necessity, employed. Constructing fictions and constructing society emerge as two forever interacting versions of the same impulse, and the para-forensic occasion, in turn, emerges as a microcosm of the transactions and negotiations by which we construct the world we live in and survive (or thrive) in the world we construct. If Sismonda plays fast and loose with the "facts" in her forensic exercise, at Arriguccio's expense, and if, as a result, she can look forward to an indefinite future of extramarital pleasure, the fact remains that her self-serving manipulation of forensic techniques rests on, and responds to, social constructions—class antagonisms, the exchange of women between men for male, but not female, advantage—that she did not create, and that can be said to have created her. As first the neglected, then the jealously guarded wife of a socially ambitious merchant, she must use all her personal resources and bend the system to her needs if she is to experience any satisfaction. The para-forensic occasion is the emblematic record of her struggle. (Of course, as already noted, Sismonda's adept use of language requires, for its success, the antecedent abuse, and subsequent silence, of her *fante;* this suppressed body of evidence, whose inscribed "text" of cuts and bruises provides unambiguous testimony about both patriarchal and hierarchal privilege, works its own powerful persuasion on the reader of the *Decameron.*)

Perhaps, when all is said and done, the para-forensic occasion in the *Decameron* is also what Victor Turner might call a liminoid moment of cultural performance: an outrageous fiction that forces us to confront, albeit in play, the extent to which our construction of society depends on our construction of fictions about society—and, in doing so, encourages us to attempt more constructive forms of such construction.[30]

Notes

1. On the *Decameron*'s reflection of its culture, see Branca, "L'epopea dei mercatanti" and "Le nuove dimensioni narrative e il linguaggio storicamente allusivo" (134–88); and "Contemporaneizzazione storica, metastorica e narrativa" (347–57); and Padoan.

2. Boccaccio would have know the techniques and categories of classical rhetoric above all through Cicero's *De inventione* and the pseudo-Ciceronian *Rhetorica ad Herennium,* both widely used in fourteenth-century Italian schools. By contrast, Aristotle's *Rhetoric,* the foundational text in Antiquity for the systematization of rhetoric as a discipline, was apparently not known to Boccaccio or his Italian contemporaries, although it had been translated into Latin at Paris, in the latter half of the thirteenth century, by William of Moerbeke. (See Murphy 89–132).

3. On the relationship between forensic rhetoric and European fiction-making, see esp. Eden. I am deeply indebted to Professor Eden for assistance with the rhetorical materials dealt with in this essay; she is, however, in no way responsible for its errors or omissions.

4. All *Decameron* quotations follow the translation by Musa and Bondanella—

modified in a few places—with page references inserted in the text. The Italian text I have used is Branca's edition.

5. All *Des tresces* quotations follow Reid's edition. For a brief list of other Eastern and Western story collections containing versions of this story, see Branca (1386 n.1). Professor Nancy Reale is currently at work on a comparative study of several versions, and has kindly shared her preliminary conclusions with me.

6. According to Tacitus (*Germania* xix), among the "Germans," "the husband punishes his wife's adultery, in the presence of her relatives, by expelling her from the household, ordering her hair to be cut off, and whipping her through the village" (in Pomeroy 212).

7. On the Devil as beguiler, see Ashley; on *engin*, see, further, Hanning, chap. 3 (esp. 106).

8. Compare *Dec.* 7.4: Tofano, having discovered that his wife, Ghita, has been making him drunk so that she can visit a lover, locks her out with the threat, "rest assured you'll never return to this house until, in the presence of your relatives and neighbors, I have paid you the kind of honor you deserve." The neighbors become involved because they cannot help hearing the abuse Tofano shouts at Ghita, a violation of domestic privacy which the novella's narrator condemns, saying Tofano wanted "to let everyone in Arezzo learn of his shame, when as yet no one actually knew a thing about it" (432). By contrast, Arriguccio breaks off his fight with Ruberto, Sismonda's lover, when the neighbors begin to show an interest in the goings-on. On the advantages and disadvantages of dealing with one's wife's kindred, see Herlihy and Klapisch-Zuber. For some of the implications of Arriguccio's announcement to Sismonda's kin that he is, in effect, separating from her, see King (42–43).

9. Later in the novella, after Sismonda has proven that the hair is not hers, thereby reducing Arriguccio to a state of amazed disbelief, she turns the strategy against him, identifying his confusion as a *signum* of the drunkenness that led him to confuse her with the prostitute he had "actually" shorn. See below, p. 277.

10. Aristotle explains that "a topic common to accuser and defendant occurs when the same thing can have been done for many reasons: the accuser should attribute an evil motive, pointing to the worse interpretation, the defendant the better motive" (*Rhetoric* III.xv.10). Referring to the use of colors in the mock-forensic exercises or *controversiae* popular in Roman schools, M. Winterbottom says, "a 'colour' was a line of approach to the case, a method of interpreting the facts that was to the advantage of the speaker" (Seneca, *Declamations* xviii). See further, Trimpi 312–15; in Trimpi's view, "if it is taken metaphorically to include all events and issues, the *color* might be considered the complete presentation of the case itself" (314)—a definition certainly applicable to Sismonda's self-serving interpretation of how Arriguccio obtained the woman's hair in his possession and what it reveals about his character and worth as a husband.

11. See *De inventione,* which explains that

what is assumed to be a "sign" will be disproved by use of the same topics [i.e. arguments] by which it is supported. For in the case of a sign, first it must be shown to be true; and in the second place to be a proper sign of the thing under discussion, as, for example, blood is a sign of murder; in the third place that it indicates that something has been done which ought not to have been done. . . . Therefore in the refutation it will be shown of each of these points that it is not a sign, or not an important one, or that *it favors one's own side rather than the opponents',* or that it is absolutely false, or that *it can be shifted so as to create a suspicion in a different quarter* [i.e., by an appropriate color]. (I.xliii.81)

Sismonda's refutation combines the arguments I have emphasized.

12. See Aristotle (*Rhetoric* I.ii.2–6); I.ii.2 characterizes these "*pisteis* provided through speech" as "artistic" *(enteknoi)*, in opposition to "inartistic" *(ateknoi) pisteis* that exist outside of speech: "for example witnesses, testimony of slaves taken under torture, contracts, and such like." The rhetorician must be able to "invent" the former and "use" the latter—as Sismonda clearly does. On uses of character and emotion in forensic narratives, with specific reference to winning the *benivolentia* of the listeners in the exordium, or introduction, see *De inv.* (I.xv.20–I.xvi.22) and *Rhetorica ad Herennium* (I.iv–v.8); and on appealing to the indignation *(indignatio)* and pity *(conquestio)* of the listeners in the peroration, see *De inv.* (I.liii–liv and lv–lvi, respectively).

13. Cottino-Jones stresses the "sharp contrast" between "Arriguiccio's exuberant and emotional character" and that of "his calm and rational wife . . ."; "once her brothers see their sister sitting unscathed, calmly sewing, their former complete faith in Arriguccio is shaken" (128).

14. Getto (185–86) offers an excellent analysis of Sismonda's "discorso di un'-inconfutabile dialettica" which anticipates several of the points made in somewhat greater detail here about its interplay of "dimostrabile" and "indimostrabile" arguments. Getto's primary interest is not in what I am calling the para-forensic dimension of the speech (and the novella that contains it), but rather in (as indicated by the title that includes his analysis) "lo scambio di illusione e realtà."

15. In medieval European society, matrons were required to conceal their hair from all but their husbands. See Régnier-Bohler: "undone hair has high erotic value; the fairy Melusine is perhaps the emblem of this form of seduction" (362). On sumptuary regulations for women, see Hughes "Sumptuary Law" (69–99). Cf. *Dec.* 8.8, where Zeppa enters his bedroom "and found his wife still adjusting the veils on her head, which had fallen off while Spinelloccio [Zeppa's best friend] was making love to her" (526).

Sismonda's letting down her hair ironically recalls the act of letting a string from her toe down to the street—in order to signal Ruberto whether or not she is available for love-making—thus evoking, even as Sismonda uses it to deny, her transgressive sexuality. (See below, p. 281.)

16. For the idea of the veiled text hiding its profound truths from the vulgar or uninitiated behind obscuring fictions, see Macrobius (I.ii.17–20); *Boccaccio on Poetry* (59–60 and 157, n. 8); and Dinshaw (20–22).

17. Cf. *De inv.*: "All argumentation drawn from these topics [concerning attributes of persons or action] will have to be either probable or irrefutable" (I.xxix.44). Behind this distinction lies the Aristotelian concept of enthymemes, the equivalent in rhetorical practice of syllogisms in logic. See *Rhet. ad Heren.*:

> Since few of the premises from which rhetorical syllogisms are formed are necessarily true . . . and since things that happen for the most part and are possible can only be reasoned on the basis of other such things . . . it is evident that the premises from which enthymemes are spoken are sometimes necessarily true but mostly true only for the most part. Moreover, enthymemes are derived from probabilities and signs, so it is necessary that each one of these be the same as each of the truth values mentioned. (I.ii.14)

Note 62 explains this last statement: "i.e., probabilities correspond to things true for the most part, signs to things necessarily true" (43). Sismonda uses the correctness of her argument from the sign to create the presumption on her brothers' part that the rest of her (undocumentable) account is equally accurate.

18. Copeland describes *circumstantiae* as "the specific questions that must be

asked of a given case in order to formulate an argument about it" (66). See further Robertson and (for Boccaccio), Olson.

19. Sismonda here strikes at the heart of a husband's obligations, according to Florentine assumptions about marriage: cf. Alberti: "Marriage, therefore, was instituted by nature . . . with the provision that there should be one constant life's companion for a man, and one only. With her he should dwell under one roof, her he should not forget or leave all alone, but to her return bearing things with him and ordering matters so that his family might have all that was necessary and sufficient" (111–12). According to Sismonda, her husband does "leave her all alone," and returns bearing another woman's hair and a false accusation against her fidelity.

20. On the continuing (selective) authority of male relatives (normally the father) over a Florentine woman even after her marriage, see Kuehn, chap. 8, "Women, Marriage, and Patria potestas in Late Medieval Florence." Kuehn summarizes: "the ideological justification for guardianship over women on the part of the jurists corresponded to the general view of women in Florence. Women were widely considered to be weaker than men, especially weaker mentally. . . . The supposed natural inferiority of women justified not only a legal inferiority but a social inferiority" (221). See, further, Maclean (72f); Martines.

On the dangers posed to (male) civil society by female sexuality and its manipulation by women, see Hughes, "Invisible Madonnas," for an account of how the Florentine chronicler Dino Compagni, "assigned the initiative for the factional strife that rent Florence in the thirteenth century . . . to a woman, Gualdrada, the wife of Fortiguerra dei Donati. . . ." According to Compagni, "Gualdrada and her daughters used their sexual powers to corrupt civil society" (31–32).

21. See Brucker (esp. 28–45, 50–56): "on one issue the Florentine aristocracy was firmly united—its intense dislike of the *gente nuova*" (52). The mother's scornful denunciation of country bumpkins who come to Florence seeking socially advantageous marriages reflects the fact that most *gente nuova* who became rich, by speculation and mercantile activity, in post-plague Florence "came from obscure backgrounds" (52), usually in the *contado* outside the city. (Cf. Dante's equal scorn for earlier newcomers who dilute the purity of the Communal stock, *Paradiso* xvi.49–57). For the career of a famous exemplar of the Tuscan *gente nuova* in the later *trecento,* see Origo; its subject, Francesco di Marco Datini, commented on his status as "an outsider, a yokel, and an upstart" in Florence (143).

22. For a reversal analogous to 7.8, see *Dec.* 7.4: Monna Ghita's relatives, believing her fiction that she has locked her husband out of the house because he comes home drunk every night, beat Tofano and take Ghita home with them.

23. See Davis (chap. 5, "Women on Top"). In *Dec.* 9.3, when Calandrino's friends convince him that he is pregnant, he laments, "Ah, Tessa [his wife], you did this to me, you're the one that always wanted to be on top . . ." (568).

24. For a near-contemporaneous tale variously linking sexual and commercial desire, see Chaucer's "Shipman's Tale." Both Cottino-Jones (128) and Getto (176) argue that Arriguccio becomes jealous after learning about Sismonda's affair with Ruberto. But other novelle of the seventh day set out to problematize male possessiveness: in 7.4, Tofano becomes jealous of Ghita "without any reason whatsoever" (431), while in 7.5, a rich merchant becomes jealous of his beautiful wife because, since he loves her and she tries to please him, he assumes other men will desire her as he does, and she will try to please them too, "an argument worthy of a wicked man of little sensitivity," as Fiametta, the narrator, declares (435). Both wives punish the unwarranted jealousy by giving it a *raison d'être.*

25. Florentine patriarchal culture regarded windows giving on the street as dangerous liminal spaces for women, offering access to men other than those chosen for them by their male kin. See de la Roncière (285–90). The merchant of *Dec.* 7.5 is so jealous that his wife does not "dare to show herself at a window or to look outside the house for any reason" (436).

26. According to Saul, medieval proponents of an aristocratic theory of gentility "had little trouble identifying [its] key attributes [as] lineage and virtue." The contrary argument—that virtue and lineage do not necessarily coincide—"was driven home mercilessly from the twelfth century onwards by a host of clerical writers whose own claims to authority rested on qualities other than lineage" (41–42). Brucker notes that for the mercantile patriciate of Florence, "membership in an old and eminent family was an essential qualification for high social standing. Florentines who complied *ricordanze* invariably made reference to the *antichità* of their house, and the imposing role their ancestors had played in the life of the city" (28). As for the *gente nuova* who came to Florence and prospered as merchants, "theirs was an isolated and vulnerable position, which they sought to bolster by forging marriage alliances with ancient families" (40).

27. On billingsgate as a component of popular cultures's carnivalesque language and deportment, see Bakhtin, chap. 2, "The Language of the Marketplace in Rabelais."

28. Cf. *Dec.*, Introduction to Day One: Pampinea, the first monarch, parcels out to the servants all the tasks necessary to keep the *brigata* well fed, well clothed, and comfortable; she does this to "allow our company to live an orderly and pleasurable existence without any shame for as long as we wish" (18). And when the servants Licisca and Tindaro invade the *brigata's* space with their noisy argument about female premarital chastity (Introduction to Day Six), "the Queen [Elissa] with a stern face imposed silence on [Licisca], ordering her not to say another word or make another sound, unless she wished to be whipped and then sent away along with Tindaro . . ." (382). The only words of the *fante* recorded in 7.8 are cries of pain; hence, we do not have corroboration in her own voice of Neifile's report that Sismonda "rewarded her with enough of Arriguccio's money to make the girl quite happy" (454).

See Hughes ("Invisible Madonnas" 48) for a brief, vivid summary of what the prosperity of the medieval Italian commune owed to female labor, often in servitude. Cf. Klapisch-Zuber. For a reading of 7.8 more unequivocally favorable to the aristocracy, see Cottino-Jones (129).

29. The institution of the *mundualdus* is explained in chap. 9, " 'Cum consensu mundualdi.' Legal guardianship of women in Quattrocento Florence" (212–37). Kuehn suggests that

> the practical restraint posed by the *mundualdus* on a woman need not have been very great or immediate, but it was there in some way. At the same time, by stipulating the need for male consent, the institution of the *mundualdus* ensured that, at the very least, the ideology of male dominance and superiority remained intact as a vital truth" (234).

30. See Turner, "Liminality."

Works Cited

Alberti, Leon Battista. *The Family in Renaissance Florence (I libri della famiglia).* Tr. Renée Neu Watkins. Columbia: University of South Carolina Press, 1969.

Anon. *Des tresces. Twelve Fabliaux*. Ed. T. B. W. Reid. Manchester: Manchester University Press, 1958.

Aristotle. *On Rhetoric. A Theory of Civil Discourse*. Tr. George A. Kennedy. New York: Oxford University Press, 1991.

Ashley, Kathleen M. "The Guiler Beguiled: Christ and Satan as Theological Tricksters in Medieval Religious Literature." *Criticism* 24 (1982): 122–37.

Bakhtin, Mikhail. *Rabelais and His World*. Tr. Helene Iswolsky. Cambridge, MA: M. I. T. Press, 1968.

Boccaccio, Giovanni. *Decameron*. Ed. Vittore Branca. *Tutte le opere di Giovanni Boccaccio*. Vol. 4. Ed. Vittore Branca. Milan: Mondadori, 1976.

———. *Decameron*. Tr. Mark Musa and Peter Bondanella. New York: New American Library, 1982.

———. *Boccaccio on Poetry*. (Preface, Books Fourteen and Fifteen of *De genealogia deorum*.) Tr. Charles G. Osgood. Princeton: Princeton University Press, 1930; rpt. New York: Liberal Arts Press, 1956.

Branca, Vittore. *Boccaccio medievale e nuovi studi sul Decameron*. 5th ed. Florence: Sansoni, 1981.

Brucker, Gene. *Florentine Politics and Society, 1343–1378*. Princeton: Princeton University Press, 1962.

Chaucer, Geoffrey. *The Canterbury Tales. The Riverside Chaucer*. Ed. Larry Benson. 3d. ed. Boston: Houghton Mifflin, 1987.

Cicero. *De inventione. De inventione, De optimo genere oratorum, Topica*. Tr. H. M. Hubbell. Cambridge, MA: Harvard University Press; and London: William Heinemann, 1949, rpt. Loeb Classical Library, 1976.

[Cicero]. *Ad. C. Herennium de ratione dicendi (Rhetorica ad Herennium)*. Tr. Harry Caplan. Loeb Classical Library. Cambridge, MA: Harvard University Press; and London: William Heinemann, 1964.

Copeland, Rita. *Rhetoric, Hermeneutics, and Translation in the Middle Ages*. Academic Traditions and Vernacular Texts. Cambridge: Cambridge University Press, 1991.

Cottino-Jones, Marga. *Order from Chaos: Social and Aesthetic Harmonies in Boccaccio's* Decameron. Washington, D. C.: University Press of America, 1982.

Dante Alighieri. *The Divine Comedy. Paradiso*. Ed. and tr. Charles S. Singleton. Princeton: Princeton University Press, 1975.

Davis, Natalie Zeman. *Society and Culture in Early Modern France*. Stanford: Stanford University Press, 1975.

de la Roncière, Charles. "Tuscan Notables on the Eve of the Renaissance." *A History of Private Life II: Revelations of the Medieval World*. Ed. Georges Duby, tr. Arthur Goldhammer. Cambridge, MA and London: Belknap Press, 1989. 157–309.

Dinshaw, Caroline. *Chaucer's Sexual Poetics*. Madison: University of Wisconsin Press, 1989.

Duby, Georges, ed. *A History of Private Life II: Revelations of the Medieval World*. Tr. Arthur Goldhammer. Cambridge, MA and London: Belknap Press, 1989.

Eden, Kathy. *Poetic and Legal Fiction in the Aristotelian Tradition*. Princeton: Princeton University Press, 1986.

Getto, Giovanni. *Vita di forme e forme di vita nel Decameron*. 2d ed. Turin: Petrini, 1966.

Hanning, Robert W. *The Individual in Twelfth-Century Romance*. New Haven and London: Yale University Press, 1977.

Herlihy, David, and Christiane Klapisch-Zuber. *Tuscans and Their Families*. New Haven and London: Yale University Press, 1985.

Hughes, Diane Owen. "Sumptuary Law and Social Relations in Renaissance Italy." *Disputes and Settlements: Law and Human Relations in the West*. Ed. John Bossy. Cambridge: Cambridge University Press, 1983. 69–99.

———. "Invisible Madonnas? The Italian Historiographical Tradition and the Women of Medieval Italy." *Women in Medieval History and Historiography*. Ed. Susan Mosher Stuard. Philadelphia: University of Pennsylvania Press, 1987. 25–57.

King, Margaret. *Women of the Renaissance*. Chicago and London: University of Chicago Press, 1991.

Klapisch-Zuber, Christiane. "Women Servants in Florence During the Fourteenth and Fifteenth Centuries." In B. Hanawalt, ed. *Women and Work in Pre-Industrial Europe*. Bloomington: Indiana University Press, 1986. 56–80.

Kuehn, Thomas. *Law, Family, and Women: Toward a Legal Anthropology of Renaissance Italy*. Chicago: University of Chicago Press, 1991.

Maclean, Ian. *The Renaissance Notion of Women*. Cambridge: Cambridge University Press, 1980.

Macrobius. *Commentary on the Dream of Scipio*. Tr. W. H. Stahl. New York: Columbia University Press, 1952.

Martines, Lauro. "A Way of Looking at Women in Renaissance Florence." *JMRS* 4 (1974):15–28.

Murphy, James J. *Rhetoric in the Middle Ages*. Berkeley, Los Angeles, and London: University of California Press, 1974.

Olson, Glending. "Rhetorical Circumstances and the Canterbury Storytelling." *SAC. Proceedings* 1 (1984):211–18.

Origo, Iris. *The Merchant of Prato: Francesco di Marco Datini*. London: Jonathan Cape, 1957; rpt. Harmondsworth: Penguin, 1963.

Padoan, Giorgio. "Mondo aristocratico e mondo communale nell' ideologia e nell'arte di Giovanni Boccaccio." *Studi sul Boccaccio* 2 (1964):81–216.

Pomeroy, Sarah. *Goddesses, Whores, Wives, and Slaves: Women in Classical Antiquity*. New York: Schocken, 1975.

Régnier-Bohler, Danielle. "Exploring Literature." *A History of Private Life II: Revelations of the Middle Ages*. Ed. Georges Duby. Tr. Arthur Goldhammer. Cambridge, MA and London: Belknap Press, 1989. 313–93.

Robertson, D. W., Jr. "A Note on the Classical Origin of 'Circumstances' in the Medieval Confessional." *SP* 43 (1946):6–14.

Saul, Nigel. "Chaucer and Gentility." *Chaucer's England: Literature in Historical Perspective*. Ed. Barbara Hanawalt. Minneapolis: University of Minnesota Press, 1992. 41–55.

Seneca the Elder. *Declamations*. 2 vols. Loeb Classical Library. Tr. M. Winterbottom. Cambridge, MA: Harvard University Press; London; William Heinemann, 1974.

Trimpi, Wesley. *Muses of One Mind: The Literary Analysis of Experience and Its Continuity.* Princeton: Princeton University Press, 1983.

Turner, Victor. "Liminality and the Performance Genres." *Rite, Drama, Festival, Spectacle: Rehearsals Towards a Theory of Cultural Performance.* Ed. John J. McAloon. Philadelphia: Institute for the Study of Human Issues, 1984. 19–41.

Contributors

JOHN M. HILL received his B.A. (1966) and Ph.D. (1971) degrees from the University of Washington, where Robert O. Payne was his undergraduate as well as graduate school Chaucer professor. For the doctoral thesis, he would have worked with Robert O. Payne on *The Canterbury Tales* had the mysteries of the social world depicted in Beowulf not seduced him. He has taught Old and Middle English literature at Smith College, The Catholic University, and the U.S. Naval Academy, where he is currently a professor in the English Department. His publications include *Chaucerian Belief: The Poetics of Reverence and Delight* (Yale, 1991) and *The Cultural World in Beowulf* (Toronto, 1995). Essays on Beowulf and on The Battle of Maldon have appeared in *Social Approaches to Viking Studies, Assays,* and *Mediaevalia.* Other essays on medieval and modern topics, often combining approaches from applied psychoanalysis, comparative ethnology, and the history of science, have appeared in such journals as *Psychocultural Review, Chaucer Review, Criticism, ELH, Enlightenment Essays,* and *American Imago.* A member of several professional societies, John M. Hill is also on the Advisory Board of *Exemplaria* and Chairman of the Board of Directors, The Writer's Center, Bethesda, Maryland.

DEBORAH M. SINNREICH-LEVI holds a Ph.D. in comparative literature from the Graduate School and University Center, C.U.N.Y. She is currently associate professor of English and comparative literature at Stevens Institute of Technology, where she directs the writing program and the Humanities Resource Center. Her doctoral work at on Eustache Deschamps' vernacular poetics was suggested to her by Robert O. Payne during a seminar on medieval rhetoric. She has published the first English translation of *L'Art de dictier* (Colleagues Press, 1994), and edited the first volume of Deschamps criticism in almost 100 years: *Eustache Deschamps, French Courtier-Poet: His Work and His World* (AMS Press, 1998). She is also collaborating on a bilingual volume of Deschamps' poetry.

A graduate of Princeton University and the University of Oxford, CHARLES A. OWEN, JR. was Professor Emeritus in English Language and Literature, the University of Connecticut. Having published more than a dozen articles in philological journals on the *Canterbury Tales,* beginning in 1953, Charles Owen came out with a mid-career summary of his Canterbury interests, *Pilgrimage & Storytelling in the Canterbury Tales: The Dialectic of 'Ernest' and 'Game'* (Norman: University of Oklahoma Press, 1977). In *The Manuscripts of the Canterbury Tales* (Cambridge: D.S. Brewer, 1991), Owen highlighted the importance of Hengwrt and rejected the notion of a single Chaucerian copy text. Since then he continued to publish essays on the plot of the tale telling game, on prosody, and on Chaucer's literary relationships with his continental predecessors. A gathering of his selected essays is forthcoming from Boydell & Brewer. Unfortunately Charles Owen did not live to see the present volume in print.

MARY CARRUTHERS was born in India of medical missionary parents, and educated in India, Canada, and the United States. Having taught at Smith College and the University of Illinois in Chicago, she is now professor of English and Director of the Center for Research in the Middle Ages and the Renaissance at New York University. She has published extensively on medieval English literature, and the history of rhetoric and language theory during the Middle Ages, including most recently *The Book of Memory* (1992) and *The Craft of Thought* (1998), both published by Cambridge University Press.

JOEL FEIMER is Professor of English at Mercy College in Dobbs Ferry, New York, where he has been teaching since 1967. His dissertation was on the theme of Medea in medieval literature, including Chaucer's use of "selective remembrance." He has published several articles on the medieval translations/transformations of classical themes and narratives. He is currently working on several aspects of Chaucer's works; the poet's presentations of the vicissitudes of refined love and their impact on the individual and society, his use of the terms "game" and "pleye" as they relate to the activities of refined love and story telling, and a comparative study of the ars poeticae of Chaucer and de Pizan.

ELLEN E. MARTIN is currently an unaffiliated scholar who works on pscychoanaltic and monastic literature as well as writing on Chaucer's dream-visions. Her essays have appeared in the *Chaucer Review,* the *Journal of Medieval and Renaissance Studies, Exemplaria,* and *Assays;* in early May, she may be found at Kalamazoo.

MARTIN STEVENS is a CUNY Distinguished Professor Emeritus. He has published extensively in all areas of medieval drama, art and literature. He is best known for editing the EETS *The Towneley Cycle of Mystery Plays,* 2 Vols, (Oxford Press, 1994); *The New Ellesmere Chaucer Facsimile,* and *The Ellesmere Chaucer: Essays in Interpretation,* (Huntington Library Press and Yushodu Company, 1995.) He is the author of *Four Middle English Mystery Cycles,* Princeton University Press, 1987; and he is the recipient of a festschrift: *The Performance of Middle English Culture,* ed. J. Paxson, L. Clopper, and S. Tomasch, Boydell & Brewer, 1998.

WILLIAM McCLELLAN is an associate professor of English at Baruch College, C.U.N.Y. He has published articles on Bakhtin's semiotic theory, and codicological studies of fifteenth-century manuscripts. He is currently writing a book-length study of the early transmission history of Chaucer's "Clerk's Tale" titled *The Griselda Complex.*

JOHANNA C. PRINS, lecturer in Dutch Language and Literature at Columbia University, has published essays on medieval literature from the Low Countries, medieval Netherlandic manuscripts and Aphra Behn. Her English translation of the medieval Dutch *Abele Spelen* is scheduled to be published shortly by Pegasus Press in the series "Medieval and Renaissance Drama Texts in Translation."

BURT KIMMELMAN is an associate professor of English at New Jersey Institute of Technology. His work has been primarily in medieval studies, as well as modern poetry. He has authored numerous articles, book chapters and reviews, and three books: *The Poetics of Authorship in the Later Middle Ages: The Emergence of the Modern Literary Persona* (1996), *The "Winter Mind": William Bronk and American Letters* (1998), and *Musaics* (1992). He is also a co-author of a textbook, *Environmental Protection: Solving Environmental Problems from Social Science and Humanities Perspectives* (1997).

SEALY GILLES is assistant professor of English at Long Island University, Brooklyn Center. She is co-editor of *Text and Territory: Geographical Imagination in the European Middle Ages* (University of Pennsylvania Press, 1998) and has published on the Old English *Orosius* and on *The Wanderer.* Her work on *The Wanderer* focuses on analogues for the poem's gnomic sequences found in homiletic literature and in Old Irish *Instructions to Princes.* Her study of the Old English *Orosius* explores the roles played by interpolation and compilation in a culture's in a culture's attempt to define itself. Dr. Gilles is currently writing on the performance of morbidity and mortality in Chaucer's *Troilus and Criseyde*.

GALE SIGAL is the Zachary T. Smith Professor of Humanities at Wake Forest University where she teaches medieval literature in the English department. She is author of *Erotic Dawn-songs of the Middle Ages: Voicing the Lyric Lady* (University Press of Florida, 1996), co-editor, with Deborah Sinnreich-Levi, of *Voices in Translation: The Authority of "Olde Bookes" in Medieval Literature: Essays in Honor of Helaine Newstead* (AMS Press, 1992) and assistant editor of *The Collected Letters of William Morris,* volume II (2 volumes), Normal Kelvin, ed. (Princeton University Press, 1984). Among her essays on medieval lyric, the most recent are "Courted in the Country; The Precarious Place of the Lady in the Medieval Lyric Landscape" in *Text and Territory,* Tomasch and Gilles, eds., (University of Pennsylvania Press, 1998) and an entry on the Troubadours, Trouveres and Trobairitz in the *Dictionary of Literary Biography: The Literature of the French and Occitan Middle Ages* Vol. 208, Sinnreich-Levi and Laurie, eds. (Bruccoli Clark Layman, 1999).

DIANE R. MARKS is an associate professor of English at Brooklyn College C.U.N.Y. where she has taught since 1979. She has published articles on courtly literature of the later Middle Ages and is the author of the biographical entry on Charles of Orleans in the *Dictionary of Literary Biography: The French and Occitan Middle Ages*. She is currently writing a book inspired by her dissertation on the English poems of Charles of Orleans. Her work has been supported by research awards from the Professional Staff Congress of C.U.N.Y., and fellowships from the National Endowment for the Humanities and the Wolfe Institute for the Humanities at Brooklyn College. This article on Petrarch resulted from a study begun at a NEH Summer Institute at Yale University.

ANNE HOWLAND SCHOTTER is professor of English and chair of Humanities at Wagner College. She has recently co-edited the medieval section of the Longman Anthology of British Literature (gen. ed. David Damrosch, 1999). She is author of articles on the Pearl-poet and medieval Latin poetry, and co-editor of *Ineffability: Naming the Unnamable from Dante to Becket*. In addition, she has received fellowships from the Woodrow Wilson and Andrew W. Mellon Foundations.

ROBERT W. HANNING is professor of English and Comparative Literature at Columbia University, where he has held a full-time appointment since 1963. Holder of degrees from Columbia and Oxford, he has been awarded Guggenheim, A.C.L.S., and N.E.H. fellowships and, most recently, a residency at the Rockefeller Foundation Study Center at Bellagio, Italy. He has been a visiting professor at Yale, Johns Hopkins, and Princeton Universities, and has directed three N.E.H. seminars for college teachers and three summer sessions of the Bread Loaf School of English at Lincoln College, Oxford. He has published *The Vision of History in Early Britain* (1966) and *The Individual in Twelfth-Century Romance* (1977) and co-translated, with Joan Ferrante, *The Lais of Marie de France*. He is completing a study of "social eloquence" in Chaucer's *Canterbury Tales* and delivered the Biennial Chaucer Lecture at the New Chaucer Society's international congress at the Sorbonne, Paris, in July 1998.

Index

Abel, 172
Abel, Elizabeth, 266 n.6
Abel plays, 22, 164–75
Abelard, Pierre, 85 n.32
Abraham, Nicolas, 124 n.6
Achilles, 76, 261
Aeneas, 75–76, 109, 113, 122, 123 n.2
Alain de Lille: *The Complaint of Nature*, 76
Alba lady, 24, 221–39
Albertus Magnus, 84
Alceste (Alcestis), 45, 88, 90, 92, 94, 188–89, 197–98, 200
Alcione (Alcyone), 22, 47, 56, 78, 80, 85 n.31
Anselm, 83 n.13, 177; *Proslogion*, 73
Antonius, Marcus, 73
Antony, 94–97, 102–3
Apollo, 122, 264
Aquinas, Thomas, 40, 83 n.13, 84 n.23, 183, 262–63; *Summa theologica*, 73
Aristotle, 34, 84 nn.23 and 29, 151, 153, 157, 161 n.3, 177, 183, 262, 275; *Ethics*, 40, 155; *Poetics*, 155; *Rhetoric*, 15, 154–55, 286 n.2, 287 n.10, 288 n.12
Arriguccio, 270–86
Ars poetica (*artes poeticae*), 29–31, 41, 186
Arthurian romances, 13
Auchinleck manuscript, 139
Augustine, 80, 179, 182, 191, 249–50, 256 n.4; *The City of God*, 100–101; *De doctrina Christiana*, 201 n.7, 202 n.19; *De mendacio*, 202 n.18; *De utilitate credendi*, 108
Avignon papacy, 254

Babylon, 98–99
Bacon, Roger, 183
Bailly, Harry (Host), 130–31, 133–34, 138, 141, 149–50, 152, 155–56, 158–60
Bakhtin, Mikhail, 23, 140, 143, 151–53, 209, 212
Barolini, Teodolinda, 259
Beatrice, 222, 266 nn.10 and 15
Bede, 118–19, 127 n.14
Benjamin, Walter, 179
Beowulf, 211
Beowulf, 76, 211, 213–14
Bernard of Clairvaux, 73, 77, 83 n.15, 260, 263
Bevis of Hampton, 139
Black Death, 136
Black Knight (Man in Black), 47–49, 53, 55–64, 67, 78–82, 102
Blanche, Duchess, 57, 63–64, 67, 78, 81–82
Bloch, Howard, 249
Bloom, Harold, 258–59
Boccaccio, Giovanni, 23, 124 n.5, 241, 250; *De casibus vivorum illustrium*, 141–42; *De claris mulieribus*, 89–97, 99, 103, 141; *Decameron*, 24, 40, 269–90
Boethius, Anicius Manlius Severinus, 31, 72, 76; *Consolation of Philosophy*, 70–71, 73, 141; *De institutione musica*, 34–36
Boitano, Piero, 127 n.13, 128 n.17
Bologna, university at, 69, 154
Bonagiunta degli Overardi, 250–51, 264
Bonaventure, 263
Boncompagno da Signa, 69–70
Boscoreale villa, 74–75
Bradwardine, Thomas, 178
Brodeur, Arthur, 213–14
Brooke-Rose, Christine, 90–91
Brooks, Mel, 135
Brussels, 165
Burke, Kenneth, 26